CUSTOMS in CONFLICT

THE ANTHROPOLOGY OF A CHANGING WORLD

edited by Frank Manning and Jean-Marc Philibert

CUSTOMS IN CONFLICT

The Anthropology of a Changing World

CUSTOMS in CONFLICT

THE ANTHROPOLOGY OF A CHANGING WORLD

edited by Frank Manning and Jean-Marc Philibert

broadview press

Cataloguing in Publication Data

Main Entry Under Title:
Customs in Conflict

ISBN 0-921149-34-4

GN
316
C87
1990

1. Ethnology. 2. Ethnology — Canada. I. Manning, Frank
E. II. Philibert, Jean-Marc, 1945-

GN316.C88   1989   306   C89 – 093688 – 9

broadview press   in the US, broadview press
P.O. Box 1243   269 Portage Rd.
Peterborough, Ontario   Lewiston, NY
K9J 7H5   Canada   14092   USA

printed in Canada

CONTENTS

INTRODUCTION

AN INTRODUCTION IS THE PLACE WHERE authors lay claim to an intellectual filiation, though ultimately it is up to the readers to decide whether the kinship is real or fictitious. The title of this book, *Customs in Conflict*, is a reference to a well-known book written some thirty-five years ago by Max Gluckman, the founder of the Manchester School of Anthropology. Given that recent ethnographies contain in general far fewer customs and a great deal more conflicts than Gluckman's *Custom and Conflict in Africa*, we should perhaps explain his presence in this book.

We, the editors of this book, have been strongly influenced by British social anthropology, in its 1960s form as well as in its more recent manifestation, and we owe a great deal of our research interests to ideas first expressed by Gluckman and later developed by his students. However, there is more to this than nostalgia: going back to Gluckman adds an historical dimension to our choice of articles as it places them in time along a theoretical itinerary that reflects important developments in the discipline.

We should perhaps start by pointing out that anthropologists no longer use the term *customs*, preferring instead to speak of practices. This follows a move away from considering traditional societies in the moral and legal terms dear to structural-functionalists, i.e. as tribal groups sharing a common world view, a common set of values and standards internalized to such an extent that individual behaviors are nearly always predictable. We no longer accept the idea that everyone is equally moved by a single set of age-old rules or *customs*.

The idea of *custom* is linked to another key anthropology concept, equally suspect today, that of the *tribe*. The idea of *tribe*, a natural grouping of people having one language, one culture, one social system based largely on kinship and one set of laws, has now come under attack as the product of early twentieth century colonialism. The model of a tribe is predicated on such a high degree of social and cultural integration as to render the existence of such social units highly improbable. Some historians now contend that anthropologists were insufficiently critical of the models presented to them by colonial administrators and by those segments of indigenous populations which stood to gain the most (or lose the least) from the colonial social formation (Ranger 1983).

Anthropologists have now abandoned the naive use of the concept of *custom* to denote the shared habits and values of traditional peoples, ironically at a time when this notion has been embraced by political elites in newly-independent countries (see Chapter 10 by Philibert). The demise of *custom* corresponds to a reappraisal of the concept of *culture* itself and a move away from a totalizing way of conceptualizing norms, values, knowledge, perceptions, etc. Anthropologists have been slow to realize that cultures never developed in a political vacuum; that the official culture portrayed in many monographs was not everyone's culture; and, what is more, that cultures can only be studied in the act of reproduction, never as already constituted, the latter view being the result of the neglect of time in structural-functionalist analyses. As Geraldine Finn sharply points out in this book, "...the *category* "Culture" is not a neutral category.... Cultural production serves someone's interests, and so does the Discourse of Culture. Culture, like Science, is not an innocent category, but rather one of exclusion, passification [sic] and mystification."

But anthropologists came slowly to this realization. What had to happen first was a shift in perspective from a consensual, largely benign, political model of traditional societies to a conflictual one, a change that took place in the late 1960s. Political elders and chiefs stopped being regarded as wise old men fulfilling an unenviable task handed to them by *custom*. Newly available knowledge of precolonial and colonial history made such a romanticized view of the traditional office holder untenable. Soon Marxist anthropologists studying African economic systems raised the issue of exploitation of juniors by elders; they were followed later by anthropologists who explored the subordinate position of women in traditional societies. It was found that not all social groups benefitted equally from the "egalitarian" social systems of traditional societies; that in fact, some had access to far fewer socially defined rewards than others. What had been considered in essence a benevolent, if paternalistic, political context in tribal groups, primarily because such societies lack our complex forms of social control and political specialization, was now perceived through the eyes of the social-political inferiors. Seen from below, the social system looked significantly less benign. This is when anthropologists discovered the role played by ideology in small-scale societies, a major focus of this book.

If there have been so many important changes, then one can legitimately ask, why go back to an old anthropologist like Max Gluckman? There are two reasons—first, because his work anticipates later developments and, second, because some of his students have been responsible for leading anthropology through these developments.

Section I of the book, *The Manchester School: Process, Meaning and Power*, traces the development of the Manchester school of Anthropology by showing how Gluckman's ideas were developed and refined by successive generations of Manchester anthropologists. Gluckman was one of the first anthropologists to show a marked interest in the material conditions of social life long before anthropologists rediscovered Marxism; to move away from an exclusive concern with the "traditional" to consider the whole colonial social order; to see social systems, not as functionally integrated wholes, but on the contrary, as the result of an uneasy truce between contradictory principles of social organization; and finally to perceive the role of ritual action in the daily ordering and re-ordering of social life.

Even though Gluckman still regarded social systems as legal-moral orders, he realized nonetheless that social morality, the set of values and rules of conduct associated with customary behaviors, was far from unambiguous. There was room there for divergent practices and plenty of contradictions. As Kapferer puts it, Gluckman "saw conflict and dispute as founded upon fundamental contradictions located at the heart of cultural/social orders" (1987: 7). If one had to summarize Gluckman's position succinctly, one could say that he took for granted what other anthropologists of his time could only conceptualize with the greatest of difficulty, namely, a social system in a perpetual state of flux. This, in a nutshell, is what distinguishes Max Gluckman from other British social anthropologists of his generation.

Another of Gluckman's enduring contributions is found in his study of ritual. For him, rituals were a way of papering over the cracks in social systems, cracks caused by the structural tensions found in societies governed by principles which, although equally valid, were pulling in opposite directions. This led to inconsistencies, indeed contradictions, in behavioral norms, which could only be overcome by ritual. "At the widest range, cohesion is stated in ritual terms—supported by mystical retribution—where values are unquestioned and axiomatic" (Gluckman 70: 23).

This is the point of departure for the analysis of ritual adopted by Gluckman's best known student, Victor Turner, who was a major conduit for the diffusion of the Manchester style of social analysis in North America. Turner's work on the properties of rituals goes much further than Gluckman's and its influence reaches well beyond the boundaries of the discipline; it is an instance of the student outdoing the master. Nonetheless, the concern for social dynamics expressed in his work is traceable to Gluckman. The first of the two articles on ritual symbolism among the Ndembu of Zambia, in which Turner outlines a framework for symbolic analysis, is still valued today.

One finds in symbolic studies carried out by British anthropologists a reluctance to look for explanations in the inner logic of the symbols themselves, or in the functioning of the mind or language; instead, the analyses pay close attention to social life and attend to the sociological as well as the semantic. Victor Turner is a case in point and his first student at Manchester, Abner Cohen, went even further in this direction by studying the political implications of cultural symbols which appear on the surface to be nonpolitical. He provides us in this second article of Section I with a brief, but useful overview of how he and others see the relationship between power and symbolism, one of the major preoccupations of this book.

In section II of this book, *The Power of Symbolism: Understanding and Constituting Society*, five authors explore how reality is symbolically constituted; how symbols carry meaning and move people to action; and how participants are transformed by ritual action. They investigate "social dramas" in contexts as varied as a West Indian Pentecostal church service, a senior citizens' center, the Rio carnival, an American jail for men, and the wonderful world of Harlequin Romances. What these studies have in common is the particular attention they all pay to the processes of creation of cultural knowledge.

The chapter starts with Frank Manning describing how members of a Pentecostal Church in Bermuda interpret the behavior of a drunk who rudely disrupts their church service. The analysis of this religious ceremony points to the role played by ritual in the construction and confirmation of cultural meanings. And yes, the drunk later came back to announce that he had indeed been saved.

Barbara Myerhoff, also influenced by Turner, gives an account of the sudden death of a 95 year old man during his birthday party at a Jewish senior citizens' center in Los Angeles. The unplanned death suddenly brings to an end the purpose of the birthday ritual and participants must quickly improvise their way out of this unsettling event. The article demonstrates how rituals are a means of adapting to the unpredictability of life itself.

Moved by an interest in performance theory, Da Matta examines a secular ritual in the form of a national celebration attracting millions of participants, the Rio Carnival. While the two previous cases illustrate how religious and quasi-religious rituals provide meaning in the face of unpredictable and disconcerting events, here the accent is on the playful creation of chaos, on standing ordinary life on its head. The result of this inversion of the social structure is the creation of a sense of Brazilian identity which challenges and overcomes in part the established social order.

John Coggeshall's article describes gender and sex relations among male prisoners, more particularly how American prison culture allows men to maintain their heterosexual identity while involved in homosexual relations. This is achieved by converting some male prisoners into culturally defined females. He goes on to examine the cultural identity of these "women" according to male-based perceptions of gender identity. We find out that sexual identity is not primarily determined by the form of sexual activity that one practices.

Geraldine Finn, who is not an anthropologist, considers from a feminist perspective popular culture in general and Harlequin Romances in particular. If these books are read in such large numbers, she says, it is because they offer ways of resolving the insoluble problems faced by many women. Ultimately, the books teach how to try to love authority and how authority loves submission.

This last article brings us to a dimension of Gluckman's work which is not readily apparent until the 1950s anthropological language has been dusted off his analyses. His notion of social equilibrium was far more complex than that of other anthropologists of his time. He was among the first to address some of the concerns we now have. As Kapferer states,

> If Gluckman was concerned with stable systems it was often in the context of how it was they resisted forces of transformation. In terms of modern sociological discourse he investigated hegemonic ideologies and the structures of practice which indeed maintained social orders of extraordinary inequality together despite themselves.... Gluckman explored the deep contradictions which threatened to blast them apart, the ideological resolution of these contradictions, and the practices which bound elements of the population in common opposition. (Kapferer 87: 17).

This is the line of inquiry pursued in the next two sections of this book which examine the link between power and ideology. They are also likely to be the parts of the book more open to contention, if only because the theoretical concerns are more recent and the ideas expressing them still sketchy.

While Gluckman investigated large "rituals of rebellion", as he called them, anthropologists now look for conflicts elsewhere, in the small unconscious routines of everyday life such as the proper way of greeting social superiors and inferiors, or how to behave as spectators at a cricket match. *Custom* is everyday practice, the domain of common sense, of what is unstated because it is so much taken for granted. Many anthropologists now take a dynamic, conflictual view of cultures: they consider cultures or sub-cultures as the terrain on which social groups vie with one another for the recognition and acceptance of their own views of the good society as the natural and, indeed, the only way of doing things. In other words, they are interested in the manner in which ideas held by various social groups become transformed into *custom*, a process riddled with tensions and contradictions. Anthropologists have now turned their attention to the complementary processes of social reproduction of cultures and cultural reproduction of social groups.

In most societies, various social groups have (slightly or significantly) different knowledge, values, world views guiding their social projects. However, not all of these ideas carry the same persuasiveness nor the same legitimacy. Social groups, whether social classes or not, compete with one another for cultural space, strive to have what they consider right and proper inscribed in a transient cultural landscape. Such groups are trying to obtain the agreement of other social groups that what they want is "just common sense". To get that consent, they must attend to some extent to the concerns of these other groups.

These ideas/ideals are redrawn and fought over in various guises in the fields of culture, education, sport, and popular literature, as well as in parliamentary bills, the Law, and forms of economic control. Gramsci called this process *hegemony*. He believed that in order to rule, social groups and classes must go beyond their narrow interests and develop a role of leadership by articulating popular aspirations. In this way, their own class interests and world view appear to represent the common will. Unlike other Marxist writers, Gramsci understood early the importance of culture. He put forward the idea that class control is also exercised in what he called the "civil society", institutions such as churches, political parties, trade unions, mass media, educational systems, and cultural organizations providing ideological ways of shaping reality.

> A hegemonic cultural order tries to *frame* all competing definitions of the world within *its* range. It provides the horizon of thought and action within which conflicts are fought through, appropriated...obscured...or contained. A hegemonic order prescribes, not the specific content of ideas, but the *limits* within which ideas and conflicts move and are resolved. (Clarke, Hall et al 1976: 39)

How social classes gain a monopoly of social authority for their own definition of reality and how they are able to perpetuate it are what Gramsci tried to understand. Adopting such a perspective, even in classless societies, takes us a long way from the politically aseptic view of culture held by older anthropologists. It points to the role played by ideology in *all* societies as one of the means through which social groups over-value their cultural products and under-value the products of other groups, such as women and juniors. It also provides us as anthropologists with a way to theorize various forms of popular culture in Western societies from sports to Harlequin Romances.

The process of ideological containment is explored in Part III, *The Symbolism of Power: Hegemonic Systems*, in which authors examine different forms of knowledge and the symbolic classifications on which they are based as part of hegemonic discourses existing both within and between societies. The concern here is with the ideological reproduction of social groups and, although ideological conflicts take place on the terrain of ideas, such conflicts are no less fierce for all that. The ethnographic reality is again varied as we move from Israeli kindergartens to South African Christian churches; from a cricket match in Bermuda to representations of the past in Disneyland and in Vanuatu, a small country in the South Pacific.

In the first article of this section, Lea Shamgar-Handelman and Don Handelman study child socialization, more particularly the celebration of religious and secular holidays in Israeli kindergartens. They argue that in such enactments allegiance to state authority is paramount; indeed, contrary to North American practice, primary social units such as the family are shown to derive their legitimacy from the state.

Jean and John Comaroff tackle in an exemplary fashion the difficult issue of establishing the links between Christianity and colonialism in South Africa. In the process, they manage to stay clear of two forms of reductionism: one that universalizes the phenomenon under study to the extent of denying any substantial role to local actors; the other, to forget that this phenomenon is part of a larger historical reality and to confine oneself to the ethnographically specific.

Next comes an analysis of the present-day invention of traditional culture in Vanuatu, a small South Pacific country. Jean-Marc Philibert argues that such neo-traditions, or *kastoms* as they are known locally, are a way for the political elite to turn their countrymen, behind their back, into citizens of a modern state under the guise of a return to a pre-colonial past. Examining this corpus of "customs", he asks if any symbol can be customized and discusses the failure to enshrine the drinking of *kava* within the field of the traditional.

Like rituals, popular sports speak a great deal about the social environments in which they are found, as anyone who has ever watched a USSR - Canada hockey game knows. Frank Manning's analysis of the structure of cricket festivals in Bermuda shows how these events dramatize the dilemma of Blacks in Bermuda politics.

Mike Wallace explores the version of American history on display in entertainment parks such as Disney's Magic Kingdom and Epcot Center in Florida. We are presented with Mickey Mouse history in both places: in the Magic Kingdom, an idyllic version of American society at the turn of the century, and in the Epcot Center, a view of the present and the future, in which social problems will be solved and consumer satisfaction guaranteed, thanks to the good will and technological power of multinational corporations.

Hegemonies give rise to counter-hegemonies, the way power necessarily produces resistance. Part IV of the book, *The Symbolic Wealth of the Weak: Forms of Resistance*, explores the ways social groups oppose the process of symbolic encapsulation to which they are continually subjected. This is a dimension of cultural reproduction that must be documented if we want to develop an anthropology which, operating through real time, gives social agents a historical role again. As Willis puts it, "Social agents are not passive bearers of ideology, but active appropriators who reproduce existing structures only through struggle, contestation and a partial penetration [understanding] of those structures." (77: 175).

The articles selected in this section outline various forms of resistance found among people as different from one another as the West African women of Sierra Leone, Skid Row Indians in Vancouver, Canadian students in a Toronto high school, Malay peasants, and South Pacific Islanders.

This section starts with a study by Rosalind Shaw of divination among the Temne, a Muslim people living in Sierra Leone. She examines the social strategies open to Temne women, as social subordinates, to restructure, if only privately, dominant conceptions of reality which are adverse to them.

Skid Row life is hard and probably hardest for Indians. But Alan Morinis argues that the behavior of Skid Row Indians must be seen as a political act by people lacking the means to conduct their protest in the conventional political arena. It is a way of rejecting the values and goals of white society "...through lifestyling on the stage of their minds and bodies. Their lives are their manifestos. Their politics is the politics of self."

Peter McLaren looks at the resistance strategies and methods of reprisal of students in a Toronto inner city Catholic high school. The school is a cultural system designed to make good Catholics and good workers out of the children of Portuguese and Italian immigrants. But it remains an ideologically contested terrain. McLaren believes that "student resistance in inner city schools has been one of the largest sustained guerilla warfare campaigns since the advent of mass literacy."

According to Jim Scott, to look for peasant resistance only in the form of dramatic acts of collective defiance is to blind ourselves to the reality of such resistance. It is found instead in the daily use of the weapons of the weak: "footdragging, dissimulation, false-compliance, pilfering, feigned ignorance, slander, arson, sabotage, and so forth." He proposes a model of peasant resistance in which individual, anonymous acts of self-defence are taken to be a form of class-based collective action.

Jean-Marc Philibert's article examines consumption at the interface of Western and Third World societies. When consuming Western goods, members of Third World societies borrow at the same time the ideas and perceptions responsible for the existence of these goods in the first place. He then considers the following questions: can the people studied by anthropologists resist ideological penetration? Do they have the cultural means to refuse or oppose foreign systems of ideas, from clothes, and educational systems, to forms of entertainment? Must the end product necessarily be a sort of self-imposed cultural subjugation?

Readers should note that all the articles in this volume have been previously published elsewhere, and have been edited here in order to highlight certain parts of the content and for stylistic consistency. While the versions found here represent an excellent overview, they are no substitute for the originals. Readers are strongly encouraged to go to the original versions of any articles they find they would like to pursue more in-depth.

All the articles are preceded by a brief summary outlining the main points of the argument. These articles have been chosen both for their theoretical contribution and for the vividness of their ethnographic description. We hope you have as much pleasure in reading them as we had ourselves.

References

Gluckman, M.
  1970 *Customs and Conflicts in Africa.* Oxford: Blackwell.

Clarke, J., S. Hall, T. Jefferson and B. Roberts
  1976 "Subcultures, cultures and class". In Hall, S. & T. Jefferson (eds) *Resistance through Rituals.* London: Hutchinson.

Kapferer, B.
  1987 "The Anthropology of Max Gluckman". In Kapferer, B. (ed) Power, Process and Transformation: Essays in Memory of Max Gluckman. Special Issues Series, *Social Analysis* No. 22.

Ranger, T.
  1983 "The Invention of Tradition in Colonial Africa". In: Hobsbawm, E. & T. Ranger (eds) *The Invention of Tradition.* Cambridge: Cambridge University Press.

Willis, P.E.
  1977 *Learning to Labour.* NY: Columbia University Press.

THE MANCHESTER SCHOOL: SCHOOL: PROCESS, MEANING, AND POWER

Ritual Symbolism, Morality, and Social Structure Among the Ndembu

Victor Turner

Victor Turner was Max Gluckman's most celebrated student. He was also a major conduit through whom the Manchester style of social analysis was introduced to North American anthropology and, later, to other academic disciplines.

Like other "first generation" members of the Manchester School, Turner began his field research in Central Africa. He chose to study the Ndembu of Zambia, among whom he did extensive fieldwork over a period of two decades, resulting in several major books. The hallmark of this work is an emphasis on the way that culture is symbolized and enacted in the processes of conflict, crisis, and conciliation that punctuate a tribal society's ongoing life. Turner later extended this approach, which he described as social dramatism, to the study of more complex societies, large-scale historical movements, and various aspects of contemporary popular culture.

The following piece is vintage Turner, a combination of rigorous ethnography, vivid description, meticulous attention to symbols and their action contexts, and an analytical focus on how meaning is brought to bear on social situations. The article deals with ritual, the principal setting in which the Ndembu apprehend and act upon their culture. Borrowing a metaphor from music, Turner suggests that ritual symbols are like notes, while the ritual as a whole is like a score. The notes give sensory form to culture, expressing it in ways that are visible, audible, and tactile. The score arranges the notes in ways that make them coherent and moving. The dramatic unfolding of ritual tends to associate meanings that are moral and ideological with meanings that are physical and

*emotional, a semantic exchange that embellishes social norms with
sensual appeal while also, at the same time, ennobling sensory
forms by giving them a normative reference. The overall significance of ritual, therefore, is that it makes moral and collective
principles appear desirable—or, at the least, acceptable. Durkheim
had earlier reached a similar conclusion, but the contribution of
Turner lay in showing how the process works in specific ethnographic settings and what it may mean in a field of conflicting
interests.*

*The present article, written originally in 1960, also outlines a
three-part method of symbolic analysis. Symbols must be examined
exegetically, i.e., how they are described and interpreted by native
informants; operationally, i.e., how they are used in ritual settings;
and positionally, in terms of their relationship to other symbols.
Turner elaborated this method in his later work, and it continues
to be regarded as a valuable organizational framework for the ethnographic examination of cultural symbolism.*

IN THIS PAPER I wish to discuss the semantic structure and properties of some of the principal symbols found in Ndembu ritual. Each
kind of ritual may be regarded as a configuration of symbols, a sort
of "score" in which the symbols are the notes. The symbol is the
smallest unit of specific structure in Ndembu ritual. The vernacular
term for it is *chinjikijilu,* from *ku-jikijila,* "to blaze a trail," by cutting
marks on a tree with one's ax or by breaking and bending branches
to serve as guides back from the unknown bush to known paths. A
symbol, then, is a blaze or landmark, something that connects the
unknown with the known. The Ndembu term comes from the
vocabulary of hunting and exemplifies the high ritual value attached
to this pursuit. Furthermore, in discussing their symbols with Ndembu, one finds them constantly using the term *ku-solala,* "to make
visible" or "to reveal," and they associate this term with aspects of
the chase. Indeed, in their ritual vocabulary derivatives of this verb
are frequent. For example, the temporary shrine erected for ritual
to propitiate the spirits of deceased hunter relatives very often consists of a forked branch taken from the *musoli* tree. Ndembu tell
me that this tree is used as a symbol in hunters' ritual because its
fruit and young shoots are much appreciated by duiker and other
woodland animals who emerge from concealment to eat them and
may be easily shot by a hidden hunter or caught in his snares. The

VICTOR TURNER

tree, they say, makes the game "visible." Hence, portions of it are used as medicines (*yitumbu*) in rituals performed to rid hunters of misfortune. It is said that these medicines will "make animals appear quickly to the hunter" when next he goes into the bush. *Musoli* medicines are also used in rituals performed to make barren women fruitful; they will "make children visible," say Ndembu.

Another use of *musoli* is worth mentioning. Ndembu have a ritual called *Ihamba*, the main aim of which is to remove by cupping horns from a patient's body the upper central incisor (also called *ihamba*) of a dead hunter's relative which has imbedded itself under the skin. The spirit, materialized as a tooth, is said to "bite" its victim because the latter has forgotten to pour out a libation of blood at its grave after making a kill, or else because there has been quarreling in the victim's village. The victim may not necessarily have been guilty himself of quarrelsome behavior, but may have been selected as a representative of the disordered kin-group. The specialist who supervises the ritual procedure usually insists on those village members who have grudges (*yitela*) against one another or against the patient (*muyeji*) coming forward and making a public confession of their hidden animosities. Only after this, he says, will the *ihamba* consent to being caught in a cupping horn. Now the principal medicine of this ritual, the one at which an invocation to the spirit is made, the one which is collected before all others, consists of the taproot of a *musoli* tree. My informants told me that the root stood for the *ihamba* tooth and that the *musoli* species was used "to make the *ihamba* tooth come out quickly," and "so that people would speak truly (*ku-hosha chalala*) and openly." Here the idea is clearly that relief is brought both to the patient and to the disturbed social group if hidden ill-feeling is brought to light.

Another derivative of *ku-solola* is "*isoli*" or "*chisoli*," terms that designate a "place of revelation." They refer to specially consecrated sites, used only in the final phases of important rituals, where esoteric rites are performed and secret matters are revealed to the initiated.

Finally, the term *Musolu* stands for a type of ritual performed only by chiefs and senior headmen to bring on or "make visible" delayed rains.

One aspect of the process of ritual symbolization among the

SYMBOLISM, MORALITY, & SOCIAL STRUCTURE

Ndembu is, therefore, to make visible, audible, and tangible beliefs, ideas, values, sentiments, and psychological dispositions that cannot directly be perceived. Associated with this process of revealing the unknown, invisible, or the hidden is the process of making public what is private or making social what is personal. Anything that cannot be shown to be in conformity with the norms or in terms of the values of Ndembu society is potentially dangerous to its cohesion and continuity. Hence the importance of the public confession in the *Ihamba* ritual. By exposing their ill-feeling in a ritual context to beneficial ritual forces, individuals are purged of rebellious wishes and emotions and willingly conform once more to the public mores.

In an Ndembu ritual each symbol makes visible and accessible to purposive public action certain elements of Ndembu culture and society. It also tends to relate these elements to certain natural and physiological regularities. Thus, in various contexts *musoli* relates the value of public confession to the restoration of health and of female fertility. This brings me to another important property of many ritual symbols, their polysemy or multi-vocality. By these terms I mean that a single symbol may stand for many things. This property of individual symbols is true of ritual as a whole. For a few symbols have to represent a whole culture and its material environment. Ritual may be described, in one aspect, as quintessential custom in that it represents a distillate or condensation of many secular customs and natural regularities. Certain dominant or *focal* symbols conspicuously possess this property of multivocality which allows for the economic representation of key aspects of culture and belief. Each dominant symbol has a "fan" or "spectrum" of referents, which are interlinked by what is usually a simple mode of association, its very simplicity enabling it to interconnect a wide variety of *significata*. For example, the associational link provided by "whiteness" enables white clay (*mpemba*) to stand for a multiplicity of ideas and phenomena, ranging from biological referents such as "semen," to abstract ideas such as "ritual purity," "innocence" from witchcraft, and "solidarity with the ancestor spirits."

When we talk about the "meaning" of a symbol, we must be careful to distinguish between at least three levels or fields of meaning. These I propose to call: (1) the level of indigenous interpretation (or, briefly, the exegetical meaning); (2) the operational

VICTOR TURNER

meaning; and (3) the positional meaning. The exegetical meaning is obtained from questioning indigenous informants about observed ritual behavior. Here again one must distinguish between information given by ritual specialists and information given by laymen, that is, between esoteric and exoteric interpretations. One must also be careful to ascertain whether a given explanation is truly representative of either of these categories or whether it is a uniquely personal view.

On the other hand, much light may be shed on the role of the ritual symbol by equating its meaning with its use, by observing what the Ndembu do with it, and not only what they say about it. This is what I call the operational meaning, and this level has the most bearing on problems of social dynamics. For the observer must consider not only the symbol but the structure and composition of the group that handles it or performs mimetic acts with direct reference to it. He must further note the affective qualities of these acts, whether they are aggressive, sad, penitent, joyful, derisive, and so on. He must also inquire why certain persons and groups are absent on given occasions, and if absent, whether and why they have been ritually excluded from the presence of the symbol.

The positional meaning of a symbol derives from its relationship to other symbols in a totality, a *Gestalt*, whose elements acquire their significance from the system as a whole. This level of meaning is directly related to the important property of ritual symbols mentioned earlier, their polysemy. Such symbols possess many senses, but contextually it may be necessary to stress one or a few of them only . Thus the *mukula* tree viewed in abstraction from any given ritual context may stand for "matriliny," "huntsmanship," "menstrual blood," "the meat of wild animals," and many other concepts and things. The associational link between its various senses is provided by the red gum it secretes, which Ndembu liken to blood. Now in the boys' circumcision ritual (*Mukanda*) the meaning of *mukula* is determined by its symbolic context. A log of this wood is placed near the site where the boys are circumcised. They are circumcised under a *mudyi* tree, which, as we shall see, stands *inter alia* for motherhood and the mother-child relationship. Then they are lifted over a cutting of the *muyombu* tree, which is customarily planted quickset as a shrine to the village ancestor spirits, and placed still bleeding on the *mukula* log. Here the *mukula* log stands mainly for two things. It represents the wish of the elders that the circumcision wounds will heal quickly (from the fact that *mukula* gum quickly coagulates like a scab). It also represents, I was told, masculinity (*wuyala*) and the life of an adult male, who as hunter and warrior has to shed blood. The rite represents (1) the removal of the boy from dependence on his mother (the passage from the *mudyi* tree); (2) his ritual death and subsequent association with the ancestors (the passage over the *muyombu* tree); and (3) his incorporation into the male moral community of tribesmen (the collective setting on the *mukula* tree where the boys are ceremonially fed as though they were infants by the circumcisers and by their fathers. Each boy is given a ball of cassava mush to be eaten directly from the circumciser's knife). In this rite the position of the *mukula* symbol with reference to other symbolic objects and acts is the crucial semantic factor.

The same symbol may be reckoned to have different senses at different phases in a ritual performance, or rather, different senses become paramount at different times. Which sense shall become paramount is determined by the ostensible purpose of the phase of the ritual in which it appears. For a ritual, like a space rocket, is phased, and each phase is directed towards a limited end which itself becomes a means to the ultimate end of the total performance. Thus the act of circumcision is the aim and culmination of a symbol-loaded phase of the *Mukanda* ritual, but itself becomes a means to the final end of turning a boy into a tribesman. There is a consistent relationship between the end or aim of each phase in a ritual, the kind of symbolic configuration employed in that phase, and the senses that become paramount in multivocal symbols in that configuration.

I should now like to consider the exegetical meaning of one of the principal Ndembu ritual symbols, the *mudyi* tree. This symbol is found in more than half a dozen different kinds of ritual, but its *locus classicus* is in the girls' puberty ritual (*Nkang'a*). The novice is laid, wrapped in a blanket, at the foot of a slender young *mudyi* sapling. Ndembu say that its pliancy stands for the youth of the girl. The sapling has been previously consecrated by the novice's ritual instructress (*nkong'u*) and her mother. They have trampled down the grass in a circle around the tree, thus making it sacred—"set apart" (*chapkumbadyi*) or "forbidden" (*chakujila*). The site, like

VICTOR TURNER

that of circumcision for the boys, is called *ifwilu* or "the place of dying." Both sites are also known as *ihung'u*, "the place of suffering" or "ordeal." *Ihung'u* is also applied to a hut where a woman is in labor. It is a "place of suffering" because the novice must not move her limbs until nearly nightfall on penalty of being pinched all over by the older women; nor may she eat or speak all day. The association of the *mudyi* tree with suffering and dying should be borne in mind as an aspect of its positional meaning.

Ndembu begin the exposition of *mudyi's* meaning by pointing out that if its bark is scratched, beads of milky latex are promptly secreted. For this reason they say that *mudyi* or "milk tree" is a symbol (*chinjikijilu*) for "breasts" and "breast milk"—both called in Chindembu *mayeli*. They go on from there to say the *mudyi* means "a mother and her child," a social relationship. They further extend this sense to signify a matrilineage (*ivumu*, literally "a womb or stomach"). A text which I collected well expresses this view:

> *Mudyi diku kwakaminiyi nkakulula hakumutembwisha ni ankukulula*
> The milk tree is the place where slept the (founding) ancestress, where they initiated her and another ancestress

> *mukwawu nimukwawu ni kudi nkaka ni kudi mama ninetu anyana;*
> and (then) another down to the grandmother and the mother and ourselves the children;

> *diku kumuchidi wetu kutwatachikili ni amayala nawa chochu hamu.*
> It is the place where our tribe (or tribal custom—literally "kind") began, and also the men in just the same way.

My informant then added the following comments: "The milk tree is the place of all mothers; it is the ancestress of men and women. *Kutembwisha*, "to initiate a girl," means to dance round and round the milk tree where the novice lies. The milk tree is the place where our ancestors slept, to be initiated there means to become ritually pure or white. An uninitiated girl, a menstruating woman, or an uncircumcised boy is called "one who lacks whiteness (*wunabulakutooka*)."

SYMBOLISM, MORALITY, & SOCIAL STRUCTURE

Contextually, a particular novice's milk tree may be termed "her matrilineage." At one phase of the ritual, the leaves of this tree are said to represent "the novice's children"—a sense that is concerned with a future wished-for state of affairs rather than with the past or present.

In other phases of the *Nkang'a* ritual the milk tree is said to stand for "the women" and for "womanhood." It also has the situational sense of "married womanhood."

Finally, the milk tree stands for the process of learning (*kudiza*), especially for learning "women's sense" or "wisdom" (*mana yawambanda*). An informant said that *"mudyi"* is like going to school; "the girl drinks sense as a baby drinks milk."

The semantic structure of *mudyi* may itself be likened to a tree. At the root is the primary sense of "breast milk" and from this proceeds by logical steps series of further senses. The general direction is from the concrete to the increasingly abstract, but there are several different branches along which abstraction proceeds. One line develops as follows: breast, mother-child relationship, matriliny, the Ndembu tribe or tribal custom of which matriliny is the most representative principle. Another line runs: development of the breasts, womanhood, married womanhood, childbearing. Yet another goes from suckling to learning the tasks, rights, and duties of womanhood. As with many other Ndembu symbols, derivative senses themselves become symbols pointing to ideas and phenomena beyond themselves. Thus "matriliny," a derivative sense from "the mother-child" relationship, and "breast-milk," by the principle of *pars pro toto,* itself becomes a symbol for Ndembu culture in its totality.

However, despite this multiplicity of senses, Ndembu speak and think about the milk tree as a unity, almost as a unitary power. They can break down the concept "milk tree" cognitively into many attributes, but in ritual practice they view it as a single entity. For them it is something like Goethe's "eternal womanly," a female or maternal principle pervading society and nature. It must not be forgotten that ritual symbols are not merely signs representing known things; they are felt to possess ritual efficacy, to be charged with power from unknown sources, and to be capable of acting on persons and groups coming in contact with them in such a way as to change them for the better or in a desired direction. Symbols, in

VICTOR TURNER

short, have an orectic as well as a cognitive function. They elicit emotion and express and mobilize desire.

Indeed, it is possible further to conceptualize the exegetic meaning of dominant symbols in polar terms. At one pole cluster a set of referents of a grossly physiological character, relating to general human experience of an emotional kind. At the other pole cluster a set of referents to moral norms and principles governing the social structure. If we call these semantic poles respectively the "orectic" and the "normative" pole, and consider Ndembu ritual symbols in terms of this model, we find that the milk tree stands at one and the same time for the physiological aspect of breast feeding with its associated affectual patterns, and for the normative order governed by matriliny. In brief, a single symbol represents both the obligatory and the desirable. Here we have an intimate union of the moral and the material. An exchange of qualities may take place in the psyches of the participants under the stimulating circumstances of the ritual performance, between orectic and normative poles; the former, through its association with the latter, becomes purged of its infantile and regressive character, while the normative pole becomes charged with the pleasurable effect associated with the breast-feeding situation. In one aspect, the tie of milk, under matriliny, develops into the primary structural tie, but in another aspect, and here the polar model is apposite, the former stands opposed to and resists the formation of the latter.

Other important Ndembu symbols have a similar polar structure. *Mukula,* for example, in the context of *Nkula,* a ritual performed to cure menstrual disorders, represents at its orectic pole the "blood of birth," while at the normative pole, it represents matriliny and also the historical connection between the Ndembu and the empire of Mwantiyanvwa in the Congo, whose first incumbent, a female chief called Luweji Ankonde, suffered from menorrhagia. The tough *chikoli* thorn tree, which plays an important role in the boys' circumcision ritual, is said to stand for "masculinity" in the moral and social sense. It is said to stand for courage (*wulobu*), skill at hunting, and for "speaking well in legal cases," but *chikoli* also has its physiological pole. To quote one informant: "*Chikoli* is a very strong tree, its wood is very hard. One name for it is *chikang' anjamba,* from *ku-kang'anya,* to fail, and *njamba,* the elephant. The elephant fails to break it. Neither wind nor rain can break it, and white ants cannot eat it. It stands upright like the male organ or a man's strong body. That is why we say it represents strength. (*wukolu*). "*Chikoli*, like *wukolu*, is derived from *ku-kola*, "to be strong or potent." I could cite many other Ndembu examples of this polarity, which I consider to be a universal feature of ritual symbols of any semantic complexity.

However, let us return to the *mudyi* tree, this time to observe what takes place near and around it on the day of the novice's ordeal, the phase of *Kwing'ija,* or "putting in," with which the girl's puberty ritual (*Nkang'a*) begins. For now we are going to consider the operational meaning of the milk tree. Immediately we are confronted with a problem. Whereas it can be argued that on the exegetic level of meaning, the structural referents of the milk tree are concerned with the harmonious and solidary aspects of groups and relationships organized by matriliny or femininity, it is immediately obvious that much of the behavior observable in connection with it represents a mimesis of conflict within those very groups and relationships.

For example, in the early hours of the morning only the senior women of the novice's own village may dance around the *mudyi* tree. Later on, only women and no men may dance there, and the women attack the men in jeering and lampooning songs. Moreover, for a long time the girl's mother may not approach the *mudyi* tree, and when she eventually does so, she is mocked by the senior women. I might also mention an episode in which all the senior women compete to be first to snatch a spoon of cassava mush and beans, called "the porridge of *chipwampwilu,*" from the ritual instructress. This porridge represents fertility and in particular, the novice's fertility. If a woman from a distant village grabs the spoon first, this is thought to mean that the novice will bear her children far away from her mother's place of residence. This episode represents competition between the principles of matriliny and virilocality. Other episodes in *Nkang'a* also signify this conflict, though most of them do not have direct reference to the milk tree.

Thus, during different episodes, the value attached to the solidarity of women is contradicted in practice by the conflict between the novice's mother and the adult women who are ritually incorporating her daughter into their married ranks and removing her from her mother's knee. It is further contradicted by the separa-

VICTOR TURNER

tion of the novice's village members from the other women, and by
the rivalry, on a village basis, between the women for the novice's
fertility, and between individual women for fertility. The unity of
the tribe is contradicted by the mobilization of the women around
the milk tree in jeering opposition to the men. The novice's ordeal,
with the threat of punishment if she moves, represents one aspect
of the conflict between senior women and girls.

What is interesting is that indigenous informants do not relate
these conflicts, stereotyped though they be, to their orthodox interpretations of the symbolism of the milk tree. Yet these mimed conflicts have to take place at the *ifwilu,* the novice's "dying place,"
which is located next to the milk tree. A psychoanalyst of the
Kleinian school might be tempted perhaps to relate the contrast
between the exegetic and operational levels of meaning, between
the emphasis on harmony and the emphasis on discord, to the
infant's ambivalent attitude to the mother's breast, which both
soothes him and arouses hostility by its capricious absences. He
might regard the lack of interpretation of the conflict behavior as
due to the psychological "splitting" mechanism which separates the
hostile from the loving attitude to the breast and thrusts this hostility
into the unconscious psyche, but it is theoretically inadmissible to
explain social facts, such as ritual symbols, by the concepts of depth
psychology. A sociological hypothesis to account for the contradiction between these levels of meaning might be advanced to the
effect that on the exegetic level, the principle of matriliny is
abstracted from its social context and appears in its ideal purity.
The conflicts within groups and relationships articulated by matriliny
which are exhibited at the operational level are not due to the structural inadequacies of matriliny or to human frailty with regard to
keeping rules, but rather result from other principles of social organization which constantly and consistently interfere with the harmonious working of matriliny. Age and sex differences cut across
matrilineal affiliation. Virilocal marriage strikes into the cohesion
of a local matrilineage. The matricentric family makes rival demands
on the loyalty of members of a matrilineage. Type-conflicts of these
kinds are acted out before the milk tree, the archsymbol of
matrilineal continuity, and of the ultimate dependence of Ndembu
society on the mother's breast. The puberty ritual asserts that
though matriliny may regularly be challenged by other principles

and trends, yet it persists and triumphs.

In conclusion, I would like to draw attention to the relationship between the milk tree symbolism and the symbolic principle of "whiteness" (*wutooka*) on the exegetic level of interpretation. At the apex of the total symbolic system of the Ndembu is the color triad, white—red—black. At certain esoteric episodes in the boys' circumcision ritual and in the initial ritual of the men's and women's funerary associations of *Mung'ong'i* and *Chiwila,* the meanings of these three colors are taught to young Ndembu. Whiteness is most commonly represented by powdered white clay (*mpemba* or *mpeza*), redness by powdered red clay (*mukundu, ng'ula,* or *mukung'u*), and blackness by charcoal (*makala*). These substances are not so much symbols as tokens of three vital principles, akin to the Hindu "strands of life" mentioned in the Bhagavad-Gita. I have collected many texts and made many observations of the use of these colors in ritual and may therefore state briefly that whiteness stands, *inter alia,* for goodness (*ku-waha*), health (*ku-koleka*), ritual purity (*ku-tooka*), freedom from misfortune (*ku-bula ku-halwa*), for political authority (*wanta*), and for assembling with the spirits (*kudibomba niakishi*). To sum up, it represents the entire moral order plus the fruits of virtue; health, strength, fertility, the respect of one's fellows, and the blessing of one's ancestors. Whiteness differs from redness in that it stresses harmony, cohesion, and continuity, while redness, associated with bloodspilling as well as with blood kinship, tends to denote discontinuity, acquired through breach of certain rules, and male aggressiveness (as in hunting, which is represented in many rituals by red clay and red symbols).

There are many symbols that Ndembu themselves class as "white things" and which they believe to be pervaded by the moral attributes of whiteness. The milk tree, representing matriliny, is one of these. For Ndembu, matriliny is what Professor Fortes has called (1949, 344), though in a rather different connection, an "irreducible principle" of social organization, through which the moral order, with all its prescription and prohibitions, is mediated to the individual. Matriliny is the framework of those aspects of Ndembu morality which the people regard as changeless and as harmoniously interrelated nodal points. It would be possible to show that the norms and values controlling those relationships derived from the tie of milk form the "matrix" of the moral order and have ideally

VICTOR TURNER

what Ndembu would regard as a "white" quality. Matriliny gives a specific form and stamp to a morality which would otherwise be imprecise and general.

References

Fortes, Meyer.
    1949. *The Web of Kinship among the Tallensi.* London: Oxford University Press.

POLITICAL SYMBOLISM

Abner Cohen

Abner Cohen was Victor Turner's first student at the University of Manchester, and he extended Turner's ideas in much the same way that Turner extended the ideas of his own teacher, Max Gluckman. Whereas Turner concentrated on ritual symbolism, Cohen deals primarily with political symbolism—or, more precisely, with cultural symbols that have political implications and functions. Anthropology's major contribution to the study of politics, he argues, lies in examining symbols that are apparently non-political— those of religion, kinship, race, ethnicity, and so on—which nonetheless impinge on politics in subtle but significant ways. "Often," he observes, "the less obviously political in form symbols are, the more efficacious politically they prove to be"

Cohen's central perspective is that human social life involves an ongoing dialectic between cultural expression and political interests. In the process, culture is politicized and politics is invested with cultural significance. Hence in order to understand the meaning and internal dynamic of political activity, one must situate it within this "two-dimensional" process. Cohen developed this perspective in his research in West Africa, and then elaborated it in his studies of racial and ethnic minorities in plural societies. This latter work, which has been taken further by other anthropologists as well as those in cognate disciplines (as seen in Sections II, III, and IV of this book), demonstrates the relevance of the Manchester tradition to the study of contemporary social issues.

Cohen discusses Marxist and neo-Marxist approaches in the piece that follows, but he is careful to avoid the reductionism into which they often fall. Ideas, he emphasizes, are neither an illusion of material conditions nor a resource that is monopolized by the ruling class. Alternately, ideas and the symbolism in which they are expressed are real phenomena that are actively contested within specific political fields by social groups with conflicting interests.

ABNER COHEN

*Hence ritual, festivity, and other modes of cultural performance
are often rife with political significance, and are themselves integral
aspects of the wider political environment.*

Much OF THE RECENT LITERATURE that bears directly on political symbolism has been surveyed in two excellent papers, the one
on "Symbolic Studies" by Turner (1975), the other on "Political
Anthropology" by Vincent (1978). In this paper I explore a number
of key conceptual, analytical, and methodological issues that are involved in this topic, covering some of the more recent publications,
including relevant Marxian literature. A good deal of the discussion
will be concerned with unfolding the political implications of cultural symbols. This is because many, indeed most, of the symbols
that are politically significant are overtly nonpolitical. Often, the
less obviously political in form symbols are, the more efficacious
politically they prove to be. The greatest contribution of sociocultural anthropology to the study of politics has been the analysis of
the political functions of symbolic, nonpolitical institutions like kinship and religion.

It is the very essence and potency of symbols that they are ambiguous, referring to different meanings, and are not given to
precise definition. The most dominant symbols are essentially bivocal, being rooted, on the one hand, in the human condition, in what
may be called "selfhood," and on the other in the relations of power.
Forms that are clearly and formally political tend to be signs, not
symbols; they lack ambiguity and are thus unidimensional. Some of
them do in time become efficacious, but only when they acquire
nonpolitical, existentialist meanings in addition to their formal connotation.

Extensive Definitions

These are categorical statements which make a number of basic
assumptions that are highly controversial. First among these is
the statement that politics refers to the distribution, maintenance,
exercise of, and struggle for power within a social unit. Power is
analytically conceived as an aspect of nearly all social relation-

ships. Even such primary relationships as those between husband and wife, father and son, or friend and friend have their own power element and thus form part of the political system in any society.

The term "power" is an abstraction referring simply to relations of domination and subordination. These are either economic relations, arising in the course of production, exchange, and distribution, or "purely political," deriving ultimately from command over organized physical force. These two types of relations, though distinct in many respects, are interrelated and in many situations inseparable. Nearly everywhere in small-scale preindustrial societies the system of land tenure, client-patron relationships, exchange, and the distribution of goods are inseparable parts of the political order. In many centralized tribal societies, the chief holds the land in trust and allocates it to his people; in exchange he is given allegiance and part of the produce, which he then redistributes. In many uncentralized societies, mythologies of kinship that are often articulated in the form of elaborate genealogies regulate the distribution of land and define political groupings at one and the same time. Similarly, in the advanced industrial societies the relationships between property owner and user, employer and employee, producer and consumer, and a host of similar relationships are maintained and regulated by the laws of the state. Economic and political interests interpenetrate each other and react on one another. They continually exert pressure on the state and the state continually exerts pressure on them.

Some Marxists would object to these formulations on the ground that all relationships of power derive from the relations of production and that the state itself is but an instrument used by the economically dominant class to develop and protect its interests and maintain the relations of production by organized coercion. Thus in their celebrated metaphor of the superstructure and infrastructure, Marx & Engels (1970) placed politics and law in the superstructure, not in the economic base. This view of the state and of politics was no doubt greatly affected by the conditions prevailing in industrializing European societies during the nineteenth century. But the state is now almost everywhere, in capitalist as in communist societies, a power in its own right, regulating the increasingly complex public services, running industries, and becoming to a large

ABNER COHEN

extent autonomous, and it is not simply the agent of one class or another. There is no evidence that it is "withering away" in communist countries.

On the other hand, as Anderson points out:

> the aftermath of the Second World War also saw the establishment, for the first time in the history of bourgeois rule, of representative democracy based on universal suffrage as the normal and stable structure of the State in all the main capitalist countries—West Germany, Japan, France, USA, England, Italy (1976: 46-48).

These are conditions unaccounted for by classical Marxism. It is probably a reflection of these developments that Althusser (1970, 1971) has modified the Marxian metaphor, giving a relative autonomy to politics and law which is separate from the superstructure (see also Milliband 1974: 51). This is not to deny that the state, while attending to universalistic functions for the society as a whole, both internally and externally, is at the same time and to a larger or lesser extent also particularistic, serving the interests of one power group or another.

The two types of power, the economic and the political, are of course distinguishable in many respects. But for heuristic purposes most social anthropologists have concentrated on the common denominator between them, namely power relations. When anthropologists study economic activity, their ultimate aim is to discover the relations of power that are involved in production, exchange, and distribution.

Power relations are objectified, developed, maintained, expressed, or camouflaged by means of symbolic forms and patterns of symbolic action, both or which are referred to here as "symbolism." In most of the systems that anthropologists have studied, kinship and ritual have been the main form of symbolism; they are deployed alternatively, or combined together as articulating principles that are dialectically related to power relations. There are of course other symbolic forms that are similarly related to power. Indeed the whole of normative culture is involved here. "Culture," writes Raymond Williams (1976: 76) "is one of the two or three most complicated words in the English language." It is a highly ambiguous term which is extensively used in many different senses and is thus too wide in its various connotations to be useful in sociological analysis. What is astonishing is that anthropologists who specialize in the analysis of culture should continue to use this term in the global, ragbag definition formulated by nineteenth century writers. In its current usage in social anthropology, the word often covers both utilitarian and normative traits, both objective and subjective phenomena.

Marxist writers use the term "ideology" as a substitute. Indeed, as Anderson (1976) points out, Western Marxists since the end of the First World War have been principally concerned with the analysis of ideology or superstructure. Literally hundreds of books and articles have recently been published on the subject, mostly attempting to define what ideology is and what Marx and his followers have said about it. The most systematic comprehensive analysis in this respect to date is that of Althusser (1969, 1971). But what is clear from reading Marxist literature is a complete lack of consensus about what ideology is and what functions it plays in society. What makes the subject more confusing is that Marx himself and even Althusser changed their views about ideology in the course of their careers. The result is that the concept is now as confused, if not more so, as that of culture. Ideology has been conceived as an epistemological concept, as the way men know their world; as a systematic body of values, norms, and beliefs; as synonymous with all culture, including ritual and ceremonial beliefs and practices. It has been described as "false consciousness" (Lukacs 1971), inspired by the ruling classes to mystify people and prevent them from uncovering exploitation, and as such it exists only in class societies (Marx & Engels 1970). Althusser (1969: 231-36), on the other hand, emphasized that ideology is an organic part of every social identity, that it is indispensable in any society, communist or capitalist. Some writers conceive ideology as expressive of, or determined by, the relations of production; others—including Althusser—regard it as relatively autonomous and as instrumental in recreating the relations of production.

One way of overcoming some of the difficulties and ambiguities involved is to apprehend culture or ideology in their manifestations in symbolic performances that are objective and collective and hence observable and verifiable, indicating normative patterns of action, in sharp contrast with utilitarian and technical patterns.

ABNER COHEN

Power relations and symbolism are present in all social relationships. This broad conception of political symbolism led me to conclude a paper on "Political Anthropology: The Analysis of the Symbolism of Power Relations" (1969) by the statement that "political anthropology is nothing other than social anthropology brought up to a high degree of abstraction." This view drew sharp criticism from some colleagues, and it will be instructive to discuss some of the arguments involved, as they will highlight the central theoretical issues in the study of political symbolism.

Politics and the Symbolism of Life Crises

If we consider the crisis of death, we shall immediately be struck by its universality and pervasiveness. "Why are we born and why do we die?" is a problem that has confronted all people in all societies at all times. It is a perennial problem in the sense that it can have no scientific solution. There have been, in fact, almost as many "solutions" as there have been cultures, and no one can tell which solution is more scientific than which. Everywhere the crisis is marked by symbolic patterns of action. The crisis is thus and to that extent irreducible; it is universal and is probably the most crucial factor in the human condition generally.

But if the symbolism of death is purely expressive of a universal, perennial human problem, we would expect it to be ceremonialized *in equal intensity* (although allowing for differences in symbolic forms) throughout humanity. A quick comparative survey of the literature, however, will immediately show considerable variations in the degree of ceremonialization. In some societies, death ceremonials are simple and brief; in others they are highly elaborate and extensive. In some cases death is considered terminal and the dead are thought to be gone forever; in other cases death is regarded as a phase in the biography of persons, after which the dead resume existence as spirits which interact with the living and affect their life in a variety of ways. In this latter case the dead, or some of the dead, are revered and feared, and extensive recurring rituals are performed for them.

A comparison between different groups will also indicate that the intensity of the ceremonials of death and of the dead is not related to the level of education or to so-called civilization. Even my own very limited ethnographic field studies demonstrate this clearly. Neither Middle East peasants nor indigenous African traders nor West Indian proletariat in London show a fraction of the elaborate cult of the dead which is practised among the highly educated and sophisticated Creoles of Sierra Leone. Indeed, among these the cult has been considerably intensified during the last three decades as more and more Creoles acquired higher education and joined the professional elite of the country.

This is not the place to give a detailed discussion of the variety of cults related to death and to the dead. What is evident from the ethnographic literature is that the intensity of the ceremonialization of this motif is closely related to fundamental politico-economic factors. The ancestors' cult reported for numerous societies, including the Chinese (Ahern 1973; Freedman 1966), the Tallensi (Fortes 1945), and the Lugbara (Middleton 1960), has been shown to be instrumentally related to the structure of the lineage system, to political alignments, territorial divisions, and the organization of authority. Among the Creoles of Sierra Leone (Cohen 1980), the intensification of the cult in the last three decades is related to the political cleavage that has developed between them and the provincials over political power and public employment, but more particularly over control of vast freehold land and housing estates in the Freetown peninsula. Comprising less than 2 percent of the population of the country, yet dominating the civil service and the professions, they believe that as long as they maintain their control over land in the most politically and economically strategic part of the country, they can maintain their privileged position. But Creole landlords are under constant pressure and sometimes temptation to sell housing and land at ever mounting prices. The only force stopping them from doing so is their fear of the dead who bequeathed to them most of this property, where the spirits of the dead continue to dwell.

In all these cases, the cult of the dead is a collective representation which constrains individuals—sometimes against their conscious wills and private interests—and its symbolism is charged with political significance. Thus the question of "why are we born and why do we die" is embedded in the very core of human nature, but the symbolic beliefs and practices that are developed to deal with it are rarely individual constructions; they are often collective

ABNER COHEN

and always loaded with meanings and functions that develop and maintain the interests of the group.

There is no reductionism here. On the contrary, the problem of death is such a deep-rooted and powerful human issue that power groups everywhere seize on it and exploit it for their ends. This is true of all societies, including the modern, officially secular communist societies. The cult of Lenin is an eloquent example. Lenin's body was embalmed, mummified, and put on display in a special mausoleum in Red Square, which is the center of all major national political gatherings. Millions of people from all over the Soviet Union go on pilgrimage to the shrine, queuing up for hours in long rows, silently watching the change of the guard, then file up to view the body in awe and respect. It was of course initially a *consciously* institutionalized cult aiming at commemorating and glorifying "the Father of the Revolution" and unifying his people behind the party that he founded. The authors of the cult might have been highly rational men who planned "scientifically" the whole procedure. But such innovators are few in number and for the millions of ordinary people, young and old, the cult is powerful principally because it is also mystically related to something rooted in their very human nature. For the leaders, the body might have been a political "sign" with specifically defined meaning, but for the masses of people it is a symbol with different connotations, some of which touch some of their innermost thoughts and feelings.

The political significance of this kind of cult can be seen even more dramatically in the development in our time of a similar practice surrounding Mao Tse Tung in China. For about three decades the communist authorities have waged a relentless war against the traditional Chinese lineage which had been the basis of regional political organization, often competing and sometimes challenging the authority of the central government. This meant an attack on the ancestors' cult which expressed and maintained the corporateness and the organizing principle of the lineage. However, the sentiment relating to the dead is not itself suppressed, but is now partly channelled to what may well become the most massive cult of the dead in history, as the communist authorities have planned and actually set up a mausoleum for Mao which would dwarf that of Lenin.

This manipulation of dead corpses to serve as dominant political symbols is successful, not for purely rational considerations. For if that were the case, a memorial picture or statue, or any monument to the dead, rather than a decaying corpse, would have been sufficient. But the sight of the corpse by the masses of visitors, amidst strictly observed silence and solemnity, the association of the mausoleum with supreme state power, the guards of honor, reverence and admiration for the deceased, all these combine significantly with the enigmatic problem of life and death to conjure up in the minds of the pilgrims a complex psychic experience which can add further to what political philosophers call "political obligation."

Other societies or groups, though, do not neglect the motif of death, but seize on other life crises to infuse power into the symbolism of political authority. Significant among these crises is the initiation of the young to adulthood. In many small-scale preindustrial societies, initiation is dramatic in the sense that it transforms, within a brief period, children into adults. It is also collective in that a whole group of children go through the process at one time. Thus almost overnight, a new generation of men or women comes into being and begins to compete with the established adults over authority and control of resources, in effect threatening to and eventually succeeding in supplanting their parents' generation. The crisis of initiation is thus essentially not individual but social. This is why it is highly ritualized and why its symbolism is of such great political potential. In some societies the crisis serves as a perpetual basis for the organization of political authority and for politicking generally. Thus in Sierra Leone and Liberia alone, there are numerous tribal societies where the initiates become incorporated as permanent members within a secret society: the Poro for men, the Sande for women. Indeed, the importance of the Poro is so pronounced that one anthropologist, d'Azevado (1973), has labelled the whole region as the "the Poro Belt."

The political significance of this cult can be seen from the way the cult is practised among the Mende of Sierra Leone (Little 1951, 1966). Here, Poro initiation is the rite of passage from boyhood to manhood. It takes place in the "secret bush," where the boys are taken and placed under the custody of Poro officials. Rituals are performed to signify the death and subsequent rebirth of the initiates, who in the process undergo physical pain and become imbued with the fear of the horrors that may be inflicted on

ABNER COHEN

wrongdoers by the masked spirits of the society. At the same time, the novices are instructed about sex and the procreation of children, duties to one's tribe and obedience to its elders, and the meaning of life and death. In this way the anxieties caused by passage to adulthood, physical pain, dramatic rituals, and the horrors behind the masks combine to leave in the initiates a deep psychic experience which remains a source of emotional and sentimental agitation that can be triggered and kept alive by the repetitive display of the symbols of the society and the performance of its rituals.

In the process, a powerful bond of loyalty is created in the initiates toward their Poro masters, who are thus loved, revered, feared, and obeyed.

While most of the initiates remain ordinary members of the Poro all their lives, a small minority continues to pursue a ritual career by undergoing further courses of instruction and being subsequently initiated into higher ritual degrees within the order. To achieve this they have to pay high fees and costs, and this means that only the wealthy and influential will rise up in the hierarchy of leadership, at the apex of which stands the "inner circle," whose members are in effect the arbiters of chiefly authority, supporting it and sometimes checking its excesses even to the extent of deposing the incumbent. Little (1965, 1966) says that among the Mende, the Poro provides the mystical element to the otherwise purely secular authority of the chief. The two hierarchies, the ritual and the secular, are in fact overlapping in roles and in personnel. The powerful men in the one tend to be the powerful men in the other.

This makes the Poro into a significant weapon in the hands of chiefly families who use it in some situations, particularly when their own interests are threatened. Such use has actually occurred on a number of occasions during the colonial and postcolonial periods (Cartwright 1970; Kilson 1966; Scott 1960). Thus, Poro organization and loyalties were manipulated in the planning and conduct of the Hut Tax War in 1898 against the British and in the organization of the riots of 1955-56. When the British established the franchise and the country gained independence, Poro institutions were used to mobilize votes in elections. Sierra Leone political parties at the time were loose coalitions without any kind of organization in the provinces and thus relied on the provincial chiefs for the mobilization of votes for them.

POLITICAL SYMBOLISM

A similar organization is based on the initiation of females into the Sande secret society, though because political power in the area is mainly in the hands of men, its political significance is less pronounced. Poro and Sande cults are also found extensively in Iberia (d'Azevedo 1973; Harley 1941; Harley 1950; Libenow 1969). Many other societies in other parts of Africa and elsewhere seize on the crisis of initiation and politicize it in the service of one interest or another.

In industrial and postindustrial societies, initiation is gradual and diffused, though it is no less politicized. Here the rising, maturing young men and women are on the one hand socialized and trained in the dominant culture of the established order and on the other radicalized by the counter-cultures of discontented groups. When they finally graduate, they begin to compete with the more senior cohorts over employment, control of resources, and political power generally. Tension is particularly high in societies increasing in population, where more men and women reach adulthood than retire or die.

Another type of life crisis that is intensely politicized is that of sudden unpredictable misfortune resulting from accident, illness, loss, and calamities of all sorts. A whole system of symbolic beliefs and practices is developed to diagnose, explain, and compensate for the misfortune. This system is concerned not with the "how" but with the "why" of the singularities of misfortune. The Azande (Evans-Pritchard 1937), for example, know the natural process by which a man is killed when a tree trunk falls on him; their concern, however, is not with the immediate natural cause but with the power that brought about such a unique combination of factors and circumstances that led this particular man to pass through that particular spot near that particular trunk at that particular moment, and so on. In many societies this singularity of misfortune is explained not as an accident but as the mystical work of witches, and no redress can be realized until they are discovered and brought to justice. Divination is called for and the witch, often a person innocent of the particular crime in question, is eventually punished. In the not so remote past, witches in Europe, North America, and Africa were even put to death.

Studies of witchcraft in a number of societies have shown that the *incidence* of accusations—i.e. who accuses whom—is not haphazard but occurs mostly between certain related categories of persons. Thus in some matrilineal systems (Marwick 1965, 1952) accusations are often made by a man against his mother's brother, from whom he would eventually inherit property and whom he would replace politically. This relationship is always fraught with tension and quarrel. When the total incidence is considered throughout the extent of the society, it will emerge as the manifestation of a struggle for power between one generation and another.

In some patrilineal societies like the Zulu (Gluckman 1956), most accusations are directed against married women by their in-laws. The Zulu tend to live in extended families consisting of father, mother, and married sons. When the father dies the sons continue to live within the same household. However, as time passes by and the families of the sons expand, the division of the household becomes inevitable. But because of brothers' solidarity, no one would dare suggest such a division. When a member of the household becomes ill, one of the wives (who because of exogamy are strangers from outside the lineage of the husbands) is accused of exercising witchcraft, and this enables her husband to claim that in order to save his brothers from her wickedness he would move with her to live in a separate household; the other brothers seize the opportunity and hive off, each to establish his own separate household.

There are many other variations in the pattern of the incidence of witchcraft accusations. In some tribal systems the chief is endowed with, among many other mystical powers, witchcraft in order to enhance further his authority. In some changing social systems, the ideology of witchcraft serves as a basis for the formation of political factions that are mobilized as "antiwitchcraft movements" whose purported aim is to combat the evil designs of witches, who are in fact their political enemies (Parkin 1968).

In some systems the emphasis is not on redressing but on averting misfortune. This is the case, for example, among a Hausa community based on long-distance trade in Nigeria (Cohen 1969). This trade is full of pitfalls and perils because of numerous factors and circumstances whose combination cannot be predicted by the trader. As a result, almost every trade expedition hovers between success and disaster. In the absence of insurance, banking, modern means of communication, swift and effective procedures of adjudication and hence security of contract, an effort is made to divine the likely outcome of every enterprise. Thus every trader has his own malam, a ritual specialist, whom he regularly consults. Consultation is not exclusively about the prospects of trade but also about every affliction or important stage in life. For example, when a new baby is born the parents consult the malam about the most propitious name to give to it. Malams thus have a strong hold on their clients. They form an order of their own, with a ritual hierarchy which is almost parallel to the political hierarchy, largely made up of the landlords of the trade, or the chief of the community, and of his advisors. All landlords and senior malams have the title *hajji,* gained after pilgrimage to Mecca. They regularly meet with the chief to deal with problems affecting the community as a whole. In these meetings decisions are conveyed to the more junior malams, who duly translate them and pass them on as ritual advice imparted to their clients. Thus the ritual activities of the malams uphold the authority of the chief and ensure the compliance of his subjects to his decisions.

Other crises of life are similarly dramatized and politicized in differing degrees of intensity. Marriage is everywhere related to the distribution of power between groups, and every marriage is thus a political event of the first order whose elements are symbolized in the ceremonials. In some systems its symbolism serves as an articulating principle of social organization, such as in the caste system or in lineage systems of different sorts (see Cohen 1974: 110-119). Even the birth of the first son is an occasion for both rejoicing and anxiety for the father, and in many systems there are elaborate customs of avoidance between the two throughout life in order to relieve tension and inhibit violence. (Fortes 1974). Among the Hausa, almost invariably a relative of the parents would by custom take the first born to raise in her or his own home. The conflict between father and first born is caused by the potential competition between the growing son and the father over property and authority. Fortes (1974) emphasized that in addition to these causes—in fact underlying them—there is a more fundamental source of anxiety felt by the father after the birth of his son. The latter transforms him into a parent and this, while being the cause for rejoicing, is also a sign that a biological replacement of him now exists.

All crises of life are interrelated and form the basis of the human condition. In all societies nearly all crises are ceremonialized, but often unequally. In some societies one crisis is emphasized and made to serve as an articulating idiom of political organization; in others two or more are equally emphasized. In the same society an affliction can be attributed to different mystical causes such as the anger of the dead or the wicked activities of witches, and it is the insight of the diviner that decides which is the relevant cause in each particular case.

The Obligatory in Symbolism

Why is the symbolism of life crises so universally manipulated in politics? First, it deals with perennial problems that are not amenable to scientific solutions and is therefore essentially ambiguous, not given to immediate searching scrutiny. This is why it is often said that one cannot argue with a ritual. For the same reasons, symbolic forms and practices are highly manipulable. The employment of dramaturgical techniques such as music, dancing, poetry, costuming, and alcohol drinking at most life crises ceremonies plays on the sentiments of the participants and sways their belief and action in this direction or that. Often in these circumstances it is not belief that gives rise to ceremonial but ceremonial that conjures up and gives definite form and structure to belief. It is reported that the prophet Muhammad once said that what concerned him was that a Muslim should pray five times a day; as to what went on in the mind of the worshipper, it was between him and Allah.

All this points out that the frequent and repetitive performance of ceremonials related to a crisis of life within a group would raise and enhance the consciousness of its members about the existential problem involved. For example, in a society where for some reasons death is not intensively and extensively ceremonialized, the reality of death is for most of the time absent from the minds of its members. In contrast, where death and the dead are heavily celebrated, as among the Creoles of Sierra Leone, the problem of existence is frequently on people's minds. For this reason it is difficult if not futile to look for basic common psychological denominators across cultures, because the intensity of feeling is itself a variable. The symbolism of life crises is like a rectangle which by definition has two dimensions, one existential, the other political. Both dimensions are to some extent manipulable. But if one dimension is reduced to nil, the shape will cease to be a rectangle and the whole reality of culture will disappear, which means that the phenomenon one is investigating would slip away. All normative culture is two-dimensional and is thus irreducible to either politics or psychology.

The second reason why the symbolism of life crises is so universally politicized is its intrinsic potential for becoming an impelling force, a valence, a categorical imperative, an "ought" that can move women and men to action spontaneously "from the inside," without the immediate incentives of reward or the threats of punishment from the outside. This feature of symbolism stands in sharp contrast with patterns of action that are contractual, utilitarian, and rational, and are implicit in purely political relations, though both types of action, the symbolic and the political, are interrelated. When a political group cannot coordinate its collective action by means of a formal association, it resorts to an informal type of organization that relies for the compliance of its members on the obligatory instead of the contractual. The obligatory, whether moral or ritual, pervades all social life. Even the most formal associations rely, in one organizational function or another, on some forms of obligation. The difference between formal and informal, between the associational and the communal, is a matter of degree. Thus social order in a modern society, whose framework is maintained by state institutions like the police, courts, laws, and the ultimate threat of physical coercion, is largely effected in day-to-day living by moral and ritual obligations that are developed, objectified, and maintained through symbolic forms and symbolic action.

To probe deeper into the nature and the dynamics of political symbolism, it is therefore essential to explore the source of the obligatory in symbolic action. Why does political man—shrewd, calculating, utilitarian—also have to be symbolist man—idealist, altruistic, nonrational? How are purely political interests transformed to the most intimate moral and ritual obligations that impel man to action without exterior constraints?

The nature of obligation has been the subject of extensive discussion and controversy among philosophers over the centuries. Two schools of thought have been evident in the continual debate: the intuitionists, who uphold the uniqueness and irreducibility of

ABNER COHEN

obligation, and the utilitarians, who deny this uniqueness and explain it away in terms of egoistic calculations of consequences aimed at maximizing benefit. In social anthropology the controversy has appeared in a number of theoretical issues. For example, is kinship an irreducible principle of social organization, as Fortes (1949) maintained, or is it only an idiom standing for political and economic interests, as Worsley (1956) and others have argued? Is society a natural system that can be studied scientifically, as Radcliffe-Brown (1952, 1957) and Fortes have contended, or is it a moral system whose study can therefore never be scientific, as Evans-Pritchard (1951, 1963) and others have argued. More recently, the utilitarian stand has received powerful support from some orthodox Marxists who interpret all normative culture as the ideology or the mystification of a dominant class, and from the anthropologists of the transactionalist school who reduce moral action to egocentric strategies directed toward the maximization of personal benefit.

But the majority of social anthropologists remain essentially two-dimensional in their orientation regarding the obligatory and the contractual as different variables intimately involved in all social relationships. Kinship relationships, for example, have both moral and utilitarian strands, and the main task of the anthropological inquiry is to isolate the one variable from the other and to show the nature of the causal or dialectical relation between them. Thus, within the main paradigm of social anthropology, the obligatory in symbolism is a phenomenon *sui generis,* having its own impelling force which, though always interrelated with the political constraints of the collective, remains essentially irreducible.

One attempt to identify and define the source of the valence, the impelling force, in symbolism is implicit in Turner's (1964) well-known distinction between the sensory and the ideological poles within the structure of the ritual symbol. In the course of ritual, the symbol effects an interchange of qualities between the two poles. Norms and values become saturated with emotion, while the gross and basic emotions aroused by the sensory pole become ennobled through contact with values. The irksomeness of moral constraint is transformed into the love of goodness. Ritual symbolism is thus a mechanism which periodically converts the obligatory into the desirable.

This is a very illuminating analysis of the manner in which sym-

POLITICAL SYMBOLISM

bols operate. But it is mainly concerned with the working of symbolic techniques such as color, music, dancing, and the use of the human body, and not the obligatory in symbols. What is more, not all symbols have material representation, and some of those that do are not particularly pleasing or desirable.

Another formulation is provided by Moore & Myerhoff (1977) who, in a discussion of secular ritual, suggest that the hold of ceremony on participants derives from its "traditionalizing effect"— a phrase they borrowed from Apter (1963)—from its potentiality for making new material traditional as well as perpetuating old traditions. Ceremony does this by employing some formal properties that mimic its message. These properties include repetition, acting, stylization, order, evocative style, and the presentation of a social message by its very occurrence. They go on to explain (Moore & Myerhoff 1977: 8)

> In the repetition and order, ritual imitates the rhythmic imperatives of the biological and physical universe, thus suggesting a link with the perpetual processes of the cosmos. It thereby implies permanence and legitimacy of what are actually evanescent cultural constructs. In the acting, stylization and presentational staging, ritual is attention-commanding and deflects questioning at the time. All these formal properties make it an ideal vehicle for the conveying of messages in an authenticating and arresting manner.... Even if it is performed once, for the first and only time, its stylistic rigidities, and its internal repetitions of form or content make it tradition-like.

Again, this sheds further light on the way symbolism operates by indicating the dynamic nature of the symbolic process, though it does not deal with the inner source of obligation, with the uniqueness of "ought." The formulation may be sufficient for the practical purposes of field study and of sociological analysis, and it may be that any further search may only lead to sheer speculative discussion. However, because the issue is so crucial for social anthropology, the inquiry is worth pursuing, as it may affect further advance in our discipline, particularly as we seek to understand *how* our two major variables are interrelated and how a change in the one affects the other.

ABNER COHEN

In an attempt to probe further in this rather meta-anthropological direction, I have focused on the dynamics of selfhood (Cohen 1977) in relation to power and symbolism. Selfhood, the "I," the oneness of an integrated psyche, is not innate in man, but is achieved in the course of interaction with significant other human beings and of developing a body of symbolic beliefs and practices, forming a world view. Almost by definition, symbolic action involves the totality of the self and not a segment or a role within it. We achieve selfhood through continual participation in patterns of symbolic activities. These are for most people provided by the interest group to which they are affiliated: the lineage, tribe, ethnic group, caste, class. When for some reasons groups cannot organize themselves as formal associations based on contract, they attempt to organize informally through the mobilization and manipulation of the obligatory, moral or ritual, in conduct. To that extent, the pursuit of the group's aims will be ensured, not by contractual mechanisms that operate on the individual from the outside through reward and punishment, but by moral and ritual obligations, by "oughts," operating from the inside and involving the total self. The self reacts to this in a variety of ways, including the creation of new symbolic patterns that are free from utilitarian interests. In time the new patterns are exploited by new or old interests and the search for new patterns can be resumed.

A Paradigm for Analysis

What the above discussion indicates is that much of the traditionalizing effect of ceremonial and of the symbolic process generally derives from some basic existential and political imperatives. In all societies people are involved in networks of primary interpersonal relationships: parenthood, marriage and affinity, friendship, brotherhood, ritual kinship, cousinhood. These relationships are developed and maintained by a complex body of symbolic beliefs and practices. People also engage in symbolic activities purporting to deal with the perennial problems of the human condition. These symbolic activities may have different social groups, or in the same group at different historical periods, but the basic themes are the same, though the intensity of involvement may vary from case to case.

At the same time, the same people are the members of interest groups with some basic organizational needs such as distinctiveness and authority. These groups may differ in size, composition, and aims, but they tend to have the same organizational requirements which, when for some reasons they cannot be met by means of formal associations, are met by some basic symbolic constructions.

Thus, despite drastic changes in power relationships and the almost endless variety of cultural traditions, there are basic symbolic forms that tend to recur in different sociocultural systems and at different historical periods within the same system. The symbolic repertoire of culture is therefore not unlimited. Furthermore, both sets of basic requirements, the existential and the organizational, tend to be met by the same set of symbols. For example, the symbolism of an exclusive cult would articulate the various organizational functions of the group, provide the members with solutions to basic existential problems, and express and maintain their members with primary, affective, moral links with other members and would thus be instrumental in the creation of their selfhoods. At the same time, the relationships may be instrumental in articulating organizational functions such as the definition of the boundaries of the group or the provision of channels for the communication of group messages.

This is indeed the very essence of normative symbols, that they cater at one and the same time to the two types of requirement. Normative symbols are thus essentially *bivocal*, satisfying both existential and political ends. This bivocal is the very basis of the "mystery" in symbolism. A man performing a ritual or participating in a ceremonial is simply unclear, mystified, as to whether his symbolic activities express and cater to his own inner needs or the organizational needs of the group to which he belongs. At times he may be inclined this way, at others that, but often he is unaware of the issue altogether. And it is this ambiguity in their meaning that forges symbols into such powerful instruments in the hands of leaders and of groups in mystifying people for particularistic or universalistic or both purposes.

There is thus a high degree of continuity of symbolic forms, even amid substantial changes in the disposition of power. But their functions within the new political context may be different. This change in function is usually effected through changes in their

ABNER COHEN

recombination within a new ideology. In the process they will undergo change in their weighting, when the significance of some forms will be heightened and exaggerated and that of others deemphasized. It is through these subtle changes in symbolic forms, in their restructuring within new ideologies, that a great deal of organizational change is effected, though a few new forms may appear here or there. Thus a great deal of organizational change is often effected through continuity of old forms.

On the basis of the foregoing discussion, it is possible to develop a tentative outline of a paradigm for the study of political symbolism. In such a paradigm, normative culture, as expressed in symbols, is considered in its relation to political organization on different levels. To simplify the discussion, a model of an interest group, such as a power elite in a contemporary state, can be taken as an example (Cohen 1971, 1980). The members of such an elite perform functions that are both *particularistic*, pertaining to their own sectional interests, and *universalistic*, pertaining to the public interest. Both types of interests are developed and maintained by means of an *organization*, which is usually complex in its structure, being partly *associational*, based on formal contractual lines, and partly *communalistic*, based on informal primary relationships [for these terms see Weber (1947: 136-39)]. The associational part is clearly visible and its observation and study pose no methodological or analytical problem. It is the communalistic part that poses a challenge to the sociological imagination.

To deal with this part methodically and empirically, we can study it in its manifestations in symbolic patterns. These can be analyzed in terms of *symbolic functions, symbolic forms,* and *techniques of symbolization.* A symbolic function, such as the achievement of communion between disparate individuals or groups, can be achieved by means of different symbolic forms, such as a church service, the celebration of the memory of an ancestor, or the staging of extensive ceremonials among overlapping groupings within the elite. Similarly, a ritual performance can employ different techniques of symbolization, such as a church service, the celebration of the memory of an ancestor, or the staging of extensive ceremonials among overlapping groupings within the elite. Similarly, a ritual performance can employ different techniques of symbolization, such as poetry, music, dancing, commensality. Different organizational functions such as distinctiveness and communication can be achieved by the same symbolic form such as kinship. On the other hand, the same organizational function such as authority can be achieved through a combination of different symbolic forms, such as kinship and ritual, as in the power of elders derived simultaneously from their genealogical position and from their monopoly of intercession with the dead on behalf of their offspring.

Such a paradigm can be significant for further meaningful research in two main directions. First, it facilitates comparative analysis across cultures and subcultures. It makes it possible to see how different symbolic forms and techniques of symbolization can be developed to achieve the same symbolic functions, and how different symbolic forms, functions, and techniques achieve the same organizational functions.

Second, it is probably a most promising device for the fruitful study of the dynamics of politico-cultural change and hence of the nature of politico-cultural causation. For although power relations and symbolic patterns of action are intimately interconnected, they differ sharply in their process of change. Marxists would refer to this as "the principle of uneven development." Changes in the relationships of power are often effected by means of symbolic continuities, not by means of new symbolic forms. An example is the manipulation of the local traditional Poro symbolic beliefs and practices in modern national election campaigns in Sierra Leone. Similar use has been made in modern contexts of such traditional forms as lineages (Cohen 1965; Hill 1963), castes, and ethnicity. On the other hand, a change in symbolic forms need not indicate a change in power relations. Thus under some new political circumstances, interest groups that in the past articulated their organizational functions in terms of ethnicity may now resort to religious symbolism as a substitute to articulate the same functions. Again, some apparent change in symbolic forms may be due only to change in techniques of symbolization. For example, facial and bodily markings to indicate sex, age, and status differences may give way under new circumstances to the adoption of different types of dress to indicate the same lines of differentiation without necessarily indicating any fundamental changes in the distribution of power or in symbolic functions.

The comparative study of such situations and developments will make it possible to probe deeper into the analysis of politico-cul-

ABNER COHEN

tural causation. Analysis in social anthropology generally has so far tended to be in terms of sociocultural correlations. We often juxtapose the social and the cultural and state that the two are interdependent without going deeper into the nature of mediation between them. But two processes may operate together epiphenomenally without any necessary direct causal connection between them. It is thus essential to attempt to show how the two variables act and react on one another.

One way of doing this is to explore the dramatic process underlying the rituals, ceremonials, and other types of symbolic activities in social life. For it is mainly in the course of such key dramatic performances that the symbolic order and the power order interpenetrate one another, so to speak, to produce, and repetitively reproduce, the bivocality and hence the mystificatory nature of the major symbolic forms. In these performances, selfhood is recreated in terms of the symbolic forms that articulate the changing organizational needs of the group; and organizational needs are thereby transformed into categorical imperatives that impel the individual to action through the inner dynamics of selfhood. In this way, the study of sociocultural causation and change becomes the analysis of the creation or transformation of dramatic forms, their production, direction, authentication, the techniques they employ, the process of acting them out, living them through, and the transformation they bring about in the relationships between the men and women involved in them.

The sociological importance of the analysis of the dramas of ritual and ceremonial has been stressed within social anthropology by a number of writers, among them Gluckman (1942, 1954, 1961), Turner (1957), Peters (1963), Mitchell (1956), and Frankenberg (1957, 1966). Turner in particular has developed dramatic analysis into an effective method for the study of the dialectical relations between politics and ritual action. It is possible that further advance can be made in this direction through a more systematic isolation and definition of the variables involved and through the application of the method to the study of symbolic action generally. This will also have the effect of rendering the vexing controversy about the difference between ritual and secular ceremonial irrelevant.

A drama is a limited sequence of symbolic action, defined in space and time, which is formally set aside from the ordinary flow of purposeful social action. In this sense the drama is not an imitation of life but a symbolic construction. It is also in a sense timeless. Ordinary social life consists of complex processes of events involving a multiplicity of actors, themes, variables, issues, and purposes in a never-ending sequence. In contrast, the drama selects a few elements that are not obviously related in ordinary life, indeed that are often contradictory, and integrates them within a unity of action and of form, a *gestalt*, that temporarily structures the psyches of the actors and transforms their relationships.

This usage of the term drama is thus narrower than the metaphorical sense in which "all the world's a stage" and the ordinary phenomenological flow of ongoing social life and social crises are treated as "theatrical" events. Turner's (1957: 19) "social drama" encompasses both a series of actual events occurring over a long period of time and involving a number of people in their daily quarrels and alliances, and the performance of ritual dramas in the narrower sense of the term, within an overall analytical framework for which Gluckman (1961) coined the term "extended case method." I am here using the term in its more restricted sense in order to highlight a number of issues involved in the analysis of sociocultural causation. The two senses of the term "drama" are of course not opposed to one another but mark differences in emphasis. For even a "pure," formalized, highly conventional drama like a church service or a wedding reception or a ball is always interpenetrated in its procedure by nondramatic events that are not formally designed as parts of the original dramaturgical script.

Politico-cultural causation operates in a continual series of dramatic performances on different levels of social organization. These performances objectify norms, values, and beliefs; interpret the private in terms of the collective, the abstract in terms of the concrete; confirm or modify relationships, temporarily resolving contradictions; and always recreate the belief, the conviction of the actors in the validity of their roles in society.

The work of the anthropologist in such analysis is akin to that of the dramatist in the Brechtian tradition (Althuser 1969: 129-51; & Lacey 1976) whose play would take a familiar, everyday event out of its ordinary ideological sequence and "throw it into crisis" by placing it in the context of a power struggle in society. In a recent study (Cohen, 1980) I attempt to do this by demonstrating how

ABNER COHEN

ordinary symbolic performances—a dancing ball, a university graduation ceremony, a funeral service, a wedding festivity—repetitively reproduce or modify power relationships and how they combine in a culture which functions instrumentally in transforming a category of senior civil servants and professionals to an interacting, cooperating, and cohesive power elite. In a more recent study I focus on a West Indian annual carnival in London, showing how in the course of about 14 years a cultural performance originally staged by a few hundred people has evolved into a massive politico-symbolic drama, mobilizing in its preparation and staging hundreds of thousands of black unemployed and semiemployed for political action.

The analysis of cultural performances as dramas is only the last stage of a long, sustained, and demanding research procedure. This is because the paradigm requires a *holistic coverage* of the social and cultural life of the group one would be studying. In order to discover the relations of power, one has to study economic and political institutions and to analyze the interconnections between them; and in order to discover the symbolic order, one has to study the major symbolic institutions because these are often complementary and interchangeable. It is only after identifying the two major variables that a final analysis and presentation of dramatic performances can be made, although a more preliminary analysis of them would have to be made in the process before this stage is reached.

This holistic coverage of both the total culture and the total power structure of a collectivity distinguishes social anthropology from other social sciences like economics and political science, each of which tends to be concerned mainly with one institution which is abstracted from the total social reality.

But because the method is so demanding, social anthropologists are forced to confine themselves to a small area of social life at a time, though without losing sight of the fact that that area is a part of ever-encompassing social units that form a total structure. How to delineate such a small area of social life, and within which total structure to consider it, are methodological problems that have been hotly debated in the literature.

POLITICAL SYMBOLISM

Toward a Universal Discipline of Sociocultural Anthropology

What is clear from the foregoing discussion is that the symbols of normative culture are almost by definition bivocal, being simultaneously both political and existential. They are not politically neutral. One result of this for the anthropological enterprise is the difficulty of establishing a science of cultural symbols, a symbolic anthropology, which seeks to study pure "symbolic systems" by discovering regular relations between symbols without systematic reference to the dynamics of power relations.

Some serious attempts to overcome this difficulty have been made by a number of anthropologists whose findings have been reviewed recently by Turner (1975). A few of these schools of thought explain the symbols of culture in terms of a system of logic which is ultimately rooted in the structure of the mind or of language. A survey of their literature will so far yield only a few, rather axiomatic, general formulations. For example, numerous studies in this field seek to demonstrate the truisms of binary or complementary oppositions: right-left, white-black, and so on. A good example can be found in a recent book, *The Reversible World*, edited by Babcock (1978), containing a collection of studies arguing the universality of symbolic inversion in all human activities, including literature, art, religion, play, relations between the sexes, systems of classification, the marking of group boundaries. The idea of inversion is also brought to bear on political action by some of the contributors. Thus Rosaldo (1978) shows how colonizers sought to enhance or justify their control of the Ilongots by attributing to them traits that are the inversion or negation of what they regarded as their own traits. The individual papers in the collection are interesting and important, each in itself, but the general argument does not add much to what was said earlier by many other writers.

A different orientation in developing a science of symbols is represented by the formulations made by Dolgin, Kemnitzer & Schneider (1977) in their lengthy introduction to a recent volume of readings. The collection contains 28 papers by different writers, including C. Geertz, D.H. Hymes, H. Marcuse, K. Marx, M. Sahlins, D.M. Schneider, and V. Turner. Many of the works are well-known masterpieces on different topics; all deal with issues involving symbolism. But the introduction seeks to develop an analysis of the common denominator between the papers, namely symbols and their meanings as considered on their own, and to offer a definition and outline of "Symbolic Anthropology." The result is a series of astonishingly obscure and mystifying formulations that in many places defy understanding, purporting to show in the end that symbolic action can be understood only in terms of other symbolic action. The confusion is not so much a reflection on the editors as on the nature of the enterprise. This is perhaps symbolized in the title of the Introduction: "As people express their lives, so they are..."—an out-of-context quote of a half statement made by Marx in *The German Ideology* (Marx & Engels 1970: 42), in effect inverting the founder of dialectical materialism into a tautologous idealist!

The endeavour to develop a science of symbols and meanings has attracted some of the most brilliant, original, and imaginative minds in anthropology. This has been its strength and also its limitation. Its strength stems from the *individual* creativity displayed in works of contemplation and vision, covering topics from art, literature, logic, linguistics, philosophy, theology, and psychology, marshalling stimulating quotations and apt illustrations, making witty statements and observations, and conjecturing meanings for symbols. Leach (Leach 1967: xvii) once said that Lévi-Strauss inspires him even when he does not understand what Lévi-Strauss is saying. In a similar fashion different readers find different points of interest and inspiration in the works of these symbologists. But when one finishes reading a work in this genre, one begins to wonder where the exposition would lead and how the inquiry could be developed further from there. So far, the different individual contributions in this field do not seem to add up to a *discipline*—a discipline in the sense of the recognition of a clearly defined problematic, a clear methodology, and a clear procedure for cumulative effort—discipline in the sense that students can acquire the knowledge and the skills that will enable them to make their own original contributions to the collective enterprise. There are of course those who argue that the study of human society generally cannot lead to the development of a discipline of this kind. But many others believe it can, or at least postulate such a possibility as a guide for systematic research.

Power and symbolism are the two major variables that pervade all social life, and social anthropology already has the possibilities for developing the study of the relations between them into a promisingly cumulative discipline with a working paradigm to guide a fairly open-ended research. What it needs further as a discipline is to be truly comparative, covering the study of urban as well as rural, industrial as well as preindustrial, communist as well as capitalist systems, demystifying in the process ideologies of all sorts, particularistic and universalistic, rendering conscious what is essentially nonconscious, and thereby throwing new light on the nature of man, society, and culture.

References

Ahern, E. M.
  1973 *The Cult of the Dead in a Chinese Village.* Stanford: Stanford Univ. Press.
Althusser, L.
  1969 *For Marx.* Harmondsworth: Penguin.
  1970 *Reading Capital.* London: New Left Books.
  1971 *Lenin and Philosophy.* New York: Monthly Review Press.
Anderson, P.
  1976 *Considerations on Western Marxism.* London: New Left Books.
Apter, D.E.
  1963 Political religion in the new nations. In *Old Societies and New States,* ed. C. Geertz. Glencoe: Free Press, Collier-Macmillan.
Babcock, B.A., ed.
  1978 *The Reversible World: Symbolic Inversion in Art and Society.* Ithaca & London: Cornell Univ. Press.
Cartwright, J.R.
  1970 *Politics in Sierra Leone 1947-1967.* Toronto: Univ. Press.
Cohen, A.
  1965, 1972 *Arab Border Villages in Israel: A Study in Continuity and Change in Social Organization.* Manchester: Manchester Univ. Press.
  1969 *Custom and Politics in Urban Africa: A Study of Hausa Migrants in Yoruba Towns.* Berkeley & Los Angeles: Univ. of California Press.
  1969 Political anthropology: the analysis of the symbolism of power relations. *Man* (N.S.) 4:215-35.

ABNER COHEN

1974 Introduction: The lesson of ethnicity. In *Urban Ethnicity,* ed. A. Cohen. ASA Monogr. No. 12, pp. ix-xxiv. London: Tavistock.
1974 *Two-Dimensional Man: An Essay on the Anthropology of Power and Symbolism in Complex Society.* Berkeley and Los Angeles: Univ. California Press.
1977 Symbolic action and the structure of the self. In *Symbols and Sentiments,* ed. I.M. Lewis. London: Academic.
1979 Variables in ethnicity. In *Ethnic Change,* ed. C.F. Keyes. Seattle: Univ. Washington Press.
1980 *The Power Mystique: Explorations in the Dramaturgy of Eliteness in Modern Africa.*

d'Azevedo, W.L.
1973 Mask makers and myth in Western Liberia. In *Primitive Art and Society,* ed. A. Forge. London: Oxford Univ. Press.

Dolgin, J.L., Demnitzer, D.S., Schneider, D.M., eds.
1977 Introduction. *Symbolic Anthropology: A Reader in the Study of Symbols and Meanings,* pp. 3-44. New York: Columbia Univ. Press.

Evans-Pritchard, E.E.
1937 *Witchcraft, Oracles and Magic among the Azande of the Anglo-Egyptian Sudan.* Cambridge: Cambridge Univ. Press.
1951 *Social Anthropology.* London: Cohen & West.
1963 *The Comparative Method in Social Anthropology.* L.T. Hobhouse Memorial Trust Lecture No. 33, Univ. London. London: Athlone.

Fortes, M.
1945 *The Dynamics of Clanship among the Tallensi.* London: Oxford Univ. Press.
1949 *The Web of Kinship among the Tallensi.* London: Oxford Univ. Press,
1953 *Social Anthropology at Cambridge since 1900,* an inaugural lecture. Cambridge: Cambridge Univ. Press.
1974 The first born. *J. Child Psychol. Psychiatry* 15:81-104.

Frankenberg, R.
1957 *Village on the Border.* London: Cohen & West.
1966 British community studies: Problems of synthesis. In *The Social Anthropology of Complex Societies,* ed. M. Banton. London: Tavistock.

Freedman, M.
1966 *Chinese Lineage and Society: Fukien and Kwantung.* London: Athlone.

Gluckman, M.
1942 *Analysis of Social Situation in Modern Zululand.* Manchester. Manchester Univ. Press.
1954 *Rituals of Rebellion in South-East Africa.* Manchester: Manchester Univ. Press.
1956. *Custom and Conflict in Africa.* Oxford: Blackwell.
1961 Ethnographic data in British social anthropology. *Sociol. Rev.* (N.S.) 9:5-17.

Harley, G.W.
1941 Notes on the Poro in Liberia. *Peabody Mus. Pap.* 19:(2).
1950 Masks as agents of social control. *Peabody Mus. Pap.* 28:(2).

Hill, P.
1963 *The Migrant Cocoa Farmers of Southern Ghana. A Study in Rural Capitalism.* Cambridge: Cambridge Univ. Press.

Kilson, M.
1966 *Political Change in a West African State.* Cambridge, Mass: Harvard Univ. Press.

Lacey, S.
1976 Brecht. *Cultural Studies 9,* pp. 124-28. Birmingham: Cent. Contemp. Cult.

Stud.

Leach, K.
   1967   *The Structural Study of Myth and Totemism.* London: Tavistock.

Libenow, J.G.
   1969   *Liberia: The Evolution of Privilege.* Ithaca: Cornell Univ. Press.

Little, K.
   1951   *The Mende of Sierra Leone.* London: Routledge & Kegan Paul.
   1965   The poltical function of the Poro (Part One). *Africa* 35:349-65.
   1966   The political function of the Poro (Part Two). *Africa* 36:62-72.

Lukács, G.
   1971   *History and Class Consciousness.* London: Merlin.

MacCormack, C.P.
   1975   Sande women and political power in Sierra Leone. *West Afr. J. Sociol. Polit. Sci.* 1:42-50.

Marwick, M.G.
   1965   *Sorcery in its Social Setting: A Study of the Northern Rhodesian Cewa.* Manchester: Manchester Univ. Press.

Marx, K., Engles, F.
   1970   *The German Ideology.* London: Lawrence Wishart.

Middleton, J.
   1960   *Lugbara Religion: Ritual and Authority among an East African People.* London: Oxford Univ. Press.

Milliband, R.
   1974   *The State in Capitalist Society.* London: Quartet Books.

Mitchell, J.C.
   1956   *The Kalela Dance.* Rhodes-Livingstone Pap. 27. Manchester: Manchester Univ. Press.

Moore, S.F., Myerhoff, B.G.
   1977   Introduction: Secular ritual forms and meanings. In *Secular Ritual,* ed. S.F. Moore, B.G. Myerhoff, pp. 3-24. Amsterdam: Van Gorcum.

Nadel, S.F.
   1952   Witchcraft in four African societies: An essay in comparison. *Am. Anthropol.* 54:18-29.

Parkin, D.J.
   1968   Medicines and men of influence. *Man* (N.S.) 3:424-39.

Peters, E.L.
   1963   Aspects of rank and status among Muslims in a Lebanese village. In *Mediterranean Countrymen,* ed. J. Pitt-Rivers. Paris: Mouton.

Radcliffe-Brown, A.R.
   1952   *Structure and Function in Primitive Society.* Glencoe: Free Press.
   1957   *A Natural Science of Society,* ed. M.N. Srinivas. Glencoe Free Press.

Rosaldo, R.I.
   1978   The rhetoric of control: Ilongots viewed as natural bandits and wild Indians. In *The Reversible World,* ed. B.A. Babcock, pp. 240-57.

Scott, D.J.R.
   1960   The Sierra Leone election, My 1957. In *Five Elections In Africa,* ed. W.J. Mackenzie, K. Robinson, pp. 168-280. London: Oxford Univ. Press.

Turner, V.W.
   1957   *Schism and Continuity in an African Society.* Manchester: Manchester Univ. Press.

ABNER COHEN

1964   Symbols on Ndembu ritual. See Ref. 19, pp. 20-51.
1975   Symbolic studies. *Ann. Rev. Anthropol.* 4:145-61.
1975   Book review. *Man* (N.S.) 10:139-40.

Vincent, J.
1978   Political anthropology: Manipulative strategies. *Ann. Rev. Anthropol.* 7:175-94.

Wallerstein, I.
1960   Ethnicity and national integration. *Cahiers d'Etudes Africaines,* pp. 129-39.

Weber, M.
1947   *The Theory of Social and Economic Organization.* New York: Free Press.

Williams, R.
1976   *Key Words.* Glasgow: Fontana.

Worseley, P.M.
1956   The kinship system of the Tallensi: a reevaluation. *J.R. Anthropol. Inst.* 86:37-75.

THE POWER
OF SYMBOLISM:
UNDERSTANDING AND
CONSTRUCTING REALITY

THE SALVATION OF A DRUNK

Frank E. Manning

Social events are often significant in both senses of the term. They are important in the context in which they take place, and they are symbolically representative of a larger field of meaning. Max Gluckman's work has inspired a rich literature dealing with the anthropological examination of religious, political, and, more recently, festive events. The close and careful study of these events enables us to see how cultural meanings are created, communicated, and changed; how they are rendered credible, questionable, or compelling; how they are brought to bear on the conditions and circumstances of ordinary life; and how they are enlisted in the service of conformity or conflict. In brief, event analysis is a window on culture itself.

In the article that follows, Frank E. Manning examines a remarkable event—the religious conversion of a drunken man at a Pentecostal revival service in Bermuda. The service was highlighted by the profuse vomiting of the drunk as he responded to the altar call, indicating that he wanted to get "saved." The pronouncements of the pastor, along with the actions and statements of the congregation, reveal both a common sense awareness of the man's drunkenness and a deeper, spiritual understanding of it as the manifestation of a dramatic struggle between Jesus and Satan, resolved by the expulsion of Satan in the guise of vomit. The man confirmed this faith on a later occasion when he returned to the church and testified that he had, indeed, been saved.

Manning's analysis focuses on the role of the Pentecostal service in constructing a complex relationship between these two levels of comprehension. The service, he argues, has two symbolic movements. The first is an alternation between playful and religious meanings. The service shifts easily between entertainment and evangelism, histrionics and holiness, enjoyment and edification. The congregation recognize this duality, as they state that they are there "to have a good time in the Lord." The second movement *is processual. As the service builds toward the climax of the altar call, it becomes increasingly less comic and more solemn. After the altar call, the service reverts to a more comic, playful form. The alternation and sequencing of these two levels of symbolic expression generate an awareness of multiple realities. The congregation consciously understand themselves as actors in a human context, but they also believe that there has been divine intervention in a human situation, demonstrating the validity of their faith. Hence the case strikingly illustrates the role of ritual in the construction and certification of cultural knowledge, while hinting at the capacity of ritual to inspire and mobilize social action.*

THE TRANSITION FROM "armchair" to "open air" anthropology in the early twentieth century had broad implications for the understanding of human thought. Before this time social theorists generally took the view that "primitive man" dwelled exclusively on a mystical plane, conceptualizing his environment and experience in magico-religious rather than empirical terms. Modes of thought alternately known as logical, rational, and scientific were believed to have developed later in the evolutionary process, bringing about eventually the modern secularization of consciousness.

The pioneer work of Malinowski abruptly challenged this position by showing that primitive peoples had a well-developed empirical science that guided their thought and action under normal circumstances. Only in situations of peril or possible failure did they resort to magic, and then as a supplement to science rather than as a substitute for it. Moreover, magic was not fused with science but remained a separate order of understanding that brought courage and confidence in time of trouble (Malinowski 1954: 17-92).

As Horton (1973: 276-284) has recently observed, the work of anthropologists, philosophers, and psychologists has broadened this perspective by indicating that the balance between empirical and nonempirical thinking seen in primitive societies has a structural analogue in modern societies. The transition from traditional to modern thought patterns is thus one of continuity rather than contrast. Yet while a fair amount of attention has been given to the logical relationship between the empirical and nonempirical levels of belief systems,[1] there has been little research that goes beyond Malinowski's psychological confidence theory in throwing light on

FRANK E. MANNING

the specific conditions that precipitate the shift of consciousness from one province of meaning to another. In particular we lack both data and theory pertinent to the movement from what Schutz (1962) described as the paramount but finite reality of common sense to the multiple other realities that intrude upon our cultural awareness.

This article explores some of these problems with reference to the plural realities that are made apparent in a Pentecostal ritual.[2] It proposes that the playful character of the ritual is an underlying condition of the phenomenological association between empirical and nonempirical meanings. The proposition is developed through a hermeneutic analysis that explores the religio-cultural context of ludic ritual symbolism and that suggests comparisons between Pentecostalism and other forms of Christianity with respect to the representation of transcendence.

The Revivalist Milieu

Bermuda, like most of the Antilles, is an example of what Cross (1950) called a "burned-over district"—an area inundated by the fervor of revivalist Protestantism. Preachers deliver sermons on streetcorners and outside bars. Weekly services take up two full pages of newspaper advertisements, and special services are given added publicity with handbills, radio announcements, and press releases. On Sunday one radio station assigns its entire air time to evangelistic broadcasts, while a second station devotes morning and evening to this type of programming. Religious arguments such as whether Saturday or Sunday is the Christian Sabbath give rise to lively pamphleteering and letters to the editor. Tracts are distributed on the streets and from door to door. Ministers and zealous laymen visit the island's three hospitals, stressing to patients the urgency of getting "saved" (converted). In short, the message and style of revivalism are encountered just about everywhere that one turns in this predominantly black, circum-Caribbean British colony of fifty-five thousand persons.

In recent decades the most successful competitor for the souls of Bermudians has been the New Testament church of God, a Pentecostal assembly affiliated with the Church of God, Cleveland, Tennessee. From a dozen devotees meeting in a coal shed in the

THE SALVATION OF A DRUNK

mid-1940's the church has grown to more than three hundred active members who now meet in a renovated theater that they rent on long-term lease. The church's strength is rooted in the black lower class. The great bulk of the membership live in an area that is characterized by low income levels, overcrowded and dilapidated housing, a relatively high percentage of tenant—rather than owner-occupied—dwellings, and the island's highest rates of female-headed households (*Happy Valley Survey* 1966). My own survey among Pentecostal males showed that nearly half had gone no further than elementary school and four-fifths were manual laborers, predominantly in service and unskilled positions; only 10 percent held white collar jobs and there was only one professional—a full-time minister.[3] The lower-class profile of the church stands in sharp contrast to the distinctively middle-class orientation of many other black congregations in Bermuda.

Much of the dynamism of the church is traceable to the pastor, a middle-aged black Bermudian who reportedly preached his first sermon at the age of five when he encountered a group of men cursing on the road and sternly warned them to repent of their sins. The episode gained him the nickname "Holy," a sobriquet that assumed irony in adolescence and young adulthood when he "backslid" (fell away) from religion to become one of the most famous "rudies" (rude boys) in his neighborhood.[4] Converted in the coal shed at the age of twenty-five, he comically remembers being thrown into a pile of coal by the force of God moving him in a new direction. He soon began preaching and in his early thirties was appointed pastor, succeeding a long line of foreign, predominantly white evangelists. A decade later he built up the church to the size where it could provide him a living, the accomplishment that revivalists regard as the indisputable proof of a man's calling to preach the gospel.

Since embracing his work full time he has developed an extensive media ministry, including radio broadcasts, a twenty-four hour telephone prayer service know as "Dial a Deliverance," and a weekly half-hour telecast featuring choral singing and a spirited sermon concluded with an invitation to come to the church for more of the same: "come out and see the Holy Ghost in operation." He publicizes special services in the newspaper with advertisements such as the following:

COME ONE 'N ALL
To
An Unusual Dramatized Sermon
The Battle of Champions
Job vs. Satan
10 Great Power Packed Rounds

A picture showed the pastor, identified as "Alias Job," squared off in boxing trunks against a lay preacher identified as "Alias Satan." The advertisement concluded:

Surely down but not out. This is a dramatized sermon of the battle Job had with the devil. You don't want to miss this event. See the pastor with boxing gear. A chance of a lifetime. It will only happen once.

The Evangelistic Service

The most popular regular service is the evangelistic meeting on Sunday night. The early arriver to the service can listen to recorded gospel music, just as he would be treated to secular music before curtain time in a theater. Ushers and usherettes in blue uniforms are busy greeting persons and assisting them to seats. Regular members generally sit near the front, many wearing buttons with inscriptions such as "Christ is the Answer," "God is Still Alive," and "J.C. is In." Infrequent attenders and those who are not converted sit further back or upstairs in the mezzanine. A few persons mill around on the street, talking in small groups and listening to the music through two large amplifiers placed above the main door.

Shortly after 8 p.m. a member of the congregation comes to the stage to begin the service. The curtain is drawn, revealing the choir dressed in one of three sets of robes and mortarboards, as well as the musicians—usually an organist, pianist, drummer, and three to six others with brass instruments. The most familiar opening hymn is the Doxology:

Praise God from whom all blessings flow
Praise him oh creatures here below

THE SALVATION OF A DRUNK

Praise him above the heavenly host
Praise Father, Son, and Holy Ghost

This single verse will be repeated twenty to twenty-five times. As the repetition progresses the congregation and even the on-lookers become kinetically involved in the rhythm. They sing loudly, clap lustily, shake tambourines and maraccas, and move from their seats into the aisles for a few dance steps. The clapping in particular is significant. As Sithole (1972: 73) has remarked in a general dis-cussion of Afro-American musical dynamics, hand clapping provides a rhythmic percussive effect that complements the regular instru-ments. Through clapping, audience participation is total; each per-son is musician as well as singer.

For the next thirty to forty minutes the service alternates be-tween prayer, congregational singing, exhortation, scripture reading, and sheer pandemonium, in no regular pattern. I was once told by a member of the congregation: "I've been coming to this church for eight years, and I still never know what's going to happen next." The fluidity of ritual form stems from the value placed on spon-taneity. Services should follow the inspiration of the Holy Ghost, not a fixed schedule devised by man. The Holy Ghost or "Spirit" is conceived as a kind of master of ceremonies who makes his will known by moving individuals to express themselves freely and in ways that may redirect a service. A "good" service is one in which the Spirit moves forcefully and dramatically and congregational par-ticipants respond without inhibition.

At about quarter to nine the collection is taken up. The service leader (who may or may not be the original leader, depending on how the Spirit has moved) makes a humorous remark such as "Oh God, please touch their hearts and touch their pocketbooks." The band strikes up a hymn in fast tempo, and the members of the con-gregation march forward and up the ramp to deposit their offerings.[5]

Soon after the collection is finished the pastor makes his first appearance, coming out from his office behind the stage. As the music and singing continues he makes sure that all is in readiness for the radio broadcast, which begins at 9 p.m. He checks the ar-rangement of the several microphones, gives last-minute instruc-tions to the musicians, and circulates among the choir and the audience, jumping, shouting, dancing, joking, and trying in other ways to amplify both volume and enthusiasm. When the service goes on the air, portable radios are passed around the church so participants may appreciate their performance.

For roughly a half hour there is a mixture of jubilant congregational singing, ecstatic shouting, and "special singing" by individuals and groups, some of them visiting from other churches. Then the pastor steps to the pulpit and begins his presentation in the following vein:

> Greetings to you here in this auditorium, as well as those who are out in radioland. By God, we are really having a ball here this evening. We are really enjoying the blessings of the Lord. Glory be to God. I trust that you have already enjoyed the Lord, and I assure you that it will get better further on.

Remarks of this type are usually followed by topical commentary. On one occasion he joked about his recent conviction in court for a speeding violation by suggesting that a "speeding demon" jumped on his foot and made him exceed the limit before he knew what he was doing. By then he had already gone through a radar trap and was being pursued by a constable.

On another occasion he observed that Bermudian women are wearing their skirts too high and thus giving unnecessary temptation to men. Regrettably, he added, a few women in the New Testament congregation must be included. To satirize them he turned his back to the audience, pulled his cassock up to his thighs, and suggestively wiggled his buttocks. This led to a broad attack on Bermudian hedonism. Instead of coming to church, he claimed, people are going to the Forty Thieves Club (a famous nightclub named after Bermuda's merchant aristocracy of forty white families). "I don't go there," he laughingly moralized, "I'm not a thief."

After ten to fifteen minutes of such commentary the pastor announces that he must get to the "Word of God." His mood and demeanor become more serious as he recites a brief prayer for divine guidance and then opens the Bible to the text that will keynote his sermon. However the sermon begins, it eventually progresses onto a constant theme: the devil is the cause of sin, the root of all evil and suffering. Rhetorical flourishes dramatize the point ("tonight I am mad at the devil.... The devil has duped, hoodwinked, and chloroformed the people of this island"), while con-

THE SALVATION OF A DRUNK

gregational approval is indicated by shouts of "Amen," "preach, pastor, preach," "it's the truth," "carry him through, Jesus" and so on. As the condemnation of Satan continues, the pastor's face becomes angry, his voice louder, his actions more demonstrative. He is now "stylin' out," letting the audience know that what is about to come is of utmost importance and to be taken earnestly (Holt 1972: 191-192). Moving from the pulpit across the stage and onto the ramp, wiping the sweat from his brow with a handkerchief, imploring God to help and hold him, he hammers home the familiar revivalist message: "the day of judgment is near; repent of your sins and turn to Jesus; better get saved."

By this point in the sermon it is usually after ten o'clock, the time when the radio broadcast concludes. There is also a change within the live audience. Nonmembers who have no immediate intention of conversion quietly get up and leave, perhaps in the same way as the catechumens of the early Roman Church left the Mass before the offertory, the beginning of the most sacred part. On the other hand, persons who have been listening to the service from the street and who feel that God is "dealing" with them may enter and take a seat.

The climax of the service is the "altar call." The pastor's directive, "let every head bow and every eye close," signals a time for prayerful solitude and private self-examination. Shifting his tone from righteous anger to soothing calm, he walks up and down the aisles pleading with those in sin to come forward and make their peace with God. The choir and congregation give support by softly singing invitational hymns such as "Almost Persuaded" and "Back to my Father at Home."

The Drunk

During this phase of the service one night a young man in a drunken stupor staggered into the church. He was assisted to the front by a member of the congregation who subsequently knelt beside him, kept him from falling over, and prayed audibly for his salvation. A few minutes later they were joined by a backslider seeking to be restored and then by a dozen other persons who were not ready to accept salvation but who responded to the pastor's invitation to come forward for special prayer.

FRANK E. MANNING

After laying his hands on the repentant backslider and praying for the others the pastor went to the drunk, who by this time was surrounded by a half-dozen men loudly imploring that he be saved. The pastor stood in front of him and spoke to the assembly:

This brother wants to be delivered tonight. This brother wants to be set free. He wants to be loosed from the enemy tonight. He's bound. He's tied.... The enemy has got him tonight. We're going to take a stand tonight against this demon, this devil. Brother, you're going to be delivered tonight.... Glory be to God. Thank you, Jesus.

At this point the drunk began to feel sicker, and they sat him down in the front row. Those around him commented that his moaning and shaking were signs of the struggle between Jesus and Satan. As the drunk leaned forward to vomit the pastor held his head and began a frenzied prayer:

The blood of Jesus is against you, demon. Right now in Jesus' name I command you, loose your hold on this man. Come out, come out, come out. [The drunk vomited, and two men went to get sawdust to cover the floor.]

He's coming out. Glory be to God. Right now the blood of Jesus prevails against you, Satan. Right now in Jesus' name I command you to loose your hold on this man.

The drunk tried to vomit again but was unable. The pastor stood over him, continuing to pray and trying to induce the vomit. Meanwhile, the congregation, elated over the first regurgitation, broke into a singing, clapping chorus:

By the blood of Jesus,
By the blood of Jesus,
By the blood of Jesus,
He's washed as white as snow.

The chorus had been sung for about ten minutes when the drunk started vomiting again. The pastor signalled the band to stop playing and exclaimed:

THE SALVATION OF A DRUNK

This is .it. This is it. I've never witnessed this before. Come out, Satan, come out.... Hallelujah! Hallelujah!... He's coming out. Glory to God. Thank you, Jesus.

The drunk wanted to vomit more but could not; again the congregation responded with a chorus:

> There is power, power, wonder-working power,
> In the blood of the Lamb,
> There is power, power, wonder-working power,
> In the precious blood of the Lamb.

The chorus was sung about fifteen minutes, during which time the drunk vomited twice more and people danced in the aisles, rejoicing in the expulsion of Satan. When he thought the vomiting was over the pastor stopped the band and spoke to the assembly:

We have witnessed a manifestation of the power of God here tonight. Jesus said, "And these signs shall follow them that believe. In my name they shall cast out devils." In the name of the Lord we've been casting out devils here tonight. Glory be to God.

God is confirming his word. Amen. He is helping us in these last days with signs. Even though in the last days we're told about abominable things...we're so glad in the last days devils are also being cast out....

At least four demons came out of this brother tonight. The last one to come out was a demon of lust. My God, brother, if you'll believe, if you'll accept what happened tonight, you'll move on through this island victorious....

You've got to realize now, when the devil comes out of you, when this [pointing to the vomit] comes out of you, every desire of the lust of the flesh, my friend, is gone. Right now your body is empty. It's clean....

And I ask you to believe, to believe that you're set free from the hand of the enemy. And while the devil has gone out, the spirit of God has come in. God wants to use you. He's brought you here for a purpose. He'll make you what he desires you to be. May God bless you tonight...[the man began again to vomit].

FRANK E. MANNING

That's it, come on. There's more there. Thank you, Jesus. In the name of Jesus the blood prevails against you, Satan.... There's more there. Come out, come out, come out...[the man vomited again, the band began another chorus].... Thank you, Jesus, thank you for the blood tonight.... Oh, my God.

The chorus was played three times, then the pastor raised his hands and spoke to the assembly:

Thank you for delivering this man, tonight, my God. Thank you for setting him free in the name of Jesus.... He feels much better now. We thank you because there's power in the blood, there's deliverance in the blood. Hallelujah! We're so glad because the lion of the tribe of Judah has broken the chains.

As the drunk slumped over in his seat the pastor seemed satisfied that the spiritual battle had exhausted him beyond the point of giving testimony. He left the drunk, returned to the pulpit, and reverted to the humorous style and mood evidenced at the beginning of his sermon. "We really felt a gush of the Holy Spirit here tonight," he quipped. He joked about the enthusiasm and histrionic behavior of some of the church members, made a few announcements about activities during the week, and finally brought the proceedings to a close with a brief benediction. It was 11:30 p.m., three and a half hours since the service had begun.

As the people were leaving the church I asked a member of the congregation if the man had been saved. "Nobody knows," he replied, "we won't know unless he comes back and gives testimony." But when the pastor joined our conversation he assured us that the man had been saved. He said that usually nobody sees the demons being driven out, "but the person feels much lighter." He ventured the view that the demons were visible this time because God wanted to show a special sign of the power of salvation. He had read about a similar incident somewhere else but said that it never happened before in his church. He also stressed the need for someone to talk to the man the next day so that Satan would not get back into him.

After everyone had left the church two members of the congregation carried the drunk out to drive him home. As they ap-

THE SALVATION OF A DRUNK

proached the car the drunk leaned over to vomit again, although this time it was only the dry heaves. "He must have been to a party before he came here tonight," commented the man holding him up. "But it doesn't matter because this won't happen again."

The drunk then turned and feebly thanked his helper, adding that he did not recognize him. "It's not important to know me," was the reply. "Just know the man I serve. Know Jesus."

As the owner of the car drove away with the drunk in the back seat, I turned to the other church member and naively asked why the man had vomited so many times. "He had too much to drink," was the simple reply. "He was really very drunk."

A Hermeneutic of Play

What is the anthropologist to make of this striking episode? The underlying motif—conversion from alcoholism—is familiar. At least two other members of the new Testament Church of God were reportedly inebriated when they were saved, and several more—including the pastor—were self-confessed heavy drinkers although apparently sober at the actual moment of conversion. Thus when the drunk returned two nights later and testified that he had indeed been saved and wished to join the church, he was only a more spectacular example of the dramatic transformation from degradation to grace that underlies the revivalist conception of conversion (see Peacock 1975). It is also notable that vomiting has precedence as a religiously significant act. Mintz (1960: 233) reports a case where Puerto Rican Pentecostals viewed a woman's regurgitations as a sign of curing and responded to them by dancing and speaking in tongues, while Hudson (1975) has recently synthesized material dealing with the purgative and divinatory symbolism of emesis among American Indians.

Yet the drunk's salvation is more than an archetype of the conversion process and an example of how vomiting can have religious implications. It is also a manifestation of how multiple modes of understanding are evoked in a specific cultural situation. An insightful approach to this phenomenon emerges from the view of Pentecostal ritual as a form of deep religious play. I will explore this approach in the following analysis, centering on the basic relationship between play and meaning.

FRANK E. MANNING

When I first told this incident to an academic audience, a waggish friend observed that Pentecostals should not be classified as "anal retentive," the syndrome commonly associated with religious believers, but instead as "oral expulsive." Quite apart from the dubious merits of Freudian analysis, this comment strikes an appropriate note for beginning a discussion of the drunk's salvation. The reference to two orifices with antithetical natural and cultural functions evokes two juxtaposed orders of meaning. The first is rooted in psychoanalytic theory and implies a serious scientific explanation. The second is rooted in scatological comedy and implies that the scientific explanation is not to be taken seriously, and perhaps not taken at all. The anal-oral comment thus exemplifies a conjunction of disjunctives, the structural essence of a joke.

The drunk's salvation is also contextualized within meaningful juxtapositions. One of these is between religious and empirical knowledge in the interpretation of the man's symptoms. Another is between evangelism and entertainment in the intentionality of the church service. A third is between cosmology and comedy in the consciousness evoked by ritual experience. I will look at these juxtapositions independently and then try to show how they are connected in ways that throw light not only on the vomiting/salvation incident but on the broadly ludic orientation of Pentecostalism.

With regard to the relationship between religious and empirical interpretations, the actors in the salvation drama were clearly aware of both the spiritual depravity and the physical condition of the drunk. From a religious viewpoint they recognized his symptoms as the manifestation of a violent struggle between Jesus and Satan, resolved when the demonic forces were driven out and the man was thereby saved. From an empirical viewpoint they knew enough to hold him up, to cover his vomit with sawdust, and to arrange eventually for his transportation home.

During the church service the religious order of meaning was dominant. It was the basis of the explicit, verbalized interpretation given to the entire incident as it unfolded between the altar rail and the front row. Accordingly, it furnished the objective pursued by the pastor, his aides, and the congregation: to get a sinful man saved. The empirical order of meaning was secondary and implicit, showing through in the actions taken to protect the drunk from injury and to salve the hygienic sensitivities of those around him by covering

THE SALVATION OF A DRUNK

the vomit.

At the conclusion of the service, however, the relationship between religious and empirical comprehension shifted. When the man leaned over to regurgitate before getting into the car, his helper commented that he must have been to a party earlier in the evening. Similarly, in response to my question about the man's condition, I was frankly told that he was drunk. The two church members were not unmindful of the religious significance of what had happened, as evidenced by their comment that the man's salvation would preclude further drunkenness as well as by their counsel to him that it is more important to know Jesus than his human servants. Yet it is quite apparent that they were now primarily aware of the man's physical incapacity and chiefly concerned with the pragmatic task of getting him safely home.

The situational shift between religious and empirical orders of meaning has been discussed by Geertz, who also notes that the phenomenon has been generally overlooked in anthropological analyses:

> The movement back and forth between the religious perspective and the common sense perspective is actually one of the more obvious occurrences on the social scene, though one of the most neglected by social anthropologists, virtually all of whom have seen it happen countless times. Religious belief has usually been presented as an homogeneous characteristic of an individual, like his place of residence, his occupational role, his kinship position, and so on. But religious belief in the midst of ritual, where it engulfs the total person, transporting him, so far as he is concerned, into another mode of existence, and religious belief as the pale, remembered reflection of that experience in the midst of everyday life are not precisely the same thing, and the failure to realize this has led to some confusion (Geertz 1966: 36).

While it seems unlikely that a devout Pentecostal's religious outlook ever recedes to the extent that it is no more than a "pale, remembered reflection" of ritual experience, Geertz' postulate is essentially applicable to the present case. In the church service, the setting of ritual, the religious order of meaning is most apparent, transforming the drunk's behavior into a cosmic struggle between Jesus and Satan, salvation and sin. Outside of ritual, in the surroundings of daily life, there is a greater manifestation of empirical understanding.

The significance of ritual lies in its components, the sacred symbolic forms and acts that fuse a religious understanding of existence with the moral directives that understanding implies. The intense and participatory encounter with these symbols afforded by ritual moves the believer into a sense of reality far different from that generated by the symbols met in other environments. In short, to take a phrase from Bellah, ritual encourages "a departure from the plane of the mundane, a departure from the plane which often arouses a sense of the uncanny, of the presence of the *mysterium tremendum*" (1970: 210).

Yet it is also clear that ritual fails as often as it succeeds. The frantic attempts at liturgical innovation in the Catholic and classical Protestant churches today derive from the recognition that much of Christian ritual has become form without meaning, a set of ossified conventions devoid of inner significance. In view of this situation one is moved to take a closer look at ritual in which an alcoholic vomiting seizure can come to represent a religious occurrence of the most profound importance.

Perhaps the most striking aspect of Pentecostal ritual in general, and the Sunday evening service at the New Testament Church of God in particular, is its obviously playful character. The service is meant to provide entertainment as well as evangelism, fun as well as salvation. Ritual symbolism conjoins histrionics and holiness, mirthful performance and solemn piety, mundane humor and hellfire preaching, enjoyment and edification. The dual orders of intentionality are condensed in the standard reason that church members give for coming out to a service: "to have a good time in the Lord."

In a formal sense Pentecostal ritual has the classic features of play identified by Huizinga (12955: 1-27). It is free or voluntary, spatially and temporally separate from other activities, technically unproductive, governed by rules and laws different from those of normal, everyday life, representative of a sense of reality that is qualitatively different from the reality of ordinary perception and experience, and marked by uncertainty. The latter feature, uncertainty, distinguishes Pentecostal ritual from its more regulated and routinized counterparts in other Christian churches. The flexibility of Pentecostal ritual allows latitude for spontaneity and individual expression and lets the service unfold in ways that are never entirely predictable.

The generic tendency of play to transcend ordinary experience and to evoke nonempirical modes of consciousness is not only a central theme of Huizinga's book but also of the many studies it has inspired—a corpus that includes the works of Caillois (1959, 1961), Rahner (1967), Cox (1969), Berger (1970), and many others writing from both social science and theological perspectives. Caillois relates this proclivity specifically to juxtaposition, which as we have seen is one of the major diacritical features of the Pentecostal ritual. In his celebrated critique of Huizinga he states:

> In this enclosure [the religious sanctuary]...regulated and symbolic movements are executed, which represent or reincarnate mysterious realities...in which, just as in play, the opposing qualities of exuberance and regimentation, of ecstasy and prudence, and of enthusiastic delirium and minute precision, are present at the same time. At last, one transcends ordinary existence (Caillois 1959: 155).

But while this line of theory brings out the formal significance of play, it stops short of indicating how this significance is articulated in actual situations. As an example of both ludic expression and transcendence, the drunk's salvation episode allows us to take this additional step and to construct a hermeneutic of play.

Symbolically, the juxtaposition of entertainment and evangelism exemplifies the coincidence of opposites that Turner (1967: 28-30, 54-55) analyzes within the framework of "polarization of meaning." He sees this ritual principle as part of the process whereby moral values are invested with sensate appeal, an exchange that renders the obligatory desirable. On the vernacular level there is a clear understanding of the same principle. The publicity efforts of the church reveal the general awareness that good music and spirited fun are a powerful enticement not only for potential converts but for those already saved. Although I never discovered whether the drunk was initially lured by such attractions or whether he merely staggered in accidentally (the former seems more probable), many members of the congregation told me they were originally drawn by the entertaining aspects of services and that religious conviction came at a later time.

A fuller significance of polarization derives from its cognitive inversion of the social order. As I have shown at length elsewhere (Manning 1973), there is a basic dichotomy in black Bermudian culture between the workmen's clubs, centers of entertainment, and the churches, centers of evangelism. Entertainment together with its accessories (liquor, dancing, sexual arousal) is the prime example of sin, while evangelism is the model of ethical behavior. By uniting entertainment and evangelism the ritual order thus transmutes the social order and formulates an alternate sense of reality.

This new reality is cosmic in scope. The congregation believes that music and dancing originated in the church but were later corrupted by their association with "the world" (environments of sin). Biblical passages such as the following are taken to illustrate the pristine character of religious worship:

> Rejoice in the Lord, O ye righteous: for praise is comely for the upright.
> Praise the Lord with harp: sing unto him with the psaltery and an instrument of ten strings.[6]
> Sing unto him a new song; play skillfully with a loud noise. (Psalms 33: 1-3).

Similarly, entertainment and worship will be rejoined in the world to be brought about by the awaited apocalypse, as the prophecies of the New Testament promise. Ritual is thus transtemporal, an embodiment of both a primeval past and an eschatological future.

The cosmic reality symbolized by social reversal is intensified by other aspects of the service. Pentecostal music and dance exemplify the ludic principle that Caillois (1961: 89-97) calls *ilinx*, or vertigo. They stimulate the euphoria that is familiar in Pentecostal ritual and that occasionally culminates in trance and in speaking in tongues (see Goodman 1973). Consider the popular hymn "God's Not Dead," usually sung during the early part of the evangelistic service. The brief lyrics are as follows:

> God's not dead, he's still alive,

THE SALVATION OF A DRUNK

God's not dead, he's still alive,
God's not dead, he's still alive,
I can feel him in my hands,
I can feel him in my feet,
I can feel him all over me.

Like all "praise and deliverance" songs (essentially, those set to a fast tempo), "God's Not Dead" is sung perhaps two dozen times over, without variation. As the repetition progresses it has an intoxicating, almost hypnotic effect. Soon the "feeling" of God in one's hands and feet which are actively engaged in beating to the rhythm) becomes for many not only a lyrical expression but an actual experience. Shouts of "Oh, yes," "I can feel him all right," and "Hallelujah" are heard throughout the church, and there is likelihood that a few persons will disengage into a kind of mesmerized delirium.

The retrospective comments of my informants indicate the intensity of ritual experience. Hymn singing was described as an occasion when "you feel like you're walking in heavenly places" and "you can really feel the presence of God." Many claimed that the Holy Ghost "takes over" during such singing and causes participants to "get high on the Spirit." Younger members of the church often compared the phenomenon to the effect of drugs, while older members likened it to alcohol—in both cases the habits they left behind at conversion. The following remark is typical:

It's like in the world. You take one drink and it makes you feel pretty good. So you take the next one and you go higher. The more you take the higher you feel. So the more you sing the higher you feel... Now some churches you could sing all day long and you wouldn't feel the way you feel after singing a song in our church.

Another comment established an insightful comparison between church music and secular music within the black cultural idiom:

Let me tell you this. Colored folk are mainly musically inclined. It's a beat that gets hold of one. Now we have a thing here called the Gombey Dance [a masquerade dance performed on the streets at Christmas]. Now they have a beat that seems to get hold of people I've seen the time when I've gone from Hamilton way down to Castle Harbour [about seven miles] just jogging behind them—just for the beat.

And it's the tempo and the beat in which things are sung at our church that makes you know it's not like a lot of other churches.

Music helps to get you worked up—worked up to a pitch or tempo where you can get with a song. It puts you in a different atmosphere. It makes you feel like you're going higher in the Lord.

Prayer has a similar effect, although its form and mood are different. Prayers are usually begun by one person, either the service leader or someone specifically asked. At first the congregation offers encouragement and agreement with shouts of "Amen," "Oh, Jesus," and the like. Before long, however, everyone begins praying individually but aloud. As volume and fervor increase, persons raise their hands to feel the "touch" of Jesus and tremble spastically when they receive it—the response that a similar congregation describes as the feeling of an "electric shock" (Keber 1971: 10). For many women the experience appears to simulate orgasm. Wildly kissing the air, they repeatedly shout "thank you, Jesus" until they finally fall to the floor in ecstatic swoon.

Like music, prayer is an important means by which participants obtain one of their chief objectives: a "blessing." Though a diffuse term with variant meanings, blessing in the ritual context signifies contact with God and the effervescence that it produces. In retrospect one informant observed, "everybody gets there praying and you come in contact with Jesus. He talks to you. And after he's finished you talk back to him. I think it's a wonderful, wonderful experience." Another man claimed that while praying, "you get a feeling, a spiritual feeling, which is out of this world."

The transcendent awareness that results from such ritual acts is itself juxtaposed to an underlying sense of comedy. As Bergson observed (and as the anal-oral joke demonstrates), "a situation is invariably comic when it belongs simultaneously to two independent series of events and is capable of being interpreted in two entirely different meanings at the same time" (1956: 23). The interplay of entertainment and evangelism in the church service provides the

THE SALVATION OF A DRUNK

double order of meaning. The comic effect is seen in the jokes, high jinks, and rollicking humor that consistently appear in all parts of the service except the final phase of the sermon and the altar call. Comedy is especially apparent in those very ritual behaviors that are most conducive to transcendent religious experience. The man who gyrates wildly from the power of God and the woman who demonstrates an orgasm with thanks to Jesus are viewed as performers, stimulated by supportive responses and applauded with appreciative laughter and jocular commentary by their ritual coparticipants.

The juxtaposition of cosmology and comedy is often centered on the Holy Ghost, who is conceived as both the most sacred and the most ludic figure of the Trinity. The unique feature of Pentecostalism, the experience of speaking in unknown tongues, is seen as the outward sign of sanctification, the spiritual baptism bestowed on individuals by the Holy Ghost sometime after their conversion. Such other valued mystical powers as divine healing and prophecy are also attributed to the Holy Ghost. My informants believed in keeping with their reading of Luke 12:10 that a curse against the Holy Ghost was the one sin that could not be forgiven. Yet the Holy Ghost is also viewed as the star of the show at church services. He animates the human performers and inspires their dramatic and comic behaviors. A striking illustration of this view of the Spirit occurred at the conclusion of a service when the pastor asked for a round of applause for God the Father. The congregation, anticipating what was to follow, clapped in a polite but restrained fashion. Next he asked for applause for God the Son, and there was a similar response. Finally he asked for applause for God the Holy Ghost; there followed a standing, cheering, shouting ovation that lasted a full fifteen minutes.

There is, however, a shift away from this comic orientation as the service moves toward its climax. The conclusion of the radio broadcast and the quiet departure from the church of those persons who do not intend to answer the altar call indicate formally that "the show is over." Deliberate comedy is subsequently suspended while all attention and effort are given to the serious task of salvation. Those who are not already committed to this task or about to be committed cease to be part of the service.

There is also a change in the usage of theological imagery. Ref-

FRANK E. MANNING

erences to the Holy Ghost tend to be replaced by references to God the Son, especially those pertinent to his redemptive sacrifice. Note, for example, the proliferation of such images as the "Blood" and the "Lamb" during the vomiting/salvation incident. This shift of images is consistent with the conceptual and affective movement of the service. The Holy Ghost, as we have seen, is the divine being who sanctifies those who have been converted and also sparks their performance abilities. Imagery of the Holy Ghost is thus appropriate in those parts of the service that are meant as a celebration of the Christian life and as a demonstration of its benefits to a wider audience. God the Son, or Jesus Christ, on the other hand, is the divine being who gave himself up to death in order that mankind might be released from inherent bondage to Satan. Images of Christ thereby work to mobilize concern for the objective of bringing the sinner to accept personally the salvation that has been made available to him.

As the service moves through this transition, the cosmological awareness generated earlier by reversal, euphoria, and ecstasy becomes focused on the evangelistic task. Hence the allegory of salvation symbolized by the vomiting seizure is taken for real; the man's moaning and shaking are seen as the struggle of Jesus against his demonic adversary, the vomit is viewed as Satan himself, and the man's weakened condition afterwards is accepted as spiritual exhaustion. But whereas cosmic reality was earlier juxtaposed explicitly with the aesthetic order of comedy, it is now juxtaposed implicitly with the empirical order of common sense. Thus the salvation incident is alternatively recognized as drunken sickness rather than as comic performance. Later, of course, the event may have been seen in a performance light, as when the entire service was recounted from the viewpoint of the Holy Ghost's theatrical attributes. But at the moment the serious urgency of salvation rather completely obscured the comical features of an entertaining performance.

The progression from levity to seriousness in the Pentecostal service is consistent with the movement of play. Huizinga (1955: 17, 21) stresses the periodic tendency of the player to become seriously engrossed in his action, an indication that play has a dimension of solemnity. Bateson describes the progression in terms of play becoming "metaphor that is meant" (1972: 183). Absorbed fully in the conceptual universe of play, one moves from seeing this universe as a symbolic construct to seeing it as the actual existential order. Hence the need for the periodic metacommunicative reminder that "this is play"—a reminder that, in the Pentecostal service, is given by the comic intrusions that bracket the more serious climax.

Analysis, of course, invites comparison. As a tentative step in this direction I would suggest the formal inversion *cum* underlying homology between the Pentecostal service reported here and the Catholic Mass. In the Mass, bread and wine are transformed into the body and blood of Jesus Christ and then consumed as communion. The change takes place at the structural climax, the consecration. According to the traditional doctrine of transubstantiation, bread and wine become the actual divine substance, not merely iconic representations of it. Yet they are recognized as retaining their former physical characteristics, such as appearance, taste, and smell.

In the Pentecostal service alcoholic vomit is transformed into Satan in the process of expulsion. The change takes place at the structural climax, the altar call. Its nature is revealed not in doctrine but in the spontaneous interpretation of the minister and other ritual actors. Finally, the transformed substance is recognized as having the physical properties of something else. Thus it is necessary to cover the vomit with sawdust in order to obscure its unsightly appearance and unpleasant smell.

Although admittedly provisional and deliberately provocative, this line of thought raises other considerations pertinent to comparative Christianity. As Norbeck (1974: 35-39) has argued, play and religion are generally overlapping entities in preindustrial societies. Not until the Protestant Reformation and its emphasis on ascetic rationality as the model of ethical behavior did play become stigmatized within Christianity as sinful. What is distinctive about Pentecostalism is that it carries the Protestant opposition to worldly indulgence to an extreme while at the same time incorporating indulgence into its ritual. Partly for this reason many adherents of Pentecostalism (including the New Testament congregation) insist that their religion lies outside the orbit of Protestantism. There may be levels of comparison between this "third force" (as Pentecostalism is commonly called) and the "first force" of Catholicism that are yet to be systematically explored.

FRANK E. MANNING

The reaction against the secularization process in classical Protestantism—the process that produced the Death of God, Christian Atheism, Demythologization, and similar theological concepts popular in the 1960's—corresponded with a new appreciation of the play element in religion and its relationship to transcendence. Perhaps the most complete statement of this perspective comes from the sociological theologian Cox (1969), who elaborates the extensive affinity between religious festivity and fantasy. Suggestively, he draws his title *The Feast of Fools* from medieval Catholicism and proposes that Pentecostalism, especially black Pentecostalism, exemplifies the festivity-fantasy (or play-transcendence) complex that is reinvigorating contemporary Christianity.

The ludic character of the Pentecostal service should not obscure the analytic separateness of play and ritual. Handelman (1976) has recently discussed the distinction in terms of contrasting metameanings. Ritual, he points out, says "let us make believe"; it is moral consecration of society's ideals. Contrastingly, play says "let us make believe"; it is an amoral commentary on society's ideals. Yet the relationship is such that the two modes of expression are phenomenologically complementary within the domain of liminality. "The experience of ritual should prepare one for play, and that of play for ritual" (Handelman 1976: 14). Hence, play and ritual are often paired in a unitary context that has the form of "play-within-ritual" (Handelman 1976: 17).

From this viewpoint the analytic juxtaposition between play and ritual stands as a kind of theoretical counterpoint to the many other juxtapositions seen in the action sequence of the Pentecostal service. All of these juxtapositions contribute to making the service both ludic and religious, an excursion into a symbol system that ranges between profound conviction and profane contrivance. The juxtapositional structure of the service seems further analogous to the philosophical essence of both play and faith. As Huizinga (1955: 1-27) realized, play is ultimately definable only with reference to its opposite, which he saw as secular, technical activity. Likewise, faith and incredulity are the disjunction celebrated in Tertullian's classic apologia: *credo quia absurdum* "I believe because it is absurd."

In conclusion, a hermeneutic of play constructed from the drunk's salvation episode gives us at least two broad insights. First, it furnishes an understanding of how modes of thought based on empirical fact are phenomenologically related to nonempirical forms of consciousness in a ritual context. Second, it throws light on the current appeal of Pentecostalism, both within its own churches and in the many other denominations where aspects of Pentecostal ritual have been introduced along with the search to rediscover transcendence.

Notes

1. Much of the relevant anthropological work has been done on African belief systems. Representative studies are those of Evans-Pritchard (1956), Horton (1962, 1967), Leinhardt (1961), and Middleton (1960). A seminal contribution to the anthropology of Christian belief systems has been made by Hudson (1972).

2. Field research was conducted in Bermuda in 1969-1970 with support from the National Science Foundation (GS-2549) and in 1976 with support from the Institute of Social and Economic Research, Memorial University of Newfoundland. I am grateful to Jean Briggs, Charles Hudson, and James Peacock for helpful comments on an earlier draft and to my wife, Gail, for helping to retrieve statistical data. Some of the data presented here are considered from a different perspective in an article I have published elsewhere (Manning 1976).

3. Although only 38 percent (nineteen of fifty) of the men in the survey were members of the New Testament Church of God, they corresponded socioeconomically to the larger sample. Bermudian Pentecostalism as a whole draws its support almost exclusively from the black lower class.

4. I have shown elsewhere (Manning 1974) that in the Antilles, nicknames are generally associated with both performance abilities and with a life style that is deemed sinful. Evangelical Christians usually avoid nickname usage because of the latter connotation. The occasional use of nicknames among Pentecostals is indicative of their having developed a performance aesthetic that is compatible with Christian practice.

5. Holt (1972: 200) reports that the congregational practice of marching to the altar rail to deposit offerings was formerly common in black American churches but is now disappearing.

6. Some Pentecostals conjecture that the "instrument of ten strings" refers to handclapping, which involves the ten fingers. This suggests an emic understanding of the rhythmic percussive effects of handclapping.

FRANK E. MANNING

References

Bateson, Gregory
1972   Steps to an Ecology of Mind. San Francisco: Chandler.

Bellah, Robert
1970   Beyond Belief. New York: Harper and Row.

Berger, Peter
1970   A Rumor of Angels. Garden City, NY: Doubleday-Anchor. pp. 61-192.

Bergson, Henri
1956   Laughter. In Comedy. W. Sypher, Ed. Garden City, NY: Doubleday-Anchor. pp. 61-192.

Caillois, Roger
1959   Man and the Sacred. Meyer Barash, Trans. Glencoe: Free Press.
1961   Man, Play, and Games. Meyer Barash, Trans. Glencoe: Free Press.

Cox, Harvey
1969   The Feast of Fools. Cambridge: Harvard University Press.

Cross, Whitney
1950   The Burned-Over District. Ithaca: Cornell University Press.

Evans-Pritchard, E.E.
1956   Nuer Religion. Oxford: Clarenden Press.

Geertz, Clifford
1966   Religion as a Cultural System. In Anthropological Approaches to the Study of Religion. Michael Banton, Ed. London: Tavistock Publications. pp. 1-46.

Goodman, Felicitas
1973   The Apostolics of Yucatan: A Case Study of a Religious Movement. In Religion, Altered States of Consciousness, and Social Change. Erika Bourguignon, Ed. Columbus: Ohio State University Press. pp. 178-218.

Handelman, Don
1976   Play, Ritual and Communication. Unpublished paper given at the International Conference on Humor and Laughter. Cardiff, Wales.

Happy Valley Survey
1966   Hamilton, Bermuda: mimeo.

Holt, Grace
1972   Stylin' Outta the Black Pulpit. In Rappin' and Stylin' Out. Thomas Kochman, Ed. Urbana: University of Illinois Press. pp. 189-204.

Horton, Robin
1962   The Kalabari World-View: An Outline and Interpretation. Africa 32: 197-220.
1967   African Traditional Thought and Western Science, Africa 37: 50-71;155-187.
1973   Levy-Bruhl, Durkheim, and the Scientific Revolution. In Modes of Thought. Robin Horton and Ruth Finnegan, Eds. Faber and Faber. pp. 249-305.

Hudson, Charles
1972   The Structure of a Fundamentalist Christian Belief System. In Religion and the Solid South. Samuel Hill, Ed. Nashville, TN: Abingdon Press. pp. 122-142.
1975   Vomiting for Purity: Ritual Emesis in the Aboriginal Southeastern United States. In Symbols and Society. Carole Hill, Ed. Athens, GA: Proceedings of the Southern Anthropological Society. pp. 93-102.

Huizinga, Johan
1955   Homo Ludens. Boston: Beacon Press.

THE SALVATION OF A DRUNK

Keber, Helen
    1971 Higher on the Hog. *In* The Not So Solid South. J. Kenneth Morland, Ed. Athens, GA: Proceedings of the Southern Anthropological Society. pp. 4-15.

Lienhardt, Godfrey
    1961 Divinity and Experience. Oxford: Clarenden Press.

Malinowski, Bronislaw
    1954 Magic, Science, and Religion. Garden City, NY: Doubleday-Anchor.

Manning, Frank
    1973 Black Clubs in Bermuda. Ithaca: Cornell University Press.
    1974 Nicknames and Number Plates in the British West Indies. Journal of American Folklore 87: 123-132.
    1976 The Rediscovery of Religious Play: A Pentecostal Case, *In* The Anthropological Study of Play: Problems and Prospects. David Lancy and B. Allan Tindall, Eds. Cornwall, NY: Leisure Press. pp. 23-30.

Middleton, John
    1960 Lugbara Religion. London: Oxford University Press.

Mintz, Sydney
    1960 Worker in the Cane. New Haven: Yale University Press.

Norbeck, Edward
    1974 Religion in Human Life. New York: Holt, Rinehart and Winston.

Peacock, James
    1975 Weberian, Southern Baptist, and Indonesian Muslim Conceptions of Belief and Action. *In* Symbols and Society. Carole Hill, Ed. Athens, GA: Proceedings of the Southern Anthropological Society. pp. 82-92.

Rahner, Hugo
    1967 Man at Play. New York: Herder and Herder.

Schutz, Alfred
    1962 Collected Papers, 1. The Hague: Martinus Nijhoff.

Sithole, Elkin
    1972 Black Folk Music. *In* Rappin and Stylin' Out. Thomas Kochman, Ed. Urbana: University of Illinois Press. pp. 65-82.

Turner, Victor
    1967 The Forest of Symbols. Ithaca: Cornell University Press.

FRANK E. MANNING

A Death in Due Time:
Construction of Self and Culture
in Ritual Drama

Barbara G. Myerhoff

Anthropological studies of funeral customs offer striking insights about the meaning of death, and the corresponding significance of life, in human societies. Barbara Myerhoff enhances this literature in her moving account of the death of a man during his 95th birthday party at a Jewish senior citizens' center in Los Angeles. The man, a prominent figure in the community, gave a ceremonial speech and then slumped in his chair, losing what he had earlier described as a battle with the Angel of Death. The guests were told to finish their dinners as the man was taken from their presence, but they quickly realized that their friend, like Moses, had died on his birthday; they had seen "a death in due time."

Appropriating the Manchester approach to event analysis, Myerhoff considers the historical process that brought the senior community into being. Its members began their lives in *shtetls*, little Jewish towns and settlements in eastern Europe. Later they immigrated to industrial cities in the United States, where they spent their working lives and raised their own families. In retirement age they moved to southern California, congregating in a heavily Jewish neighborhood of Los Angeles that is served by the center. A shared attachment to *yiddishkeit*—Jewish folk culture—is their common link to the past, while their children and grandchildren represent changes in their lives and a view of the future.

Birthday parties, which Myerhoff describes as rituals, are highly significant events, as they are organized both to celebrate Jewish folk culture and to provide an occasion when the seniors can be honored by younger members of their families. The occurrence of death at such a time is ironically fitting, as it concludes a particular *human biography by relating it dramatically to past and future, culture and community. A festive event staged to affirm life becomes instead a commemoration of it. The singularity of an individual death is diffused among the collectivity, investing the trauma with a sense of both social and cosmic design.*

Generalizing from the incident, Myerhoff considers the capacity of ritual to create meaning and transform situations. Ritual, she points out, is paradoxical. It is consciously contrived and produced by humans, but it is meant to represent transcendent truths. Ritual conveys its truths successfully when it is performed in a way that sustains this precarious relationship to reality and that enables its participants—actors and audience alike—to preserve the sense that they are involved in an authentic experience. An unplanned event is especially problematic, because the response to it must be improvised; it cannot be scripted or rehearsed. This same consideration applies to the previous paper by Frank Manning, who examines the appearance of a drunk during a Pentecostal church service. The vomiting of the drunk, like the death of the man celebrating his birthday, are unplanned and unsettling incidents. In both cases, however, the ritual participants rise to the occasion, transforming a potentially chaotic and disruptive situation into one that is highly meaningful and memorable. Such events demonstrate that ritual performance is not only an expression of culture, but also a means of adapting it creatively to the unpredictable circumstances of life.

"When the fig is plucked in due time it is good for the tree and good for the fig."

HUMANKIND HAS EVER CHAFED over its powerlessness when facing the end of life. Lacking assurance of immortality and insulted by the final triumph of nature over culture, humans develop religious concepts that explain that, if not they, someone or something has power and a plan. Thus death is not an obscene blow of blind chance. No religion fails to take up the problem, sometimes affirming human impotence thunderously. Nevertheless, people yearn for a good death, timely and appropriate, suggesting some measure of participation, if not consent. Occasionally, a subtle collusion seems to occur when human and natural plans coincide, revealing a mysterious agreement between mankind, nature, and the

BARBARA MYERHOFF

gods, and providing a sense of profound rightness and order that is the final objective of religion, indeed of all cultural designs. Belief and reality are merged at such times and death is more partner than foe. The questions of supremacy and power are rendered irrelevant, and an experience of unity and harmony prevails.

This essay describes such an event, tracing its origins and its consequences over a period of several months.[1] The entire sequence is treated as a single event, a drama of several acts. It is a social drama in Victor Turner's sense, but it is more strikingly a cultural drama, illustrating how a group draws upon its rituals and symbols to face a crisis and make an interpretation. It handles conflicts, not of opposing social relationships, but of opposition between uncertainty and predictability, powerlessness and choice. A final reconciliation is achieved when the community selects from and modifies its prevailing conceptualizations, using some traditional materials, improvising and developing others, until it has made a myth of a historical episode and found messages of continuity, human potency, and freedom amid threats of individual and social obliteration.

Death as a Cultural Drama

Jacob Kovitz died in the middle of the public celebration of his ninety-fifth birthday, among friends and family gathered to honor him at the Aliyah Senior Citizens' Community Center, which had become the focus of life for a small stable, socially and culturally homogeneous group of elderly Jews, immigrants to America from Eastern Europe. The case is remarkable for several reasons: it illustrates the use of ritual to present a collective interpretation of "reality", and it demonstrates the capacity of ritual to take account of unplanned developments and alter itself in midstream into a different event. Further, it illuminates how one man can make himself into a commentary upon his life, his history, and his community, mirroring his social world to itself and to himself at the same time. The case is an example of the transformation of a natural, biological event—death—into a cultural drama, shaped to human purpose until it becomes an affirmation rather than a negation of life.

Though quite rare in our times, such deaths are not unprecedented. The French social historian Philippe Ariès (1974) refers to ritualized, ceremonial deaths as "tamed," and points out that in the Middle Ages, knights of the *chanson de geste* also tamed their deaths. Forewarned by spontaneous realization of imminent departure, the dying person prepared himself and his surroundings, often by organizing a ritual and presiding over it to the last. Death was a public presentation, often simple, including parents, children, friends, and neighbors. Tamed deaths were not necessarily emotional. Death was both familiar and near, evoking no great fear or awe. Solzhenitsyn, too, as Ariès notes, talks about such deaths among peasants. "They didn't puff themselves up or fight against it and brag that they weren't going to die—they took death calmly.... And they departed easily, as if they were just moving into a new house." Death was not romanticized or banished. It remained within the household and domestic circle, the dying person at the center of events, "determining the ritual as he saw fit." (1968: 96-97)

Ritual is prominent in all areas of uncertainty, anxiety, impotence, and disorder. By its repetitive character it provides a message of pattern and predictability. In requiring enactments involving symbols, it bids us to participate in its messages, even enacting meanings we cannot conceive or believe; our actions lull our critical faculties, persuading us with evidence from our own physiological experience until we are convinced. In ritual, doing is believing. Ritual dramas especially are elaborately staged and use presentational more than discursive symbols, so that our senses are aroused and flood us with phenomenological proof of the symbolic reality which the ritual is portraying. By dramatizing abstract, invisible conceptions, it makes vivid and palpable our ideas and wishes, and, as Geertz has observed, the lived-in order merges with the dreamed-of order. (1966) Through its insistence on precise, authentic, and accurate forms, rituals suggest that their contents are beyond question authoritative and axiomatic. By high stylization and extraordinary uses—of objects, language, dress, gestures, and the like—ritual calls attention to itself, so that we cannot fail to see that its contents are set apart from ordinary affairs.

Ritual inevitably carries a basic message of order, continuity, and predictability. Even when dealing with change, new events are connected to preceding ones, incorporated into a stream of precedents so that they are recognized as growing out of tradition and experience. Ritual states enduring and underlying patterns, thus

BARBARA MYERHOFF

connecting past, present, and future, abrogating history and time. Ritual always links fellow participants but often goes beyond this to connect a group of celebrants to wider collectivities, even the ancestors and those unborn. Religious rituals go farther, connecting mankind to the forces of nature and purposes of the deities, reading the forms of macrocosm in the microcosm. And when rituals employ sacred symbols, these symbols may link the celebrants to their very selves through various stages of the life cycle, making individual history into a single phenomenological reality.

Ritual appears in dangerous circumstances and at the same time is itself a dangerous enterprise. It is a conspicuously artificial affair, by definition not of mundane life. Rituals always contain the possibility of failure. If they fail, we may glimpse their basic artifice, and from this apprehend the fiction and invention underlying all culture.

> Underlying all rituals is an ultimate danger, lurking beneath the smallest and largest of them, the more banal and the most ambitious—the possibility that we will encounter ourselves making up our conceptions of the world, society, our very selves. We may slip into that fatal perspective of recognizing culture as our construct, arbitrary, conventional, invented by mortals. (Moore and Myerhoff 1977: 22)

Rituals then are seen as a reflection not of the underlying, unchanging nature of the world but of the products of our imagination. When we catch ourselves making up rituals, we may see all our most precious, basic understandings, the precepts we live by, as mere desperate wishes and dreams.

With ritual providing the safeguards of predictability, we dare ultimate enterprises. Because we know the outcome of a ritual beforehand, we find the courage within it to enact our symbols, which would otherwise be preposterous. In ritual, we incorporate the gods into our bodies, return to Paradise, and with high righteousness destroy our fellows.

What happens when a ritual is interrupted by an unplanned development, when it is not predictable, when accident rudely takes over and chaos menaces its orderly proceedings? What do we do if death appears out of order, in the middle of a ritual celebrating

A DEATH IN DUE TIME

life? Such an occurrence may be read as the result of a mistake in ritual procedure, as a warning and message from the deities, or as a devastating sign of human impotence. But there is another possibility. The unexpected may be understood as a fulfillment of a different, loftier purpose, and a new, higher order may be found beneath the appearance or may take account of reality and thereby fulfill its purposes. Thus a new meaning and a new ritual emerge, made from older, extant symbols and rites.

Ethnographic Setting

Before describing the birthday party, some social and historical background is necessary. At the time of this study, the relevant community consisted of about 4,000 people at the most. These individuals were spread over an area of about six miles around the Aliyah Center; the center membership included 300 people, about 200 of whom were present at the birthday party. The great majority of people belonging to the center were between 85 and 95 years old. Most had been residents in the neighborhood for 20 to 30 years.

Nearly all of them had lived as children in the little Jewish towns and settlements of Eastern Europe known as *shtetls*. Yiddish was their mother tongue and Yiddishkeit, the folk culture built around the language and customs of the *shtetl,* was a major emotional and historical force in their lives, though their participation in and identification with it varied in intensity throughout the life cycle. In great numbers, these people and others like them had fled their original homes, intent on escaping the extreme antisemitism, intractable poverty, and political oppression, which were becoming increasingly severe around the turn of the century.

As adolescents and young adults, they came to the new World and worked as small merchants, unskilled laborers, craftsmen, and artisans in the Eastern industrial cities of America. On reaching retirement age, with their children educated, married, and socially and geographically remote, they drifted into their present community, drawn to the mild climate, the ocean, and the intense Yiddishkeit of the area. Now they were isolated and old, but freed from external pressures to be "American." In this condition they turned more and more toward each other, revived Yiddish as their preferred language, and elaborated an eclectic subculture, which combined elements from their childhood beliefs and customs with modern, urban American practices and attitudes, adapting the mixture of their present needs and circumstances.

These circumstances were harsh. Family members were distant or dead. Most of the group were poor, very old, and frail, suffering from social and communal neglect, extreme loneliness, and isolation. As a people, they were of little concern to the larger society around them. Their social, political, physical, and economic impotence was pronounced, and except on a very local level, they were nearly invisible.

Added to these afflictions was their realization that the culture of their childhood would die with them. The Holocaust wiped out the *shtetls* and nearly all their inhabitants. The center members clearly apprehended the impending complete extinction of themselves as persons and as carriers of a culture. The group was entirely homogeneous in age, and except for ceremonial occasions, no real intergenerational continuity existed. Their own membership were being depleted constantly, and there were no others to replace them. Death and impotence were as real as the weather, and as persistent.

Moreover, the social solidarity of the group was weakened by the members' ambivalence toward one another, due in part to enforced association and perhaps, too, to displaced anger. Their cultural traditions inclined them to a certain degree of distrust of nonkin, and despite the stability, homogeneity, and distinctiveness of past experiences, their circumstances, and extensive time spent together, they had less than entirely amiable feelings for each other. Factions, disagreements, and longstanding grudges marred their assemblies, most of which took place in secular and sacred rituals within the center building and on benches outside it.

But despite their ideological discord they were united by their common past. This was expressed as Yiddishkeit, in reference to the local customs, language, and beliefs that characterized these people's parental homes and early life in the *shtetl.* Very few were orthodox in religious practices. They had broken with strict religious Judaism before leaving the Old Country. A great many were agnostic, even atheistic and antireligious. But all were passionately Jewish, venerating the historical, ethnic, and cultural aspects of their heritage. Most had liberal and socialist political beliefs and had been active at one time or another in the Russian Revolution, various workers' movements, labor unions, or similar political activities. Since the Holocaust, all were Zionists, despite some ideological reservations concerning nationalism. For them Israel had become an extension of their family, and its perpetuation and welfare were identified as their own. This constellation of beliefs and experiences —the childhood history of the *shtetl*, Yiddish language and culture, secular and ethnic Judaism, and Zionism—were the sacred elements that united them.[2]

The subculture the group had developed comprised several distinct layers of historical experience: that of Eastern Europe, where they spent their childhood; of Eastern America from the turn of the century until the 1930's and 1940's, where they spent the latter part of their lives. Though there were many discontinuities and sharp disruptions during these 80 to 95 years, there were some notable cultural and social continuities, particularly between childhood and old age. These continuities seem to have helped them adapt to their contemporary circumstances. Not surprisingly, many of their rituals and symbols emphasized those situational continuities.

It is likely that the elders would not have elaborated this subculture had they remained embedded in a context of family and community. Their very isolation gave them much freedom for originality; they improvised and invented, unhampered by restraints of their original traditions and social disapproval of authorities. They had only themselves to please. For the first time since coming to America, now in old age they were able to indulge fully their old love of Yiddish and Yiddishkeit without fear of being ridiculed as greenhorns by their sophisticated, assimilated children. Now living again in a small, integrated community that emphasized learning, and where Yiddishkeit flourished and individual freedom and autonomy were exercised in isolation from mainstream society, they were able to revive their earlier responses to conditions they had known before. Their present poverty, impotence, physical insecurity, and social marginality repeated *shtetl* existence. Such continuity is adaptive despite its painful contents. People who have always known that life was hard and fate unreliable, if not downright treacherous, are not surprised to encounter these hazards again.

BARBARA MYERHOFF

They know how to cope with them and are not discouraged. They never expected life to be easy or happy. "Happiness," said Sarah, "happiness is not having a broken leg."

Dramas of Existence, Arenas for Appearing

Ritual is a form by which culture presents itself to itself. In ritual, not only are particular messages delivered, but the ritual also creates a world in which culture can appear. Further, rituals create a setting in which persons can appear, by appearing in their culture, by devising a reality in which they may stand as part. In their rituals, we see persons dramatizing self and culture at once, each made by the other. There is a satisfying replication: Jacob made up himself and his interpretation of his life through his autobiographical writings. He performed the final chapter when he died. Center members make up a world, which they enact. They enact their own existence as individuals as they participate in that world. Jacob's death strengthened the center members' construction by making it more real, and by implying through his awesome performance that their constructed world was validated by divine or at least supernatural approval.

Center life, though vital and original, was conspicuously made-up. It was an assembly of odds and ends, adaptations and rationalizations built out of historical materials that were used to deny that their present life was an accommodation to desperate circumstances. It was further strained by the necessity of binding together people who had not chosen to be with each other, who were rejected by their kin, and who had lost most of those peers whom they regarded as truly like-minded. All culture is an invention, made-up in this sense, but greater depth of time and fewer contradictions often make its work easier than it was here. Only continual and protracted ceremonies could keep center members from appreciating their differences; only regular, elaborate rituals could convince them that their way of life was real—a given and not a construct.

The center provided a stage for the dramatization of their collective life, and also a place in which they could dramatize themselves as individuals. In it, they could appear, become visible, as continuing, living people. Without the center they were so cut off from human contact that it was possible to doubt their own existence. They needed each other as witnesses, particularly because in extreme old age the senses no longer give powerful messages of vitality. For many, sight, hearing, taste have faded. Wakefulness has merged into dozing. Memory has overtaken the present and blended with dream. There is no one to touch them or whom they touch. They must reassure themselves of existence by receiving verification from outside their bodies. Their peers are only minimally useful in this; first, because they too are less acute and responsive; second, because they are in competition with each other for attention and often withhold or manipulate it to control one another.

The desire for attention is the dominant passion or dynamic force that gives the community its unique form. The attention of outsiders in general, and younger people in particular, is eagerly sought. The center people turn to them in an attempt to make a record of their existence and to leave behind with another a record that they have been here. Having a photograph taken, being interviewed and tape-recorded, even being listened to by someone who will return to the outside world and who will remember them after they are gone is urgent. By these activities the center people create arenas for appearing. Being overlooked is worse than being regarded as difficult, foolish, irrational, or selfish. Neglect is more unbearable. Naturally, if they can, they prefer to be seen as worthy and important, but in this they require certain uncommon attributes: a willing audience, a command of themselves, and demonstrable accomplishments.

Lacking assurance that their way of life will continue, finding no consolation that a God would remember their name, unable to draw on their own bodies for evidence of continuing vitality, they turn to each other as unwilling but essential witnesses to their dramas of existence. In their ceremonial life they created themselves, witnessed each other, proclaimed a reality of their own making.

Jacob was one of the most fortunate members of the community. He had the wherewithal to stage a drama not merely of existence but of honor. With his large, successful family, his accomplishments, and his command of himself, he was able to mount an exalted, ambitious proclamation on the meaning and value of his life.

For many years, birthdays had been celebrated by the members in their small, dilapidated center. These were collective occasions, grouping together all those born within the month—modest, simple affairs. Only Jacob Kovitz had regular birthday parties for him alone and these parties were great fetes. This reflected his unusual standing in the group. He had served as its president for several years, and even after leaving the community to live in a rest home, he returned frequently and had been named president emeritus. He was the oldest person in the group and the most generally venerated. No one else had managed to provide leadership without becoming entangled in factional disputes. Jacob regarded himself, and was generally regarded by others, as an exemplar, for he had fulfilled the deepest wishes of most people and he embodied their loftiest ideals.

Jacob Kovitz enjoyed the devotion of his children, four successful, educated sons, who demonstrated their affection by frequently visiting the center and participating in many celebrations there. At these times they treated the members with respect and kindness, and they were always generous, providing meals, entertainment, buses for trips, and other unusual kindnesses. Moreover, when the sons came they brought their wives, children, and grandchildren, many of whom showed an interest in Judaism and Yiddishkeit. Family was one of the highest values among all the old people, and here was a family that all could wish for.

Jacob himself had been a worker. He had made and lost money, but never had he lost his ideals and concerns for charity and his fellows. Without a formal education he had become a poet and was considered a Yiddishist and a philosopher. He was not religious but he had religious knowledge and practiced the life of an ethical and traditional Jew. Jacob was a courageous and energetic man. After retirement he became active in organizing senior citizens' centers, and he drew the attention of the outside world for what his people regarded as the right reasons. All this he managed with an air of gentleness and dignity. Without dignity, no one was considered worthy of esteem by them. Without gentleness and generosity, he would have aroused sufficient envy to render him an ineffective leader. He was accepted by everyone in the group, a symbol and focus of its fragile solidarity.

Jacob also symbolized a good old age. He advised his followers on how to cope with their difficulties, and he demonstrated that old age was not necessarily a threat to decorum, pleasure, autonomy, and clarity of mind.

Following the program suggested by Moore and Myerhoff, (1975) the ritual of Jacob's party-memorial is described in three stages: (1) its creation, (2) its performance, and (3) its outcome, sociologically and in terms of its efficacy.

Creation of the Ceremony

The explicit plan in the design of the ceremony specified a format with several ritual elements that had characterized Jacob's five preceding birthday parties. These were: (1) a *brocha*, here a traditional Hebrew blessing of the wine; (2) a welcome and introduction of important people, including the entire extended Kovitz family, present and absent; (3) a festive meal of kosher foods served on tables with tablecloths and flowers and wine, paid for mostly by the family but requiring some donation by members to avoid the impression of charity; (4) speeches by representatives from the center, sponsoring Jewish organizations under which the center operates, and local and city groups, and by each of the Kovitz sons; (5) entertainment, usually Yiddish folk songs played by a member of the family; (6) a speech by Jacob; (7) a donation of a substantial sum to the center for its programs and for Israel by the family; (8) an invitation to those present to make donations to Israel in honor of the occasion; and (9) a birthday cake, songs, and candles.

The format had a feature often found in secular ritual dramas. Within it fixed, sacred elements alternated with more open, secular aspects, as if to lend authenticity, certainty, and propriety to the open, more optional sections. In the open sections, modifications, particularizations, and innovations occur, tying the fixed sections more firmly to the situational details at hand, together providing a progression that seems both apt and traditional. In this case, for example, the *brocha*, songs, donations, and toasts are predictable; they are unvarying, ritual elements and symbolic acts. The personnel, as representatives, are also symbolic, signifying the boundaries of the relevant collectivities and the social matrix within which the event occurs, but the specific contents of their speeches are less predictable, although they inevitably repeat certain themes.

In this case the repeated themes of the speeches touched on the character, accomplishments, and personal history of Jacob; the honor he brought to his community and family; the honor the family brought to their father and their culture; the importance and worth of the attending center members; the beauty of Yiddish life; the commonality of all those individuals, organizations, and collectivities in attendance; and the perpetuity of the group and its way of life.

The style of the ceremony was another ritual element, familiar to all those who had attended previous parties, and familiar because it was drawn from a wider, general experience—that of many public festivities among strangers and mass media entertainment. It reached for a tone that was jovial, bland, mildly disrespectful, altogether familiar, and familial. It was set by a master-of-ceremonies (a son, Sam) who directed the incidents and the participants, cuing them as to the desired responses during the event, and telling them what was happening as the afternoon unfolded. Despite a seemingly innocuous and casual manner, the style was a precise one, reaching for a particular mood—enjoyment in moderation, and cooperation, unflagging within the regulated time frame. Things must always be kept moving along in ritual; if a lapse occurs, self-consciousness may enter, and the mood may be lost. This is especially important in secular rituals, which are attended by strangers or people from different traditions, to whom the symbols used may not be comprehensible. Ritual is a collusive drama, and all present must be in on it.

In this case specific direction was unusually important. The old people are notoriously difficult to direct. They enter reluctantly into someone else's plans for them; for cultural and psychological reasons, they resist authority and reassert their autonomy. For biological reasons, they find it hard to be attentive for extended periods of time and cannot long delay gratification. Programs must be short, emotionally certain and specific, skillfully interspersing food and symbols. The people can be engaged by the calling of their names, by praise, and by identifying them with the guest of honor. But their importance must not be inflated overmuch for they are quick to perceive this as deception and insult. Furthermore, the old people must not be too greatly aroused, for many have serious heart conditions. Perhaps it was the intense familiarity with their limits as an audience or perhaps it was the uncertainty that underlies all secular ceremonies that caused the designers to select as the master of ceremonies a directive leader, who frequently told the audience what was occurring, what would come next, and reminded them of what had occurred; reiterating the sequences, as if restatement in itself would augment the sense of tradition and timelessness that is sought in ritual.

The affair was called a birthday party, but in fact this was a metaphor. The son Sam said in his speech, "You know, Pa doesn't think a birthday is worth celebrating without raising money for a worthy Jewish cause." The event had a more ambitious purpose than merely celebrating a mark in an individual life. The birthday party metaphor was used because it symbolized the people's membership in a secular, modern society. But as only a birthday , it had little significance to them. None of them had ever celebrated their birthdays in this fashion. Indeed, it was the custom to remember the day of their birth by reckoning it on the closest Jewish holiday, submerging private within collective celebrations. More importantly, the event was a *simcha,* a *yontif,* a *mitzvah*—a blessing, a holiday, a good deed, an occasion for cultural celebration and an opportunity to perform good works in a form that expressed the members' identity with the widest reaches of community, Israel and needy Jews everywhere.

Its most important message was that of perpetuation of the group beyond the life of individual members. This was signified in two ways, both of which were innovations and departures from Kovitz's usual birthdays. First, temporal continuity was signified by the presence of a group of college students, brought into the center during the year by a young rabbi who sought to promote intergenerational ties. It was decided that the young people would serve the birthday meal to the elders as a gesture of respect. That a rabbi was there with them was incidental and unplanned, but turned out to be important. Second was Jacob's announcement that he was donating funds for his birthday parties to be held at the center for the next five years, whether he was alive or not. Occasions were thus provided for people to assemble for what would probably be the rest of their lives, giving them some assurance that as individuals they would not outlive their culture and community.

Another of the repeated ritual elements was the personnel involved. Most of these have been identified, and reference here need be made only to two more. These were the director of the center

BARBARA MYERHOFF

and its president. The director, Abe, was a second-generation assimilated American of Russian Jewish parentage. A social worker, he had been with this group a dozen years and knew the people intimately, usually functioning as their guardian, protector, interpreter, and mediator. He, along with Jacob and his sons, developed the format for the ceremony and helped conduct it. The president, Moshe, was a man of 82, with an Hasidic background.[3] He was a religious man with a considerable religious education, and a Yiddishist. It was to him that questions about Judaism and its customs were likely to be referred. After Jacob he was the most respected man in the group, and one of Jacob's closest friends.

Antecedent Context of the Ritual

Everyone at the center knew that Jacob had been sick. For three months he had been hospitalized, in intensive care, and at his request had been removed by his son Sam to his home so that he could be "properly taken care of out of the unhealthy atmosphere of a hospital." Before Jacob had always resisted living with his children, and people interpreted this change in attitude as indicative of his determination to come to his birthday party. The old people were aware that Jacob had resolved to have the party take place whether he were able to attend or not. People were impressed, first, because Jacob had the autonomy and courage to assert his opinions over the recommendations of his doctors— evidently he was still in charge of himself and his destiny—and second, because Jacob's children were so devoted as to take him in and care for him. But most of all they were struck by his determination to celebrate his birthday among them. They were honored and awed by this and waited eagerly for the daily developments about the celebration: details concerning Jacob's health, the menu for the party, the entertainment—all were known and discussed at length beforehand.

As the day grew close, much talk concerned the significance of the specific date. It was noted that the celebration was being held on Jacob's actual birthday. The party was always held on a Sunday, and as the date and day coincided only every seven years, surely that they did so on this particular year was no accident. Again, they noticed that the month of March was intrinsically important in the

Hebrew calendar, a month of three major holidays. And someone said that it was the month in which Moses was born and died. He died on his birthday, they noted.

The atmosphere was charged and excited before the party had even begun. Abe, the director, was worried about the old people's health and the effects on them of too much excitement. There were those who insisted that on the birthday they would be told Jacob had died. Jacob's friend Manya said, "He'll come all right, but he is coming to his own funeral."

And what were Jacob's thoughts and designs at this point? It is possible to glimpse his intentions from his taped interviews with a son and a granddaughter. In these, common elements emerge: he is not afraid of death but he is tormented by confusion and disorientation when "things seem upside ways," and "not the way you think is real." Terrible thoughts and daydreams beset him, but he explains that he fights them off with his characteristic strength, remarking, "I have always been a fighter. That's how I lived, even as a youngster. I'd ask your opinion and yours, then go home and think things over and come to my own decisions." He describes his battles against senility and his determination to maintain coherence by writing, talking, and thinking. He concludes,

> I was very depressed in the hospital. Then I wrote a poem. Did you see it? A nice poem. So I'm still living and I have something to do. I got more clearheaded. I controlled myself.

Jacob had always controlled himself and shaped his life, and he was not about to give that up. Evidently he hoped he might die the same way. "I'll never change" were his last words on the tape.

It was difficult for Jacob to hold on until the party and to write his speech, which seemed to be the focus of his desire to attend. Its contents were noteworthy in two respects: first, his donation and provision for five more parties; and second, his statement that whereas on all his previous birthdays he had important messages to deliver, on this one he had nothing significant to say. Why, then, the desperate struggle to make this statement? The message, it seems, was that he could and would deliver it himself, that he was still designing his life and would do so to the end. The preparations for and the manner of the speech's delivery conveyed and paralleled its message.

BARBARA MYERHOFF

The Performance of the Ritual

The day of the party was fair and celebrants came streaming toward the center out of their rented rooms and boardinghouses down the small streets and alleys, several hours too early. That the day was special was clear from their appearance. The women came with white gloves, carrying perfectly preserved purses from other decades, and wearing jewelry, unmistakable gifts from their children—golden medallions bearing grandchildren's names, "Tree of Life" necklaces studded with real pearls; Stars of David; a gold pendant in the form of the letter *Chai*, Hebrew for life and luck. All were announcements of connections and remembrance. Glowing halos from umbrellas and bright hats colored the ladies' expectant faces. Men wore tidy suits polished with use over well-starched, frayed shirts.

The center halls, too, were festively decorated and people were formally seated. At the head table was the Kovitz family and around it the dignitaries. Jacob, it was learned, was behind the curtain of the little stage, receiving oxygen, and so the ceremony was delayed for about half an hour. At last he came out to applause and took his seat. Music called the assembly to order and people were greeted with *shalom*, Hebrew for peace. The guest of honor was presented, then introductions followed, with references to the Kovitz family as *mispoche* ("kin"), the term finally being used for the entire assembly. By implication, all present were an extended family. Each member of the Kovitz family was named, even those who were absent, including titles and degrees, generation by generation. The assembly was greeted on behalf of "Pa, his children, his children's children, and even from their children." The religious *brocha* in Hebrew was followed by the traditional secular Jewish toast *Le' Cheüm*. Sam set out the order of events in detail, including a specification of when Jacob's gift would be made, when dessert would be served (with speeches), when the cake would be eaten (after speeches), and so forth. The announcement of procedures was intended to achieve coordination and invite participation. The audience was appreciative and active. People applauded for the degrees and regrets from family members unable to attend, and recognized the implicit messages of continuity of tradition, respect from younger generations, and family devotion that had been conveyed in the first few moments.

The meal went smoothly and without any public events, though privately Jacob told the president, Moshe, that he wished people would hurry and eat because *"Malakh-hamoves* [the Angel of Death, God's messenger] is near and hasn't given me much time."

As dessert was about to be served, Sam, acting as master of ceremonies, took the microphone and began his speech, in which he recounted some biographical details of Jacob's life and certain cherished characteristics. He emphasized his father's idealism and social activism in the Old Country and in America, and spoke at some length about the courtship and marriage of his parents. Though his mother had died 24 years ago, she remained a strong influence in keeping the family together, he said.

During Sam's speech, Jacob was taken backstage to receive oxygen. People were restive and worried, but Sam assured them that Jacob would soon return and the program continue. Eventually Jacob took his seat, leaning over to tell one of the young people in English, and Moshe in Yiddish, that he had little time and wished they would hurry to his part of the program, for now, he said, "Ich reingle sich mutten *Malakh-hamoves.*" ("I am wrestling the Angel of Death.")

The program was interrupted briefly when all those in charge recognized Jacob's difficulty in breathing and gave him oxygen at his seat. A pause of about ten minutes ensued. The thread of the ritual lapsed entirely while people watched Jacob being given oxygen. Moshe and Abe were worried about the impact of this sight on the old people. The previous year someone had died among them and they had been panic-stricken. But now all were rather quiet. They talked to each other softly in Yiddish. At last Sam took the microphone again and spoke extempore about his father's recent life, filling the time and maintaining the ritual mood until it became clear that Jacob was recovering. Sam told the group that maybe his wife's chicken soup—proper chicken soup prepared from scratch with the love of a Yiddishe mama—had helped sustain Jacob. This was received with enthusiastic applause. Most of those in the audience were women and their identity was much bound up with the role of the nurturant, uniquely devoted Jewish mother. In fact, the earlier mention of the importance and remembrance of the Kovitz mother had been received by many women as a personal tribute. They also appreciated the appropriateness of a daughter-in-law showing this care for a parent, something none of them had experienced. Sam went on to explain that since leaving the hospital Jacob had "embarked on a new career, despite his old age." He was teaching his son Yiddish and had agreed to stay around until Sam had mastered it completely. "Since I am a slow learner, I think he'll be with us for quite awhile." This too was full of symbolic significance. The suggestion of new projects being available to the old and of the passing on of the knowledge of Yiddish to children were important messages.

Sam went on, extending his time at the microphone as he waited for a sign that Jacob was able to give his speech. By now Sam was improvising on the original format for the ritual. He made his announcement of the gift of money, half to the center for cultural programs, half to Israel, reminding the audience that Jacob did not believe a birthday party was worth celebrating unless it involved raising funds for deserving Jewish causes.

Still Jacob was not ready, so the microphone was turned over to Abe, who improvised on some of the same themes, again and again, touching important symbolic chords. He, like Sam, referred to Jacob as a stubborn man and to Jews as a stiff-necked people, tenacious and determined. He reassured the assembly that they were important people and would be remembered, that outsiders came to their center to share their *simcha* and appreciate their unique way of life. They, he said, like Jacob, would be studied by scientists one day, for a better understanding of the indivisibility of mental and physical health, to see how people could live to be very old by using their traditions as a basis for a good and useful life. He finished by emphasizing Jacob's most revered qualities: his devotion to his people, his learning and literacy, and his courage and dignity. He was an example to them all. "And," he went on, "you, too, you are all examples."

At last the sign was given that Jacob was ready. Abe announced the revised sequence of events: Jacob's speech in Yiddish, then in English, then the dignitaries' speeches, then the cake. Jacob remained seated but began his speech vigorously, in good, clear Yiddish.[4] After a few sentences he faltered, slowed, and finished word by word. Here are selections from his speech in translation:

Dear friends: Every other year I have had something significant to say, some meaningful message when we came together for this *yontif.* But this year I don't have an important message. I don't have the strength.... It is very hard for me to accept the idea that I am played out.... Nature has a good way of expressing herself when bringing humanity to the end of its years, but when it touches you personally it is hard to comprehend.... I do have a wish for today.... It is that my last five years, until I am 100, my birthday will be celebrated here with you...whether I am here or not. It will be an opportunity for the members of my beloved center to be together for a *simcha* and at the same time raise money for our beleaguered Israel.

The message was powerful in its stated and unstated concepts, made even more so by the dramatic circumstances in which it was delivered. Jacob's passion to be heard and to complete his purpose was perhaps the strongest communication. He was demonstrating what he had said in the earlier interviews, namely, that he sustained himself as an autonomous, lucid person, using thinking, speaking, and writing as his shields against self-dissolution and senility.

Jacob finished and sat down amid great applause. His and the audience's relief were apparent. He sat quietly in his place at the table, folded his hands, and rested his chin on his chest. A moment after Sam began to read his father's speech in English, Jacob's head fell back, wordlessly, and his mouth fell open. Oxygen was administered within the surrounding circle of his sons as Abe took the microphone and asked for calm and quiet. After a few moments, his sons lifted Jacob, still seated in his chair, and carried him behind the curtain, accompanied by Moshe, Abe, and the rabbi.

Soon Abe returned and reassured the hushed assembly that a rescue unit had been called, that everything possible was being done, and that Jacob wanted people to finish their dessert.

Be assured that he knew the peril of coming today. All we can do is pray. He's in the hands of God. His sons are with him. He most of all wanted to be here. Remember his dignity and yours and let him be an example. You must eat your dessert. You must, we must all, continue. We go on living. Now your dessert will be served.

BARBARA MYERHOFF

People complied and continued eating. There were many who quietly spoke their certainty that Jacob was dead and had died in their midst. The conviction was strongest among those few who noticed that when the rabbi and Moshe left Jacob behind the curtain, they went to the bathroom before returning to their seats. Perhaps it was only hygiene, they said but it was also known that religious Jews are enjoined to wash their hands after contact with the dead. Hence the gesture was read as portentous.

The room was alive with hushed remarks:

He's gone. That was how he wanted it. He said what he had to say and finished.

It was a beautiful life, a beautiful death.

There's a saying, when the fig is plucked in due time it's good for the fig and good for the tree.

Did you see how they carried him out? Like Elijah, he died in his chair. Like a bridegroom.

He died like a *tzaddik*.[5]

Moses also died on his birthday, in the month of Nisan.[6]

Order was restored as the dignitaries were introduced. Again the ritual themes reappeared in the speeches: Jacob's work among senior citizens, the honor of his family, his exemplary character, and so forth. A letter to Jacob from the mayor was read and a plaque honoring him proffered by a councilman. Then a plant was given to his family on behalf of an organization, and this seemed to be a signal that gifts were possible and appropriate. One of the assembled elderly, an artist, took one of his pictures off the wall and presented it to the family. A woman gave the family a poem she had written honoring Jacob, and another brought up the flowers from her table. The momentum of the ritual lapsed completely in the face of these spontaneous gestures. People were repeatedly urged by Abe to take their seats. The artist, Heschel, asked what would be done about the birthday cake now that Jacob was gone, and was rebuked for being gluttonous. With great difficulty Abe regained control of the people, reminding them sternly that the

ceremony had not been concluded. There remained one dignitary
who had not yet spoken, Abe pointed out, and this was insulting to
the group he represented.

Abe was improvising here, no longer able to utilize the
guidelines of the birthday metaphor. The ceremony threatened to
break apart. In actuality, Abe was worried about letting people go
home without knowing Jacob's fate. It would be difficult for him to
handle their anxieties in the next few days if they were left in
suspense. No one wanted to leave. The circumstances clearly called
for some closure, some provision of order. The last dignitary began
to talk and Abe wondered what to do next. Then the phone rang
and everyone was still. The speaker persisted, but no one listened.
Abe came forward and announced what everyone already knew.

> God in his wisdom has taken Jacob away from us, in His
> mystery He has taken him. So you must understand that
> God permitted Jacob to live 95 years and to have one of
> his most beautiful moments here this afternoon. You
> heard his last words. We will charter a bus and go together
> to his funeral. He gave you his last breath. I will ask the
> rabbi to lead us in a prayer as we stand in solemn tribute
> to Jacob.

People stood. About a dozen men drew *yalmulkes* out of their
pockets and covered their heads. The rabbi spoke:

> We have had the honor of watching a circle come to its
> fullness and close as we rejoiced together. We have shared
> Jacob's wisdom and warmth, and though the ways of God
> are mysterious, there is meaning in what happened today.
> I was with Jacob backstage and tried to administer external
> heart massage. In those few moments with him behind the
> curtain, I felt his strength. There was an electricity about
> him but it was peaceful and I was filled with awe. When
> the firemen burst in, it felt wrong because they were big
> and forceful and Jacob was gentle and resolute. He was
> still directing his life, and he directed his death. He shared
> his wisdom, his life with us and now it is our privilege to
> pay him homage. Send your prayers with Jacob on his final
> journey. Send his sparks up and help open the gates for

him with your thoughts. We will say Kaddish. *"Yitgadal veyitakadash shmeh rabba...*[Sanctified and magnificent be Thy Great Name]."[7]

The ritual was now unmistakably over but no one left the hall. People shuffled forward toward the stage, talking quietly in Yiddish. Many crossed the room to embrace friends, and strangers and enemies embraced as well. Among these old people physical contact is usually very restrained, yet now they eagerly sought each others' arms. Several wept softly. As is dictated by Jewish custom, no one approached the family, but only nodded to them as they left.

There were many such spontaneous expressions of traditional Jewish mourning customs, performed individually, with the collective effect of transforming the celebration into a commemoration. Batya reached down and pulled out the hem of her dress, honoring the custom of rending one's garments on news of a death. Someone had draped her scarf over the mirror in the ladies' room, as tradition requires. Heschel poured his glass of tea into a saucer. Then Abe took the birthday cake to the kitchen, and said, "We will freeze it. We will serve it at Jacob's memorial when we read from his book. He wouldn't want us to throw it away. He will be with us still. You see, people, Jacob holds us together even after his death."

Finally, the center had emptied. People clustered together on the benches outside to continue talking and reviewing the events of the afternoon. Before long, all were in agreement that Jacob had certainly died among them. The call to the rescue squad had been a formality, they agreed. Said Moshe,

You see, it is the Jewish way to die in your community. In the old days, it was an honor to wash the body of the dead. No one went away and died with strangers in a hospital. The finest people dressed the corpse and no one left him alone for a minute. So Jacob died like a good Yid. Not everybody is so lucky.

Over and over, people discussed the goodness of Jacob's death and its appropriateness. Many insisted that they had known beforehand he would die that day. "So why else do you think I had my *yalmulke* with me at a birthday party?" asked Beryl. Sam commented, "After a scholarly meeting it is customary to thank the man.

Jacob was a scholar and we thanked him by accompanying him to Heaven. It's good to have many people around at such a time. It shows them on the other side that a man is respected where he came from." Bessie's words were "He left us a lot. Now the final chapter is written. No? What more is there to say. The book is closed. When a good man dies, his soul becomes a word in God's book." It was a good death, it was agreed. Jacob was a lucky man. "Zu mir gezugt" "It should happen to me" was heard from the lips of many as they left.

Two formal rituals followed. The funeral was attended by most of the group (which, as promised, went in a chartered bus), and a *shloshim* or thirty-day memorial was held at the center, when the birthday cake was indeed served, but without candles.

At the funeral, the young rabbi reiterated his earlier statement concerning the electricity he had felt emitting from Jacob just before he died, described how Jacob used his remaining strength to make a final affirmation of all he stood for, and revealed that, at the last moment of his life, Jacob—surrounded by all the people he loved—believed in God.[8] In his eulogy, Jacob's son Sam said, "In our traditions there are three crowns—the crown of royalty, the crown of priesthood, and the crown of learning. But a fourth, the crown of a good name, exceeds them all." Spontaneously, at the graveside, without benefit of direction from funeral officials, many old men and women came forward to throw a shovel of earth on the grave, sometimes themselves tottering from the effort. Each one carefully laid down the shovel after finishing, according to the old custom. Then they backed away, forming two rows, to allow the Angel of Death to pass through. They knew from old usage what was appropriate, what movements and gestures suited the occasion, with a certainty that is rarely seen now in their lives. Moshe, one of the last to leave, pulled up some grass and tossed it over his shoulder. This is done, he explained later, to show that we remember we are dust, but also that we may be reborn, for it is written: "May they blossom out of the city like the grass of the earth."

A month later, the *shloshim* was held. In it a final and official interpretation of Jacob's death was forged and shared. He was a saint by then. He must be honored, and several disputes were avoided that day by people reminding one another of Jacob's spirit of appreciation and acceptance of all of them and his wish for peace

BARBARA MYERHOFF

within the center. The cake was eaten with gusto as people told and retold the story of Jacob's death.

The Efficacy of the Ritual

How shall the success of a ritual be estimated? How is one to decide if it has done its work? These are among the most complex and troublesome questions to be faced in dealing with this topic. It is not impossible to examine efficacy in terms of the explicit intentions of the performers. But it is necessary to go beyond this and inquire, too, about its unintended effects and the implicit, unconscious messages it carries. Then, one may ask, for whom did it work? For there may be many publics involved. In religious rituals even the deities and the unseen forces are addressed and, it is hoped, moved by the performance. The official plan for a ritual does not tell us about this. Many levels of response may be specified, for this is not given by the formal organization of a ritual. Sometimes audiences or witnesses are more engaged by watching a ritual than are its central subjects and participants. When we inquire about conviction, it is necessary to ask also about the degree and kind of conviction involved, since a range of belief is possible, from objection and anger if the ritual is incorrectly performed, through indifference and boredom, to approval and enjoyment, and finally total and ecstatic conviction. The long-range as well as immediate effects of the event must be taken into account since rituals have consequences that reach past the moment when they occur; their outcome is usually to be known only in due time. It is impossible to take up all these questions. The fieldworker never has such complete information. And the symbols dealt with in ritual are by definition inexhaustible in their final range of referents. Subjects cannot verbalize the totality of their apprehensions in these areas because so much of their response is unconscious. Inevitably there are blanks in our inquiry, and ultimately the fieldworker interested in such questions takes responsibility for interference in explanation, going beyond the observed behavior and "hard" data; to do otherwise would mean losing all hope of understanding the issues that make ritual interesting in the first place. In discussing ritual, an analysis of outcome is always an interpretation and an incomplete one.

All rituals are efficacious to some degree merely by their taking place. They are not purposive and instrumental, but expressive, communicative, and rhetorical acts. Their stated purpose must be regarded not as an illustration of a piece of life but as an analogy. No primitive society is so unempirical as to expect to cause rain by dancing a rain dance. Not even Suzanne Langer's cat is that naive. A rain dance is, in Burke's felicitous phrase, a dance with the rain, the dancing of an attitude. The attitude is the one described earlier—collectively attending, dramatizing, making palpable unseen forces, setting apart the flow of everyday life by framing a segment of it, stopping time and change by presenting a permanent truth or pattern. If the spirits hear and it rains, so much the better, but the success of the ritual does not depend on the rain. If a patient at a curing ceremony recovers, good, but he or she need not do so for the ritual to have successfully done its work. A ritual fails when it is seen through, not properly attended, or experienced as arbitrary invention. Then people may be indifferent enough not to hide their lack of conviction; their failure or refusal to appear to suspend disbelief is apparent and the ritual is not even efficacious as a communication.

In the case of Jacob's death, matters are complicated because two rituals must be considered: the intended birthday party, a designed, directed secular affair with nonreligious sacred nuances, transformed spontaneously by a collectivity into a nonplanned, fully sacred religious memorial.

The birthday party, as far as it went, was a success. It is hard to imagine how it could have failed to make its point and achieve its purposes, which were entirely social. It was convincing to all concerned and received by the audience with appreciation and cooperation. It demonstrated social connections and implied perpetuity of a collectivity beyond the limited life span of its central figure. It honored the man Jacob and his friends, values, and traditions. It reached beyond its immediate audience to include and allow for identification with a wider, invisible Jewish community. The goals of the birthday party were relatively modest and not unusual for secular ceremonies of this sort. The turning point occurred when Jacob died; the message and impact of the day's ceremonies took on a new dimension, and the sacred ritual replaced the social, more secular one.

BARBARA MYERHOFF

In dying when he did, Jacob was giving his last breath to his group, and this was understood as a demonstration of his regard for them. His apparent ability to choose to do what is ordinarily beyond human control hinted at some divine collaboration. The collective and spontaneous reversion to traditional religious death rituals was hardly surprising. Death customs are always elaborate and usually constitute one of the most long-lasting and familiar areas of religious knowledge. According to some authorities, saying Kaddish makes one still a Jew no matter what else of the heritage one has relinquished (see Zoshin 1974). The saying of Kaddish makes palpable the community of Jews. According to the rabbi at the party-memorial, the Kaddish always includes not only the particular death at hand but all a person's dead beloved and all the Jews who have ever lived and died.[9] Mourners coalesce into an *edah*, a community, connected beyond time and space to an invisible group, stretching to the outermost reaches of being a people, *Kol Israel*—the ancestors, those unborn—and most powerfully, one's own direct, personal experiences of loss and death.

For religious and nonreligious alike that day the Kaddish enlarged and generalized the significance of Jacob's death. At the same time, the Kaddish particularized his death by equating it with each person's historical, subjective private griefs, thus completing the exchange between the collective and the private poles of experience to which axiomatic symbols refer. When this exchange occurs, symbols are not mere pointers or referents to things beyond themselves. A transformation takes place: "symbols and object seem to fuse and are experienced as a perfectly undifferentiated whole." (Langer 1942) Such transformations cannot be planned or achieved by will, because emotions and imagination, as D.G. James (1937) observes, operate more like fountains than machines. Transformation carries participants beyond words and wordbound thought, calling into play imagination, emotion, and insight and, as Suzanne Langer says, "altering our conceptions at a single stroke." Then participants conceive the invisible referents of their symbols and may glimpse the underlying, unchanging patterns of human and cosmic life, in a triumph of understanding and belief. Few rituals reach such heights of intensity and conviction. When this occurs, all those involved are momentarily drawn together in a basically religious, sometimes near ecstatic mood of gratitude and wonder. That Jacob's death was a genuine transformational moment was attested to by a profound sense of *communitas* and fulfillment that people appeared to have experienced with the recitation of the Kaddish.

We are interested in the unintended, implicit messages conveyed by ritual as well as the planned ones. Therefore, in this case it must be asked, What were the consequences of the set of items that suggested uncanny, inexplicable factors—Jacob's seeming ability to choose the moment of his death, and the prophecy of his death in the form of a dream? The questions are particularly important because ritual is supposed to deliver a message about predictability and order, and here were intrusions beyond human control and therefore disorderly and unpredictable.

Paradoxically, these very elements of the uncanny, mysterious, and unpredictable made the ritual more persuasive and more convincing rather than less so. All these surprises were clothed in a traditional idiom, and while perplexing were not unfamiliar. There were well-used accounts for such matters; there were precedents for prophetic dreams, the presence of the Angel of Death, the deaths of the *tzaddikim,* and of Moses. Conceptions existed for handling them, and if most people involved did not deeply believe in the dogma, they were not unwilling to consider the possibility that explanations previously offered, though long unused, might have some validity after all.

Renewed belief in God at the end of life is hardly rare, and indeed it might even be that people were more reassured than frightened at the turn of events of the day. When a man dies, as Evans-Pritchard reminds us, a moral question is always posed: not merely, Why does man die? But why this man and why now? In our secular society, we are often left without an answer, and these celebrants, like most who have abandoned or drifted away from their religion, were ordinarily alone with these questions, dealing with ultimate concerns, feebly and individually. The result of Jacob's death, however, was the revival of the idea, or at least the hope and suspicion, that sometimes people die meaningfully; occasionally purpose and propriety are evident. Death in most cases may be the ultimate manifestation of disorder and accident but here it seemed apt and fulfilling. More often than not death flies in the face of human conception, reminding us of our helplessness and ignorance. It finds the wrong people at the wrong time. It mocks our sense of justice. But here it did the opposite and made such obvious sense that it came as a manifestation of order. It helped fulfill the purposes of ritual, establishing and stating form drawn forth from flux and confusion.

Remarkably enough, in this ritual the distinction between artifice and nature was also overcome. The ritual, though unplanned, was not susceptible to the danger of being recognized as human invention. Ironically, because no one was clearly entirely in control—neither Jacob nor the designers and directors—and because it unfolded naturally, the ritual was received as a revelation rather than as a construction. It did not suffer the usual risks of ritual, displaying the conventional and attributed rather than intrinsic nature of our conceptions. Had there been no intimations of the supernatural, the death would probably have been frightening, because it would have exaggerated mortal powers beyond the credibility of the people participating. The hints of mystery suggested powers beyond Jacob's control, making a religious experience of one that otherwise might have been simply bizarre. Despite the party and the resultant radical change of course, the celebration that occurred had that very sense of inevitability and predictability of outcome which is the goal of all human efforts in designing and staging a ritual.

Ritual, Time, and Continuity

Any discussion of ritual is also a discussion of time and continuity; when the ritual in question deals with death and birth, the themes of time and continuity are thrown into high relief. Ritual alters our ordinary sense of time, repudiating meaningless change and discontinuity by emphasizing regularity, precedent, and order. Paradoxically, it uses repetition to deny the empty repetitiveness of unremarked, unattended human and social experience. From repetition, it finds or makes patterns, and looks at these for hints of eternal designs and meanings. In ritual, change is interpreted by being linked with the past and incorporated into a larger framework, where its variations are equated with grander, tidier totalities. By inserting traditional elements into the present, the past is read as prefiguring what is happening in the here and now, and by implication the future is seen as foreshadowed in all that has gone before. Religious rituals are more sweeping than secular ones in this elongation of time and reiteration of continuity. The latter usually confine themselves to remembered human history, whereas the former transform history into myths, stories with no beginning and no end. Then time is obliterated and continuity is complete.

To do their work rituals must disrupt our ordinary sense of time and displace our awareness of events coming into being and disappearing in discrete, precise, discontinuous segments. This discontinuous experience is our everyday sense of time, used to coordinate collective activities; it is external in origins and referents, and does not take into account private responses, stimulation, states of mind, or motivation. Public chronological time is anathema to the mood of ritual, which has its own time. Rituals sweep us away from the everyday sense and from the objective, instrumental frame of mind that is associated with it. By merely absorbing us sufficiently, ritual, like art, lets us "lose ourselves" and step out of our usual conscious, critical mentality. When successful, ritual replaces chronological, collective time with the experience of flowing duration, paced according to personal significance; sometimes this is so powerful that we are altogether freed from a sense of time and of awareness of self. This is ritual time, and it must be present to some degree to mount the mood of conviction concerning the messages contained in a ritual.

But ritual is still a social event, and it is necessary that, within it, individuals' temporal experiences are coordinated somewhat. They must be delicately synchronized, without obliterating the individual's sense of an intense personal experience. Ordinary time is suspended and a new time instituted, geared to the event taking place, shared by those participating, integrating the private experience into a collective one. These moments of community built outside of ordinary time are rare and powerful, forging an intense communion that transcends awareness of individual separateness. Continuity among participants prevails briefly, in a sometimes euphoric condition, which Turner has described at length as a state of *communitas*, (Turner 1971) and which Buber calls *Zwischenmenschlichkeit.*

Continuity of self may occur in rituals, especially rites of passage marking stages in the individual life cycle, and this produces yet another experience of time. Personal integration is achieved when the subject in a ritual retrieves his or her prior life experiences, not as past memories, but as events and feelings occurring in the present. Then the person is a child or youth once more, feeling one with earlier selves, who are recognized as familiar, still alive, coherent. Coherence of the "I," a sense of continuity with one's past selves, is not inevitable, as James Fernandez points out. The chaos of individual history, especially when that history has been great and often marked by numerous social and cultural separations, may be acute. The burden of memories weighs heavily on the elderly: the necessity for integration of a life is often a strong impulse. Reminiscence among the old is not merely escapism, nor the desire to live in the past.[10] It is often the reach for personal integration and the experience of continuity, and for the recognition of personal unity beneath the flow and flux of ordinary life.

Because ritual works through the senses, bypassing the critical, conscious mind, it allows one to return to earlier states of being. The past comes back, along with the ritual movements, practices, tastes, smells, and sounds, bringing along unaltered fragments from other times. Proust was fascinated with this process (see Myerhoff and Tufte 19). His work examines how the past may sometimes be recaptured with all its original force, unmodified by intervening events. This may occur when the conscious mind with its subsequent interpretations and associations is bypassed. Experiences of past time come back unaltered, often as spontaneous responses to sense stimuli; as Adam Mendilow describes this process, it occurs when the chemistry of thought is untouched by intervening events and the passage of time.[22] These numinous moments carry with them their original, pristine associations and feelings. This is timelessness and the past is made into present. It is, says Mendilow, a kind of

> hermetical magic, sealed outside of time, suspending the
> sense of duration, allowing all of life to be experienced as
> a single moment.... These are pinpoints of great intensity,
> concentrations of universal awareness, antithetical to the
> diffuseness of life. (Mendilow 1952: 137)

These pin-points of timelessness are beyond duration and change. In them one experiences the essence of life—or self—as eternally valid; simultaneity has replaced sequence, and continuity is complete.

Conceivably, any kind of ritual has the capacity to retrieve a fragment of past life. Rituals associated with and originating in childhood are more likely to do so, and these especially carry opportunities for finding personal-historical continuity. Two characteristics of these rituals are salient here: first, their intensely physiological associations; and second, their great power and immediacy, coming as they do from the individual's first emotional and social experiences. They are absolutely basic, arising in the context of nurturance and dependence, evoking the familiar, domestic domain, utterly fundamental, preceding language and conception. In our world of plural cultures, the first domestic nurturant experiences are often associated with ethnic origins, bound up with first foods, touch, language, song, folkways, and the like, carried and connoted by rituals and symbols learned in that original context. Ethnic ritual and symbol are often redolent of the earliest, most profoundly emotional associations and it is often these that carry one back to earlier times and selves.

Consider the statement made by one of the old men present at Jacob's birth-death ritual.

> Whenever I say Kaddish, I chant and sway, and it all comes back to me. I remember how it was when my father, may he rest in peace, would wrap me around in his big prayer shawl. All that comes back to me, like I was back in that shawl, where nothing bad could ever happen.

The Kaddish prayer was probably the most important single ritual that occurred the day of Jacob's death. It was the most frequently and deeply experienced aspect of Jewish custom for the people there, the most ethnically rooted moment, sweeping together all the individuals present, connecting them with earlier parts of self, with Jacob the man, with each other, and with Jews who had lived and died before. The life of the mortal man Jacob was made into a mythic event, enlarging and illuminating the affairs of all those present. Here is ritual achieving its final purpose of transformation, altering our everyday understanding in a single stroke. Ultimately, we are interested in ritual because it tells us something about the human condition, the mythic condition, and our private lives all at once. It demonstrates the continuity between

BARBARA MYERHOFF

one human being and all humanity. It does more than tell us an eternal tale; it sheds light on our own condition. Jacob's death did this.

Jacob, when the celebration ended, had become a point from which radiated the enlarged meanings of his life and death, as well as the immediate ones, the grand and the minute, the remote and the particular, all implying each other, until continuity had become total unity.

Jacob's death could not change the harsh realities. But if people lived only by harsh realities there would be no need for rituals, for symbols, or for myths. The power of rituals, myths, and symbols is that they can change the experience we have of the world and its worth. Jacob's death rites may be considered an extraordinarily successful example of ritual providing social, cultural, biological, and spiritual continuity. More perpetuation, more connection, more interdependence, more unity existed when the day was over, making the oblivion of an individual and his way of life a little less certain than anyone had thought possible that morning.

Notes

1. The methods used to gather information for this essay included participant observation, interviews, tape recording, group discussions, films, and still photography. I taped and photographed the event described and later had access to 8-mm film footage taken during the celebration by one of those attending. I interviewed Jacob Kovitz many times before he died, and interviewed members of his family before and after. The final interpretation I developed was discussed with the family, who had no objections to it, though it varied in some points with their own. All names used, including that of the center, have been changed.

2. Here I am distinguishing between "religious" and "sacred" and treating them as categories that may exist independently or be joined. Where ideas, objects, or practices are considered axiomatic, unquestionable, literally sacrosanct, they are "sacred," with or without the inclusion of the concept of the supernatural. Their sacredness derives from a profound and affective consensus as to their rightness; their authority comes from their embeddedness in many realms of tradition. Over against the sacred is the mundane, which is malleable and negotiable. When sacredness is detached

from the religious, it refers to unquestionably good and right traditions, sanctified by usage and consensus.

3.   Hasids (Hasidim) were, and are, a deeply religious, semi-mystical group practicing a vitalized, fervent form of folk Judaism originating in Eastern Europe during the mid-eighteenth century.

4.   All these people are completely multilingual and use different languages for different purposes, with some consistency. For example, political and secular matters are often discussed in English; Hebrew is used to make poems, reminiscences, and arguments and bargaining. Yiddish, the *mamloschen,* punctuates all the areas, but appears most regularly in times of intense emotion. It is also used most in conversations about food, children, cursing, and gossiping. For some, Yiddish has connotations of inferiority since it was associated with female activities, domestic and familial matters (in the *shtetls,* few were educated in Hebrew and so Yiddish dominated the household). It was the language of exiles living in oppression and, later, of greenhorns. For others, the Yiddishists in particular, it is a bona fide language to be treated with respect and used publicly. Careful pronunciation, proper syntax, and avoidance of Anglicized words are considered signs of respect for Yiddishkeit. On the whole, Jacob was always careful in his Yiddish, and this was seen as an indication of his pride in his heritage.

5.   A *tzaddik* in Hasidic tradition is a saintly man of great devotion, often possessing mystical powers. It is noted that important Hasids sometimes died in their chairs, and it is said that they often anticipated the dates of their death. There is also a suggestive body of custom surrounding the symbolism of the chair, which figures importantly in at least two Jewish male rites of passage. In Hasidic weddings it is customary for the bridegroom to be carried aloft in his chair. And an empty chair is reserved for the prophet Elijah at circumcisions; this is to signify that any Jewish boy may turn out to be the Messiah, since Elijah must be present at the Messiah's birth.

6.   In fact, Moses died on the seventh of Adar. He did, however, die on his birthday; he was allowed to "complete the years of the righteous exactly from day to day and month to month, as it is said, the number of thy days I will fulfill" (Talmud Bavli Kaddushin 38A). Hence the tradition in folklore that the righteous are born and die on the same day. Elijah did not die in his chair, however. He is believed to have "been taken up by a whirlwind into Heaven," passing out of this world without dying. His "passage" was not a normal death in any event, and this is probably why his death was brought up in this discussion. These points were clarified in personal communication by Rabbi Chaim Seidler-Feller of Los Angeles.

7.   In Jewish mysticism, represented in the Kabbalah, a person's soul or spirit is transformed into sparks after death. "Kaddish" is a prayer sanctifying God's name, recited many times in Jewish liturgy; it is known also as the Mourner's Prayer and recited at the side of a grave.

8.   Others disagreed with this and were certain that Jacob died an agnostic. They did not confront the rabbi on the matter, however; said Heschel, "If it makes the rabbi happy, let him believe it.".

9.   The rabbi was in attendance fortuitously that day, in his capacity as leader of the young people. Without him the Kaddish would not have been said. His unplanned presence was subsequently interpreted by many as another sign that the memorial was meant to take place when it did.

10. See R.N. Butler, "The Life Review: An Interpretation of Reminiscence in the Aged," in B.L. Neugarten, ed., *Middle Age and Aging* (Chicago, 1968), for a discussion of the therapeutic functions of reminiscence in the elderly.

BARBARA MYERHOFF

References

Ariès, P.
1974 *Western Attitudes toward Death from the Middle Ages to the Present.* Baltimore: Johns Hopkins University Press.

Fernandez, J.
1974 "The Mission of Metaphor in Expressive Culture", *Current Anthropology* 15 (2): 119-133.

Geertz, C.
1968 "Religion as a Cultural System", Banton, M. (ed) *Anthropological Approaches to the Study of Religion.* London: Tavistock Publications.

James, D.G.
1960 *Scepticism and Poetry.* London: Allen & Unwin.

Langer, S.K.
1957 *Philosophy in the New Key.* Cambridge, Mass.: Harvard University Press.

Mendilow, A.A.
1952 *Time and the Novel* London: P. Nevill.

Moore, S.F. & B.G. Myerhoff
1975 *Symbols and Politics in Communal Ideology.* Ithaca: Cornell University Press.

Moore, S.F. & B.G. Myerhoff (eds)
1977 *Secular Ritual.* Amsterdam: Van Gorcum.

Moore, S.F. & V. Tufte
1975 "Life History as Integration: Personal Myth and Aging", *Gerontologist 15: 541-543.*

Solzhenitsin, A.
1968 *Cancer Ward.* NY: Dial Press.

Turner, V.
1971 "An Anthropological Approach to the Icelandic Saga," T. Beidelman (ed) *The Translation of Culture: Essays to E.E. Evans-Pritchard* London: Tavistock Publications.

Zoshin, J.
1974 "The Fraternity of Mourners," J. Riemer (ed) *Jewish Reflections on Death.* New York: Schocken Books.

CARNIVAL IN MULTIPLE PLANES

Roberto Da Matta

---

*R*ecent anthropological emphasis on the cultural dynamics of contemporary societies has fostered a growing interest in national celebrations and ceremonies, sporting and entertainment spectacles, and other popular performances that claim the attention, and sometimes the active participation, of millions of people. Studies of these massive "secular rituals" and their entangled relationship to the cross currents of the contemporary world have drawn inspiration from the early Manchester ethnographies of traditional ritual in the context of social change and political conflict. Max Gluckman himself is fondly remembered for "persuading" his students to attend local football matches as anthropological observers, and his final published article was a preliminary attempt to develop a comparative understanding of sport within the framework of modern performance genres. Victor Turner, Abner Cohen, and many other anthropologists influenced by Gluckman played major roles in broadening this thrust and helping to integrate it with similar interests in other academic disciplines.

In the following piece Brazilian anthropologist Roberto da Matta examines his country's **Carnaval**, perhaps the most renowned of all national festivals. Drawing heavily on Turner's ideas about ritual liminality, da Matta proposes that carnival "dislocates" and subsequently "recategorizes" the Brazilian cultural universe. This complex symbolic process is achieved through the inversion of social structures and behavioral norms. Women and men exchange roles, sexual intimacy and other activities ordinarily restricted to the privacy of the house are instead performed in the public domain of the street; the urban environment is transformed from a place of instrumental, individualistic work to one of expressive, socially oriented play. Hence the cultural vision that is constructed in carnival is the negation of ordinary reality. At the same time, carnival establishes and sustains a deep, rather *metaphysical sense of Brazilian identity and self-understanding. Carnival also exhibits political potential, fashioning a populist alternative to the hierarchical domination of church and state. It is the one cultural performance in Brazil that lacks an official patron, because it is understood as being collectively "owned" by the people and expressive of their interests, values, and sensibilities.*

Read in conjunction with the previous essays by Manning and Myerhoff, Da Matta's analysis exposes the variability of ritual performance. In the earlier essays, ritual serves to make sense of unpredictable and problematic events, evoking a religious faith that resolves social chaos and human uncertainty. In the case of carnival, however, ritual performance works much differently. It creates chaos—or "madness," as carnivalists often say—by dissolving the boundaries and reversing the norms that structure everyday life. In the end, though, the contrived chaos of carnival yields a form of cultural awareness that transcends and potentially resists the established social order.

Their difference notwithstanding, the three essays have much in common. In particular, each draws attention to the importance of play in cultural performance. Whether it is central or peripheral, the element of play is frequently crucial in the social and symbolic processes of performative genres. While play may appear inconsequential, it should always be taken seriously by the anthropologist.

IN PREVIOUS WORKS I have examined the Brazilian *Carnaval* in its general and globalizing aspects. Here I wish to consider Carnival in its regional character and to discuss a group of problems related to the transformation of the everyday world into an "inverted universe." I shall take as a basis certain fundamental categories of the Brazilian social universe and certain processes of ritualization and symbolization.

In Jorge Amado's *O Pais do Carnaval* (The Country of Carnival), the central character, Paulo Rigger, says at a crucial moment, "I only felt Brazilian twice. Once, in Carnival, when I danced the samba in the street. The other when I beat Julie, after she deceived me." The quotation is filled with significance. First, at the time of this novel, the nation was searching for the essence of what was truly Brazilian. In this context, Paulo Rigger's outburst (or discovery) is as highly provocative as it is revealing. To be Brazilian for him is the equivalent of "dancing the samba in the street" (*sambar na rua*) and adopting the patriarchal behavior—typically heavy-handed and authoritarian—of "beating French mistresses" every time they deceive one. And, I should add, Julie deceived Paulo, the individualist son of a plantation owner, with one of his employees— a virile and muscular black who never experienced the existential dilemmas of his boss.

The quotation implies a certain tragedy in discovering oneself as a Brazilian. In other countries self-identification raises questions of a civic nature, referring to flags, hymns, crowns, or heroic struggles, but for our character, who is here a paradigm, to be Brazilian is to dissolve oneself in the multitudinous disorder of dancing the samba in the streets and in savagely beating a European mistress. Thus, in the case of Brazil, the process of identification brings to the surface Carnival and the control of feminine sexual favours.

The House and the Street

Paulo Rigger's identification as a Brazilian involves two social domains. One of them is evidently the street, where the hero danced the samba (his partner was a mulatto woman). The other is the domain of the house—of the bedroom, to be precise— where the deceiving French mistress was eventually beaten. The opposition between street and house is basic and can serve as a powerful instrument in the analysis of the Brazilian social world, and above all in the study of its ritualization.

The category "street" indicates the world with its unpredictable events, its actions and passions. The category "house" pertains to a controlled universe, where things are in their proper places. The street implies movement, novelty, and action, while the house implies harmony, warmth, and calm. Furthermore, in the street one works; at home one rests. The social groups that occupy a house are radically different from those of the world of the street. In the home we have associations ruled and formed by kinship and "blood relations." In the street, relationships are those of patronage and have an indelible character of choice, or imply the possibility of choice. In the house, relations are ruled "naturally" by the hierarchies of sex and age, with males and the elderly taking precedence. In the street some difficulty may be encountered in localizing and discovering the hierarchies, as they are based on other principles. Although both domains should be governed by a hierarchy based

ROBERTO DA MATTA

on respect, the concept of respect in the Brazilian social universe is above all characteristic of the relations between parents and children, especially in the relation between father and son.

As a consequence of this, in the street one must take care not to violate unknown or unperceived hierarchies. Similarly, care must be taken to avoid the circle of people who would trick, mislead, or dominate one, since the basic rule of the street is to deceive and to take advantage of others. *Malandragem*—taking advantage of others—is the Brazilian art of using the ambiguous as an instrument for survival. In the street the world is seen as a Hobbesian universe, where everybody tends to be in some kind of competition against everybody else, until some form of hierarchy can appear and impose order.

But in the house everything is the inverse. Here space is rigidly demarcated, divided into verandas, parlors, dining rooms, kitchens, bathrooms, bedrooms, and invariably the servants' area and service areas. Space is demarcated in such a way that the house as a whole is a grouping of spaces where greater or lesser intimacy is permitted, possible, or prohibited.

The opposition of street and house separates two mutually exclusive domains. Yet they can be interrelated in a complex way, since they may be expressed both in the form of a clear opposition and in terms of gradations in a continuum. The spatial division of the Brazilian home itself suggests the possibility of gradation, of compromise and mediation. The veranda is an ambiguous space between the house and the street, generally facing the street. The parlor, although within the house, is also an intermediate space, since it is where visitors are received. Also ambiguously situated between the interior and exterior worlds are the windows. From these one can see the street, with its movement, its constantly parading figures. It was from the windows that the girls of the house could enter into visual contact with their boyfriends, as Thales de Azevedo has observed. It is evident that certain areas of the house permit the world within to communicate with the world without, and thus the feminine (which is always under control) with the masculine.

In addition, the kitchen is a special place, exclusively feminine and, even today, in this era of modernization and change, an area separated from the rest of the house and generally hidden—as op-

CARNIVAL IN MULTIPLE PLANES

posed to the kitchen in North American and European houses. Still
another ambiguous precinct is "the service area" or the "servants's
area" (*dependências da empregada*). This space relates the world of
the house with the street, and with work, poverty, and marginality.

The distinctive feature of the domain of the house seems to be
control over social relations, which implies a greater intimacy and
a lesser social distance than elsewhere. The house is the seat of "my
family," "my people," or "mine own," as people say colloquially in
Brazil, but the street implies a certain lack of control and a distancing between self and others. It is the locale of punishment, of "life's
toils," and of work. The street is where one encounters what the
Brazilians call the hard realities of life. It is an area of confusions
and novelties, where robberies occur and where it is necessary to
walk carefully, suspicious and alert. In sum the street, as a generic
category in opposition to the house, is a public place, controlled by
the government or by destiny—those impersonal forces over which
we have minimal control.

In this sense the street is equivalent to the category scrub land
(*mato*) or forest (*floresta*) of the rural world, or to the "nature" of
the tribal world. In each case we are speaking of a partly unknown
and only partly controlled domain peopled with dangerous figures.
Thus it is in the street and in the forests that the deceivers, the
criminals, and the spirits live—those entities with whom one never
has precise contractual relations.[1]

The category "street" thus expresses both a particular place and
a complex social domain. One says in Brazil: "I'm going to the
street" thus indicating that one is going to the commercial heart of
the city, or to a city in the case of a person who lives in a town or
on the limits of an urban area. In the same way the expressions
"street kid" (*moleque de rua*) and "out on the street" (*jà para a
rua*) are very powerful and offensive expressions, designating in the
first case a person without any family roots or moral scruples and
in the second anyone without a precise social position. Hence, to
throw somebody "out of the house" is synonymous with removing
that person from a precise social network or from a group of marked
moral positions. To leave one's house in Brazil is a difficult choice,
even a punishment, depending upon the situation.

The category "street" can be divided into two others: the
downtown area (*centro*) and the plaza. In fact, in the Brazilian urban

ROBERTO DA MATTA

world, we always have the house (as a term referring to the place where one engages in greater intimacy), the plaza, and the downtown area. The plaza represents the aesthetic aspects of the city: it is a metaphor of its cosmology. In it are located the gardens and the buildings most basic to the social life of the community—the Church, representing religious power, and the government offices, representing political power. In contrast, commerce is centralized downtown, in the area where impersonal transactions take place. Evidently, in many cities the downtown coincides with the plaza. What is basic, however, is to maintain a separation between the domain of power (temporal and religious) and the domain of the economy. The spheres may be complementary; they are not identical. (Gluckman 1962) The domain of the plaza is an arena for encounters, a place where various social segments may or may not appear in a structured way as in civic rituals. In the downtown area of a city, in opposition to the plaza, the rules of encounter, of hierarchial complementarity, are not obeyed. Instead, it is the locus of individualism, born of the impersonal and competitive laws that regulate supply and demand.

The duality of street and house is confirmed by the existence of complete sets of roles, objects, and actions that must appear in one or the other domain. Beating and scolding, for example, are actions that should occur in the private part of the residence, where this kind of intimacy can occur. The opposite is the case in political conflicts, which, in principle, should occur in the streets and above all in the plazas, near the government buildings. Sleeping, eating, bathing, sexual relations, and other modes of obtaining physical satisfaction should occur in the universe of the house, where people recuperate from the wear and tear of daily life. Everything that pertains to the use, care, and recuperation of the body, and as a consequence implies rest and renewal is related to the domestic world. Actions that speak more of the external aspects of social life are related to the public world, the world of the street.

In Jorge Amado's book, Paulo Rigger beats his mistress in the house and participates (*brincar,* literally, "to play") in the Street Carnival. "Street" here refers to the streets of the downtown area of the city. But the more or less perplexed tone of his observation permits us to say that in this case we are confronting a strong opposition. In fact, the place of a mistress is in the street, not in the house. And the place to sing and dance the samba, particularly in the case of the upper class, is in a house or a club, never on the street. In the characterization of *O Pais do Carnaval* we can thus see that Jorge Amado is using an inversion, removing objects that should be in the house to the street (dance and song), and putting objects that should be in the street in the house. Thus Julie, the French mistress, comes to have a permanent relationship with the hero. The inversion is so symmetrical that we cannot avoid seeing it as an intuitive and commonplace dramatization.

Dialectics, Symbolization, and Ritualization

The heart of the symbolizing process is the passage of an object or its appearance in a different domain. This would seem to be important because we speak about symbols but in general do not specify the conditions that transform a mere object—a piece of leaf, a stone, a gesture, a book, an animal—into a symbol. But the change or passage of an element from one domain to another is the fundamental part of the process of symbolization. Van Gennep raised the important question of rites of passage, but I believe it is important for us to retain the concept of movement, process, and dislocation, inherent in this perspective, rather than cling to the categorical term ritual. Understanding dislocation as the critical mechanism in the transformation of objects into symbols is basic to the understanding of what is a rite. This perspective permits us to see ritual as something that is created and no longer to see it simply as a finished and definitive type of social action, as is common in social anthropology. If, as I suggest, we must ask ourselves how a given object has become a symbol and under what conditions this was possible, we must also ask under what conditions a given set of social actions is transformed into a ritual.

Through the work of Victor Turner we know that the processes of symbolizing and ritualizing are interrelated and "go together." I suggest that in both processes we have a phenomenon of consciousness, that is, of being aware. This is, in fact, the only common denominator that I can see in the so-called world of ritual, constituted, as it is, by an infinite number of qualifications. In this way to ritualize—just as to symbolize—is fundamentally to dislocate an

ROBERTO DA MATTA

object from its place, a process that brings a clear consciousness of the nature of the object, of the properties of its original domain, and of its adaptation to its new locale. Thus dislocations bring on a consciousness of all the reifications of the social world, whether arbitrary or necessary. For this reason the world of theater, with its artificiality and arbitrariness, is able to move us. Through the artificial, we end up being moved by and, ourselves mobilizing the real world, which is completely dislocated on the stage through the agency of actors.

Clearly one of the critical problems raised by the dialectic of street and house is to know which objects pass from one to the other domain and under what circumstances this occurs. One should ask when it is possible to modify the domestic world or the public world, whether to transform one of these domains into the other, or simply to emphasize one of them. Here, when we raise the problem of dislocation and of mediation, we are seeking the metaphor— the essential and critical link between these domains within the basic code that governs Brazilian culture. In this way we can suggest that there are situations in which the house extends itself into the street and into the city in such a way that the social world is centralized by the domestic metaphor. On the other hand, we could have inverse situations, when the street and its values tend to penetrate the private world of the residence, with the world of the house being integrated into the metaphor of public life. It is also possible for the two worlds to be related through a "double metaphor," with the domestic invading the public and, in turn, being invaded by it. In this case, society creates a special space and time, truly intermediate between the intimacy of the house and the respectability of the street. We shall see how this occurs in the case of the Brazilian Carnival.

Basic Forms of Dislocation

A basic relationship exists between social domains and the roles, ideologies, gestures, and objects contained in them. The basic concern is to discover the points of origin of a few of the social dislocations. We know that a complex society is filled with diverse movements and passages. In everyday life these passages are indelibly marked by the dialectical rhythm of home and work. We call this frenetic movement rush hour. What we mark and are conscious of is not the moment of passage but rather the impulse to move on—the rush. What is important is the leaving or arrival.

In the daily world, then, what we consider basic is what occurs either at work or at home. The dialectic is really that of the poles standing in opposition and in frank comparison, competition, or reciprocity: when we are at work we think about our home, our beer, and our favorite chair, whereas when we are at home we talk about our work and our co-workers.

In the ritual world, or rather in the dislocated world of ritual and consciousness, there is a fundamental difference: it is the travel that becomes important. In this context the leaving and arrival are less important than the movement itself, which becomes the ritualized element and, for this reason, is raised to consciousness. We have, therefore, a continuum that goes from the most unconscious and banal travels (such as our frequent rush hours) to the quasi-epic journeys, the wanderings of a pilgrimage, where the fundamental thing is to travel and progress (Turner 1974, 1978). Daily travel is functional, rational, and operational, since it has a specific aim: work, shopping, business, or study. But in ritual travel, or rather in the conscious travel of ritual, the aim and the travel itself become more or less the same. Thus the normal daily dislocation is inverted, since one no longer concentrates on only the goal but also the travel itself. In ritual travel, what one looks for at the point of arrival is nothing concrete, palpable, or quantifiable, but instead blessings, cures, and signs of faith.

Within the Brazilian social world there are other kinds of journeys, in addition to pilgrimages, each kind clearly expressing the point of departure and point of arrival and, thus, each capable of creating (or inventing) diverse ritual moments. In pilgrimages, as I said above, a man transforms himself into a pilgrim. He leaves his house, where he is personalized by a network of kinsmen, *compadres,* and friends with whom he has relations of complementarity, and goes to encounter his diffuse companions of faith. The intention of the journey seems to be gradually to replace ties of substance with social and political ties of a more universal order, provided by religion. The problem is thus to transform the son of so-and-so into someone much more generalized, such as "son of God" and brother of all the other pilgrims, no matter how bad his material, moral, and

ROBERTO DA MATTA

spiritual condition may be. The pilgrimage implies a dislocation, a journey that relates the most intimate with the most universal until one can return again to intimacy, since when the travel is successful, one has again reached a formerly lost intimacy with God and through that with all the rest of mankind, including one's family.

The second type of journey is the procession. In this way of moving we have a basic variation of the pilgrimage. For while in the pilgrimage it is we who go, as Turner has said, to the encounter with the center, here it is the center (represented by the image of the saint) that leaving its sacred niche, comes to encounter us. Therefore, we may or may not leave our houses, and if we do so, we take part in an orderly group with a clearly defined center, namely, where the saint and the authorities are located.

In the Brazilian case, processions—like military parades—take familiar trajectories, sanctifying streets and alleyways of residential neighborhoods or the periphery of the city. Generally, processions avoid the commercial *centro*, a universe profane to the point of being in competition with the values and ideals of faith. Thus the procession passes through streets where families can see and thereby receive the saint in their residences. In the procession, it is the sacred that enters into the houses and, according to the religious specialists, into the hearts of each of the spectators and participants in the procession. This being the case, a procession is a moment in which the saint, being above everyone, overcomes the dichotomy of house and street, creating his or her own social domain. Carried on a litter and raised higher than the surrounding crowd, the saint is actually elevated and above others, uniting the believers into a brotherhood as they transfer (often with sincere and perturbing emotion) their sentiments of filiation during the moment of passage. Thus the saint, in passing, creates relationships that are often sparked by the faith-filled gaze of the devotees. The corporality of the saint grows and crystallizes during the very moment of the passage. As the saint passes and is seen, the faithful may transfer temporarily their group, class, or social loyalties to this new focus. This is what occurs, perhaps, when people say they were blessed by a saint. What is involved is a redefinition: group and other loyalties are dissolved in favor of an intimate, visual, penetrating, and affective relationship. Further, by means of the saint, a relationship develops that includes all of those who are following as well as those

CARNIVAL IN MULTIPLE PLANES

who are watching. It is precisely in these moments that miracles and favors from the saint may appear in the world of men.

Here the streets are transformed and the frontiers between street and house are weakened. In processions, no one refuses water to the participants, and the whole space is occupied by those who are related to the saint. The atmosphere is one of the transferring of loyalties and of opening oneself to the sacred domain. Thus windows and doors should remain open. Curtains and the best embroidered linen, as well as festival vases of flowers, are placed in the windows and on the verandas. All this is done so that the saint can "see" the house, in a dramatization of opening and of the relational domain that should pertain among men and their saint, even in their residences, where people have their strongest loyalties. We have, thus, the sacred, the saint, entering and being received into the houses.

A second form of procession is the military parade. Here, too, men walk as in a procession, with one person behind the other, all going forward. But it is curious that we use the expression *parade* (Portuguese *parada,* from the verb *papar* "to stop") to designate this form of the relationship between the world of the house and the public universe. There are two starting points in parades: the soldiers begin from their barracks and the onlookers from their residences. The dramatic moment of a parade is the demonstration of force, when the men who are armed and prepared for war present themselves in uniform with their formations completely coordinated, and are applauded. In contrast with processions and their open and emotive movements, there is an absolute control of movements in the parade. In parades there is also an emphasis on division and separation. This is a fundamental point: in a procession people can enter or leave the whole because it is formed of a nucleus surrounded by a fluctuating, diffuse area. But in parades this never occurs. In this kind of event there are only two camps: those who are qualified to be inside the order and the rigid hierarchy of the event and those who are outside the isolating ropes and can only see what goes by in the street. The dramatization of the military parade is thus the hierarchical separation of positions. In the case of Brazil and other peripheral countries, the Armed Forces appear as the most crystalline personification of the state in its most ordered, disciplined, obedient, and powerful aspect. Perhaps for this

ROBERTO DA MATTA

reason parades in Brazil nearly always occur in the very heart of the city. The people who take the complementary role to the marchers—the onlookers—must leave their homes to see the parade. We have, then, the superordered military on the march, all clearly differentiated by their corporations, armed and uniformed, silent and absolutely solemn. And on the other hand, separated by ropes, we have the people as a crowd—undifferentiated, talking, moving about, impressed by the military and the discipline of the movements, and accompanied by their most precious possessions: their admiration, their obedience, and their children, who are having their first lessons in practical citizenship.

During a parade the center of the city is reconquered by order and molded in a civic and moralistic way, losing in the process the characteristics of its daily life of highly individualistic economic transactions. The important figures in the parade are the authorities, motionless in a reviewing stand, watching the contingents pass by. The focuses are the flag and the other national symbols, incarnate in the persons who occupy high places in the structure of power that is the state. The rigid separation between the massed crowds of onlookers and the authorities and soldiers clearly reveals the skeleton and the drama of a society: the street and the plaza are taken from the people and become the domain of soldiers who, armed and uniformed, are renewing their ties of loyalty with the authorities. Here the opposition between house and street is mediated by a rigid social body, strongly divided, with the houses being virtually dragged into the public world that recruits them, as it did with the soldiers. Whereas the participants act as "brothers" in the religious procession, here they are "fellow citizens," some of whom occupy high places in order, while others fill the humbler roles of undifferentiated onlookers. Still others, the soldiers, are the third part and the key to the setting: they are materializations of pure power, or rather of power in its most instrumental and open—or brutal—form: armed and prepared for war. And in this case, to make way for the parade is, in fact, to keep the people far from the plazas and streets, reaffirming that in this social world the role of the masses is that of onlooker.

Finally, a third form of procession is the *desfile*, which literally means to "walk in a file." It is applied primarily to the processions in Carnival.

CARNIVAL IN MULTIPLE PLANES

The Invention of Carnival

One of the characteristics of the Carnival *desfile* is that it is part of the so-called Street Carnival. This is opposed to the closed forms of Carnival, which occur in private clubs. These latter are in fact "House" Carnivals (*carnaval caseiro*): before balls in private clubs became popular, around 1840 in Rio de Janeiro (Eneida 1958), Carnival took place in private houses without any public observation. It was a family and neighborhood festival, very similar to its original form, the famous *entrudo* from Portugal. The Street Carnival, in contrast with a Club Carnival, is a classic segmentation. In the street, Carnival assumes the form of an open encounter, in Rio de Janeiro dominated by the *desfile* of the Samba Schools. In the clubs the ambience is more clearly defined, since the physical space itself is private. To view this segmentation as rigid, however, would be a mistake. In fact it takes only a little reflection to see that there is a correspondance between street and club. They both repeat in their respective contexts the same oppositions. Thus in the open street Carnival, the *desfiles* of the Samba Schools or *blocos* involve a closure of the Carnival space since they are clearly defined associations of persons who come together to perform a *desfile*. When they pass by there is a clearly defined public that only watches the performers who display themselves. And here, too, there are gradations.

By the same logic, in the Club Carnival, the closure is relative for two reasons. First, one must purchase admission to the balls, a typical feature of Carnival events.[2] Second, inside the club, a structure is created that again represents the opposition. In the clubs there is a stage where the orchestra sits. There is a large hall where people individually or collectively participating in Carnival can enter and leave as they wish. Finally, along the walls of the hall there are tables and chairs and, raised above the tables on a platform, the "boxes." These are closed spaces with tables and chairs. There is thus a repetition of the logic of the Street Carnival with more or less well ordered spaces and planes. In the hall, which is the arena of the festival, the plane is either individual or collective. Here we have an open structure, like the street itself, with a permanent *desfile* of celebrants (called *foliões*, "crazy people"), "playing" alone, in couples, or collectively. They circulate slowly around the hall in such a way that everyone is seen by everyone else, including those who are at the tables and in the boxes. The space occupied by the tables and boxes is a much more private and less open plane, for here there are corporate groups of people, usually families or groups of couples who are friends. The area of table and box thus symbolizes the house, the place from which people observe the others passing by. In the case of the boxes, the space is even more closed, and people there can be seen even better by those who are on the floor of the hall or elsewhere in the club. From the box, to the table, to the hall we have a perfect continuum. The continuum can always be reformulated in terms of "play in the hall" in opposition to "play in the box." Here we can observe the same oppositions we have seen between street and house. In addition, at the tables and in the boxes one can rest: drinking, eating, and ceasing to dance and sing in the characteristic way that is "playing Carnival." To renew the body at the table thus brings this area still closer to the features of the house as a social category. The hall, then, is like the street—a place where energy is spent to be later renewed at a place of rest.

Thus Carnival, like daily life, has two fundamental planes: the street and the house, but each has the central elements of the *desfile*. In the club people circulate in the hall; in the street people are incorporated in groups. There is a true equivalence between the closed space of the clubs and the similarly closed space of a corporation. The more closed a Carnival corporation, the closer it is to the reality of the hall of a club because the greater will be its capacity to use a part of the street for itself alone.

A SPECIAL SPACE

Whether it be in the street, alley, plaza, avenue, club, school, or home, Carnival requires its own space. Even in the club, with its own closed space, it is necessary to prepare that space. To this end the walls are decorated with motifs related to Carnival. A South Seas beach, Rio in an earlier era, designs that recall paintings by Picasso, or even a Dante's Inferno, transform the club. Thus, even when space is clearly demarcated, within it another space is created, designed exclusively for Carnival.

The same thing happens with urban space. The commercial center of the city is closed to traffic so that people, whether or not they are associated with the typical corporations of Carnival such as the *blocos* and Samba Schools, can occupy it without difficulty. The street or avenue is thus domesticated. Most of the time, the streets of Rio and other Brazilian cities are deadly areas, with automobiles moving at high speeds. During Carnival, however, these tense, high-speed areas take on the aspect of a medieval plaza, where people walk in place of cars, watching or taking part in the festivities. The business district is transformed into a place for all the encounters and dramatizations typical of Carnival.

The center of the city becomes really the center in spite of the holiday. In Rio de Janeiro and other cities the normal movements of holidays are inverted during Carnival. Instead of people leaving for the beaches or the more festive and leisure-oriented neighborhoods, they move toward the center of the city, just as they do on a workday. Further, during Carnival the actual process of going to the city center is festive (and highly conscious), with people singing, dancing, and beating samba rhythms in the buses and trains. Such an event is obviously not due to a sudden improvement in urban transport during Carnival, but to the fact that the interior space of the transport is transformed into a Carnival space. The bus or train is no longer transporting workers who must be in the office or factory at a fixed hour, but celebrants who ensure that things will begin only when they arrive. The moment of passage into an overloaded public transport, in the everyday world considered one of the most hellish of urban infernos, becomes a moment of great creativity during Carnival. It is a moment to be lived intensely, through smiles, jokes, and body contact. It is conscious movement from place to place, and for precisely this reason it is highly ritualized and inverted. This is very different from the travel to work, which cannot be "enjoyed" because during it we are in an empty moment of time, time that has to be killed. (Goffman 1967; Bajtin 1974)

The urban world is set aside for Carnival. But that is not all. This area itself has many spaces within it. Entire streets take on an almost private aspect, similar to the houses along them. With their own lighting and decoration, these streets open themselves to the houses and have their own *desfile* and costume competitions. Similarly, the entire city is reordered in such a way that the downtown becomes a multitude of small niches, little plazas, where people can meet and have their own small carnivals. The mayor's

ROBERTO DA MATTA

office undertakes the decoration of the city, creating these spaces by erecting stands on the corners of certain avenues and contracting musical groups to play on them. Rio de Janeiro, seen as a megalopolis in the everyday world, is suddenly changed into a great number of Carnival subdivisions, each with its own stand, band, and celebrants. The usually impersonal and unarticulated city becomes personal, communitarian, and, above all, creative, allowing for the differences of neighborhoods, classes, and social categories. But all of this variation is within a single style: the Carnival style.

The movement of Carnival does not differ from other ritual movements, since all require a special place for their realization. The clear contrast, however, between the Carnival *desfile* and military parades and religious processions is in the size of the area and its period of occupation. In parades and processions the public space (streets, avenues, alleys, and plazas) is occupied for a few hours —a morning or an afternoon. In Carnival, however, this occupation lasts for at least three days. There is also a long period of preparation. For this reason a special transit plan, which requires considerable elaboration (especially in a large city like Rio de Janeiro) is devised and implemented. In addition to the smaller platforms mentioned above, a gigantic grandstand is erected to enable people to watch the *desfile* of the Samba Schools on Sunday. The grandstand holds a total of 60,000 people, and includes bathrooms and medical services for the onlookers. Seats in the grandstand are hierarchically divided by price. There are also expensive boxes for small groups of persons and places for the press and for visitors. The space here is clearly marked, with the street itself being occupied by the common people, who come to live in it. The *desfile*, involving about 12,000 people in the case of the Samba Schools of the first group, occurs inside a virtual canyon of watchers.

Instead of frenetic and deadly rides in automobiles, we have in Carnival an inverted movement, without goal or single direction. The peripatetic movement of Carnival is highly ritualized because it is highly self-conscious. It is not very important where one wishes to go or how one gets there, what becomes important is simply the act of going without direction, enjoying the act of walking, occupying the streets of the commercial heart of the city, the locale of impersonal and inhuman laws of transit in the daily world.

In the Carnival of 1977, I saw people sleeping, urinating, and

CARNIVAL IN MULTIPLE PLANES

making love on the benches in the little plazas in the center of the city. I also saw people with their families, including wives and children, camped out in the middle of the city. Seated in collapsible aluminum chairs with bottles of water and coolers of beer, they unselfconsciously watched the steady file of groups of celebrants and Carnival *blocos*. Nearby, children were sleeping in the family car. It was like an inverted picnic, taking place in the middle of the savage and devouring asphalt, which was for the time transformed and domesticated. Rio Branco Avenue, the Brazilian Wall Street, was transformed into a row of houses, with the spirit characteristic of streets in the small towns of Brazil. I noted this same transformation on Cinelândia, a plaza located at the end of Rio Branco Avenue. In the everyday world this is a meeting place for homosexuals and is therefore normally avoided by families.

On Rio Branco Avenue, where people usually walk rapidly, preoccupied with the act of arriving, I met people walking without the least signs of preoccupation. No one was looking for anything or hurrying to reach an appointment, concerns that make us forget the pleasure of the act of moving. On the contrary, everyone became part of a single unit with the common goals of Carnival. During Carnival one looks for "happiness," "a smile," "music," and sexual pleasure in these moments. The thousands of people become a single crowd called simply "the people" or "the masses." They search together for these goals, which still elude the politicians and the urban planners. Fundamentally people pursue pleasure and luck, happiness and well-being. It is precisely this that impedes corporate precision and leads to the remarkable openness that ends up uniting (as in a truly religious moment) the people as simple celebrants—as members of a single human species in its eternal search for happiness and as Brazilians. The social roles of family member, resident of a neighborhood, or member of a race or an occupational or social category are sifted to leave only the pure truth: we are all this, but only this: men and women looking for pleasure within a certain style, and because of this, we are equally Brazilians.

A MULTIPLE SPACE

On Rio Branco Avenue and Cinelândia the street becomes the

ROBERTO DA MATTA

stage of a theater whose performances have no fixed text. Spontaneous dramatizations are improvised by those in costume. There is an intense participation between the "actors" and "spectators." Everyone can mix and change places in the modification of fixed social positions that, for Bajtin (1974), characterizes truly popular spectacles, where the people represent themselves. Here, too, the roles of actor and spectator are spontaneously questioned. One sees the maternal figure, the ideal housewife who cares for her husband and her children by day and at night watches a soap opera on television. Woman is seen as a generic category in the Brazilian culture, strongly (though paradoxically and simultaneously) associated with the world of sin (by means of the prostitute) and with that of purity (by means of the Virgin Mary). All of these characters are represented by men—some homosexuals, some not—dressed as women. So dressed, they arouse both envy and condescension. It is common for onlookers to shake their heads in disapproval, but to watch closely these men who, dressed as women, bring into play the basic figure of the world of the house. One of these men was dressed as a pompous grande dame, with jewels, furs, and makeup incapable of hiding her age, bringing into play both social class and femininity. Another, elsewhere in the plaza, brought to the fore (through inverted and grotesque imitation) the mysteries and complications of feminine physiology: feigning menstruation and revealing to the onlookers the proper means of indicating that condition. Others, in groups, provoked the onlookers, involving them in moral harangues and commentaries on the enormous number of homosexuals in the modern world. At play were two opposite domains. On the one hand there was the universe of the street, to which the homosexuals belong. On the other hand there was the universe of the house, anchored in its strict customs and morality of the family, where there is only room for the dichotomies that guarantee the reproduction of the system: man and woman, elderly and young.

On the other side of the street, a few meters farther along, and within the same space, two young women were walking. They were dressed as seducers, wearing clothing that did not cover, but instead revealed. There, in the middle of the multitude they were not assaulted. On the contrary, they assaulted the men, the Brazilian *machos* who during Carnival let their masks fall and showed themselves to be incredibly and surprisingly timid in sexual encounters. Farther along were four or five youths dressed as Arabs. Each had a long robe and carried a briefcase. Their faces were serious and they carried on their backs a sign that read Owners of the World. At another corner, an elderly gentleman solemnly puffed a pipe and looked on the passing spectacle with a grave face. He was an executive, with his characteristic briefcase. But he had no pants. And thus he demonstrated, as Bajtin has shown, that Carnival is the glorification of things that occur from the waist down, in opposition to the repressive and hierarchical world of the bourgeoisie, where the soul has a hypocritical primacy.

Faced with all of this, we are obliged to forsake our traditional roles. We cease to *be* and instead *live* the moment of communitas (Turner 1969). In Carnival, in its typical space, the instant overcomes time and the event becomes more than the system that classifies it and gives it a normative meaning. It is for this reason that the word most often heard is "craziness" (*loucura*). "This is crazy!" we say to each other, looking upon the scene. It is crazy because all space is inverted, dislocated, and everything is called into question. Crazy because we are in the street and it has suddenly become a secure and human place. Crazy, finally, because our social world, which is preoccupied with hierarchies and the logic of knowing one's place, is offering more openings than we can possibly take advantage of.

A RITE WITHOUT A PATRON

In addition to creating this space, which generates a carefree ramble, without goals and highly conscious, ritualized, and euphoric, Carnival is a moment without a patron. It is for everyone. This appears to be basic, for in a society such as Brazil everything is normally under the rigid control of dominant codes. As a consequence one cannot (perhaps, one should not) allow a festivity without a patron, a subject, a center, or an owner, as is commonly said in the rural and urban regions of Brazil. In fact, it is common, when speaking of ritual moments, to say "Who is the owner of the festival?" or "For whom is this festival?" Reunions of a collective character (above all, those that are

ROBERTO DA MATTA

programmed) would have a center, a subject, or a destiny for which they take place. This is precisely what occurs in religious processions, when homage is presented to a saint, commemorating the date of his or her birth, death, or passion. It is also what happens in military parades, when a national or regional hero is commemorated on the date of his birth or of his heroic act. The same occurs in *passeatas* ("protest marches"), where the purpose of the march is to demonstrate against some attitude considered unjust by the marchers, here called *manifestantes,* a word with negative connotations in Brazil, kingdom of conformity. As in the religious processions and the parades, the intention of the group is clear: to commemorate and to protest. In sum, the meaning of the festival, the march, the reunion is known. It is precisely this that provokes people to congregate, to gather together, and finally to incorporate themselves; individuals must have a common goal in order to transform themselves into a body, a group, or an association.

If a ritual has a subject or an owner, that becomes the focal point. It provides at the same time a motive, meaning, and unity. But who is the owner of Carnival? To this people reply, "Each plays Carnival as he can," because "Carnival belongs to everybody." Carnival is perhaps the only national festival without an owner.

In the innocence of the sayings above, there is a strong distributive, democratic, and naturally compensatory content. This in a society extremely devoted to the imposition of forms and fixed formulas—largely with a definite juridical format—on ways of doing, reproducing, commemorating, and ritualizing. Both in the street and at home the Brazilian is normally subject to fixed rules that demand a constant relationship between him and his group. The intention of the Brazilian social order is to make the individual dissolve and disappear. When faced with a conflict between his individual will and a course of action dictated by norms and rites, the Brazilian oscillates, conciliates, and interprets. He is never the true controller of himself but rather is controlled by laws, norms, and decrees.

At home he is subject to the rigid code of love and respect to his family, a group seen as inevitable and inescapable, in which he is a perpetual dependent and in which his individuality is frequently dissolved. Yet it is within the family that one learns to be "somebody" and becomes a *person,* specifically, an integral member whose

CARNIVAL IN MULTIPLE PLANES

absence would be felt by the group through "longing" (*saudade,* from the Latin *solitate,* solitude). The world of the family and of the house is focused on the complementarity between rules and men, events and classifications, elderly and young, masters and servants, men and women, parents and children, respect and obedience, blood and social relations.

The world of the street is the opposite. Here the individual is torn loose from his moral and complementary group and subjected to the impersonal codes of traffic, of supply and demand, of the municipality and the state. It is not an accident that in this hostile world, which is nearly always lacking in hierarchy and complementarity, the Brazilian uses rites of distancing and reinforcement. These are implied in the expression "Do you know to whom you are talking?" which is used whenever anyone feels himself being crushed by impersonal norms and wishes to demonstrate that, after all, he is "someone."

In Brazil, therefore, it is essential to ritualize every passage between the domains of house and street. To prepare to leave the house is a way of making reflexively conscious (thus ritualizing or dramatizing) this passage from a secure place, where complementarity and hierarchy reign, for another, far more individualistic place, where one is anonymous. Dress and appearance (which includes the way of walking, speaking, and gesturing) help to maintain one's position as the member of a house. The preoccupation with clothing and appearance, above all in the act of going (or being) in the street, demonstrates the desire to mark the body with social indicators. This prevents anonymity and serves as an instrument to permit the establishment of hierarchy and to create spaces where each person can perceive and know "with whom he is talking," especially in the individualized universe of the street.

To remain outside of some encompassing and hierarchical totality leaves the person subject to definition by impersonal laws: religion (as with the law of human charity) or the state (by means of laws that protect the individual). But neither the law of charity nor the laws of the state link the individual to a concrete and present social group. On the contrary, they link him as an individual to abstract entities, such as Humanity or the People. To be in this anonymous situation, in the middle of the "lonely crowd," is a situation that every Brazilian seeks to avoid. The pattern is rather to

ROBERTO DA MATTA

demonstrate systematically that one is confronted with a special case, by a person who is not one's equal. To accept the contrary profoundly threatens a person's self-esteem. The Brazilian multitude thus always looks for the axes of hierarchy and complementarity, attempting to avoid impersonal submission to more general norms that make individuals equal to one another.

We can therefore say that all social situations have some owner in Brazil. If it is not a concrete person, it is a saint. If not a saint, then a hero, or even some abstract social domain itself. Always some code must be imposed so that the situation can be read and classified.

But in Carnival the laws are liminal. It is as if a special space had been created away from the house and above the street, where everyone could be without their preoccupations with their groups of birth, marriage, and occupation. Being above and away from the street and the house, Carnival engenders a festival outside of the everyday social world without the individual being subjected to the fixed rules of belonging or of being somebody. For this reason everyone can change groups and everyone can cut in and create new relationships and unsuspected solidarity. In Carnival, if the reader will permit a paradox, the law is to have no law. This is the inverted ideology of the festival.

Obviously this does not mean there are no regularities or fixed procedures in Carnival. The general principle of no law is homologous with refusing to treat the celebration as belonging exclusively to a certain group, segment, or social class. Because of this, Carnival is multiple and permits the exercise of an extreme degree of social creativity. In it we celebrate diffuse and inclusive things, such as sex, pleasure, happiness, luxury, song, dance, and joking. All of this is summarized for us in the expression "to play Carnival." If Carnival celebrated sexual union (and not sex), it would be centered in a structure and would be the festival of couples and of union. The owner or patron would be the institution of marriage (this routine of sex; this machine of social reproduction). If, on the other hand, Carnival celebrated belonging to a permanent group—for example, through commensality—it would have the family as its owner. Its world would then be that of the house and it would be limited to an exclusive group. Similarly, if Carnival were a festival of wealth—and not luxury—it would have as a subject a social class.

CARNIVAL IN MULTIPLE PLANES

Furthermore, if Carnival were centered in discursive speech and on walking—instead of on song and dance—it would be a ritual of order, a ceremony of reinforcement and structure. But the focal point of this ritual is the human universe at large, with its perennial suggestion of inclusiveness and community. For all of these reasons, Carnival cannot have an owner.

This claim makes possible the observation that all other festivals in the Brazilian social world have an owner or a patron. In the same way, a festival without an owner is primarily a festival of the destitute and of the dominated, for in the daily world they possess nothing (except their bodies and their labor, their mystical powers and their hunger to live). They can only be the center of an inverted and paradoxical festivity, one that does not involve law and owners but that can be possessed only by those who have nothing. It is for this reason that Carnival can be the subject of all the social projections. It appears, therefore, as an immense social screen, where multiple visions of social reality are projected simultaneously.

Conclusion

In the course of this essay I have tried to show how Carnival redefines the Brazilian social world. For this it was not enough simply to show that during Carnival the world is inverted. It was necessary to indicate the course or orientation of this inversion, since both the rule and the cultural domains and objects on which the rule operates are basic.

This being the case, I began with the opposition between street and house. The Brazilian social world molds itself around this complex and *segmentary dichotomy*. The ritual sphere elaborates these domains, either in an attempt to transcend or in an attempt to separate or reinforce the two worlds. In religious processions the house is invaded by what happens in the plaza, in the churchyard, and in the street, while in military parades the house simply disappears as a category, since the event occurs in the very center of the city, necessitating a dislocation and transforming all the members of a family into Brazilian citizens. In Carnival, everything occurs as if society were finally able to invent a special space where street and house encountered each other. The festival has public aspects (such as the *desfile* and formal groups), but it also allows a number

ROBERTO DA MATTA

of gestures and social actions that in general occur only in the house.

This dislocation of objects (social roles and values) from one domain to another allows the elaboration of a few basic hypotheses on the definition of symbol, ritual, and drama, as well as on their fundamental principles.

The ritual universe (as well as that of drama) is that of visible things, of correct things (prescribed, even if shocking or uncommon) and therefore of things that are set apart and dislocated. It is on stage that open and cruel murder is allowed; in the stadium that—through highly individualistic and fair competition—a hierarchy is established; and in Carnival that we allow a confusion of the rules of hierarchy. Thus, if the ritual world has a grammar, it is certainly not that which governs the sequence of actions in the everyday world. The sequence of ritual could be created on the consistent and obstinate use of three well-known social principles (and consistency and obstinacy are two characteristics always necessary for a "ritual action"): inversion (which engenders joking), reinforcement (which leads to respect), and neutralization (which leads to avoidance or social invisibility). Each allows the dilation, recutting, exaggeration, and turning inside out of the routines of the daily world—just as do good directors of theater or cinema, these shamans of the contemporary world. Because of the necessary consistency in the application of a rule (activated in an absolute and obsessive way), rituals frequently need special spaces, programmed and established beforehand. Ritual thus demands a preparation (which helps its consistency) and obviously a high degree of understanding of what will happen, while the routines of the daily world simply occur: they are seen as "natural" and thus tend to become automatic. In rituals the routine is interpolated, inverted, and reinforced. The aim is a search for consistency that, in fact, is never obtained in "real life"—whether because actors are never pure instruments of rules and of society (they also have their own interests), or because the rules themselves are contradictory. This is why we speak of daily life as "hard," "difficult," and "deceiving." And the way these contradictions are confronted is through locating their institutionalization at the level of "nature" through an enormous and systematic automatization and reification.

In ritual, however, everything happens differently. Here it would seem that we wish for the consistency that all the idealized versions of the social world appear to reveal. For this reason rituals demand preparation—as do spectator sports, cinema, and theater. And since we want a consistent world—opposed to the automatization of the everyday—we radicalize life in rituals, making it take on again a shine, rigor, certainty, and contrast. We create, then, a special space where the routines of the daily world are broken and where it is possible to observe, discuss, or criticize the real world seen standing on its head. For this reason, rituals should always be studied in contrast to the everyday. Both are part of the same structure, like the two faces of the same coin, and expressions of the same social principles. In fact, rituals are equally part of the social world, but they are moments in which sequences of action are broken, dilated, or interrupted through the dislocation of gestures, persons, ideologies, or objects.

Take, for example, the case of an ordinary man during Carnival. In the morning he remains in bed, recuperating from the events of the preceding night, when he enthusiastically celebrated in the street or in a club until the small hours. He thus ceases to prepare himself for work or for leisure (for Carnival is not a common holiday). At noonday he eats very little, since Carnival does not mark the meal through special foods, as occurs in many Brazilian rituals. On the contrary, it is time to eat little and celebrate a lot, in a typical attitude of "castigating" the body. After all, the word "carnival" comes from a Latin phrase meaning literally "to take away the meat." In the same way it is precisely because there is no special food that families are isolated. Carnival does not promote family reunions in the houses, but rather reunions of individuals in the streets. Thus there is nothing to hold a person at home. In the afternoon our actor takes a bath (an essential operation for leaving the house) and goes to the street, where he will stay until the next day. Asked where he is going, he will say simply that he is going to see Carnival. In fact, the whole point of the festival is precisely in not knowing what will happen in a world where adventure is finally radicalized because petty bourgeois social life (constructed on small contrasts between right and wrong, sin and virtue, certainty and uncertainty) is suspended and inverted. The actor does not cease sleeping, eating, relating to others, entering and leaving the house, changing clothes, and so on. But now his world comes to be lived with a clear element of decision and consciousness. And more, life

ROBERTO DA MATTA

comes to be evaluated through such motivations as "to have fun," "to have adventure," "to make something happen," which are paradoxical because opposed to the daily world. If in the real world I look for certainty, in Carnival I am radically convinced that I will encounter uncertainty. This, without a doubt, is one of the paradoxes of the ritual world. Ritual and film reveal that what is important is not "rationality" or "knowledge" or "moral basis" or the moment of arrival. What is important is the means, the way, the journey.

The sequence is thus dislocated. Our actor no longer wakes up to rush to work in the "natural" sequence of his daily shuttling between house, work, and house, since he leaves the house to take part in a Carnival *desfile*. The street where he celebrates, the commercial heart of the city, the onlookers who observe and applaud—the whole world around him is turned into his house. The order of things is dislocated and everything becomes full of emotion, allusive, symbolic, and representational. While the daily *desfile* is painful and functional, since it has definite objects and its means are equal to absolutely precise ends, the ritual *desfile* is pleasurable, open, and without rigidly defined objectives. In the first case, what is important is to leave and to arrive, regardless of how one arrives. In the second, inversely, what is basic is how one goes, never where one arrives. This is what characterizes the "symbolic wandering." It is like a curing ritual. The basic object of the cure is to make the patient live. And to live is to be subject to everything. When some theoreticians of ritual ask why such a complex mode is developed only to relate such a simple message, they forget that at the rational, intellectual, distant level, which is uninterested in symbolic march, everything really is painfully simple. It is as if the researcher were only interested in the entrances and exits, never in the heart of things, the centers, the disproportions between the means and ends. This *disproportionality* is precisely what characterizes the logic of the symbolic.

CARNIVAL IN MULTIPLE PLANES

Notes

1. For a study of these entities in the Amazon region, see Da Matta 1973.
2. In contrast to the ball of the daily world, the Carnival Ball is a source of profit for many clubs. This being the case, they "open" up during Carnival. The Yacht Club of Rio de Janeiro, for example, which is a closed association of the upper class, in Carnival promotes its famous Hawaiian Ball, usually open to anyone who can buy an entrance ticket.

References

Amado, J.
    1970   *O Pais do Carnaval*. Sao Paolo.

Bajtin, M.
    1974   *La Culture Popular en la Edad Media y Renacimiento*. Barcelona.

Da Matta, R.
    1973   "O Carnaval Como um Rito de Passagem". *Essaios de Antropologia Estrutural*. Petropolis.

De Azevedo, T.
    1975   *Namoro a Antiga: Tradicao e Mudanca*. Salvador.

De Castro, E.V.
    1975   "O Devido Respeito." Programa de Pos-Graduaco em Antropologia Social. Rio de Janeiro: Museo Nacional.

Eneida
    1958   *Historia do Carnaval Carioca*. Rio de Janeiro.

Gluckman, M.
    1962   "Les Rites de Passage." *Essays on the Ritual of Social Relations*. Manchester: Manchester University Press.

Goffman, E.
    1967   *Interaction Ritual*. Garden City, NY: Anchor Books.

Turner, V.
    1964   *The Ritual Process*. Chicago: Aldine.
    1974   *Dramas, Fields and Metaphors*. Ithaca: Cornell University Press.

Turner, V. & E.
    1978   *Image and Pilgrimage in Christian Culture* NY: Columbia University Press.

ROBERTO DA MATTA

THOSE WHO SURRENDER ARE FEMALE: PRISONER GENDER IDENTITIES AS CULTURAL MIRROR

John M. Coggeshall

---

*T*he distinction between biology and behavior is crucial to an understanding of the social personalities of men and women. Margaret Mead's **Sex and Temperament in Three Primitive Societies**, a study of New Guinea published originally in 1935, stands as a pioneering anthropological account. In a later preface to the book she writes, "I found three tribes all conveniently within a hundred mile area. In one, both men and women act as we expect women to act—in a mild parental responsive way; in the second, both act as we expect men to act—in a fierce initiating fashion; and in the third, the men act according to our stereotype of women—are catty, wear curls, and go shopping, while the women are energetic, managerial, unadorned partners" (Mead 1950: vi). While undoubtedly oversimplified, this ethnographic comparison makes the important point that it is culture, not nature, which shapes the roles that men and women play in society.

The Manchester tradition of anthropology, which highlights the significance of power, is one means of grounding Mead's insights in a wider context. This approach leads us to examine the social personalities of men and women—and, more especially, their roles vis-a-vis each other—with reference to such factors as inequality, domination, dependency, and resistance. Further refinements of Mead's theme flow from recent studies emphasizing the situational flexibility of male and female identities as well as the myriad ways in which culture influences the interactive relationship of men and women.

In the following essay John Coggeshall applies these and similar insights to the study of sexual relations among male *prisoners. Prison culture, he points out, involves the "conversion" of genders, a semantic process whereby "Dominant males...redefine submissive males as incipient females." In the relations that ensue, the dominant partners play stereotypical male roles of protection, aggression, and sometimes brutality, while the submissive partners render both sexual and "domestic" (cell cleaning, grooming, food serving) services to the men whom they describe as both lovers and "daddies." These conditions constitute a means through which sexual relations of an objectively homosexual nature are culturally reconstructed according to the male norms of heterosexuality. As Coggeshall concludes, "Hated and abused, desired and adored, males as females in prison occupy an important niche: they are the women of that society, constructed as such by the male-based perception of gender identities." In effect, prison culture offers a caricature of patterns that are all too easily recognizable in the wider society.*

YOU ARE HERE TO SEE THE SHOW?" the inmate leered. The focus of attention was the tall, slim blond then receiving her food in the cafeteria line. The kitchen workers in the medium-security prison filled her plate with polite deference, and as she walked between the tables her fine blond hair bounced over her shoulders. "Make you want to leave home?" a guard teased. His comment clarified the significance of the events that the guards, staff, and inmates had just witnessed. The object of interest was genetically a male, but reconstructed as a female according to the perception of gender within prisoner culture. Behind bars, certain males become redefined as females. The process by which this transformation occurs illuminates gender perceptions in prisoner culture as well as the larger issue of gender inequality in mainstream society.

Gender Identity, Roles and Statuses

An understanding of the gender redefinitions in prisoner culture requires a conception of gender itself as primarily a cultural construct; cultures define male and female (Mukhopadhyay and Higgins 1988: 485). This approach follows the contemporary deconstructionist movement in the social sciences and humanities, which sees gender as mutable and malleable, depend-

JOHN M. COGGESHALL

ing on the social context. Moreover, this perspective shifts the emphasis from exclusively female studies to *both* male and female studies, for quite frequently an understanding of one requires at least a consideration of the other.

For example, many Western cultures view genders as dichotomous, despite obvious contradictions in these restrictive cultural categories (Grimm 1987: 67-68). The dichotomy further enhances gender identities (Devor 1987: 13-14, citing Bem 1981) because the contrastive elements mutually exclude each other. One is either male or female. The two genders exist in binary opposition, each defining and being defined by the other.

In American culture, the dualistic contrast of gender identities reinforces a contrast in roles as well (see Brandes 1980: 6 for a European example). Masculine identity embodies personal characteristics such as success and status, toughness and independence, aggressiveness and dominance. Moreover, masculinity is defined in contrast to femininity; being male assumes *not* being compliant, dependent, or submissive, and not being effeminate in physical appearance or mannerisms (Herek 1986: 568).

Most American heterosexuals assume that males engaging in homoerotic sexual behavior would describe themselves as both homosexual in sexual orientation and "feminine" in gender identity (Read 1980: 16). But this assumption is patently false. Jack Weatherford (1986), in a study of an urban red-light district, described numerous instances of homoerotic behavior between males who still identified themselves as heterosexuals. Similarly, in the street life described by Reiss (1967), teenagers permit adult males to fellate them for money. However, the "peers" do not equate this homoerotic behavior with a feminine, or even homosexual, identity (*idem*: 225, 201).

Although American culture assumes homosexuals adopt and retain dichotomous "masculine" (insertor) or "feminine" (insertee) roles, "the terms active or passive partners, masculine or feminine role," simply have no meaning for homosexual dyads (Hooker 1967: 182). Nearly all male homosexuals know they are men, as do their lovers (Read 1980: 105, 110). Nevertheless, they sometimes adopt exaggerated female roles, ridiculing women while reaffirming their masculine identity in binary contrast (*idem*: 98). This denigration of women by men to enhance or supplement a male identity requires

THOSE WHO SURRENDER ARE FEMALE

closer scrutiny.

While in some cultures males and females retain relative status equality, no cultures elevate women politically or economically at the expense of men (see Mukhopadhyay and Higgins 1988 for a summary of gender status research). On the other hand, many cultures denigrate and devalue women (Sanday 1981: 33-34). While gender inequality correlates strongly with overall social inequality and male domination appears correlated with overall aggression and socially-approved violence, research still seeks to discover why women as a group always lose status when gender inequality occurs.

However, gender inequality need not necessarily imply sexual antagonism and violence (Davis and Whitten 1987: 77). Cultures differ in the degree, severity, and consequences of male control of economic and political power (Mukhopadhyay and Higgins 1988: 466-67). The pertinent issue pertains to the factors that transform gender inequality (when it does occur) into the degradation, humiliation, and sexual assault of women.

Some researchers have proposed psychological explanations for the male domination of females. Early formulations of this idea emanated as a reaction to Freudian theory. Instead of the androcentric assumption of penis envy as universal, Horney (1926: 330-331) argued that males envied the procreative powers of women and thus denigrated them. Chodorow (1974) felt that male insecurity stemmed from difficulties in establishing separate gender identities. More recently, Kittay (1983: 95, 121) suggested that because males cannot reproduce while women can, male "womb envy" led directly to the oppression and exploitation of women (see also Mukhopadhyay and Higgins 1988: 482-3). It is their envy and fear of that which they cannot control which lead men to humiliate and denigrate women (See Brandes [1980: 76] for a European example).

Other researchers have suggested that where a culture's value system condones, or at least does not strongly discourage, male sexual antagonism against women, such a system provides at least implicit acceptance of the brutalization of women. Cross-culturally, evidence indicates that the lower the status of women, the greater the sexual aggression of men (Baron and Strauss 1987: 480-81). Many cultures, such as those of Western Christianity, emphasize male domination symbolically through all-powerful male deities, providing a "script" for male control (Sanday 1981: 215-16; McBride

JOHN M. COGGESHALL

and Castelli). In such societies, sexual aggression both reflects the lower status of women and contributes further to the gender inequity (Baron and Strauss 1987: 481). The cultural misconception is that women are submissive and, therefore, males can dominate them. But, through this process of dominion, males find women to be submissive. The vicious circle of control and violence is completed.

In American culture, physical and sexual violence against women has been directly associated with the cultural devaluation of women (see for example Scott and Tetreault 1987: 379; Silbert and Pines 1984: 864; Schur 1984: 150). In actuality, rape represents only the tip of a chilling iceberg of male psychological and physical oppression of women, a terrible "extension and distortion of...the approved patterns of sexual behavior in our society" (Schur 1984: 148). For this sexual aggression to decline, dramatic modifications in values and behavior must occur, including the elimination of male perceptions of women as property to be possessed and as conquests to be dominated (*idem*: 156).

Finally, the economic inequality of men and women may reinforce the tendency toward male domination (Mukhopadhyay and Higgins 1988: 463; Schlegel and Barry 1986: 149; Sacks 1974: 221-222). Where men exercise economic control over women, they also control women's sexuality (Schlegel and Barry 1986: 147). When coupled with a value system emphasizing male domination, the male control of female economic power leads directly and frequently to the oppression and sexual domination of women by men, a pattern that may justify aggression and even rape.

Gender Concepts in Prison

Prison provides a social microcosm of the consequences of gender inequality in American culture. Inmates face antagonism from guards, violence from fellow inmates, and deprivation from incarceration itself. One means by which male inmates retaliate is to humiliate and assault their fellow inmates sexually. However, not all inmates face these attacks. By a complicated cultural process described below, certain inmates become redefined as women in prison. This metamorphosis allows males engaging in homoerotic behavior to retain a heterosexual identity, and it also justifies the brutalization of these inmates who have been redefined as females. As will be shown, sexual roles and behaviors in prison reflect those in American culture.

Victims of sexual assault in men's prisons "are perceived as those who are (or [who] may be) willing to occupy the passive role" (Nacci and Kane 1984: 46-47). According to attackers, victims appear "weak and attractive (i.e. a *logical stand-in for a woman*)" [emphasis added] (*ibid.*); see also Wooden and Parker 1982: 3). In prison, "the supreme act of humiliation is to be reduced to the status of a woman" (Cardozo-Freeman 1984: 400). In turn, the perception of female passivity justifies male domination: victims are said to have asked to be raped through "sexually stimulating behavior or appearance or negligence in self defense" (Nacci and Kane 1984: 49). In other words, victims of sexual assault are seen as defenseless, vulnerable females, and forced sexual intercourse is the weapon of offense (*idem*: 47; Jackson 1974: 377).

Why "female" inmates become "logical" targets reveals much about American culture in general as well as prisoner culture in particular. In the sexual domination of female substitutes, inmate exploiters gain power and self-esteem: "To express your machismo you must have people without it" (Jackson 1974: 377; Nacci and Kane 1984: 47; Nacci and Kane 1983: 33). The dehumanization of one gender by another enhances the latter's esteem. In prisoner culture, as in American culture in general, men "seek to preserve a threatened identity by retaliating by force" against those without power, that is, women (Sanday 1981: 210).

In sharp contrast, sexual victimization does not occur in women's prisons (Giallombardo 1966: 98). Despite the parallel oppression and dehumanization of incarceration, female inmates do not retaliate in exactly the same ways. In women's prisons, homoerotic dyads are extremely common and are seen by inmates "as a meaningful personal and social relationship" (*ibid.*) Frequently, these dyads involve the gender roles of stereotypical American culture: dominant "husbands" control submissive "wives" (Giallombardo 1966: 148-49; Burkhart 1973: 371; Williams and Fish 1978: 547-48). While economic exploitation occurs (Williams and Fish 1978: 549-50), and while jealousies and indiscretions sometimes spark violence (*idem*: 551), the ideal relationship is based on romantic love (Giallombardo 1966: 125). In fact, couples with a mutually compatible relationship gain the greatest prestige.

Giallombardo (1966: 17, 130) further suggests that sexual exploitation occurs only in men's prisons because American culture expects men to be aggressive and women passive. More specifically, Wooden and Parker (1982: 44) argue that prison sexual aggression replicates "sexual patterns and ethnic differences" among lower-income groups. Cardozo-Freeman feels that male inmates react violently because of the dehumanization of the social situation: "the state 'screws' the prisoner; he, in turn, does the same to his fellow prisoners" (1984: 400). Gang rapes become, at least in part, a reflection of displaced antagonism against a repressive society.

Gender Perceptions in Male Prisoner Culture

For inmates, the concept of female emerges from the concept of the male. To borrow a polysemic metaphor, the rib for Eve's creation is taken from Adam's side, and draws both its cultural significance and social status from the extraction. Woman is defined in contrast to man, and takes a lesser place at his side. In prison, males create females in their opposite image, and thereby dominate and subjugate them.

The fieldwork for this study was conducted in two medium-security Illinois state prisons over a two-year period. During that time three university-level courses were taught to forty-four adult inmates, whose racial and ethnic characteristics were generally representative of the non-prison population and whose criminal offenses were representative of other prison populations. Student-inmate perceptions provided a portion of the data, supplemented by observations of, and conversation with, guards, staff, and prisoners. After having received some instruction on data collection, one student-inmate, Gene Luetkemeyer (now released), volunteered to collect additional information. His nine detailed interviews of various inmates, identified below by pseudonyms, significantly enhanced the scope and detail of the study.

Prison culture is extremely complex and deserves much more detailed study by anthropologists (see for example Goffman 1961; Giallombardo 1966; Davidson 1983; Cardozo-Freeman 1984; Fleisher 1989; see Coggeshall 1988: 6 for further research suggestions). This paper concentrates on prisoner cultural views, that is, on the views of inmates themselves.

Various estimates exist on the amount of homoerotic activity in prison. As with most research on human sexual activity, "It is difficult to find out just how much activity actually goes on, and impossible to find out who does what to whom" (Jackson 1974: 375). Tommy, a self-described homophobe, believes that about 33% of prisoners engage in homoerotic activity, while Spankie, a self-described homosexual, suggests about 50% (Jackson [1974: 375] and Nacci and Kane [1983] citing Buffum [1972]). Paul and Sandy, homosexual lovers, estimate that 65% of prisoners engage in homosexual activity, an assumption supported by Doctor B., an incarcerated physician (Davidson 1983: 75). While not all inmates accept or condone homoerotic behavior, the vast majority see it as at worst an unpleasant necessity and at best as an acceptable alternative.

A small percentage of inmates do not condone or participate in homoerotic activity because for them such participation implies a feminine identity, even if one actor occupies the dominant role exclusively. For example, Tommy considers any homosexual act to be reciprocal, that is, both dominant and submissive: "if you pitch, you catch," he feels; "there's none of this 'being a man one day and a freak the next' business" (see also Jackson 1974: 375).

On the other hand, Spankie estimates that about 96% of sexual participants are "bi-sexual," giving as well as receiving pleasure. In other words, many inmates variously adopt both an "inserter" and an "insertee" role for sexual gratification and emotional bonding (see also Jackson 1974: 373, 398-403). In such relationships, though, genders remain distinct, differentiated not on methods of sexual gratification and not necessarily on "active" or "passive" sexual participation, but primarily on the basis of control of the relationship. In fact, domination defines the structure of the relationship which distinguishes the genders.

In prisoner culture, males have a gender identity quite distinct from females. Robert, an inmate, describes "a big...macho, weightlifting, virile, Tom Sellek-type guy" as a typical male. Weight lifters seem to predominate in this category, for strength suggests masculinity. Men vigorously protest sexual advances from other males by exhibiting a willingness to fight. Men are also perceived as those who can keep, satisfy, protect, and control, women.

In direct contrast to the male definition of masculinity, men see women as passive and subordinate. Terms from inmate folk vocabulary (Luetkeyeyer 1987) support this view. According to male inmates, women exhibit certain typical behaviors and characteristics. As Robert commented, women are "sweet and charming", "fluid of movement", with "seductive gestures". Doctor B. believes that he himself exhibits such effeminate qualities as "mild manners" and a "passive demeanour".

Primarily, women are defined by men on the basis of their sexuality. Sandy, a male perceiving himself as female, views promiscuous women as "tramps" or "whores". On the other hand, Sandy equates her distinguished status in prison to that of any well-respected woman in the world outside of jail:

> If you want to be treated like a lady and get respect, you've got to demand that respect.... If you whore around,...you'll get no respect. But if you are true to your daddy, carry yourself well, have a dignified demeanour, you'll be treated with respect.

According to inmates, some genetically female prison employees reinforce these stereotypes. Women work as wardens, guards, staff, and teachers, so that numerous female role models exist for the inmates. Prisoner culture suggests that these women cannot resist being sexually attracted to inmates, due to the diversity of males from whom to choose and the relative lack of female competition in prison.

Of course, nearly all female staff resist inmate advances. By inmate definition, then, they cannot be women. Such "unsexed" women, far from challenging gender constructs, on the contrary reinforce them. Female guards, staff, and teachers occupy positions of authority over inmates, decidedly atypical for women from a prisoner's perspective. Moreover, most female employees deliberately dress to de-accentuate anatomical differences for their own professionalism and safety. Because these women control men, dress as non-women, and act in a professional, non-enticing manner, they do not fit the inmate perception of women at all. Thus they cannot be women and must be homosexuals, or "dykes" as the convicts term them. To inmates, this can be the only explanation for women who do not act like women.

THOSE WHO SURRENDER ARE FEMALE

Prisoner gender concepts maintain distinct boundaries even when faced with apparent contradictions. In the mutually-exclusive dichotomy of gender definitions in prisoner culture, members of one gender who act like those of another are placed into the proper category. Thus women who control men are reclassified as "dykes" (non-women), and men who submit sexually are reclassified as "girls" (non-men).

However, since the "girls" of prisoner culture have been males at one time, this presents "real" men with a gender identity problem: the need to reconcile sexual activity with other males with a masculine self-concept. This adjustment is accomplished by means of a unique folk explanation of the etiology of gender development and orientation. Basically, dominant males in prison redefine submissive males as incipient females.

In prisoner culture, certain males are believed to have a deep-seated proclivity for being female; they are, in effect, trapped between male and female, needing to be released to achieve their true gender identity. Inmate terms for this metamorphosis reveal the gender ambiguity: males "turn out" these non-males, transforming them into the cultural equivalent of females. Certain males become redefined from the dominant male perspective as females trapped in male bodies. Such individuals figuratively "turn out" to be females, reconstructed according to the prisoner cultural stereotypes of the female. They thus become their true selves at last.

This transformation creates additional complications in gender identity for such inmates. Men readjusting their sexual orientations face a reassessment similar to the adjustments Goffman has described (1961: 146-69). These individuals must reconcile past heterosexual behavior and male identity with present homoerotic behavior and a feminine identity. The newly-created female must convince herself that this had been her true identity all along, and that she now has adopted the normal role befitting her gender identity. As might be expected, this role acceptance creates difficult psychological problems for such inmates, and not all reconcile themselves easily to this transition.

Vindication for the transformation comes as those forced to become females remain so. The inmate's acceptance of a "woman's" new gender identity and associated behavior justifies the conversion

JOHN M. COGGESHALL

for the rest of the prison population. If a new woman had no natural proclivity or had not been submissive and thus by definition female, she would never have embraced a feminine identity. The inmate culture produces the following false syllogism: those who surrender are weak, and females are weak by nature, therefore those who surrender must be female.

In fact, the structure of the relationship defines gender identity and role, not the forms of sexual gratification. "Real" men may engage (surreptitiously) in either active or passive homoerotic behavior with their "ladies" or "girls". Nevertheless, the former retain a heterosexual gender identity because they control their partners, both socially and sexually. Because the latter *are* controlled, they are by cultural definition female.

Folk conceptions of the etiology of gender support this perspective on gender transformation. For example, Tommy believed that all humans are "conceived as female, then either, as fetuses, develop male genitalia or not". Some perpetuate this ambiguous fetal identity into adulthood. Those who do, even unconsciously, can be transformed or "turned out" by stronger, i.e. male, inmates. Not resisting, or not resisting aggressively enough, merely validates this hidden gender identity. In inmates' views, it is only appropriate that those trapped in the wrong gender be released, to unfetter their true natures. The gender conversion, through whatever means (trickery, coercion, or rape), only restores the natural order.

Once the metamorphosis has taken place, most inmates agree that it can never be reversed (see also Davidson 1983: 75). In effect, individuals have been restored to their true feminine nature. In prisoner culture, most retain that identity throughout their incarceration.

A note about inmate terminology is in order here. As discussed above, homosexual identity and homoerotic behavior are not always correlated, and homosexuals are not simply passive or effeminate. However, gender identity in prison replicates the masculine or feminine dichotomy in American culture. By necessity, though, sexual gratification becomes primarily homosexual. Thus, in prisoner culture, inmates designate males engaging in homoerotic but primarily dominant sexual relationships as heterosexuals, while males in homoerotic but primarily passive relationships are termed homosexuals. This preserves the gender dichotomy found in

THOSE WHO SURRENDER ARE FEMALE

American culture (see also Nacci and Kane 1983: 35). Hereafter, the term "homosexual" refers to the inmates' category of a male transformed into a female. As noted earlier, social control, not gender identity or sexual gratification *per se,* define gender categories and their status in prisoner culture.

Prisoner culture divides homosexuals into several types (see also Jackson 1974: 373-4, 1978: 260; Cardozo-Freeman 1984: 369-403), each defined on the basis of degree of sexual promiscuity, amount of self-esteem, and severity of coercion used in the transformation. Generally, status declines as promiscuity and the intensity of coercion used in the conversion process increase.

The highest status category of homosexuals in prison contains "queens" or "ladies", those who have come out both voluntarily and willingly. Spankie defines queens as those who think of themselves as women and who thus behave as such. Prisoner cultural belief suggests that these individuals had been homosexual before incarceration but had not felt comfortable in "coming out". Prison provides them with the freedom to do so. Such individuals maintain a high status by remaining in control of their own lives and of their own gender identity.

For example, Sandy had been a female impersonator before imprisonment and had voluntarily turned out immediately upon entering prison. She feels that she has a certain amount of class and thus a high status. She always has and always will select her own lovers. Granted, she admits, she draws part of her status from her current lover Paul, a well-respected but retired gang leader. But Sandy feels she also has her own status, determined by her "dignified demeanour". Her self-confidence has allowed her to maintain a secure and stable identity and status in prisoner culture.

While other inmates volunteer to be females (in effect selling their male identities for rare or contraband goods), many are forced to become homosexuals against their initial will. According to an inmate, "Everyone is tested. The weak—of personality, personal power, willingness to fight, physical frailty, timidity—are especially susceptible." He adds, "Respect is given to one who can control the life of another." Those unwilling or unable to control others are thus themselves controlled. According to inmate cultural rules of gender identity, those who dominate, by natural inclination, are males, and those who submit, by natural temperament, are females.

JOHN M. COGGESHALL

Individuals forced to adopt a female role have the lowest status and are termed "girls," "kids," "gumps," or "punks" (see also Reiss 1967: 218). These individuals are kept in virtual servitude, as a sign of the owner's power and prestige. A gump may also have been tricked into surrendering his male identity by initially trusting an older "friend" who gradually drew the novice into a debtor situation where the only repayment is through submissive sex. A punk, most agree, initially hesitates, and is turned out by forcible rape and continued domination.

However created, homosexuals perform numerous functions. Generally, the higher the status, the more control one has over one's activities. High status individuals such as Sandy select their own lovers and live as wives and husbands in what Jackson (1974: 373) termed a "parody" of heterosexual relationships. In these situations the submissive partner provides stereotypical female services such as laundry, cell cleaning, grooming, and sexual gratification for her dominant "daddy".

Those with less status perform the same tasks but less voluntarily and with less consideration from their daddies. For example, Robert forced his kid to perform "certain menial functions" such as cleaning his cell. This established Robert's prestige *vis a vis* other inmates. As one of Cardozo-Freeman's (1984: 370) informants commented, "a punk in the bunk is like a crack in the shack [a woman at home].... They wash your clothes, they clean the house, [and] make your bed...."

Once an inmate has been forced to adopt a submissive lifestyle, the more intense the nightmare of domination becomes. For example, in a maximum security prison one inmate has been forced to fellate an entire row of inmates in the prison theatre. Another inmate recalled the capture of a first-offender by a convict in a county jail, who then forced the "girl" to submit to sex with anyone he sent. Gumps might be required to render sexual services to a gang chief and then passed down to a trusted lieutenant or to gang members for their enjoyment. A particularly attractive kid might be put "on the stroll," forced to be a prostitute for the financial benefit of the gang.

As valuable profit-making enterprises, kids may be sold to gangs by specialists who have trained or recruited them. Particularly attractive or submissive individuals bring high prices, as much as $100 in a cash-poor prisoner economy where money cannot be easily acquired. Economically productive kids can also be won or lost through gambling, or traded from owner to owner like property. "Gumps are bought and sold and traded between gangs like baseball players under contract," an inmate observed.

Hated and abused, desired and adored, males as females in prison occupy an important niche: they are the women of that society, constructed as such by the male-based perception of gender identities. In prison, as Dr. B. observes, actual females are termed "holes" and "bitches," reflecting the contempt in which they are usually held in the minds of lower class men. He adds, a homosexual "is likely to receive much of the contempt (and) pent-up hostility that would otherwise be directed at women." Herein lies the key to unlocking the deeper significance of gender construction and maintenance in prisoner culture.

Recall the general inmate perception of gender in prisoner culture. As Cardozo-Freeman (1984: 394) noted, submissive homosexuals "are seduced, raped, beaten, forced to please men, often in degrading ways and against their will, (and) assigned the usual drudgeries real women have always been assigned...." Even such a high-status individual as Sandy commented that homosexuals in prison have "far less respect; (you are) kept in your place, have no rights, your opinions and viewpoints are not acknowledged." While Sandy was saying this, her lover, Paul, interrupted and forced her to modify her opinion.

In prisoner culture, homosexuals are owned and protected by "daddies." In exchange, homosexuals provide sexual gratification and menial labor upon demand. Many are forced to sell their bodies for material objects or for protection from physical harm. Homosexuals are also viewed as being emotional, helpless, and timid. Best suited for certain tasks, homosexuals provide domestic and personal services for their daddies, serving their every whim.

Above all, homosexuals in prison are seen as sexual objects, to be used, abused, and discarded whenever necessary. Passive recipients of male power, they are believed to enjoy being dominated and controlled. In fact, males are considered to have done them a favor by releasing their female identities through rape. In prisoner culture, "no" means "yes," and resistance to sexual advances can be ignored as merely teasing taunts or further proof of weakness. A homosexual's wants and self-concept matter little, for in prison power is the main ingredient of sexuality.

Ultimately, in whose image and likeness are these "males and females" created? Genetically female staff and administrators do not fit the stereotypical gender view, and thus provide no role models for "females" in prison. The female role models for prison homosexuals are not women but male perceptions of women. Males themselves sculpt the image of female in prison, forming her from the clay of their own impressions. Males turned out as females perform the cultural role allotted to them by "real" males, a role of submission and passivity. In actuality, males produce, direct, cast, and write the script for the cultural expression of gender identity behind bars.

Implications for American Culture

In prison, woman is made in contrast to the image and likeness of man; men establish their own identity from this juxtaposition. In prisoner culture genders are dialectical; each pole draws meaning from a negation of the other. As discussed earlier, this dichotomy parallels the value system in many cultures, enhancing and reinforcing maleness at the expense of femaleness and the powerful at the expense of the powerless. Gender differences in many cultures come to be gender inequalities. By means of male domination, women remain in a culturally-defined place of servitude and submission. In turn, males interpret women's powerless position as justification for the continued exploitation of females.

It is precisely this concept of gender identity and status inequality that has proven most disquieting regarding the position of "males as females" in prison. Granted, prisoner culture presents a shockingly distorted view of American culture. Nevertheless, one sees in the mirror of inmate culture a shadowy reflection which remains hauntingly familiar. As "males as females" are viewed by males in prisoner culture, so are females perceived by many males in American culture. Gender roles and attitudes in prison do not contradict American gender concepts, they merely exaggerate grossly the domination and exploitation already present.

Thus the gender status of "males as females" in prison presents

THOSE WHO SURRENDER ARE FEMALE

not an anomaly but a caricature. Although aberrant and grotesque, the relationship between "girls" and the "daddies" in prisoner culture unfortunately provides a reflexive discourse on gender relationships in American culture today.

References

Baron, Larry and Murray Straus (1987). Four Theories of Rape: A Macrosociological Analysis. *Social Problems* 34:467-89.

Bem, Sandra (1981). Gender Schema Theory: A Cognitive Account of Sex Typing. *Psychological Review* 88:354-64.

Blackwood, E. (editor) (1985). Cross-Cultural Perspectives on Homosexuality. *Journal of Homosexuality* 11.

Brandes, Stanley (1980). Metaphors of Masculinity: Sex and Status in Andalusian Folklore. *Publications of the American Folklore Society* (n.s.) Vol. 1. Philadelphia: University of Pennsylvania Press.

Buffum, Peter C. (1972). *Homosexuality in Prison.* Washington, D.C.: U.S. Department of Justice.

Burkhart, Kathryn (1973). *Women in Prison.* Garden City, NY: Doubleday and Company.

Cardozo-Freeman, Inez (1984). *The Joint: Language and Culture in a Maximum-Security Prison.* Springfield, IL: Charles C. Thomas.

Chodorow, Nancy (1974). Family Structure and Feminine Personality. In *Women, Culture, and Society,* ed. by M.Z. Rosaldo and L. Lamphere, pp. 43-66. Stanford: Stanford University Press.

Coggeshall, John M. (1988). Behind Bars: Transformations in Prison Culture. Paper presented at the American Anthropological Association annual meeting, Phoenix, AZ.

Davidson, R. Theodore (1983). *Chicano Prisoners: The Key to San Quentin.* Prospect Heights, IL: Waveland Press.

Davis, D.L. and R.G. Whitten (1987). The Cross-Cultural Study of Human Sexuality. In *Annual Review of Anthropology,* ed. by B. Siegel, A. Beals, and S. Tyler, pp. 69-98. Palo Alto, CA: Annual Reviews Inc.

Devor, Holly (1987). Gender Blending Females: Women and Sometimes Men. *American Behavioral Scientist* 31(1):12-40.

Fleisher, Mark (1989). *Warehousing Violence.* Frontiers of Anthropology, Vol. 3. Newbury Park, CA: Sage.

Giallombardo, Rose (1966). *Society of Women: A Study of a Women's Prison.* New York:

John Wiley and Sons.

Goffman, Erving (1961). *Asylums: Essays on the Social Situation of Mental Patients and Other Inmates.* Garden City, NY: Anchor Books.

Grimm, David (1987). Towards a Theory of Gender: Transsexualism, Gender, Sexuality, and Relationships. *American Behavioral Scientist* 31:66-85.

Herek, Gregory (1986). On Heterosexual Masculinity: Some Psychical Consequences of the Social Construction of Gender and Sexuality. *American Behavioral Scientist* 29:563-77.

Hooker, Evelyn (1967). The Homosexual Community. In *Sexual Defiance*, ed. by J. Gagnon and W. Simon, pp. 167-184. New York: Harper and Row.

Horney, Karen (1926). The Flight From Womanhood: The Masculinity-Complex in Women, as Viewed by Men and by Women. *International Journal of Psycho-Analysis* 7:324-339.

Jackson, Bruce (1974). *In the Life: Versions of the Criminal Experience.* New York: New American Library.

Jackson, Bruce (1978). Deviance as Success: The Double Inversion of Stigmatized Roles. In *The Reversible World: Symbolic Inversion in Art and Society,* ed. by B. Babcock, pp. 258-275. Ithaca, NY: Cornell University Press.

Kittay, Eva Feder (1983). Womb Envy: An Explanatory Concept. In *Mothering: Essays in Feminist Theory,* ed. by J. Trebilcot, pp. 94-128. Totowa, NJ: Rowman and Allanheld.

Luetkemeyer, Eugene (1987). Terms. Unpublished manuscript.

Mukhopadhyay, Carol and Patricia Higgins (1988). Anthropological Studies of Women's Status Revisited:1977-1987. *Annual Review of Anthropology* 17:461-95.

Nacci, Peter and Thomas Kane (1983). The Incidence of Sex and Sexual Aggression in Federal Prisons. *Federal Probation* 47(4):31-36.

Nacci, Peter and Thomas Kane (1984). Sex and Sexual Aggression in Federal Prisons: Inmate Involvement and Employee Impact. *Federal Probation* 48(1):46-53.

Read, Kenneth (1980). *Other Voices: The Style of a Male Homosexual Tavern.* Novato, CA: Chandler and Sharp.

Reiss, Albert, jr. (1967). The Social Integration of Queers and Peers. In *Sexual Deviance,* ed. by J. Gagnon and W. Simon, pp. 197-228. New York: Harper and Row.

Sacks, Karen (1974). Engels Revisited: Women, the Organization of Production and Private Property. In *Women, Culture, and Society,* ed. by M.Z. Rosaldo and L. Lamphere, pp. 207-222. Stanford: Stanford University Press.

Sanday, Peggy Reeves (1981). *Female Power and Male Dominance: On the Origins of Sexual Inequality.* Cambridge: Cambridge University Press.

Schlegel, Alice and Herbert Barry III (1986). The Cultural Consequences of Female Contribution to Subsistence. *American Anthropologist* 88:142-150.

Schur, Edwin (1984). *Labeling Women Deviant: Gender, Stigma, and Social Control.* New York: Random House.

Scott, Ronald and Laurie Tetreault (1987). Attitudes of Rapists and Other Violent Offenders Toward Women. *Journal of Social Psychology* 127:375-80.

Silbert, Mimi and Ayala Pines (1984). Pornography and Sexual Abuse of Women. *Sex Roles* 10:857-68.

Weatherford, Jack M. (1986). *Porn Row.* New York: Arbor House.

Williams, Vergil and Mary Fish (1978). Women's Prison Families. In *Justice and Corrections,* ed. by N. Johnston and L. Savitz, pp. 541-552. New York: John Wiley and Sons.

THOSE WHO SURRENDER ARE FEMALE

Wooden, Wayne S. and Jay Parker (1982). *Men Behind Bars: Sexual Exploitation in Prison.* New York: Plenum Press.

JOHN M. COGGESHALL

WOMEN, FANTASY AND POPULAR CULTURE: THE WONDERFUL WORLD OF HARLEQUIN ROMANCE

Geraldine Finn

Coggeshall's article shows how gender identity is a function of power in prison culture. Geraldine Finn also examines the issue of gender and power, this time, in what seems the gentler context of a made-for-women form of popular culture, Harlequin Romances. The question she asks is, Why does a type of literature so many consider unworthy appeal to so many women?

The first point she raises is why female fantasies such as Harlequin Romances should be considered less worthy than male fantasies like Star Trek for instance. How does one account for the different evaluation of cultural products made for different publics, in this case men and women? This leads her to consider the ideological content of Culture from the point of view of gender and to raise the issue of cultural power, the focus of the next section of this book.

Next, she examines Harlequin Romance from the perspective of the writings on fairy tales. She claims that plots are almost always structured the same way: a young, beautiful, competent woman is forced to confront a dark and mercurial man, a Heathcliff character in a position of authority over her. At the end of a long period of resistance, the heroine is brought to her knees and finally succumbs to a crisis of nerves and/or mental and emotional exhaustion and/or a slight accident. While she is unconscious and no longer herself, the man's cruelty is unexpectedly revealed as true and passionate love. Finn believes that the reading of this never-changing plot allows women to retrace their own transition from a carefree and independent youth into a dependent and trapped adult.

If there is escapism in looking for personal rather than political and social solutions to these problems, at least such books acknowledge in ways that no other cultural forms do the real contradictions in women's lives. The books may tell female readers how to love a man who is not only feared and hateful, but who also controls her life; they may show how to love authority and how, in return, authority loves submission and dependence. Nonetheless, for Finn, Harlequin Romances are "as complex, contradictory and challenging as the lives of the women who read them and regularly tax their imaginations and intellects in their efforts to construct acceptable meanings from unacceptable facts".

OVER THE LAST SEVERAL YEARS feminists in the United States and Britain have begun to pay attention to popular culture forms which address themselves specifically to women as women: to day-time TV, for example, talk shows and soap operas, women's magazines and girls' comics, "women's" movies and selected (teeny-bopper) pop music, advertising, and, of course, gothic and romantic novels.[1] Most of the research focuses on the content and ideology of these various cultural products to show how their form and message work together to reproduce and reinforce current ideals of femininity, and to reconcile women to them: domesticity, motherhood, sexuality, economic dependency, subordination, self-sacrifice, and so forth.[2]

These "entertainments" command women's allegiance because they address real contradictions in women's lives and in the feminine ideal we expect ourselves to fulfill and be fulfilled by. They also offer solutions to these contradictions, albeit imaginary, false and momentary ones: how to find and hold a husband, for example, without appearing to be thus engaged; how to be sexy without being cheap, submissive without being servile, competent without being threatening, economically and socially dependent without being emotionally dependent, loving without being smothering, encouraging without demanding; how to be mother, mistress, maid and wife at once and feel honored, gratified and fulfilled in being so privileged; how to be responsible for the personal happiness and success of others without the political, economic, or social power that makes it possible; how to love and nurture without being loved and nurtured in return; how to be 50 and look 35, a terrific and

GERALDINE FINN

constant cook and wear size ten; how to be interesting, "alive" and "aware" when you spend the better part of every waking day in the company of small children (or in a female job ghetto) doing routine tasks which must be repeated every day, every hour, even every minute, every week and every year; how to feel like a member of a human community when you are isolated in your nuclear home (or on a conveyor belt); how to transform three meals a day, the family wash, the agony of birthdays, annual "family" holidays and Christmas into "fun" for you too!

Soap operas, romantic novels, women's magazines variously and differently address these very real contradictions and conflicts which structure the everyday lives of everyday women—though they seldom name the problems they explore as directly as I have done above. In fact, they carefully isolate and separate the various issues from the larger context of women's lives precisely to obscure the contradictions involved in following all the prescriptions for femininity and fulfillment. Most notable, for example, is the separation of sex from motherhood. For instance, in women's magazines sexual and romantic concerns are contained within the parameters of fiction or the letters page (Dear Abbey, or Dear Dr. X). Similarly, in the "traditional" Harlequin Romance (economic competition has spawned new variations) the narrative always ends with marriage, children are never mentioned (not even in romantic anticipation) let alone featured in the story, and all family connections and responsibilities are kept to the absolute minimum. In addition, the heroine is often an orphan and living in some strange and unfamiliar environment and the family connections of the hero are always remote.

The solutions these various cultural products offer women are imaginary, false and fantastic. While the problems and the pain they address are *collective* and rooted in the general social structural conditions which determine the personal possibilities of particular women the solutions offered are always *individual*. All these cultural forms personalize the political in this way and in the long-run, therefore, only add to the burden of femininity which they may momentarily alleviate. They perpetuate the myth that female failure is personal and accidental and not intrinsic to the social system itself. In this sense they fail to direct women to the real causes of their pain: the economic and political organization of production and reproduction which co-operate to guarantee the division of labour between the sexes and the structural domination of one over the other.

Research into the mode of production of popular culture aimed at women suggests the same structure of male dominance and female subordination in the forces and relations of cultural production, distribution and consumption as in Western societies more generally (see Jensen 1984). Yet, the most important aspect of the popular culture industry, from the point of view of those of us trying to develop revolutionary cultural theory and praxis, continues to be the least researched aspect of the field; that is, how these cultural products *are actually used and considered by the people who participate in them.* None of us is a passive consumer of culture, and no cultural object has meaning-in-itself, neither *Hamlet* nor *Dynasty* nor *Harlequin's.* In every case, cultural meaning is constituted historically and individually, in action and in relationships with others.

We are all *doing* something when we listen to a record, turn on the radio or television, read a book—whatever. However, we may not all be doing the same thing. I went to soccer games on Saturday afternoons to "hang out"; my father probably went to watch the match. Nevertheless, in one respect we were doing the same thing; we were both engaged in the practice of winning meaning and creating space for ourselves from within the social and cultural environment which to some extent we shared. Because all of us are differentially situated in that environment according to specificities of gender, race and class, the meanings and space we seek and require from and within it will be different. We cannot presume to know *a priori* what others differently placed from ourselves make of the same cultural phenomenon.

To someone who does not read Harlequin Romances self-indulgently for pleasure, for example, they may all seem alike and equally boring and pointless, because the characters are all types which are both predictable and unchanging and, until recently, all the stories have tended to have similar endings (more on this in a moment). Conversations with women who read them—sometimes as many as nine a week—however, reveal that plot and character development are not so important to them as "the unreal, fantastic shape of the story itself," which gives pleasure by providing an "escape," both literally and figuratively, from the "pressures" and "ten-

GERALDINE FINN

sions" they experience in their daily lives. As Janice Radway notes:

> The act of reading them literally draws the women away
> from their present surrounding. Because they must
> produce the meaning of the story by attending closely to
> the words on the page, they find that their attention is
> withdrawn from concerns that plague them in reality. One
> woman remarked with a note of triumph in her voice: "My
> body may be in that room, but I'm not." (1983: 58)

The women interviewed by Radway explain that they feel "refreshed and strengthened" by their vicarious participation in the romantic fantasy: "where the heroine is frequently treated as they themselves would most like to be loved." (See also Radway 1984)

The fact that many, and certainly the best, of the romance writers are drawn from the ranks of their readers is also politically relevant and an important consideration in any evaluation of the emancipatory potential of these kind of novels. For it means that here, in this particular cultural form, women address women as equals, speak to each other's shared pains and desires, and nurture each other through their collective participation in the production of a fantasy which consoles and strengthens at the same time as it provides a brief respite from the constant demands and contradictions of female being.

It was tempting in preparing this paper to review the current research on Harlequin Romances in greater detail, some of which has been schematically indicated above, and to engage with some of the controversies which this research has generated—to convey the richness, complexity, specificity and importance of this particular cultural phenomenon which reaches so many women and is both widely enjoyed and heavily criticized. There are, for example, women who argue that Harlequin Romances are "pornography" and, depending on their sexual politics, deplore or applaud them on that account. Others emphasize the continuity and similarity between Harlequins and "serious" literature, like the novels of Nathaniel Hawthorne, Jane Austen, the Brontë sisters, or Margaret Atwood. Some emphasize the expressive, independent, rebellious and, therefore, emancipatory tendency in the novels; others their usual recuperation of the heroine within the structure of withdrawal from the public world to the private domestic space circumscribed by one man.

I decided to resist this temptation and add fat to the fire by trying to situate Harlequin Romances within the discourse of Culture in general, and literary and popular culture in particular. In so doing I want to emphasize three general truths about our Culture and our concepts which my own research into the recent literature on popular culture, leisure and ideology thrust upon me: i) the specificity of women's cultural experience as a structured absence rather than a presence; ii) the specificity, therefore, or women's struggle for meaning, space and self-respect within the confines of that cultural space; and iii) the resulting inadequacy and partiality of the concepts, categories and meanings produced to understand that Culture in our absence.

I am certainly not the first to observe that Culture is not neutral; but we need to be reminded, it seems, that the *category* "Culture" is not a neutral category either. Cultural production serves someone's interests, and so does the discourse of Culture. Culture, like Science, is not an innocent category, but rather one of exclusion, passification [sic] and mystification (Finn 1982). Of course, I cannot pretend to defend these claims adequately here, in the preamble to a brief discussion of Harlequin Romances. I can only indicate how I would argue the case were I called upon to do so.

Culture and Exclusion

Like Art, Science, Reason, and Sex, Culture is a normative and not a descriptive category. It tells us how to behave towards a particular practice, people or product (with some kind of reverence or respect), but not much about that which is selectively included in its category. Culture always designates that which distinguishes Man from Nature, for example; but not all men and not all human beings and human activity are included. Women and women's praxis have always been defined and produced as Culture's Other—a part of Nature to which Culture is traditionally opposed and which Culture attempts to tame, domesticate, conceal, control or annihilate in its professed project of "human" development, emancipation, self-creation or expression. In the discourse of Culture, as in the discourses of Science, Art and Sex, men are its agents or subjects, and women their

GERALDINE FINN

objects, the raw material of an essentially male cultural praxis: artifacts, mediators. In fact, if Levi-Strauss (1969) is to be believed, women are the very medium of exchange between groups of men by and in which Culture itself is at once constituted and instituted.

Not surprisingly, the way women win meaning *for themselves*, as subjects, *within* Culture has no or very little cultural presence, and even less recognition *as* Culture. This is as true of popular culture and alternative and dissenting culture as it is of mainstream or official "high" Culture. Even women artists, novelists, musicians and intellectuals in our own time, who explicitly attempt to address women as women in their work must also produce *for men* and include them in their address. For it is men who mediate women's cultural presence, men who are the watchdogs of Culture. They control the norms of Culture—what is to count as art, literature, music, as well as the means and methods of its production. (The same is true, of course, of Science and Sex.)

Women's magazines and women's pages in men's newspapers are two of the few examples of cultural production where women address women—but they do so only through the mediation of men. In both cases, the words usually must first be approved by men to get published at all, and the words have a public presence which makes them easily accessible to men for their approval or censure. Not surprisingly then, in both cases, women tend to address women in their ideologically correct political relationship to men and economic and cultural production; that is, as wives, mothers and domestic (and sometimes sexual) labourers.

Harlequin Romances as Popular Cultural Forms

Our own Culture is dominated by a capitalist and masculine hegemony. Harlequin Romances, like every other popular cultural form, both express and reproduce this order of dominance. Harlequins, however, are somewhat unique. Because they escape the scrutiny of the public, they engage much more directly and exclusively with the realities of women's *personal* experience than any other cultural product I know. Women address women's *private* pains and passions *privately* in Harlequins, in ways that more public forums like television shows, records and movies could never do. Harlequins (and similar pocketbook romances) do not need to seek men's collective approval or assuage their collective vanities as do these other more public forms. The market-segmented logic that is the basis of their commodity form opens up a unique space for women in their private cultural use.

Like all novels, Harlequins can take certain liberties because they are produced and consumed *alone,* away from the peering and judgemental eyes of others; and this in fact, is one of their biggest selling points. The fantasy world of Harlequin Romance is a world into which the reader can *disappear* and mercifully escape the relentless destiny of women, which is to be always the site of other people's wills and determinations not one's own, as well as the permanent sight/site of male objectification, manipulation and exploitation. Women in their roles as wives and mothers have little private life in the real world: they exist for others, not for themselves.

In the world of romance novels they can imagine, however, that they have a rich self-existence. Because such novels do not seek legitimation as "literature," they are even freer to engage more directly, more fancifully and more exclusively with women's subjective experience than other novels which must include male subjectivity in their address if they want to be published or critically acclaimed. The largely male entrepreneurs who mediate Harlequins, by contrast, are not concerned with "standards," but with sales. They do not care what women are saying to women, or how they are saying it, just so long as women continue to buy their product.

Such romances, therefore, are uniquely placed to tell us something which other cultural products can't about how women experience our Culture and attempt to win space and meaning for themselves within it; about how they reconcile themselves to its contradictions so they can live out their lives with some semblance (or illusion) of coherence, control, integrity, dignity, purpose and pleasure. The fact that there are so many women who read these romances and read so many of them, often compulsively and obsessively, testifies to the enormity and extent of women's personal needs and frustrations, as well as to the difficulty women must experience in meeting them and wrestling an acceptable meaning for themselves from and within their everyday lives.[3] For every day the effort must be ritually renewed, just as faith in God is renewed through daily prayer.

GERALDINE FINN

In my opinion, though this would not be shared by all researchers, the principle contradiction which Harlequin romances have traditionally attempted to resolve (magically, as we shall see) is that of loving a feared and hateful man who has control over you and upon whom you are ultimately dependent. Others have argued that the central task of such romances is to enable women to enjoy sex, without assuming responsibility for it; to show them how they can get a husband without appearing to want one; to resolve "the fundamental contradiction in women's lives: the conflict between intimacy and power in any female/male relationship." (See Patterson 1981). I think all these are true characterizations of the Harlequin experience, but they could all be subsumed under the central problematic described above: that of loving a feared and hateful man who has control over you and upon whom you are ultimately dependent.

Surely this is the central prescription of contemporary femininity, the particulars of which may change according to historical, economic and ideological circumstances. The representation of sex, for example, is a relatively new feature in these romances, corresponding to the "trickle-down" of the sexual orthodoxy of the 1960s and 1970s, prescribing frequent and varied sexual activity for "healthy" couples and sexual pleasure for women as well as men. Women have to learn these new tricks which have been thrust upon them as part and parcel of their femininity, and are expected of them by their husbands. The substitution of sexual passion for romantic love in some Harlequins of the 1980s caters to this new demand on women by showing them how to "re-read" their own responses to others as an explicitly sexual response indicative of sexual need and sexual passion, where before they would have "read" only tenderness and selfless love.

Until just recently all Harlequins have generally had the same plot structure.[4] A plucky, independent, young heroine meets an older, rich, powerful and at first hated hero. The bulk of the novel consists in tracing the struggle between these two: their mutual misunderstandings and conflicts, and his eventual victory over her determination to resist him and his taunts and temptations. She finally realized that he loved her all the time and that his strange and often hostile behavior was an expression of his fear that his love would not be reciprocated or of his hurt after a previous love affair. The story always ends with the promise of marriage and the heroine tenderly wrapped in the hero's gentle and careful embrace—regardless of any sexual passion which may have preceded it. The reader, of course, knows what will follow the marriage: dependency, domesticity, motherhood—the very things she turns to Harlequins to escape from. But reading the romance allows her to re-read and reconstruct the circumstances which brought her to this point in her life, without at the same time forcing her to confront its betrayal of her dreams.

Although all Harlequin Romances are alike in this respect (and in others as we shall see), they are also very different and their readers are often highly discriminating about authors and characters, just as habitual readers of science fiction profess to be. In fact, the plots of Harlequin Romances are no more repetitive, predictable, fantastic or politically reactionary than are the plots of Dr. Who or Star Trek—fantasies which address men specifically as men and for that reason alone command greater respect and recognition in our cultural calculus of value. This is reflected in the massive public and private expenditure and sophisticated technology which these productions entail and in the fact that men and women alike, conservatives, liberals and revolutionaries, are not ashamed to admit to enjoying them and celebrating them publicly in ritual displays of their support and satisfaction. By contrast, Harlequin Romances, and by association those who read them (or perhaps the determining relation is really vice versa?), are often dismissed with contempt and regarded as pariahs; a status reflected in their contrasting economic relations of production and consumption. They are extremely cheap and consumed in private, uncelebrated by public recognition, left behind in laundromats and bus stations, given free in packets of soap powder and readily discarded in garbage cans and rummage sales.

I would like to exploit this contrast—between the Star Trek/Dr. Who phenomenon and Harlequin Romances, between male and female popular fantasies, and elaborate upon it further. Ernst Bloch once made an important distinction between myths and fairy tales (cited in Jameson 1972: 69). He suggested that whereas myths reflect the warrior-class and the priesthood, fairy tales are the narrative expression of the poorer classes. The acquisition of honor and glory is central to myth; access to material wealth is central to the fairy tale.[5]

If we acknowledge the male as the site of coincidence between patriarchal and capitalist relations, i.e., as the site for women to gain access to social and cultural presence and power, then Harlequins can be seen as fairy tales: the narrative expression of the culturally dispossessed. Among other things this expression magically transforms women from a prior condition of social and cultural exile and impoverishment into meaning, Culture, and social wealth through their association with a particular man. Fantasies, like Star Trek and Dr. Who which are addressed to men's hegemonic masculinity can then be seen as equivalent to myths, within which men compete against other men for glory and honor, secure in the knowledge of their inherent Cultural control and the legitimacy of their Cultural presence. In both cases men and women differentially win meaning for themselves as individuals from the contradictions and struggles specific to their daily lives.

Harlequin Romances share the following features with fairy tales: they are to all intents and purposes *anonymous* and they are *fantastic*. Yet, their anonymity and fantasy are radically different from those associated with traditional fairy tales addressed to a subjectivity which is for the most part presumed to be male. This point requires clarification.

Consider, first, the question of anonymity. Harlequin Romances are characterized by anonymity of both character and author. Although they are novels, they are not like novels of the "malestream" Culture where invention and authorship are considered important and rewarded accordingly, though they do have named authors who have distinctive styles and followings. In this respect, Harlequins are more like collective tales than individual narrations: more like *langue* than *parole*. Their focus is likewise more synchronic than diachronic: concerned with affirmation, confirmation and accommodation rather than with exploration, development or explanation, as we would expect from an "ordinary" novel.

In addition, there is a complete lack of specificity in the Harlequin romance, of context as well as of character. The heroine likely has no history (no past or future), experiences no maturation, never has children and rarely has parents. The tale merely requires that she be young, pretty and alone, separated from her family and thrown into an unfamiliar situation in which she must fend for herself, both materially (for survival) and socially (for emotional support). Likewise, the hero, who appears from nowhere, is mysteriously wealthy and mysteriously interested in intruding himself upon the heroine's consciousness and heart.

In the *Morphology of the Folk Tale*, Vladimir Propp (1968) argued that characters in folk tales have only three attributes: a name and external appearance, particularities of introduction into the story, and a dwelling place. It is precisely the same in Harlequins. Both hero and heroine apparently fall in love with physical appearance alone, for they learn nothing of each others' history or personality. All they know about the other is what particular detail brought them to the exotic place where they meet and ultimately fall in love. But, surprisingly, much is made of houses and dwelling places, especially interiors which are often described in loving and careful detail. The hero always has some large house somewhere, which is surprisingly well appointed with domestic and homely attributes—and he can usually cook. Commentators have suggested that this house signifies to the heroine (and the reader) the place which she will eventually presume in his life, the promise of marriage and mutual domestication. It is always a high spot in the story when the heroine discovers the home behind the man.

Now consider the question of fantasy. Harlequin Romances are fantastic in two precise ways: (1) they rely on the intervention of magic for the resolution of the initial situation of lack—lack of legitimacy, sense (sens/direction), love; and (2) they have the form, not of a story or an anecdote, but of wish-fulfillment, for the end is given in the beginning and what interests us, as readers, is the *how* rather than the *what* of its achievement. We know that the heroine will marry the hero, and that his apparent brutality, indifference and contempt will be ultimately revealed as manifestations of love. We also know that her corresponding plucky resistance to his authority will finally be undermined by that knowledge.

What we are interested in is the *how* of this transformation. For, if it can be done in fiction, maybe it can be done in fact, too? Maybe our own experience of intimidation and confusion in response to a dominant man, and his cold and cruel indifference to us, could also be transformed into an expression of mutual "love?" Fantasy is, after all, precisely what reality can be confused with. It is through fantasy that our conviction of the worth of reality is es-

GERALDINE FINN

tablished." (See Cavell 1979). The fantasy in Harlequins is not so much in the point of departure—the confrontation of innocence with a cold, authoritative, scornful, older, richer man; but in the mode of resolution; in the interpretation of this dynamic as love and/or sexual desire.

The magic intervenes on two levels: on him and on her. And in both cases the magical agent is the same: love and/or sexual desire; which appearing without apparent rhyme or reason or personal choice, magically transforms the meaning of the couple's struggle into Romance and its sense (sens/direction) into Marriage. In spite of the heroine's wilful and determined resistance to this hateful and domineering stranger whom she did not invite into her life, she finds herself in mid-story quivering with excitement at the very idea of him or the thought of his presence. The fear and humiliation his scornful and taunting behavior caused in her at first is subtly transformed into the thrill of love, or more recently, sexual desire; a crudely physical condition of extreme agitation which reduces her, without the intervention of her will, to a puppet of *his* will, to total self-effacement (literally as well as figuratively as we will see) and total self-sacrifice. He, meanwhile, begins by being cool, condescending, bemused and even sometimes cruel and hostile towards the heroine and is transformed into a gentle, loving and nurturing mother/father figure about six pages from the end of the story.

This magical transformation in the hero occurs in response to the heroine's ultimate loss of control. In her efforts to resist the hero and assert her independence from him she eventually oversteps herself and gets herself into a situation from which she must be rescued. Only then does the hero give any indication of his secret love for her: when she is helpless, dependent on him, and most importantly, temporarily *unconscious*—of him, her effect on him and his response to her. She may literally leave the conflict situation and move to some other place and some other interest, or, as is often the case, she has some kind of accident which leaves her unwell or unconscious.

In her absence the world of struggle is transformed—as if by magic, for her action has nothing to do with it—from one in which she was alone, confused and embattled into one in which she is wanted, loved and nurtured. And she returns, or reawakens, to find herself cradled in the warm and safe embrace of the very same man who had previously caused her so much grief. The reader's pleasure in the transformation of the heroine's world is presumably enhanced by her own "disappearing" act which reading Harlequin Romances offers her. Temporarily absent from the "stresses" and "tensions" of her life she can imagine that it too will have been magically transformed when she returns to it.

Significantly, the hero's love is usually expressed in terms of the heroine's irresistible appearances—when she is defeated, dependent and hardly conscious, remember—and never in terms of her personality or competence. It is her body eviscerated of mind which he cradles so lovingly in his arms at the end of the story. When the heroine was assertive, competent and independent, he scorned and mocked her; when she is immobilized, passive and dependent, he loves her—indeed, desires her passionately. It is this near-necrophily, this sado-masochistic message of traditional Harlequin Romances which has led some feminists to regard them as pornography.

It is interesting to note the transformations and reversals which occur in the standard fairy tale formula when the tale is addressed to women, and the specificity and demands of our social reality (as opposed to men's), which is taken as the "cultural" norm. According to Frederic Jameson (1972), the hero in the beginning of the folk tale is never "strong enough to conquer by himself." He "suffers from some initial lack of being" (the realistic point of departure) which the intervention of a donor and a magical agent remedies by fantastic means. In Harlequin Romances, by contrast, the heroine in the beginning is not *weak* enough and suffers from an initial surfeit of being for a woman, whose social and cultural destiny is subordination to Man in general and economic and social dependence on one man in particular in marriage. The plot in her case, therefore, is constituted by her inevitable loss of control and she wins (recognition, a husband, love, meaning, sens/direction) only by losing (consciousness, self, strength, independence). In the traditional folk tale there are several well-distinguished *dramatis personae:* the hero, the villain, the donor of the magic agent, the dragon, the false hero and the princess—the hero's reward. The appropriate behavior of the hero towards each one is clearly delineated. He complies with and is deceived by the villain; tested and then assisted by the donor; struggles and defeats the dragon; discloses the false hero and wins and weds the princess.

GERALDINE FINN

Things, needless to say, are more complicated in the usual Harlequin Romance where winning is losing and victory is defeat and we are looking at life and the production of meanings from the point of view of the would-be princess and not the man that marries her. Here the politics is personal not public and the oppressor localized in the home and family (in father, husband, brother or son). For women, men cannot be so easily differentiated into friends and foes, nor evils objectified in dragons. It is often immediate, particular, familiar men who oppress, control and terrify us, not a distant patriarch or an identifiable elite.

It is quite appropriate, therefore, that the male hero in women's tales should play *all* these parts simultaneously. Although he is the hero, the good guy, he is also the villain. For at the beginning of the story he deceives the heroine, teasing, cajoling, lying, and challenging her into dealing with him, and making her believe that he despises and dislikes her. And it is his contradictory and confusing behavior towards the heroine that motivates the narrative and the series of trials which are ultimately "resolved" in marriage. He is also the donor, the one who possesses the magic agent and passes it on to the heroine, enabling her success: that is, sex or love, which makes all meaningful and at the same time brings her to a place of submission before him and thus to "success" as a woman. He is also the dragon against whom the heroine must struggle and lose, in order to win her place beside this Prince in marriage. (Her own strength and spirit of independence could also be seen as the dragon which she must conquer to be fulfilled as a woman: her struggle with the hero is thus the means to that end).

The hero is, at the same time, the false hero. For, at first, she mistakes his overt scorn and dismissal for indifference or hostility (silly, foolish woman!), until her moment of helplessness and submission, whereupon he shows his "true" self and reveals himself as her Prince, her reward and her saviour. Little wonder the heroine is confused about the appropriate response to make to this man, and by implication all men, and keeps making mistakes in her efforts to assume the correct behavior in his presence. And no wonder, she must lose consciousness as her end in marriage approaches—how else could life with such a man be tolerated?

Some Harlequins actually begin with marriage, but it is a marriage in name only. Hero and heroine scarcely know each other, appear never to have consummated their sexual relationship, have no children, do not live together and are socially, geographically and emotionally estranged. Apart from this wrinkle, however, these stories have the same plot structure as other Harlequin Romances: the independence of the heroine and the indifference of the hero are gradually revealed as mere appearances and the struggle between them finally resolves in their reunion in a loving and, therefore, "real," marriage. It is once again the *how* and not the what of this transformation that interests the reader: how a lonely, sterile, and loveless marriage can be changed into a passionate and "true" union of husband and wife. And it is love once again that is introduced as the magical agent of this transformation.

Harlequin Romances are neither shallow nor simple; rather, they are as complex, contradictory and challenging as the lives of the women who read them and regularly tax their imaginations and intellects in their efforts to construct acceptable meanings from unacceptable facts. Although the resolutions in these romances are unreal, the central contradiction they address is real enough for many women: how to love a loveless, fearsome and authoritarian man upon whom you are dependent. That they are written and read in such quantities testifies to the fact that women are not entirely defeated by their circumstances, nor entirely reconciled to their fate, nor entirely convinced by the white-wash of male-stream ideology which attempts to naturalize it.

For the most part, Harlequins have never presented men in a very good light. Until the magic moment of his transformation, the hero is consistently hateful and hated, brutal and feared. He frequently incites the heroine to anger and rage and she is never afraid to confront him with her criticisms. The reader's sympathies are always with the heroine at these times and her outbursts against him clearly permit women to express and enjoy their own rage against men vicariously, without the enormous risk that this would entail were they to attempt to do so in their own lives.

On the other hand, the heroines are always presented in a very good light, at least until the very end. They are independent, self-sufficient, uncomplaining, intelligent, competent, if naive, young women, with adequate jobs and income, and no apparent desire or need for a man. They hold their own in arguments against the hero, never cry, never feel sorry for themselves or whine, and explicitly

GERALDINE FINN

chastize themselves when they do begin to weaken and have to confess to themselves their mysterious attraction to this magnetic man. They are brought to their knees through a series of accidents and coincidences which are more a consequence of destiny than design, and to which they finally succumb as they succumb to the hero's embrace at the end of the story.

What the romance provides is an acceptable interpretation of how we women get from there to here: from the independence, innocence and freedom of girlhood, to the jaded subordination of marriage, without our appearing to have collaborated in the process. These romances also provide us with an object-lesson in rereading the loveless behavior of many men so that it conforms more closely to the romantic ideology of marriage and our own frustrated dreams therein.

Like pornography, however, Harlequin Romances largely mistake the problem for the solution, and exacerbate the initial condition by recommending more of the same. Pornography gives men a diet of exaggerated masculinity to alleviate the intolerable and contradictory existential problems which masculinity itself produces. Harlequin Romances offer women a diet of femininity to solve the problems femininity generates. But it is too simple to say of Harlequins that they produce false consciousness, for they mix the true with the false, the emancipatory with the mystifying. Unlike pornography, for example, Harlequins announce themselves as fantasy and the women who read them do not confuse the world of Harlequin with the real world in which they must negotiate their real relationships with men. They turn to Harlequins for escape and comfort from that world, *not* for exemplary practices they can bring back to it.

The professed fantasy of pornography, on the other hand, is implicitly denied by the reality of the "models" used in its production, by the biographical and documentary mode of its narrative, by the concrete and immediate sexual response it explicitly calls forth in its clientele and by the material circumstances and context of its modes of production, distribution and reception (in magazines with "features" and advertising, for example). And men do confuse the pornographic world with the real world and do use pornographic practices as examples in their real relationships with others.

Harlequin Romances are one of the few popular cultural forms that address women as women *and* as subjects. For not only is the heroine self-defined and self-determined, but the woman who reads about her must also participate actively and personally in the production of the story's meaning. By excluding the family from the story, Harlequins also, uniquely I would say, constitute both heroine and reader as female beings *for themselves* rather than as beings for others, and provide women with one of their rare opportunities for taking time out *for themselves* and by themselves to devote themselves self-indulgently to pursuing their own pleasure. Harlequins are also one of the few non-feminist cultural forms, and perhaps the only popular one, that speaks to women's rage against men and provides women with a space and a place within which their rebellion against male dominance and the cultural expectation of female subordination and passivity can be safely expressed.

Thus, there is much more to Harlequin Romances than romance. Although their resolutions are fantastic and their heroines ultimately recuperated into traditional marriages, the bulk of the tale concentrates on the struggle against this inevitable destiny. The fact that so many women take pleasure in reliving this struggle— over and over again—should give us cause for hope rather than despair. For it means they have not been defeated by their pain, nor anaesthetized against it. As Tania Modleski (1980) has noted, "It is not high art alone which keeps alive the desire for a world different from the one in which we live."[15] Nor is it high art alone which expresses our desire for freedom and our freedom for desire.

Notes

1. See, for example, Nina Baym, "Hawthorne's Women: The Tyranny of Social Myth," *Centennial Review,* Vol. 15 (1971) and *Women's Fiction* (Ithaca and London: Cornell University press, 1978); Muriel Cantor (with Suzanne Pingree), *The Soap Opera* (Beverly Hills: Sage, 1983); Dorothy Hobson, *Crossroads: The Drama of a Soap Opera* (Eyre: Methuen, 1982); Clair Johnston, *Notes on Women's Cinema* (London: Society for Education in Film and Television, 1973); Ann Kaplan, *Women and Film*

(Methuen, 1983); Annette Kuhn, *Women's Pictures* (Routledge and Kegan Paul, 1982), and "Women's Genres," *Screen,* Vol. 25, No. 1 (January-February 1984); Tania Modleski, "The Disappearing Act: A Study of Harlequin Romances," *Signs, Journal of Women and Culture in Society,* Vol. 5, No. 3 (Spring 1980), and *Loving with a Vengeance: Mass-Produced Fantasies for Women* (Hamden, CT: Archon Books, 1982); Joanna Russ, "Somebody is Trying to Kill Me and I Think it is My Husband: The Modern Gothic," *Journal of Popular Culture,* 4 (September 1973).

2.   In addition to the writers noted above, see Ann Douglas, "Soft Porn Culture," *New Republic* (August 1980); Dorothy Hobson, "Housewives: Isolation and Oppression," in *Women Take Issue* (cccs Series, Hutchinson, 1978), and "Housewives and the Mass Media," in *Culture, Media and Language* (cccs Series, Hutchinson, 1980); Angela McRobbie, "Girls and Subcultures: An Exploration," in *Resistance Through Rituals* (cccs Series, Hutchinson, 1976), Working Class Girls and the Culture of Femininity," in *Women Take Issue* (cccs Series, Hutchinson, 1978), "Settling Accounts with Sub-cultures: A Feminist Critique," *Screen,* 37 (April 1980), and (with Trisha McCabe), *Feminism For Girls: An Adventure Story* (Routledge, 1981); Laura Mulvey, "Visual Pleasure and Narrative Cinema," *Screen,* 16(3) (Autumn 1975), and "Afterthoughs on 'Visual Pleasure and Narrative Cinema'," *Framework,* 1516/17 (1981); Lillian Robinson, *Sex, Class and Culture* (Bloomington: Indiana University Press, 1978); Anita Burr Snitow, "Mass Market Romance: Pornography for Women is Different," *Radical History Review,* 20 (Spring/Summer 1979); Janet Winship, "A Women's World: 'Woman'—An Ideology of Femininity," in *Women Take Issue* (cccs Series, Hutchinson, 1978), and "Sexuality for Sale," in *Culture, Media and Language (cccs Series, Hutchinson, 1980).*

3.   For example, Harlequin alone sold 168 million new copies in 1979, translates its writers into 16 languages, and as of this writing, runs a subscription service offering its readers six new romances a month at the 1982 price of $1.50 each. In addition, Harlequins are recycled several times through second-hand book outlets and exchanges.

4.   I am indebted to Harlequin author, Claire Harrison for pointing out recent changes in the Harlequin "formula." In personal communication she has noted that my version of the traditional Harlequin plot:

> ...certainly was the standard plot of the pre-1980 Harlequin, and I'm sure that you will still find some on the shelves, but many books now don't conform to that "formula" and, therefore, don't fit into your philosophy. In my books, heroines are older, heroes are younger and rarely "feared and hateful." The story is, of course, the boy meets girl plot—that is after all the essence of romance, but there is a wide variety of stories within the basic framework. And, contrary to what you have stated, there are any number of books that include children, and the marriage-in-name-only plot is now a very rarely used device. And, if you follow the genre closely, you will find authors who do not ignore a heroine's past, rarely make her an orphan, and allow her to develop in maturity as the story progresses. And, as for the heroine reverting to a submissive child from an independent woman, I could argue about that for hours, but perhaps my best evidence is that I recently sold a *Harlequin Presents* to my editor in which the hero is forced to give up his career in order to be with the heroine who is a pediatrician and will not leave her practice to be with him.

Claire Harrison does not offer any suggestions about *causes* for recent revisions to the long-standing Harlequin "formula," and there is every reason to believe that the elements of anonymity and fantasy outlined in the paper at hand continue to play a prominent role in Harlequin books. It is likely that most of the changes which have occurred in the Harlequin formula have been a response to increased economic competition in the romance fiction market in the 1980s. This competition has led to a reconsideration of the romance fiction audience as a cluster of slightly differing market "segments" rather than a homogeneous block of female readers. Set in this context, the "traditional" formula has been adapted in keeping with marketing strategies designed to identify and target specific segments (e.g., young professional women, adolescent girls, middle-aged wives and mothers).

5.   Thanks to Eleanor Shapiro, Earlham College, Indiana, for pointing this out to me (in personal conversation).

References

Cavell, S.
    1979   *The World Viewed: Reflections on the Ontology of Film*. Cambridge, Mass.: Harvard University Press.

Finn, G.
    1982   "Women and the Ideology of Science," *Our Generation*. 15(1).

Jameson, F.
    1972   *The Prison House of Language*. Princeton: Princeton University Press.

Jensen, M.
    1984   *Love's Sweet Return: The Harlequin Story*. Toronto: The Women's Press.

Levi-Strauss, C.
    1969   *The Elementary Structures of Kinship*. Boston: Beacon Press.

Modleski, T.
    1980   "The Disappearing Act: A Study of Harlequin Romances", *Signs*, 5(3).

Patterson, J.
    1981   "Consuming Passion", *Fireweed*, 11.

Propp, V.
    1968   *Morphology of the Folktale*. American Folklore Society.

Radway, J.
    1983   "Women Read the Romance: The Interaction of Text and Context", *Feminist Studies*, 9(1).
    1984   *Reading the Romance: Women, Patriarchy, and Popular Literature*. Chapel Hill: University of North Carolina Press.

GERALDINE FINN

THE SYMBOLISM
OF POWER:
HEGEMONIC SYSTEMS

Holiday Celebrations in Israeli Kindergartens: Relationships Between Representations of Collectivity and Family in the Nation-State

Lea Shamgar-Handelman and Don Handelman

Created, conveyed, and socially situated through cultural performance, ideological systems exercise enormous influence in human affairs. Ideology validates the social structure, legitimizes political authority, sanctifies ecclesiastical jurisdiction, and, above all, issues the myriad meanings that establish compatibility and mutual reinforcement between a society's particular brand of common sense and its deeper beliefs and values. The comprehensive and resilient influence of ideology leads to the concept of hegemony as used by Gramsci and others who have sought to explain the complex relationship between culture and power. Hegemonic theory addresses the issue of how dominant ideologies acquire, manifest, and maintain diffuse cultural significance, the quality that enables them to elicit broad and seemingly voluntary acceptance, even among those whose material and political interests are poorly served.

The study of childhood socialization—the means by which children are introduced to their culture and taught to accept its precepts and standards—is an important area in which anthropology has contributed to an understanding of ideological transmission. Lea and Don Handelman here examine the socialization process in Israel, focusing on kindergarten celebrations of religious and secular holidays. The Israeli case, they suggest, is particularly intriguing and crucial because the role of education has been "...less the replication of social order than the construction of an ideological blueprint that contributes to the very creation of the *state." In this regard the state of Israel is similar to other new nations faced with the need to develop ideological forms to express and enhance their identity, interests, and aspirations.*

Using as a point of departure the Manchester tradition of ceremonial analysis, the Handelmans examine both the content of kindergarten celebrations—what is said and done—and the overall form, which they term the "architectonics of enactment"—the dramaturgical principles of setting, style, and sequencing. They argue persuasively that these celebrations exalt the paramountcy of the state relative to other social entities to which children owe allegiance. The family, for example, is depicted as deriving its legitimacy from the state and remaining dependent on the state, not as a primary social unit with its own inherent justification. Even on the observance of Mother's Day, the role of the mother is subordinated to that of the teacher, who represents state authority. The authors conclude that symbolic socialization of this type facilitates the transition of children from the status of offspring to that of citizens—an observation which implies that kindergarten celebrations are the functional equivalent of rites of passage. These rites function to prepare children for the rigors of universal military service and other onerous demands that the Israeli state imposes on its adult citizens. In effect, the hegemony of state ideology owes its vitality to a process that begins in kindergarten.

THE OBJECT OF EDUCATION, contended Durkheim (1956: 71), "is to arouse and to develop in a child a certain number of physical, intellectual, and moral states which are demanded of him by...the political society as a whole." Mechanisms of education, he added, are among the major means through which "society perpetually recreates the conditions of its very existence" (1956: 123). Durkheim conjoined two themes that are salient for the modern Western nation-state. First, that the political economy of education, especially formal education, is a crucial expression of the ideology and authority of the state. Second, that the reproduction of social order depends, in no small measure, on the exercise of the power of education through the requisite apparatus of the state.

In the case of Israel the tasks of formal education were less the replication of social order than the construction of an ideological blueprint that contributed to the very creation of the state. The fusion of political ideology and formal organization, in order to in-fluence the maturation of youngsters who were the future generation of citizenry, began in the kindergarten.[1] For example, a veteran Jewish kindergarten teacher[2] reflected, as follows, on the intimate ties that developed between the Jewish community, the *yishuv*, in pre-state Palestine and the kindergarten system. These were bonds, she enunciated, between a form of early-age education and "the ideas and aspirations that lifted the spirits of those parts of the nation that rebuilt the ruins of its homeland and rejuvenated this." The Zionist dream of returning to work the land of Israel, she added, "brought the garden into the kindergarten" (Fayence-Glick 1957: 141). As in numerous other aspects of the nation-building of Israel, that of the kindergarten was linked very closely to the practice of proto-national ideology.

Very young children experience and learn the lineaments of personhood and world through the family arrangements into which they are born. In these contexts they are enculturated into a sense of hierarchy and status, of order and division of labor, of sentiment and loyalty, through notions of kinship and familism that come to be the natural ordering of things. Only later is the child made to realize that parental superordination is itself subordinate to the idea of a wider social order; and that on numerous occasions loyalty and obligation to the collectivity transcends that of familial ties. This transition, however obvious, is crucial to the reproduction of the social orders of the state.

Bluntly put, all children must learn that their parents are not the natural apex of hierarchy and authority; and that the rights of the collectivity can supercede those of the family. This is integral to the process of maturation in the nation-state. In present-day Israel the young child's entry into the kindergarten is the onset of extended periods in educational settings that are regulated and supervised by organs of the state. The youngster is moved slowly during this lengthy transition from his embeddedness within home and family until, at the age of 18, he enters the army for compulsory service. At this time he is given over wholly by his parents to the authority and service of the state. The transition is one from offspring to citizen.

With regard to this transition, kindergartens in Israel are of especial interest, since their annual round is punctuated by numerous ceremonial occasions that, on a wider scale, are of import to the religious and civic cultures of nation and state.

HOLIDAY CELEBRATIONS IN ISRAELI KINDERGARTENS

Anthropologists are very well aware that ceremonials, whether sacred or secular, are concentrated foci of the explicit and implicit, yet selective, production, display, and manipulation of symbolic forms and sentiments (Turner 1982; Manning 1983; Moore and Myerhoff 1977). During such occasions other themes and qualities of the everyday live-in world are held in abeyance (Handelman 1982, 1983, 1984). Whether an analysis stresses the semiotics of ceremonial structure (Geertz 1972), or the dramatistics of enactment (Turner 1974), the ritualism of ceremonialism is patterned to communicate in enhanced and pointed ways, regardless of the size or scope of the occasion.

Holiday celebrations in Israeli kindergartens are in keeping with these attributes of ceremonialism. Given the early ages of the young participants the messages of these celebrations, at least the explicit ones, are presented in quite clear-cut ways. Through such occasions children are involved, outside of their homes, in focused representations of culture that, in general, are considered to be of significance to aspects of the nation-state. On an explicit level many of these occasions celebrate versions of tradition and historicity of the Jewish people, and of the renewal and coherence of the Jewish state. Scenarios emphasize the joint effort, the consensus of cooperation, between kindergarten and parent, state and citizen, in order to inform the maturation of the child with experiences that begin to situate his personhood in relation to directives of the past and expectations of the future. On a more implicit level the "hidden agendas" of such scenarios unearth the more problematic relationship between state and family.[3] Thus numerous celebrations can be understood as versions of the relationship between representations of collectivity and family, through which youngsters are shown, and are encouraged to experience, that the superordination of the former supplants that of the latter.

Kindergarten and Celebration in Israel

The first kindergarten in Palestine was established in 1898, and it was intended as a preparatory class for elementary school. The language of instruction was German, translated into those of the pupils. The first Hebrew-speaking Zionist kindergarten was opened in 1911. Unlike its predecessors it was an autonomous unit for early-age education. In the context of Zionism this kindergarten, its successors, and local seminaries for kindergarten teachers, all freed Hebrew early-age education from the domination of foreign theories of pedagogy. These kindergartens gave especial attention to the cultivation of the Zionist spirit: for example, to the values of working the land and building the nation. (Faylance-Glick 1957: 141).

By 1919 there were thirty-three Jewish kindergartens in Palestine, with a total of 2,525 pupils. Some coordination of kindergarten policy and curricula was instituted during the period of the British Mandate, on the part of the educational department of the Zionist governing bodies of the *yishuv*. Nonetheless, the prevalent pattern was of a variety of kindergarten frameworks, Zionist and other, that were subsidized in part by numerous sources, and whose programs of instruction were supervised in varying degrees.

With statehood, in 1948, kindergarten education was centralized. The Law of Obligatory Education, promulgated in 1953, made kindergarten mandatory for children at age 5, and placed the supervision of kindergartens under the aegis of the national Ministry of Education. Numerous kindergarten classes were opened for children from the age of 2 and above. From the 1920s until the present the demand for places in kindergartens almost always exceeded those available. In 1982-83 some 250,000 children, between the ages of 2 and 5, were enrolled in 2,035 kindergartens. Of those aged 2, 63.6 percent were enrolled; while for those aged 3 and above the equivalent proportions were over 90 percent (*Statistical Abstract of Israel* 1983: 654).

Throughout the period of Zionist early-age education, teachers insisted that the kindergarten was to be used to inculcate the meaning of Zionist existence, and to teach somewhat vague notions of Israeli "culture," not only to children but also to their parents, many of whom were recent immigrants from diverse cultural backgrounds. The kindergarten was conceived of as an instrument of national purpose: one that would help to transform the child into an Israeli person different from that of his parents; moreover, a person who would re-enter the home to influence parents to alter their own attitudes toward the rearing of children.

Writing of the Mandatory period, Katerbursky (1962: 56), a veteran educator, stated: "The obligation of the kindergarten is to uproot bad habits that the children bring from home." This was attempted, for example, through parent-teacher meetings and through instructional sessions in preparation for holiday celebrations. Katerbursky (1962: 58) added: "We understand that the parents, especially the mothers, are still very distant from understanding many of the educational...[and] social problems of education; and we will have to educate them as well." When the occasion allowed, mothers were given instructions on how to behave towards their children, on correct attitudes towards the development of the child, on how leisure time with children should be spent, and on the kind of cooking that children would enjoy eating at home. Although such exercises were phrased in the idiom of mutual understanding between teachers and parents, it is clear that the former regarded these goals as integral to their pedagogical mandate. (Katerbursky 1962: 64).

These themes of inculcation hardly changed after statehood. If anything they intensified with mass immigration and a more centralized educational bureaucracy. Numerous books of instruction and advice for kindergarten teachers were published. These attest to differing perceptions over aims held by kindergarten and home, although these were ameliorated by the rhetoric of mutual cooperation disseminated by educators. We note again an emphasis on the need to educate parents as well as children (Rabinowitz 1958), and, for that matter, to enlist the youngsters as allies in this endeavor. For example, one educator put this forcefully: "Our influence on the surrounding can be great with the help of our faithful partners, the children, if only we will know how to inject into the home one common version of customs.... It is not the first time in the history of this country that the child fulfills an important role in educating the nation.... That is why we can hope that in the new assignment of the 'ingathering of the exiles' (*kibbutz galuyot*)...the child will fulfill his mission and will not disappoint us" (Zanbank-Wilf 1958: 57). Less direct but cognate sentiments are expressed in other such didactic manuals (Naftali and Nir-Yaniv 1974; Shemer 1966; Ministry of Education and Culture 1967).

In more recent instruction books the teacher is featured as a touchstone of tradition. Parents, however, have undergone the traumatic social and cultural dislocations of immigration that destroyed the traditional atmosphere of holidays in the Jewish home. The teacher also is a source of modernism: of the creation of new patterns of celebration through the borrowing of elements from different Jewish traditions, in order to bring the holiday anew, through children, to homes bereft of such ceremonial occasions (Rabinowitz 1958b). No matter how naive such attitudes appear to be, they reflect the cultural melting-pot notions of Zionism. These often emphasized that immigrants would have to begin again to build a tradition in common, in order to create a new Jewish personhood in the resurgent homeland (Ben-Yosef 1957).

Therefore serious thought is given to the planning of ceremonials in the kindergarten and instructional books offer various scenarios for their enactment (Rabinowitz 1958c). These are designed less to instruct didactically or to encourage reflection. Instead emphasis is placed on the arousal of emotion through symbolic forms that evoke collective sentiments. In general there is a profusion of what Langer (1953) called "presentational" symbolism: media that engage the senses more than the critical faculties of mind. Participants should experience enactments by living through their symbols, rather than as spectators. Instruction books note, for example, that the kindergarten child needs the emotional experience of a holiday, not a logical explanation or historical exposition. Ideally the celebration should be a "common experience" that "uplifts the spirit" and that encourages feelings of togetherness (Rabinowitz 1958a, 1958b).

In the views of kindergarten educators the arousal of such sentiments is induced if scenarios are well-designed, so that their enactment is left less to chance. The architectonics of celebration should be logical and holistic, with defined segments of opening, elaboration, and closing (Fayence-Glick 1948). Attention should be given to one or more major ideas or motifs, to scheduling in relation to calendrical cycles, to the sequencing and progression of the program, and to overt symbols. Often these symbols are both "living" and "lived through," such that the physical positioning of the participants itself creates symbolic formations. The symbol comes alive, and participants live through this both as a collectivity and as individuals. Such devices powerfully invoke a metonymy between motifs of celebration and their being experienced, and a synecdoche in which each part of the collective entity replicates and signifies the coherence and unity of the whole.

Kindergarten Celebrations

The occasions to be discussed are representative of the range of Jewish holidays celebrated in Israel, in terms of their traditional or modern roots. Given the paucity of information available on kindergarten celebrations, we prefer to inform the reader with a sense of the variation among such occasions, rather than to limit our focus to one or two categories of holiday. The first two of our cases, Hannukah and Purim, are traditional holidays, but not holy Days of Rest. Both commemorate victories: Hannukah of the Maccabees and of the rededication of the Temple in Jerusalem, and Purim the saving of the Jews of Persia through the influence of Queen Esther. Both are celebrated, in varying degrees in home and synagogue, and Purim also in the street. Our analysis of a Hannukah celebration demonstrates the implicit manipulation of hierarchy, such that the family unit is shown to be encompassed by the collectivity. The case of Purim that we discuss brings out an implicit assumption that the maturation of children moves them from a condition closer to nature to one of civilization, and so toward their assumption of citizenship in the future. The third case, Mother's Day, is borrowed from modern Western popular culture, and is a wholly secular occasion of no official standing. The implications of our case suggest that it is the collectivity that mandates the legitimacy of the family unit, and not the reverse which is closer to the viewpoint of the family. The fourth case, Jerusalem Day, is a secular state commemoration of the reunification of Jerusalem following the 1967 Six-Day War. Our analysis of this case points to the symbolic forging of direct links between the collectivity and the child as future citizen, without the mediation of the family. All of these cases offer implicit versions of hierarchical relationships between collectivity and family that should reverse the early-age experiences of the child. However, we stress here that, in the first few years of education, youngsters experience dozens of such celebrations. Explicit themes, contents, and organization vary within and among kinds of celebrations. Yet the types of implicit relationships between collectivity and family that emerge from our cases likely have a cachet of relevance that extends to numerous other kindergarten celebrations. For the child, it is the cumulative ac-

LEA & DON HANDELMAN

cretion of such experiences that has enculturative impact.

All the celebrations described took place on the kindergarten premises (although others, not discussed here, sometimes were taken outside). The kindergarten is defined as "the child's world," and the only adult that has a legitimate place within it is the teacher—the representative of the collectivity. Parents (and other adults) always are only guests in the kindergarten. Nothing better symbolizes this attitude than the chairs in the kindergarten. In all kindergartens visited, no more than one or two full-size chairs were found. That is to say, as a rule, the teacher sits in a full-size chair and, "at her feet," as it were, the children on small chairs. When parents are invited to the kindergarten, be it to a celebration, to a parent-teacher meeting or to their child's birthday party, they always are seated on children's chairs. Thus a parent in the kindergarten always occupies a child's place.

Prior to the celebrations, the children were given explanations in their respective kindergartens with regard to the character of the holiday concerned, its significance for the people of Israel or for the children themselves (as in Mother's Day), its dominant symbols, and some rudimentary historical background. Where the celebration involved more complicated enactments by the children, these were rehearsed beforehand. All the actions that took place in these celebrations were in accordance with the explicit instructions and orchestration of the teacher, unless otherwise specified.

Hannukah: Hierarchy, Family, and Collectivity

Hannukah, the Festival of Lights, commemorates the victory of the Maccabees over the Seleucids, and their rededication of the Temple in 165 B.C. According to the *Talmud*, in the Temple there was only enough undefiled oil for one day of lamp-lighting. Miraculously the oil multiplied into a supply sufficient for eight days. Hannukah is celebrated for eight consecutive days in the home, primarily by the lighting of an additional candle each day, in an eight-branched candelabrum, the *hannukiah* (pl. hannukiot). An extra candle, the *shamash*, is used to kindle the others. Hannukah celebrates liberation from foreign domination: it is a triumph of faith, of the few over the many, of the weak over the strong. In present-day Israel the martial spirit of this holiday casts reflections on the struggle of the Jewish people to create a unified homeland.

Books of instruction suggest that the major motif be heroism in Israel. The enactment should evoke the emotional experience of the occasion. The central symbols of the celebration should be the hannukiah, candles, tops,[4] and, according to some, the national flag. The locale of the party should be filled with light, just as the shirts or blouses of the children should be white, to create an atmosphere of joyous luminosity. The best time is late afternoon or early evening, for these hours evoke the uplifting illumination of the holiday from the midst of darkness and the depths of despair; and they connect the kindergarten to the home, where candles may be lit soon after. Scenarios suggest that a central hannukiah be lit by an adult; that the parents light the small hannukiot made by their children; that the children form "living hannukiot"; and that parents and children dance or play games together (Rabinowitz 1958c). Certain of these elements were incorporated into the example described below.[5]

Description. The party began at 4:30 P.M. Thirty-two children, aged 4 to 5, and their mothers sat at tables placed along three walls of the room. Only a few fathers attended. A name-card marked the place of each child. The tables were covered by white tablecloths. At the center of each were a vase of flowers, bags of candies, and candles equal to the number of youngsters at that table. Before each child stood a little hannukiah made by that youngster. On the walls and windows were hung painted paper hannukiot, oil pitchers, candles, and tops, all of which had been prepared in the kindergarten. Against the fourth wall was a large hannukiah, constructed of toy blocks covered with colored paper, which supported eight colored candles and the shamash.

An accordionist played melodies of the holiday, and the mothers joined in singing and in clapping. The teacher welcomed all those present and, at a prearranged signal, her helper extinguished the lights. Each mother lit a candle and aided her child to kindle his own little hannukiah. The room lights were turned on. A father lit the large hannukiah of toy blocks, and recited the requisite prayers. As he did so, the teacher told the children: "Remember, when father says a blessing, you must sit quietly and listen to the blessing." More holiday songs followed.

LEA & DON HANDELMAN

The teacher announced: "Now we want to make a living hannukiah. A living hannukiah that walks and sings, a hannukiah of parents and children." She arranged the mothers and their children in a straight line, so that each child stood in front of his mother. An additional mother-child pair, the shamash, stood some feet to the side. Each mother held a candle, and each youngster a blue or white ribbon. Each child gave one end of his ribbon to the child-shamash. In this formation all children were attached to the shamash by their ribbons, and each mother to her own child. The mother of the shamash lit the candles held by the others. The lights were extinguished, the room lit by the living hannukiah in the gathering darkness of late afternoon. The accordionist played a melody of the holiday, "We came to chase away the darkness," as each mother walked around her child. The lights were turned on. The mothers returned to their seats as a group, followed by their children.

The children and mothers of one table returned to the center of the room and were told by the teacher: "The children will be the spinning tops. Get down, children." They fell to their knees, bent their heads, and curled their bodies forward. Each mother stood behind her child. The teacher declared: "The whole year the spinning tops were asleep in their box. From last year until this year, until now. And the children said to them, 'Wake up, spinning tops. Hannukah has come. We want to play with you.'" To a background of holiday melodies the teacher moved from child to child, touching their hand. With each contact a child awakened, stood up, raised his arms, and began to spin. Each mother spun her child, first clockwise, then counterclockwise. Next the mothers became the tops, spun by their children in one direction and then the other. The teacher told the second table: "You'll also be spinning tops. Each mother will spin her own child and when I give the signal, change roles. Alright? Let's start.... The children are the spinning tops...the parents are the spinning tops." Those at the third table followed.

Mothers and children held hands, formed an unbroken circle, and danced round and round the teacher. Only one father joined the circle. More singing, and food, followed. As 6 P.M. approached, the teacher gave the participants permission to leave; and the party broke up.

Discussion. This ceremonial is composed of three major segments, the overt symbolism of which is quite explicit. The first focuses on the serious traditionalism of the holidays, primarily through the emblem of the hannukiah. This segment brings out the connectivity between past and present. The second works through the make-believe of the spinning top, and evokes the relationship between present and future.

The initial segment proceeds through a series of candle-lightings: mother helps her child to kindle the small hannukiah, father lights the large hannukiah, and the candles are lit on the living hannukiah. These actions and others are embedded in the melodies and songs of the holiday that tell of heroism, victory, and the illumination of darkness. These themes weave together emotion and experience to carry the past into the present. The blue and white ribbons of the living hannukiah are the official colors of the modern state, and of its flag. In the living hannukiah ancient triumph is fused with modern renaissance. Collectivity is dedicated to temple, temple to collectivity.

Here the idea of family is central. The enactment replicates symbolic acts—the kindling of candles and prayers—that should take place within the home, and that delineate familial roles and an elementary division of labor. Thus it is apt for mother to help her small child, in this instance to light the hannukiah. Moreover, it is appropriate for father, the male head of household, to recite the prayers that accompany this act, on behalf of the family. Here one father does this on behalf of the assembly. The symbolism of this enactment then transcends the level of the family. The "living hannukiah" encompasses all of the mothers and children, while respecting the singularity of individual families, represented here by the dyads of mother and child. Each mother stands behind her child and walks around and encompasses the latter, delineating the family unit. This living hannukiah is a collective symbol that also is a symbol of collectivity, while this collectivity itself is constituted of smaller family units.

The living hannukiah projects into the present the significance of past heroism and dedication. This is done through the living bodies of mothers and children, who themselves compose the shape and the significata of this central symbol. Thus the collectivity is presented as living through family units, just as the latter live within and through the former. Each is made to be seen as integral to the other. However the connotation is that the collectivity is of a higher order than the individual family, since here it encompasses the latter.

In contrast to the seriousness of the first segment, the second is playful. Its motif is the top, a child's holiday toy that itself is inscribed with Hebrew letters that denote the miraculous—the multiplication of oil, and perhaps the victory itself. But in this segment commemoration and tradition are not marked. Instead the make-believe is evoked, slumber is shattered, and the participants act joyously in the holiday mood. Again the focus is that of the family unit, represented by dyads of mother and child. The hierarchy at the close of the first segment is kept. The teacher activates each child, and the latter performs under the direction of mother.

But in this make-believe segment, mother and child reverse roles: the former becomes the sleeping top that is awakened and directed by her child. Unlike the inscription of tradition in the first segment, the playful is full of potential, as is the youngster who eventually will exchange the role of child for that of adult. As a mature adult the child will become a parent, bringing into being and controlling children of his own. This segment projects the child, as parent-to-be, towards a future in which he will replace his parents and will replicate their roles and tasks. Through the two segments past and future are joined together with a sense of the movement of generations. Whereas the first segment recreates family and collectivity in the images of tradition, of the enduring past, the second segment demonstrates the transitoriness of particular parents and the direction of succession. For the child the experience may evoke some feeling that his own parents are not timeless monoliths that will continue to structure his world indefinitely.

The second segment closes and the third starts with an unbroken circle dance of mothers and children who revolve about the axis of the teacher.[6] This formation is a restatement of the relationship between family and collectivity. The circle dance, however, blurs the distinctiveness of particular families and, within these, of parents and children, adults and youngsters. The delineation of family units has disappeared. Instead, all are closer to being discrete and egalitarian individuals who themselves are part of a greater and embracing collectivity. This formation connotes the connectivity of present and future citizens, and their orientation towards an axial center.

In this and in other kindergarten celebrations the teacher is the sole arbiter and the ultimate authority. She is seen by children to control parental figures before their very eyes. We argue that the teacher is a statist figure, perhaps the earliest representation of authority outside the home that very young children encounter. In these celebrations she is not an alternative source of authority to that of parents, as she may be perceived by children in the daily life of the kindergarten. Instead she is the pinnacle of hierarchy that supercedes and that subsumes the family. Thus the whole enactment is framed by the architectonics of hierarchy that are external to, but that act upon, the family unit. All actions of such celebrations, regardless of their explicit content, are embued with this quality of hierarchy.

The implicit messages of this Hannukah celebration are about hierarchy from a more statist perspective. The first segment constructs a version of the superordination of roles within the family, and then embeds the latter within a version of collectivity. The second deconstructs the centrality of family status and transforms hierarchical relationships among family members. The third emphasizes equality among citizens, all of whom are oriented towards the statist figure of the teacher.

In the first segment the child is dependent upon, and subordinate to, his mother in order to light the little hannukiah. In turn, both of them are dependent upon the figure of the father in order to light the large hannukiah and to recite prayers on behalf of the whole family. This series is an accurate rendition of the comparative status of elementary roles within the family. Family units then are made to constitute a symbol of the collectivity, the living hannukiah. The collectivity is seen to exist as a coordinated assemblage of families. Here individual families are dependent upon and are subordinate to the collectivity in order to relate to one another, and in order to create an alive and enduring vision of tradition and belief. The first segment builds up the symbol of the hannukiah in increasing degrees of encompassment and hierarchy. The apex is the living of this collective emblem. Integral to this are the ribbons, in the national colors, held by the children. Thus the hannukiah itself is embued with the symbolism of statehood, while implicit in this more traditional collective emblem is a more modern version.

The second segment begins with an expression of hierarchical family roles. The dyad of mother and child delineates the coherence of the family unit. The mother directs the movements of the spinning top, her child, in an accurate depiction of status and authority in relation to her offspring. But their reversal of roles is, at one and the same time, a representation of independence and of equality. The autonomy of children, and their founding of families, is expected to be an outcome of maturation. Through this process children partially are freed of their subordination to their family of procreation, and thereby are inculcated in their obligations of citizenship to the nation-state. As citizens, all Israelis are the theoretical equals of one another and are subordinate to the state without the intervening mediation of the family. In the third segment, the circle dance, there is no characterization of the family unit: the unbroken circle evokes egalitarianism and common effort and all the dancers are oriented towards their common center. Orchestrating their actions stands the teacher, just as the state stands in relation to its citizens.

Like the hannukiah alive, the circle dance is a living collective symbol. But each is in structural opposition to the other. The hannukiah depends on the family and on its internal hierarchy for its existence. The circle dance eliminates the specificity of the family unit and simultaneously relates each participant in equality to all others and to a statist apex of hierarchy that is not representative of family. In the sequencing of this celebration the unbroken circle with its apical center supplants the cellular hannukiah, just as, for children, with time the state will supercede their parents as the pinnacle of authority.

Purim: The Evolution of Maturity

Purim commemorates the deliverance of the Jews of Persia from the evil designs of their enemies through the persuasions of Esther, the Jewish queen of the Persian monarch. This story is read in the synagogue and the holiday is celebrated by a festive family meal, and by the exchange of gifts of food among relatives and friends. An especially joyous holiday, it is the only time in the ritual calendar when some license in dress and behavior is encouraged. Secular celebrations take the form of dressing up in costume and attending parties.

Instruction books designate the holiday as an entertainment, with children in costume and parents in attendance. Little mention is made of the traditional significance of the holiday and scenarios for its celebration rarely are given. It is left to the teacher to decide on the measure of organization desired. The example we discuss is in keeping with such advice. Its explicit enactment is intended to entertain and to amuse the youngsters and their mothers. However, in this there is a degree of implicit patterning that connotes the role of the kindergarten in the maturation of children. Of this the teacher denied any conscious knowledge.

Description. This celebration was held for three year-olds. Some two weeks prior, at a meeting of mothers and teacher, the teacher requested that the children be dressed in animal costumes. Her reason was that such figures were closest to the world of the child, and therefore more comprehensible to the youngsters. If this were not possible, then the child should be dressed as a clown. A few days before the party each mother informed the teacher of the costume her child would wear, so that the teacher could prepare her program.

The party took place in the late afternoon, at the onset of the holiday. Mothers and children were arranged in a wide semi-circle, facing an open area where the teacher stood. Mothers sat on the tiny kindergarten chairs, their offspring on the floor before them. Music of the holiday played in the background.

The celebration consisted of two loosely articulated segments, separated by an intermediate segment of an unbroken circle dance. In the first the children showed their costumes before the assembly in a set order of presentation. In the second, five mothers who were dressed as clowns performed a rehearsed dance and song. The teacher, dressed as a clown, organized the presentation of costumes in terms of a simple narrative. Many years ago, she said, there was a king, and she called out a boy dressed as a king. He was joined by a girl dressed as a queen. In their court, continued the teacher, there was a zoo full of animals. She called out the inhabitants of the zoo. As each kind of character came forward a song that described its typical movements or activities was sung. The following was the order of appearance. Five cats walked on all fours and meowed. Then three rabbits hopped out. A bear fiercely lumbered forth and was introduced as a "teddy-bear." Three dainty dolls came forward and were described as living in cardboard boxes. All of these dwelled in the royal zoo. The teacher told a soldier, a policeman, and a cowboy to come out, introduced them as the "royal guard," and marched with them around the semi-circle. This ended the narrative of the zoo within the royal court. The remaining children, all dressed as clowns, were called forth. After this, all the mothers and children formed an unbroken circle, with the teacher in the center, and danced to the melody of a song about a little clown.

The teacher announced that the performance of the children had ended. She requested the performing mothers to sing. Each of their costumes was of a single color, and their song described the activities of clowns dressed in each of these colors. They sang in a line, with the teacher at their head. Food followed, and the party ended.

Discussion. Unlike the previous Hannukah celebration, this one of Purim was not considered to have any coherent scenario or explicit significance. The intention was to have fun and to give the youngsters the opportunity to play make-believe characters. The teacher had hoped that all of these characters would be animals—in her view, close to the world of the child. Faced with a mixed bag of costumes, she used a simple narrative to order their appearance. On a more implicit level this ordering is of direct relevance to our contention that kindergarten celebrations, in various ways, are engaged in the symbolic representation of rudimentary socialization, in the direction of adulthood and citizenship.

The teacher recasts the kindergarten as the court of a king and queen. This role-play is in keeping with the story of Purim, of Queen Esther and her Persian monarch. But from this point on there are no further connotations of the text of the holiday. Nonetheless, monarchy and court are emblematic of hierarchy, or moral order, and of social control. In short, these are symbols of maturity and of statehood that exist above and beyond those of home and family. A zoo is situated within the court and is filled with characters. In Israel, zoos are institutions where wild animals, instinctive and unconstrained in their nature, are locked in cages, artifacts of civilization that place external restraints on these creatures. This is a popular view of the zoo. In the teacher's view small children are close to the world of animals and so are driven by their instincts and are not governed by the obligations of maturity and by the norms of civilization. In the enactment, children-as-animals are placed in a zoo, itself within a court. Through these metaphors the kindergarten is represented, on the one hand, as a locale of moral order with connotations of ultimate authority and so of statehood, and on the other as a place of confinement for those who have yet to learn internal restraint.

The order of appearance of the inhabitants of the zoo suggests strongly that the more "natural" state of youngsters is conditional. Their sequencing projects a developmental image of enculturation, of moving towards maturity within metaphors of hierarchy and control. The first animal to appear is the cat. Although cats in Israel are sometimes pets, the cities of the country are pervaded by a profusion of alley cats that are undomesticated, fierce, and wary of humans. Even as a pet the cat is a comparatively independent and autonomous creature. These are the primary stereotypes of the cat in Israel. In her narrative the teacher describes the children-as-cats as "looking for friends." That is, these make-believe cats desire to establish relationships, with the connotation of becoming more domesticated through sociation.

The next is the rabbit. In Israel this creature usually is found in the wild, and sometimes as a pet. In either case it is thought of as a timid, passive, and docile creature—a vegetarian in contrast to the more predatory cat. Although wild, the rabbit is more easily caged and controllable than is the cat. The rabbit is followed by a child dressed as a bear. However enthusiastically he plays this gruff bear, the teacher turns this wild and fierce creature into a "teddy-bear." Unlike cat and rabbit, the teddy-bear is a child's plaything. As a toy it is the human product of its natural counterpart—that is, a copy. Its animalism is man-made. A product of culture, it is a fully-controlled and domesticated creation, in contrast to cat and rabbit. Still, the teddy-bear retains its animal form.

The doll appears next. This is again a child's plaything and is man-made. Yet, unlike the teddy-bear, it is created in a human image, and its attributes of behavior are largely those of a person. According to the narrative the doll lives in a cardboard box, its own enclosure that is somewhat more akin to a home than is a cage. Where the teddy-bear is a play upon nature, the doll is a reflection of humanity and civilization. Of all the zoo creatures to appear, the doll is the most domesticated and restrained. These controls are

LEA & DON HANDELMAN

inherent in, and emerge from, its human form and its attributes of culture. They are not a shell of strictures imposed from without, as in the case of cat and rabbit, nor an intermediate being, a domesticated animal, like the teddy-bear.

Left with a soldier, a policeman, and a cowboy, the teacher organizes them into a "royal guard." These are not inhabitants of the zoo, but stand outside it, and close and complete the framework of social control introduced by the royal figures. Like the latter the royal guards are fully human figures whose roles embody a regimentation of maturity and order. They are guardians of moral codes against the predations of more impulsive natural beings. Such associations are reinforced as the teacher takes these guardians by the arm and they march together. As she had not done with those within the zoo, the teacher identifies herself with children who, by being given roles of control and order, play themselves as they should become in the future—as mature adults.

Wittingly or not, the teacher has brought into being a small drama about the evolution and the enculturation of humanity and hierarchy that leads to maturity and the assumption of responsibility beyond that of the familial. Framed at the outset and at the close by human figures with statist and hierarchical connotations, the characters of the zoo are transposed from the wild to the tame, from creatures of instinct to artifacts of culture. Just as their mothers watch this encoding from the periphery, these youngsters see their mothers watching this happen to them. The children experience a brief metaphor of how they are perceived to be by the teacher and of what they are expected to become.

The figure of the clown was intended by the teacher as a fallback costume for the children. Clowns were not included in court and zoo, but were presented afterward. On the face of it, these residual figures have no logical connection to prior actions in the sequence, nor to those that followed. In overt terms these clowns, like those of the clown-stereotypes that they copy, are simply unabashed figures of fun that are in keeping with the good humor of this holiday. Nonetheless, the deeper structure of the clown type likely makes these figures the most complex of the celebration. (Willeford 1969).

These clown costumes, like those of numerous clown stereotypes, are composed of variegated elements that do not compose any simple pattern of symmetry and homogeneity, as do the other costumes. The elements of these clown costumes are without gender; they contrast with one another to a degree; and so, in theory, this kind of configuration should encourage an attitude of reflection toward the complexity of the overall composition. The clown is a human figure, but it is an experimental one that is constructed more self-consciously. In other words, the clown figure plays with potentials, and with the axiomatic and the taken-for-granted in human existence (Willeford 1969; Handelman 1980). Ironically, clowns are more figures of maturity than are authoritarian monarchs and regimented guards. The maturity of the clown is, in part, related to a freedom of action that accrues when self-discipline is more assured; and when one is well-aware that one is not that which one plays at. This is the maturity of adulthood, of the teacher and the performing mothers, all of whom are dressed as clowns. In our view, the appearance of the clowns, following on the characters of court and zoo, represents the completion of maturation. In a way, it signifies a reward that maturation carries with it—the freedom of action.

The appearance of the child-clowns is followed by a circle dance of all mothers and children. As noted, the connotations of this formation are of collectivity, egalitarianism, and joint effort. But there is no delineation here of the family unit, nor of the special bond between mother and child. Thus the teacher reunites the children with persons who first and foremost are adults, rather than mothers, after these little people have been represented as trained and developed in an idiom of social order. This process is validated in the second segment of the celebration. The teacher and clown-mothers perform a dance and song. The figure of the clown appears here as the apex of authority and maturity, with the teacher at its pinnacle. On this note the celebration ends.

In our view the entire enactment is an extended metaphor of a process of maturation that the child will undergo in order to turn into an adult member of a wider collectivity. The children are presented, through court and zoo, in different stages of development. These characters are superceded by the more complex figures of the child-clowns. The character of the clown, with its connotations of freedom tempered by self-discipline, is used to free all the children to rejoin the adults in an egalitarian circle dance. Thus the enactment is projected towards a future in which youngsters take their place of equality alongside their parents. The child-clowns also bridge the two segments. They share their figuration with teacher and performing mothers. The child-clowns blend fairly easily into the figures of the clown-mothers, who are adults indeed, and with that of the teacher-as-clown who here is at the apex of childhood.

Mother's Day: The Creation of Family and Intimacy

This party was celebrated together by some forty children aged 3, 4, and 5, who belonged to three separate classes of the same kindergarten. The explicit aim of the teacher was to have the youngsters demonstrate their love and respect for their mothers. This included the giving of gifts by the child to his mother. However the sequencing of enactment conveys a more implicit pattern: that it is the collectivity, represented through the teacher, that brings into being the affective bonds of the mother-child relationship.

Description. During the prior week each child prepared a present for his mother: a piece of shaped dough, decorated, baked, and lacquered. A small hole allowed this to be hung on string, like a pendant. Each gift was wrapped, together with a greeting card. On the morning of the celebration vases of flowers were placed on tables, as well as an additional flower intended for each mother. The children arrived at the usual early hour; their mothers were invited for midmorning. The small kindergarten chairs were arranged in a large unbroken circle. An accordionist provided music.

Each mother was seated, with her child before her on a cushion. The teacher stood in the center of the circle. From the outset she instructed the children on how to greet and to behave towards their mothers. "Come children," she cried, "let's say a big 'hello' to mother! Let's give mother a big hug! Let's sing together, 'What a Happy Day is Mother's Day'." After the singing each child was handed a flower. They sang together, "A Fine Bouquet of Flowers for Mother." "Give the flower to mother," said the teacher, "and give kisses to mother." Each child turned, gave his mother the flower, and kissed her.

The mothers stood and were arranged in pairs. Each pair faced one another and together held their two flowers. The children

formed a large circle and, holding hands, walked around all the pairs
of mothers and sang. Mothers and children sat and sang together.
The teacher said a few words to the youngsters on the importance
of being nice to mother. The children stood, faced their mothers,
and sang: "Let's bless Mother, blessings for Mother's Day. Be happy
in your life, for the coming year. Arise and reach 120 years."[7] The
teacher instructed: "Give mother a big hug and sing, 'My dear
mother loves only me, yes only me, yes only me'." After they had
done so, she added: "Now smile at mother."

The mothers closed their eyes and each child gave his mother
the present made especially for her; and according to instruction,
gave her "a very warm kiss." The children sang together, while the
mothers hung the pendants around their necks. Each mother and
child formed pairs and danced and sang together. The lyrics concerned physical coordination of the "look up, look down" variety.
The teacher enunciated the lyrics, so that they became instructions
for movement that were followed with accuracy. All returned to
their places. Since the day was Friday, said the teacher, she and the
children were going to teach the mothers a song with which to welcome the Sabbath. After this singing the teacher announced that
the "ceremony" was completed.

One mother stood and declared: "We want to say that it's true
that we're the children's mothers. But we want to thank and to give
a present to the real mother of the children while they're in the
kindergarten. We want to give her this bouquet of flowers." A
youngster was given the bouquet and presented it to the teacher,
while the mothers applauded. Snacks were offered by the teacher,
and the party closed.

Discussion. The explicit scenario of this celebration is clear.
The children show their affection for their mothers in order to
honor them. These qualities of emotional closeness are expressed
through various media: song, dance, gifts, and numerous tactile gestures. According to the teacher the use of different media was intended to declare emphatically the strength and the vitality of the
mother-child bond. The sequencing of these numerous acts was not
meant to convey an implicit significance. Instead their purpose was
to lengthen the celebration, and so to give the children many opportunities to demonstrate their appreciation.

In our view there is a more implicit patterning in this sequence:

one that projects the creation of the familial bond out of collective formations, under the supervision of the teacher. The major social formation consists of an outer circle of mothers, an inner circle of children, and the teacher in the center. Each concentric circle constitutes a category of person—that is, mother and child. The child is situated between mother and teacher. Although each child is placed close to his mother, the affective expression of this dyad is orchestrated wholly by the teacher.

The initial stress in the ceremony is on the delineation of the social category of motherhood. Mother first is welcomed as something of a "stranger," and the youngsters are told exactly how to show affection towards her. ("Let's say a big 'hello' to mother! Let's give mother a big hug!"). Such instruction may well be necessary to coordinate the actions of participants, especially when half of them are little children. Yet such directives also impress that an acquaintanceship is being formulated, that the category of children is being introduced to that of mother. It is as if, within the kindergarten, the abstract category of mother is being made real for that of the child. The intimate affection of the mother-child bond, one that precedes the kindergarten experience, is re-presented here as the creation of the teacher.

The first gift follows: a flower given to the child by the teacher, that he in turn presents to his mother. This gift is standardized for all of the mothers. Like gifts generally, its symbolic value establishes a relationship. Of common worth, this gift forges the same kind of relationship between each child and each mother. This rather impersonal gift serves to mediate into existence the category of mother and to articulate it to that of the child. This gift accords motherhood to each woman, through the proof of her status—her child who is the giver of the gift. In contrast to the developmental cycle of the family, here it is the alliance of teacher and child that forms and activates the category of motherhood. But the source of the gift is the statist figure of the teacher, and so the category of mother, and its articulation to that of the child, is shaped at her behest.

Subsequent actions support this line of interpretation. After the first gift the seamless circle of seated mothers is fragmented. The mothers forms pairs: each couple holds jointly their gifts of flowers, and is connected through these. In other words, through the medium of the gift each mother is transposed: from being a member within the category of mother to becoming individuated, a person and a mother in her own right. As such she represents the motherhood and the nurturance of a family unit. Moreover, connections between families as discrete entities are delineated, as mothers jointly clasp their gifts. Yet these particular families still are denied children of their own. The youngsters are kept in their categorical formation that encircles these mothers. This implies that, from a more collectivist perspective, personhood develops within categorical boundaries: that, first and foremost, people are members of social categories, and only then are they accorded the status of persons with their own unique attributes.

The participants resume their original formation. The children stand as a category, face the mothers, and sing their blessings. They then sing, "My dear mother loves only me, yes, only me, yes, only me." This act marks the beginning of a transposition whereby each child is told to recognize the especially intimate and affective bond between himself and his mother. This shift is realized through the personalized gift that each child had prepared especially for his mother. This second gift mediates the creation of a unique relationship between a particular youngster and mother. Just as previously the mother was accorded personhood in her own right, so now is her child. The category of child is fragmented; mother and child are united, and the family unit is delineated.

This intimate bond is represented further as the concentric formation breaks up, and as each mother and child form pairs and dance and sing together. Each pair, like each family, is a separate and distinct entity. However its unity depends on the teacher, who tells each pair exactly how to coordinate their movements in unison. The special bond that is crucial to the existence and to the reproduction of the family is under her control. This is emphasized as teacher and children teach the mothers a song with which to welcome the Sabbath. The ceremony to welcome the Sabbath within the home, on behalf of family and household, is exclusively the domain of the wife and mother. Her expertise, should she do this rite, likely is garnered from sacred texts and from having watched her own mother. No external intervention is required. Here she is treated as if she were ignorant of one of the essential ritual elements that maintain the integrity of the traditional home. Instead it becomes incumbent on a representation of collectivity in alliance with its wards, the children, to impart such knowledge to mother and home.

From the perspective of family and home the implicit patterning of the whole ceremony recasts and reverses the normal progression of the domestic cycle for it is the collectivity that creates the family. The usual view of parents, and the one that the little child first experiences, is that in the beginning there is the family; that into this nexus the child is born and within it matures; and that with time he leaves and establishes his own home. But here the progression is as follows: first the collectivity exists and is composed of social categories of people. Links are forged between the categories, and from these there emerge discrete social units, or families. These are accorded the right to bear and to raise children; and from this there emerges the special bond between mother and child. In this process the rights of, and obligations to, the collectivity are shown to be paramount.

Jerusalem Day: Statehood and Citizenship

After the 1967 Six-Day War, Jerusalem Day was promulgated as a civil state holiday to commemorate the reunification of the capital of Israel. It is celebrated primarily through official receptions and other functions, which include a festive mass march around the environs of the city. The major thoroughfares are decorated with the national flag and with the banner of Jerusalem, a golden lion (the emblem of the ancient kingdom of Judah) rampant on a white background with blue borders. Jerusalem is the central place of the Jewish nation and state. The city was divided, from 1948 until 1967, into western and eastern sectors, the former within Israel and the latter controlled by Jordan. Within the eastern sector is Mount Moriah, the Temple Mount, the site of the first temple built by Solomon, and of the second, destroyed by the Romans in 70 A.D. This defeat spelled the onset of the Diaspora, the widespread dispersion of the Jews into exile from ancient Israel.

Circumventing part of the western and all of the southern borders of the Mount are walls that survived the Roman sack. These remnants of the outer ramparts of the second temple complex are all that was left of that edifice most sacred to Judaism. A short stretch of the western rampart is called the Wailing Wall, but is

known in Israel as the Western Wall. For reasons overly complicated to discuss here, the Western Wall, long a site of worship, has
become since 1967 the most significant symbol of the State and of
Judaism. The Wall has become evocative of a nation whose flores-
cence as a state awaited the return of its people. It is symbolic of
a continuity that is perceived to have endured throughout the absence of Jewish sovereignty for close to 2000 years. Therefore it
connects and condenses, as does no other physical presence in
modern Israel, the glory and then the desuetude of the past and
the national redemption of the present. We raise these points because much of the symbolism of this kindergarten celebration is
focused on the Western Wall.

Description. Three classes of 3, 4, and 5 year-olds, totalling
some sixty youngsters who belonged to the same kindergarten, par-
ticipated. The celebration took place in the open courtyard of the
kindergarten on the morning of Jerusalem Day. Parents were not
invited. The courtyard was decorated with national flags and with
cut-outs of the lion of Jerusalem. Most of the children were dressed,
as asked to, in blue and white clothing. Each was given a small lapel
pin that depicted the lion. Each class was seated along one side of
the courtyard, with the teacher in the center and an accordionist
nearby.

The ceremony opened with songs whose respective themes
were: the ancient kingdom of Israel, rejoicing in Jerusalem, and the
re-building of the temple. In a brief peroration the teacher declared
that Jerusalem was and always would be the capital of Israel; that
this day marked the liberation of East Jerusalem and the reunification of the city by the Israel Defence Forces; and that this day was
celebrated by everyone throughout the country.

The teacher told a story taken from a booklet of legends about
Jerusalem. The narrative spoke of a lonely wall, dark with age, and
laden with the memories of the great temple, and of the free nation
that dwelled here. Enemies burned the temple and drove out the
Jews. They tried to destroy the wall, but their tools broke. The gentiles used the wall as a rubbish heap in order to obviate its presence.
For centuries, in their hatred of the Jews, they dumped their garbage about the wall, until it disappeared from sight.

One day a diaspora Jew came to see the wall, but all denied its
existence. He came to a great mound of rubbish and there learned

of the custom of obliterating the Jewish wall. He swore to save it.
A rumor spread that precious metals were buried there. The
populace swarmed to sift through the garbage, found some coins of
value, and uncovered the top stones. Happy, the Jew kissed the
wall. The next morning another rumor spread that treasure was
buried at its base. People excavated the rubbish and gradually the
whole of the wall was revealed. No treasure was found except for
that of the Jew—the Wall itself. Yet the Wall still was filthy; but a
miracle occurred. Clouds gathered and rain poured, cleansing and
purifying the Wall. And the Jew gave thanks for this salvation.

Dancing, and carrying toy blocks, the 3 year-olds built a wall of
roughly their own height. The other youngsters formed a circle, held
hands, and revolved singing and dancing around this model. With
this the celebration ended.

Discussion. Unlike the previous three celebrations, in this one
no reference is made to the family, nor for that matter to any social
units that may mediate between nation-state and citizen. Their
relationship is direct, immediate, and hierarchical. Here the family
unit of the child not only is superceded but is rendered irrelevant
to the nation-state. The nation is presented as the redeemer of the
state, and the state as the protector of the nation. Both depend on
the faith and loyalty of the citizenry.[8]

The courtyard is decorated in emblems of statehood and it acquires the semblance of an official locale. The outfits of the
youngsters are standardized through colors that shape these
children into living emblems of the state. Thus their bodies are inscribed with signs of citizenship, of belonging to the collectivity.
Each child appears as a small part that embodies the greater whole,
itself composed of many such components. In other words, the ideal
relationship between citizen and collectivity is one of synecdoche.
This relationship is not manipulated during the ceremony, but is
repeated in various ways.

The opening songs lay out the connectivity of the past, present,
and future; although the words of each have in common references
to verities that are held eternal. The first is about King David, who
made Jerusalem the capital of ancient Israel. The second rejoices
in Jerusalem eternal. The third tells that the temple, a metaphor of
the nation in its reborn homeland, will be rebuilt. The words of the
teacher situate these sentiments within the reality of present-day

Israel. The assembly celebrates the reunification of the eternal capital of the nation-state, as do all of its citizenry on this day. Moreover this deed was accomplished by citizens in the people's army of the Israel Defence Forces, in which all these youngsters will serve on their completion of high school. Collectivity and citizenship are presented in and through one another in mutual interdependence.

The primary message of the narrative of the rediscovery of the Wall is that the Jews must defend their patrimony, otherwise they will lose this. The tale is an allegory: the world of Israel, signified by the Wall, must be demarcated clearly from that of non-Jews who threaten its integrity and viability. This is the logic of nation and state, at their boundaries, and it is one that resonates strongly with aspects of the historical Jewish experience. In terms of nationhood then, one either is a Jew or one is not. In terms of statehood, one either is a citizen or one is not. In the ideology of the nation-state these two dimensions of inclusion-exclusion become almost isomorphic. The outer boundaries of the permissible are set by the collectivity, to which the desires of the citizen are subordinate. This is perhaps the highest level of contrast between "inside" and "outside" that is set for the Jewish citizen of modern Israel; and this is a lesson that youngsters will have reason to learn in numerous contexts beyond that of the family in years to come. At this level of contrast, the hierarchy, values, and relationships of the family always are of lesser relevance.

The tale posits a series of contrasts between Jew and gentile that derive from a simple postulate: that the Wall, and by analogy the nation and state, are indestructible and enduring despite all the depredations of enemies throughout the centuries. This is its internal and eternal truth. By comparison all else is transitory. The Jew who returns to his source, across the gap of generations, is motivated by ideology. His is the wisdom of spirituality. The gentiles who try to destroy his roots are driven by materialism. He uses their cupidity to reveal the glory of the Wall and his spirituality helps to bring about its cleansing.

The closing enactment brings the message of the story into existence through the cooperative efforts of the children, just as the living Shield realized the prophecy of the poetic doves. The youngsters build the Wall from the ground up, just as modern Israel was redeemed through the joint efforts of its citizenry. The simulated labors of the children signify that which will be expected of them when they attain adulthood and full citizenship. The children dance in an unbroken circle around the completed Wall. Again their formation evokes egalitarianism, synchronization, connectivity, and perhaps the outer boundary of statehood that must be drawn and protected by its citizenry. Once more the center of the circle is filled, here by the model of the Wall—an emblem that is hierarchical and authoritative and, above all, a symbol of the Israel nation-state.

Conclusion

In the world of the little child the kindergarten celebration is among the very few categories of occasion when the order of things that structures the wider social environment directly intersects with, and dominates, that of the home. In part this is evident through explicit symbolism. Yet perhaps more profound in their impact are the architectonics of enactment. Their significance derives from the very ways in which people in unison are mobilized, organized, and synchronized in social formations in order to accomplish the more explicit scenarios of celebration. The lineal progressions of such formations constitute their own implicit sets of messages; and it is these that we have addressed here.

These celebrations, and numerous others like them, make extensive and intensive use of living formations. Some of these take the shape of explicit symbols, like the hannukiah and the Shield of David. Others, like the unbroken circle and the dyad, remain more implicit. In either instance these are highly powerful media. Through them the meaning of things is turned into the shape of things. The shape of things is graspable by the senses, as is the case of icon and emblem. Yet in such latter instances these shapes still are largely external to the human body, to the source of emotions and feelings. But one grasps the shape of things in living formations by living through them. This is a more sensual experience, one that engages the senses more fully to create a holistic experiential environment. Architects sometimes write of haptic space, of coming to know the shape of space and the feelings this engenders through the sense of touch. Through living formations the visual, the auditory, the tactile, and perhaps the olfactory senses are all "touched" by the shape of things. The meaning of form and the form of meaning become inextricable.

The sequencing of formations, in keeping with premises of lineality, are at the experiential heart of the kinds of enactments that we have addressed. Indeed, as noted, they are intended to touch the heart of the little child, and so to impress upon his being lessons that otherwise may remain more exterior to his sense of self. In particular we have stressed certain themes that will be adumbrated for the child in numerous ways and contexts in the years to come: for example, the relationship between hierarchy and equality. The interior hierarchy of the family is supplanted and is subsumed by the superordination of the collectivity. The collectivity, the nation-state, is superior to each of its citizens; yet they compose it, and it exists only through their cooperative efforts. In relation to one another, as citizens, they largely are equals. So too, as children grow, they will succeed and replace their parents, both as heads of family and as citizens. These processes depend on the proper outcome of that of maturation: the parent should infuse the child with internal restraint and with a sense of responsibility towards the collectivity and its component units. In turn, all of the above seems to evoke elementary patterns of social boundedness, and of the categories and entities that these demarcate and define. Thus boundaries between people, as members of categories and persons, between family and collectivity, and between the nation-state and whatever lies without are taken apart, constructed anew, and, in essence, shown to exist.

Such messages are essential to the reproduction of social order. In kindergarten celebrations they are communicated in ways that make them easy to grasp for the little child. Youngsters are full of feeling, but they have yet to develop the kind of critical attitudes that can buffer personal choice against the demands of group pressure and the inducements of collective sentiments. Socialization through celebration, as instruction books for kindergartens note, is first and foremost an appeal to the emotions of little children. Thus moods and feelings about collectivity, centricity, control, and cooperation are communicated early on to Israeli youngsters. These sentiments were crucial to the periods of the *yishuv* and the early state, years of self-defense for survival and growth. Yet one should inquire whether the emphasis today on these and related values survives primarily through inertia, and through the inability of the apparatus of education and polity to check the viability of its own involution. The further growth of the nation-state may depend as much on the teaching of critical perspectives and of personal choice as it does on values that continue to close the collective circle.

Notes

1. Both in the pre-state and post-state periods there is no especial distinction between nursery school and kindergarten. Youngsters may be in kindergarten at age 2, and at age 6 continue on to elementary school.

2. The Hebrew term for kindergarten teacher, in the feminine gender, is *gannenet*. Its meaning is literally that of "gardener." The connotations of the term, as in English, are those of one who is an active agent in the processes of growing, of cultivating, and of taming. The term likely is a translation of the German *kindergertnerin*, a gardener of children, and is distinguished clearly in Hebrew from "educator" (fem. *m'khanekhet*) and "teacher" (fem. *mora*). The Hebrew term for kindergarten, *gan yeladim*, again is a translation from the German.

3. Our usage is analogous to that of "hidden curriculum" (Gearing and Tindall 1973:103), although we stress more the contested relationship between parents and state that is implicit in the maturation of youngsters, from offspring to citizens.

4. On each of the four sides of the Hannukah top is inscribed the first letter of each of the Hebrew words, "Ness Gadol Haya Po" (There was a great miracle here). Spinning the top is a popular children's game. Regardless of which side remains uppermost when the top topples, its letter signifies the integrity and unity of the whole message, as does the top in its circular spinning.

5. In order to avoid confusion it should be noted that the *hannukiah* is distinguished from the *menorah* (the candelabrum) that appears as the official emblem of the state of Israel. The hannukiah has 8 candles (excluding the shamash) to commemorate the eight days for which the miracle of Hannukah supplied oil for the 6 candles of the menorah of the Temple on Mount Moriah.

6. In modern Israel the circle dance became a popular form through which to express egalitarianism and the dynamism of enduring bonds between persons who, through their cooperative efforts, forged the embracing collectivity of which they were a part.

7. The age to which, tradition has it, Moses lived; and a customary greeting of well-wishing.

8. We should mention that other such celebrations did not ignore the family, but involved it in the scenario. In some cases, fathers were invited to reminisce about their experiences as soldiers fighting for Jerusalem; while in others parents were asked to tell about life in Jerusalem under siege during the War of Independence. In these

instances the stress was on the obligation, transferred from parents to children, to serve the country under any circumstances.

References

Ben-Yosef, Yitzhak
1976. "Ha'khag k'besis ha'khinukh" (The Holiday as a Basis of Education). In *Sefer Hayovel Shel Histadrut Hamorim (Book of the Fiftieth Anniversary of the Teachers' Union)*. Tel Aviv: Histadrut Hamorim B'Eretz Yisrael. pp. 305-8.

Doleve-Gandelman, Tzili
1982. "Identité Sociale et Cérémonie d'Anniversaire dans les Jardins d'Enfants Israéliens." Unpublished Ph.D. Thesis. Paris: Ecole des Hautes Etudes en Sciences Sociales.

Durkheim, Emile
1956. *Sociology and Education*. Glencoe: Free Press.

Fayence-Glick, S
1948. "Khanuka B'gan Ha'yeladim" (Hannukah in the Kindergarten). *Oshiot* 2:28-39.
1957. "Gan Ha'yeladim B'Eretz Yisrael" (Kindergartens in Eretz Yisrael). In *Sefer Hayovel Shel Histadrut Hamorim (Book of the Fiftieth Anniversary of the Teacher's Union)*. Tel Aviv: Histadrut Hamorim B'Eretz Yisrael. pp. 132-44.

Gearing, F.O., and B. Alan Tindall.
1973. "Anthropological Studies of the Educational Process." *Annual Review of Anthropology* 2:95-105.

Geertz, Clifford
1972. "Notes on the Balinese Cockfight." *Daedalus* 101:1-37.

Handelman, Don
1980. "The Ritual Clown: Attributes and Affinities." *Anthropos* 76:321-70.
1982. "Reflexivity in Festival and Other Cultural Events." In *Essays in the Sociology of Perception*. Ed. Mary Douglas. London: Routledge & Kegan Paul. pp. 162-90.
1983. "The Madonna and the Mare: Symbolic Organization in the Palio of Siena." In *Spectacle—An Anthropological Enquiry*. Ed. Victor Turner and Masao Yamaguchi. Tokyo: Sanseido. pp. 153-84.
1984. "Inside-Out, Outside-In: Concealment and Revelation in Newfoundland Christmas Mumming." In *Text, Play, and Story* (1983 Proceedings of the American Ethnological Society). Ed. Edward Bruner. St. Paul: West Publishing.

Katerbursky, Zivya
1962. *B'netivot Hagan (The Ways of the Garden)*. Tel Aviv: Otsar Hamoreh.

Langer, Susanne
1953. *Feeling and Form*. London: Routledge & Kegan Paul.

Manning, Frank E., ed.

1983. *The Celebration of Society*. Bowling Green: Bowling Green University Popular Press.

Ministry of Education and Culture
1967. *Hannukah, Khag Ha'urim (Hannukah, Feast of Lights)*. Jerusalem: Ministry of Education and Culture.

Moore, Sally Falk, and Barbara Myerhoff, eds.
1977. *Secular Ritual*. Assen: Van Gorcum.

Naftali, Nitza, and Nekhama Nir-Yaniv, eds.
1974. *Pirkei Hadrakha: Me'onot Yom (Subjects of Instructions: Day-Care Centers)*. Jerusalem: Ministry of Education and Culture.

Rabinowitz, Esther
1958a. "Hakhag B'gan Ha'yeladim" (The Holiday in the Kindergarten). In *Khagim U'moadim Bakhinukh (Holidays and Times in Education)*. Ed. Esther Rabinowitz. Tel Aviv: Urim. pp. 39-44.
1958b. "Hakhag, Mashmauto V'erko Bakhinukh" (The Holiday, its Meaning and Value in Education). In *Khagim U'moadim Bakhinukh*, pp. 9-57.
1958c. "The Place of the Holiday in the Kindergarten." In *Khagim U'moadim Bakhinukh*, pp. 141-46.

Shemer, Aliza, ed.
1966. *Darkei Avoda B'ganei Yeladim (Ways of Work in Kindergartens)*. Tel Aviv: Tarbout V'khinukh.

State of Israel
1983. *Statistical Abstract of Israel* (no. 34). Jerusalem: Central Bureau of Statistics.

Turner, Victor W.
1974. *Dramas, Fields and Metaphors*. Ithaca: Cornell University Press.

Turner, Victor W., ed.
1982. *Celebration: Studies in Festivity and Ritual*. Washington, D.C.: Smithsonian Institution Press.

Willeford, William
1969. *The Fool and His Sceptre*. London: Edward Arnold.

Zanbank-Wilf, Aliza
1958. "Hagan K'markiv B'yetzirat Avirat Khag Babayit" (The Kindergarten as a Component in Creating a Holiday Atmosphere at Home). In *Khagim U'moadim Bakhinukh*, pp. 57-59.

CHRISTIANITY AND COLONIALISM
IN SOUTH AFRICA

Jean and John Comaroff

This article by Jean and John Comaroff on the impact of Christian missionaries on the Tshidi—a Tswana speaking group of South Africa—not only exemplifies the theoretical approach developed in this reader, but also illustrates one direction anthropology will undoubtedly take in the 1990s. As such, it warrants reading at two levels at once: (1) as an empirical contribution to a particular ethnographic-historical problem, i.e. as assessment of Protestant evangelism in South Africa; (2) as a theoretical solution to the related problems of level of analysis and of agency when trying to understand the local manifestation of a world-wide phenomenon such as colonialism.

The anthropological literature on Christian evangelism is polemicised around the issue of whether or not missionaries were anything more than agents of imperialism. This reduces a very complex social and cultural phenomenon to an entry on the plus or minus side of the historical ledger. Thankfully, the Comaroffs are careful not to join this debate.

Their article is made up of three sections. The first one examines the history of involvement of Methodist missionaries in formal political processes. It is presented in the form of three vignettes, each illustrating a different principle. The first vignette describes the unwitting intervention of evangelists in local politics. Following the Methodist view of the complementarity of church and state developed in nineteenth century Britain, missionaries endeavored to respect the power of local Tshidi chiefs. They wanted only the freedom for converts to practise Christianity. However, the unintended result of conversion was an erosion of the spiritual nature of traditional political power. In other words, when the evangelical message was inserted into the local culture, it undermined the secular authority of chiefs by separating for the first time religion from politics.

The second vignette describes the conscious political involvement of a missionary who tried to protect the Tshidi from the grasping Boers. His solution was to propose the creation of a Tshidi state under the protection of Britain. Lacking the power and influence to bring about these changes, his plans came to nought.

The last vignette shows the systematic political action of a third missionary who believed that the only way to preserve the people from both the English and Boer predators was to have Britain administer the Tshidi territory as a protectorate. He also failed in his efforts at humanitarian imperialism. And the Comaroffs conclude, in short, that "even the most politically active and imperialistically driven missionaries were relatively ineffectual in the *realpolitik* of empire."

The second part of the article is concerned with changes which, though not of a political nature, nonetheless fostered the penetration of colonialism. Missionaries introduced new agricultural methods, new standards of dress, new styles of houses and a new form of marriage as mission culture revolved around "nuclear family, private estate, marriage as a sacred contract between individuals." Besides introducing literacy, they also brought in notions of time derived from the Industrial Revolution. The impact of these Western imports was to transform Tshidi consciousness slowly, and to begin a "conversation" between these two social and cultural worlds. In the process, the Tshidi internalized the missionaries' categories and values and eventually made themselves into the image of Protestants. The incorporation of the Tshidi in the colonial world resulted as much from cultural borrowing as from political coercion. By helping to transform the Tshidi conceptual system, missionaries thus played a decisive role in furthering colonialism.

However, the story does not end here and we move to the last section of the article. Missionaries were unable "to deliver the liberal democracy promised by their ideology and implied by their practices...at the level of explicit power, they could be neither imperialists nor liberators." Trained to enter a Christian state or at least the social system associated with Methodism in nineteenth century Britain, the Tshidi found the colonial reality altogether different. They then turned to the Bible to find out what was wrong; indeed, Christianity became their "language of protest". In time, other forms of resistance and protest emerged. Yet, for a while, opposition to colonialism could only be phrased within the terms of orthodox Protestantism. As the authors conclude,

"The ultimate power of Christianity in South Africa is enshrined in the fact that it took many decades for

> blacks to cast aside the language and ideology of the mission...to move...from revelation to revolution."
> Anthropologists have been dissatisfied with a world system approach which, at the limit, treats historical processes like colonialism as if they had the ineluctable force of natural laws. The Comaroffs have found a way to explore colonialism in its specific South African form which does not universalize this historical phenomenon. They have done it in a way which, without denying the formal political structure and obvious forms of political coercion, emphasizes the more subtle, unconscious, everyday practices particular to the Tshidi and their Methodist evangelists. In this way, the Tshidi, though robbed of almost everything else, are no longer robbed of their history.

Introduction

ALTHOUGH THE LITERATURE ON MISSIONS in Africa is very large, many have commented on the relative lack of systematic analyses of the evangelical encounter; analyses that go beyond detailed, if often sensitive, chronicles of events and actions (Heise 1967; Beidelman 1982: 2ff.; Etherington 1983; Ranger n.d.; cf. Shapiro 1981: 130). Indeed, the emerging picture is one of bewildering factual variation and a lack of theoretical convergence. Moreover, as Beidelman (1982: 7) implies, the subject has lent itself to polemical debate rather than careful scrutiny. This is well exemplified in the South African literature, our present focus, where much of the discussion until quite recently cast those who stressed the philanthropic role of missionaries (Wilson 1969, 1976; Sillery 1971) against those who condemned them as agents of imperialism (for example, Majeke 1953; Dachs 1972). Much of that debate was addressed to the issue of "Whose side was the missionary really on"—and, by extension, "Whose ends did he serve?"—thus translating a complex historical problem into a crude equation of cause and effect (cf. Bundy 1979: 36ff.) Few would any longer debate the historical role of the missionary in these terms. Nonetheless, as Ranger notes in an extended review of the literature, another unfortunate tendency still remains.

JEAN & JOHN COMAROFF

An oddity of most recent historiography of early mission Christianity is that it has greatly overplayed the manifest political and economic factors in its expansion and greatly underplayed the cultural and the religious...[Even the formal church historians have] hardly discussed the impact of missionaries and their African catechists on the cultural imagination of Africa [n.d.: 36].

In this essay, we seek not only to examine the cultural implications of the mission, but also to inquire how they might be related to the sphere of manifest political processes. Rather than seek generalizations in the historical record, however, we analyze one instance of Protestant evangelism in Africa as a problem in the interplay of power and meaning. We stress the singularity of the case: the missionary project was everywhere made particular by variations in the structure of local communities, in the social and theological background of the evangelists, and in the wider politico-economic context and precise circumstances within which the encounter took place. If anything more general emerges from this study, then, it does not lie at the level of events and actions; instead, it concerns the generic nature of mission agency in the colonial process. This involves two interrelated dimensions. One is the capacity to act in the domain normally defined as "the political," the arena of concrete, institutionalized power relations. The other is the ability to exert power over the common-sense meanings and routine activities diffused in the everyday world. Both dimensions are simultaneously material and symbolic, and the relationship between "religion" and "politics" plays itself out in each.

The analysis has three steps. In the first, we show that it is impossible to arrive at any consistent conclusion about the purely "political" aspect of the role of the missionary among the Tswana, of his activities in the institutional arena of tangible power relations. For, from this standpoint, both the motivation and the consequences of his part in the imperial project remain variable and indeterminate—just as imperialism itself appears more inchoate, less crushingly methodical than is often allowed. But this poses an immediate question. If it is true that there is no consistency at this level, does it not follow that the labors of the evangelists are best treated in an idiographic manner? Can we do no more, at this stage, than seek their relevance in the uniqueness of each missionary encounter, as

Beidelman (1982: 29f) seems to suggest?

In the second step of the analysis we begin to show that the role of missionary does in fact yield to systematic accounting in the Tswana case; that here, as elsewhere, it was both a vital and a consistent element in the colonial encounter. In order to do so, however, we reexamine the nature of their power to affect the course of history. For power, the capacity to impose the conditions of being on others, does not reside solely in palpable forces of influence. As Marx and Weber noted long ago, it has a second, less visible aspect. This involves the incorporation of human subjects into the "natural," taken-for-granted forms of economy and society. And these forms lie not just in the institutional domain of "politics," but also in such things as aesthetics and religion, built form and bodily presentation, medical knowledge and the mundane habits of everyday life (Bourdieu 1977: 184f.). The construction of the subject in this mold, moreover, is rarely an act of overt persuasion. It requires the internalization of a set of values, an ineffable manner of seeing and being. As others have observed (Schapera 1958; Etherington 1978: 116; Bundy 1979: 41ff.), it is precisely here that the evangelist left his mark most deeply in southern Africa. For, while the colonial process often entailed material dispossession, even brute force, a critical part of the subjection of native peoples lay in the subtle colonization, by the missionary, of indigenous modes of perception and practice.

This, however, raises a final issue. On one hand, we show that the part of the missionary in the "political" domain was variable and indeterminate; on the other, we suggest that his efforts were decisive in the imposition of a new mode of being. Neither of these observations is novel, of course, although the exact contours of the present case are not a mere repetition of a universal process. What we seek to do here, however, is to explore *how* these two dimensions of historical agency relate to one another. As we shall indicate in the last section, the disjuncture between them underlines the double-sided role of the mission in the colonial process. For, ironically, the evangelist failed where he hoped most to succeed—in creating a unified black Protestant church in a South Africa built on Christian principles—yet succeeded where his actions were least tangible; in restructuring the native conceptual universe in important respects, he laid the ground for its integration into the industrial capitalist world. Yet, while the signs and practices instilled by the mission came to underpin the new order, they also exposed its contradictions, and gave rise to more than one language of protest. In this way, orthodox Christianity was also to provide the instruments of its own negation.

The Politics of Christianity

We begin, then, by examining the part played by missionaries in the 19th-century political life of a Tswana people, the Barolong boo Ratshidi (Tshidi). The Tshidi, who lived along the Molopo River that today divides Botswana from South Africa, first met the Congregationalists of the London Missionary Society (LMS) in the 1820s. The latter had set up a station in the nearby Batlhaping chiefdom; and, while they did not labor among the Tshidi, their presence in the region had much to do with the eventual founding of a Methodist mission to the Barolong.

It is impossible to know how the Tswana first perceived the Christian message; the evangelists suggest that they paid it little attention (Dachs 1972: 648). But chiefs were quick to see temporal advantages in the presence of the mission, and made incessant requests for goods and military aid. The missionaries put this down to the unenlightened greed of the savage—his "carnal view of spiritual things" (Broadbent 1865: 178)—and yielded to many demands in the hope that it would prepare the way for their sacred task.

The Europeans did not merely bear valued goods, however; they also gained repute for their technical skills—in irrigation and the sinking of wells, for example—and for the patent superiority of their guns in a theater of spears. As a result, they themselves became a prized resource (Schapera 1958: 5) and, before long, chiefs were actively engaged in competing for them—and in preventing others from doing likewise, often by resort to malicious slander.

The Tshidi had also tried to attract a missionary, but ironically their first sustained contract with the Methodists came almost by accident. In the early 19th century, the rise of the Zulu state had effects that were to be felt throughout the hinterland of southern Africa. Marauding "tribes" fell upon their agrarian neighbors, razing their settlements and seizing their stock. This swelling wave of destruction, known indigenously as *defikane* (upheaval), overtook the Tshidi as well. Having been attacked by the fearsome Batlokwa, they were expelled from their home on the Molopo River and sought temporary refuge with another Barolong group, the Seleka.

Amidst this unrest, the Methodists had been looking for a settled place to work and, just before the arrival of the Tshidi, had thrown in their lot with the Seleka. They were to accompany the Barolong on a series of defensive migrations, and to help them secure land from the Sotho chief, Moshweshwe. This site, Thaba 'Nchu, became the refuge of the chiefdoms for almost a decade. In fact the Seleka were to remain there permanently. There, in 1837, the Barolong met the Boers, who had embarked on their own epic migration, the Great Trek, to escape the liberalism of the Cape Colonial government. It was there, too, that the Wesleyan mission set up its area headquarters. Eventually, the Tshidi departed this refuge to return to their former territory. Soon after they had resettled, Chief Montshiwa, who had recently succeeded to office, decided to recruit an evangelist (*moruti*, teacher). Rev. Joseph Ludorf arrived at his capital in January 1850. For the first time, the Tshidi had a missionary to themselves.

It is not possible to detail the history of the Tshidi mission here. Hence, we offer three vignettes, each representative in its own way, that should serve to make the point. One tells of the intrusion of the Methodists into the internal political life of the chiefdom; the second recounts a dramatic instance of their participation in relations among southern Tswana and the settlers of the region; and the third concerns the intervention of an influential evangelist in transactions among the local population, the colonial state, and capitalist interests.

Samuel Broadbent and the "Native Dance"

The first vignette typifies a recurring conflict: Samuel Broadbent (1865: 187) recalls that, when he heard the sounds of the "native dance" in the royal court, he went out "to oppose it, and preach to those...willing to hear." The "dance" refers to rainmaking rites, which the missionaries recognized to be important not only to the fabric of "heathen" belief, but also to the power of the chiefship. Although aided by specialist rainmakers (*baroka*), often recruited from far afield, chiefs were themselves responsible for bringing rain; in fact, their authority was intimately connected to their ritual success, and some were famed practitioners of the art. *Pula,* which meant both "rain" and "well being," appeared conspicuously in the symbolism of political ceremonial, and rulers always greeted the people *"ka* [with] *pula"*.

Broadbent was not the only one to see rainmaking as a critical impediment to the spread of the gospel; almost every missionary felt compelled to act against it. Among the Tshidi, such efforts were to have palpable results. Later, when a small Christian congregation took root, its members refused to take part in these and other communal rituals, such as male initiation. Montshiwa insisted that they do so, declaring that he would tolerate the church only if they complied. But the converts continued to resist, and the dispute led quickly to a deep cleavage between the "people of the word" and the ruler; an effect that occurred throughout southern Africa. Wittingly or not—the methodists varied greatly in the degree to which they understood the implications of their actions—the attempt to subvert "heathen ceremonies" sharpened a contradiction in their own project. It was a contradiction that was to have consequences far beyond their control.

On the one hand, the Methodists had always worked under the aegis of the chiefs, soliciting their patronage and showing them deference. This was not just a matter of political opportunism, although it was difficult to work where a ruler put obstacles in their path. It was also rationalized in terms of a stated commitment to the complementarity of church and state, of divine and worldly power. Thus, while they argued for religious freedom for their converts, invoking the precept of individual self-determination, they avoided any hint of challenge to the "secular" legitimacy of the chiefship itself. Indeed, *pace* the "missionary imperialist" thesis— which holds that the Protestants among the Tswana, finding local sovereigns an increasing thorn in their side, took steps to limit their power—all evidence suggests that the Wesleyans desired a strong polity under a head, pagan or Christian, who could sustain order, and so provide a stable context for their efforts. Even if they had wished to dismantle the office, however, the events set in motion by their actions were to make any such intervention irrelevant.

For, on the other hand, by advancing the cause of Christianity as they did, the Wesleyans, like other missionaries in Africa (see for example, Ekechi 1972: 36ff.; Beidelman 1982: 25), eroded not only the spiritual aspect of the chiefship but its entire foundation. In seeking to restore religious authority to God, they drove a wedge between two dimensions of power and legitimacy which, for Tswana, were indissoluble. That is why, once they saw that the missions were there to stay, rulers worried about the long-term implications—notwithstanding the material benefits they might gain. The point, however, was not merely that the missions undermined royal sovereignty by opposing communal rites that were essential to the ruler's control over people and property. Nor was it that Christianity threatened the relations of inequality and servitude which made possible the extraction of labor and tribute. It was rather that the unravelling of *puso* (government)—and its division into discrete domains of religion and politics, chapel and chiefship—engendered a new pluralism. For whatever the intentions of the mission, its converts remade the political sociology of the church in their own image. Around it they created another center, with its own leadership, power relations, and symbolic resources; and, in so doing, they expressed in Christian idiom long-standing tensions surrounding the chiefship. The intrusion of Christianity, in other words, attacked the real basis of the office: its *exclusive* dominion over the political process and, with it, every sphere of social life.

In sum, where before the chiefship was the epicenter of the social and symbolic world, it now became one of two foci of authority. Nor was the church any less "political" than the royal court. Indeed, its first native leader, Molema, later made a direct bid for chiefly office, and for a century his descendants were to challenge the legitimacy of the ruling line. But the final irony was that, once he had gained supremacy in the church and had built a firm power base, Molema rejected the missionaries, making it hard for them to work among Tshidi. It was Montishiwa, the heathen chief, who fostered their presence, and who, when Molema died in 1882, declared "religious freedom"; being continuously harassed by the Boers, he was more than ever in need of an agent and an adviser. On his initiative, too, Methodism finally became the "state" religion. Thus it was that a pagan ruler ended up in alliance with the evangelists that his Christian brother had cast aside.

The implication is clear: from the viewpoint of the missionaries, their involvement in the internal politics of the Tshidi was always indirect, almost incidental. The intention of opposing the "native dances," seen largely as an act against "heathenism," was to reclaim religion for God and to leave secular authority intact. But, given the indigenous political culture, this was impossible, and set in motion a process that had very mixed, contradictory consequences (see Linden 1977 for a strikingly similar analysis). By fracturing the chiefship and creating a practical distinction between the "political" and the "religious", it produced a dualistic order with competing foci of power relations. Moreover, it put the evangelists themselves in an equivocal political position, placed between a weakened ruler who courted them and a strong local congregation that was much less inclined to do so.

One thing is clear, however. The missionaries rarely escaped being caught in the fissure that they had created between church and chiefship. Neither the motivation nor the effect of their entry into internal politics, then, is reducible to the simple terms of colonial domination that some scholars have described (for example, Temu 1972: 9, 132; Dachs 1972); a view that, in any case, has been increasingly qualified of late (see, for example, Strayer 1978: 101).

Joseph Ludorf and the "United Tswana Nation"

The second vignette begins with the discovery of diamonds in 1867 at Hopetown on the Orange River, some 200 miles south of the Molopo region. Later, major finds were also made along the not-too-distant Vaal and Harts Rivers. Almost immediately, six parties laid claim to the territory: the Boer Republics of the Orange Free State and Transvaal, which fought the dispute in alliance with one another, and four indigenous peoples.

The Barolong case at Bloemhof was led with "skill and devotion" by the Reverend Ludorf, former missionary to the Tshidi, who was drafting a manifesto and constitution for a "United Barolong, Batlhaping and Bangwaketse Nation." Its capital was to be at Klipdrift, in the awarded territory, and he was to be its "commissioner...and diplomatic agent." In this spirit, he wrote to the chiefs, evoking Isaiah:

And now chiefs: rulers of the land, I appeal to you. Awake:

arise and unite soon before your trophy is torn asunder by wolves; come ye together, make protective laws; stop all breaches and gaps and close your ranks. Safeguard the heritage of Tau your ancestor. Hear ye chiefs: Come together and unite [Molema 1966: 66-67].

This must rank as one of the more remarkable documents of South African mission history. Ludorf was convinced that the Republics would try to make it impossible for the chiefs to take possession of the land, and he was correct; the next decade was a period of unremitting hostility. Most immediately, it is clear that he envisaged an independent confederation of southern Tswana states with a formal government. This, in his view, was the only way to avoid Boer oppression. The "United Nation" was not to be absorbed into the empire either. Ludorf wanted it protected, not colonized, by Britain. The plan came to nought, though; ignored by the Crown and derided by the Boers, the evangelist took ill and died a few weeks later.

Here, then, is the odd spectacle of a missionary defending Tswana from Boer subjugation by striving to found an *autonomous* state in the crevice between settler colonialism and British imperialism. By doing so, however, he denied himself the support and resources necessary to achieve his goals—even if he had lived longer. Ludorf's lead was not followed by other evangelists. Not only did his action openly violate the separation of church and state, and thus contravene official policy; it also highlighted the fact that the missions lacked the real power to engage in such pursuits with any hope of success. Still, his campaign was not dismissed as frivolous or misguided by his colleagues. From their perspective, the protection of Tswana from Boer "enslavement," from "tribal" wars, and from unscrupulous freebooters was vital to their work. In this situation, it was difficult to avoid being drawn into "politics." And where it happened, it made as much sense, in principle at least, to promote an independent native state as it did to call for British overrule. Both courses fell within the compass of mission ideology: it was a question on which reasonable men could, and did, disagree. The role of the missionary in concrete political process, in other words, was *intrinsically* indeterminate. Methodism did not, because it could not, mandate any one course of action.

JEAN & JOHN COMAROFF

John Mackenzie and the "Imperial Factor"

The final vignette narrates a different, yet complementary, story. It involves John Mackenzie of the LMS, who worked primarily among the Ngwato rather than the Tshidi, but who had great impact on the political destiny of all Tswana. Indeed, if anyone might properly be termed a "missionary imperialist" it was he.

The bitter hostilities that followed the diamond field dispute gave the missionaries cause to fear for the lives and property of their congregants. Then, in 1878, amidst the turmoil, there was an uprising on the part of some Tswana groupings to the south of the Tshidi. During the rising, the LMS station at Kuruman was attacked. Thus, when the Boers persisted in occupying land given to the chiefdoms, Mackenzie decided that only firm political measures would stop them. He had long entertained hopes of imperial intervention. These now crystallized into a complex plan for implementing a form of indirect rule. Like Ludorf, he believed that a political solution had become unavoidable; but his schemes involved the full weight of the Crown.

In contrast to most of his contemporaries, Mackenzie argued that blacks should eventually enjoy equal rights in a federated, nonracial South Africa, the goal being to assure that "class would not be arrayed against class; the hatches would not be battened down over the heads of blacks, to be opened in bloodshed at some future period" (quoted in Sillery 1971: 51). To this end, the Tswana ought not to be governed by any colony, English or Dutch, but directly by imperial rule from London. Note the distinction between colonialism and imperialism here: it was crucial to the actors of the period, as it determined who would actually wield authority over the natives—and to what end. Mackenzie was an unyielding imperialist. He urged Britain to annex the borderland in order to stop freebooters and colonists from dispossessing the Tswana and reducing them to servitude. Mackenzie's preference for imperial rulers, rather than whites of settler or colonial origin, was phrased in language remarkable for the time. In his view, "one class of farmers" could not "legislate for another and unrepresented class." Because both the whites and the blacks were agriculturalists, the former could not oversee the latter without conflict of interest (see Sillery 1971: 52).

Mackenzie pressed his plan on British authorities whenever possible, and found a sympathetic ear in Sir Bartle Frere, High Commissioner and Governor of the Cape, who conceded that the
regulation of the frontier was beyond the scope of his colonial administration. The missionary persuaded him of the material and
humanitarian advantages of an imperial presence, and this was conveyed to London. Although wary of the plan at first, the Colonial
Office slowly warmed to it. Frere went as far as to invite Mackenzie
to be Commissioner for Bechuanaland when a protectorate was
created, and the LMS was asked for its approval. But the directors
rejected "such a corporeal union of Church and State."

Mackenzie renewed his campaign with yet greater vigor. A complicated story, its next stage included a furlough in England in 1882-
84, during which he canvassed widely and, with other humanitarian
and economic interest groups, formed the South African Committee. Through a series of Conventions and parliamentary debates in
the aftermath of the first Anglo-Boer War of 1880-81, the Committee tried to affect foreign policy, using the press, the public platform, and personal influence. Its efforts were finally rewarded,
though it took an offer from the Cape Colony to shoulder part of
the administrative cost before Gladstone's government would agree
to establish a protectorate in Bechuanland. When it did, in 1884,
Mackenzie was invited to become the resident Deputy Commissioner. He accepted, and duly left the LMS (Dachs, ed. 1975:
164ff.).

In South Africa itself, the appointment was condemned by the
Boers, for obvious reasons, and by many English-speaking Cape par-
liamentarians. Some of these politicians enjoyed the support of the
local Afrikaner Bond, and were particularly anxious that its members not be offended. Among them was Cecil Rhodes, already a
magnate and a cabinet minister, whose own expansionist agenda at
the time required amicable relations between the colonies and
republics. For him, the "Imperial Factor" represented by Mackenzie
was anathema: he envisaged an African dominion securely under
the control of interests at the Cape. Bechuanaland, a vital link in
its establishment, had thus to be absorbed by the Colony. The
Governor and High Commissioner, Sir Hercules Robinson, con-
curred, leaving MacKenzie isolated and powerless.

Mackenzie's first goal was to settle outstanding disputes among the chiefdoms, the Transvaal, the white farmers, and the freebooters. The latter repeatedly raided the Tlhaping Tshidi. He proceeded to castigate the whites, to try and restore land they had taken from the Tswana, and to plead for armed help to quiet the troubled region. This further alienated the Boers, the Cape government, and the High Commissioner. As the situation degenerated, his requests met with increasingly irritable rejection from Robinson, who eventually recalled him for consultation and asked Rhodes to act in his stead. Mackenzie never did return to office. In the face of growing hostility, the missionary resigned.

This fragment underlines the sheer complexity surrounding the political agency of missionaries in colonial southern Africa. It does so precisely because John Mackenzie was emphatic in presenting himself as a truly "humane" imperialist; although, of course, the imperialism for which he fought was barely recognizable in Cape Town, or even in London, where the cause of native rights was never a high priority, and where the evangelist was treated as anything from a mild irritation to a dangerous subversive. The primary relevance of his historical role to our analysis here is twofold.

One dimension concerns Mackenzie's encounter with the LMS position on the "corporeal union of Church and State." In order to influence policy, an evangelist had not just to defy official mission ideology; he had somehow to penetrate government circles. This, after all, was the bitter lesson of many unsuccessful entreaties to Whitehall and the Cape on the question of native rights. It is no coincidence that the most visible "missionary imperialists" were those who left the Society and took administrative positions. But, in so doing, they found themselves politically isolated. On one hand, they received no open support from their colleagues, who wished not to be tainted by association with government. Yet on the other, they were not career politicians and had no autonomous power base. However charismatic an evangelist might have been, in other words, the nature of his relationship to formal political institutions limited his influence.

In short, even the most politically active and imperialistically driven of missionaries were relatively ineffectual in the *realpolitik* of empire. The majority, of course, had no overt part in it anyway. And when they did, their intentions were often perverted in unexpected ways.

All this, in turn, raises a second point, one which we first encountered in Ludorf's case. Even where missionaries wished to exert influence in the public domain, nothing in their Christianity per se prescribed one political doctrine above all others. This is hardly surprising, since the colonial history of southern Africa involved a long and sometimes acrid argument; an argument that, in the rhetoric of the time, cast metropolitan imperialist against settler colonialist, capitalist against philanthropist, and, on occasion, mercantilist against industrialist. Nor were the disagreements trivial, since they implied very different destinies for the victims. Yet there was nothing in nonconformist dogma that determined the stand to be adopted by the missionaries in the debate. They could—indeed, they had to—take sides. But the moment they did, they lost any *collective* identity in the political process. The "role of the missionary," in short, became indeterminate.

This is not to say that missionaries were never catalysts, or that they did not connive in the cause of the European domination of southern Africa (see, for example, Bundy 1979: 36ff.). Nonetheless, as actors in the domain of formal politics, their generic role was necessarily equivocal. As the three vignettes suggest, they varied widely in their efforts to wield temporal influence. And for good structural reasons, they were rarely potent figures in the political arena, the consequences of their actions in that domain often being beyond their control. Moreover, far from speaking with a single voice, they expressed a variety of attitudes. As all this suggests, in summary, the position of the missionary in the realm of institutional political processes could not but be uncertain in its contemporary impact and ambiguous in its historical implications (cf. Crummey 1972: 150f.) But this, as we have said, is only one part of a more complex story.

The Method in the Mission

We turn, then, to the second level of the missionary project distinguished above—that which lay implicit within the very nature of evangelical practice, and which, in its challenge to the Tswana world, laid down the terms of colonial subjection (cf. Bohannan 1964: 22f.).

The Tswana system, c. 1830, was founded on a set of contradictory sociocultural principles. An agnatic ideology existed side by side with a form of endogamy that limited the emergence of descent corporations, and bred a field of ambiguous social relations. What is more, forces for political centralization and hierarchy were opposed by tendencies toward the dispersal and individuation of households. As we show elsewhere (for example, J.L. Comaroff 1982; J. Comaroff 1985), the conflicts generated by this structure had to be addressed in everyday practice—practice that, in turn, gave shape to communities on the ground.

The reproduction of centralized chiefdoms, and the social order at large, involved politico-ritual processes which imposed an authoritative imprint on the everyday world. Crucial here was the molding of the person and his or her experience in the context of mundane activity. Hence, built form and the organization of space marked out an asymmetrical opposition between the center of the polity (embodied in the chief and his court) and its productive periphery (the domestic unit whose material form invoked the female body). This spatial logic was reinforced by a division of labor in which women's labor and reproductive power subsidized the male construction of the social community.

Men represented themselves and communal values through the pliable medium of cattle, which served as both a currency and an icon of politico-economic relations. The husbandry and exchange of stock enabled the transaction of reproductive rights, the siphoning of ancestral power, and the creation of bonds of inequality and dependency. Thus the circulation of beasts complemented cultivation and nurture, and sustained the contrasts between center and periphery, politics and production, chief and commoner, male and female. And while the polity constantly threatened to fragment under the weight of its internal contradictions, the tendency was countered, for the most part, by the repeated symbolic restatement of established hierarchical arrangements. Further, this scheme implied a mode of being in which material objects were not definitively set apart from human subjects. Products embodied the social processes of their own construction (cf. Taussig 1980: 36), and "time" and "work" were immanent features of such processes themselves (J. Comaroff 1985: 127). Visible and invisible forces in the world existed in a reciprocal relationship, and material and moral being were interdependent. If chiefly potency waned, so did the productive capacity of the community. If polluting sexuality over-flowed moral bounds, the land as a whole would be "spoiled."

It was into this world, this meaningful terrain that "comes without saying because it goes without saying" (Bourdieu 1977: 167), that the nonconformist evangelists entered in the 19th century. While the literature on missions in colonial Africa affirms that their sway in matters specifically "religious" and "political" varied widely (see, for example, Crummey 1972: 150f.; Strayer 1978: 100ff.), many accounts speak similarly of their thoroughgoing influence on different aspects of the everyday world (see, for example, Schapera 1936: 228f.; Bohannan 1964: 22; Ekechi 1972: 16f; Etherington 1978: 115f; Beidelman 1982: 11, 26f, 133f.; MacGaffey 1983: 113f.) Their effect on Tswana social life was indeed pervasive. But it was in the *total* configuration of their imprint on seemingly disparate aspects of the mundane that their true impact lay (cf. Bundy 1979: 37). The seeds sown in the humble soil of everyday Tshidi practice were to mature and to change local horizons irreversibly; "God's gardeners"—as they liked to call themselves—did more than just prepare the ground for colonial penetration.

The implicit structures of the Methodist mission originated in late 18th-century British nonconformism, the product of the radical reorganization of productive relations set in motion by industrialization. Directed at the emerging working and middle-classes of the northern river valleys, its message was of salvation attainable through arduous and methodical self-construction. Its rhetorical forms were cast in the factory and the foundry, and its model of orderly process was that of the self-regulating market. Wesley's creed celebrated an individualistic, free enterprise of the spirit. Money, "that precious talent which contains all the rest" (Warner 1930: 155, quoting Wesley), featured prominently, being the sanctified currency of what had become a moral economy. This creed was a particular transformation of the Protestant ethic: it naturalized the essential categories and relations of industrial capitalism, centering its discourse upon the values of wage labor and private property, and discouraging any activity designed to subvert the divinely wrought inequality of the workplace (Warner 1930: 125, 146f.). But its primary focus was the subject divided, charged with the duty of creating an immortal self, and submitting the body, now shameful and transient, to sober constraint.

JEAN & JOHN COMAROFF

We shall trace the impact of this ideology on the Tshidi by examining the introduction of a set of key practices which gave coherence to the mission project throughout the colonial epoch. For, while thwarted in their early effort to gain converts—apparently by the natives' "carnal view of spiritual things"—the Christians proceeded to set up, piece by piece, the necessary techniques of "cultivation": the practical and social tools that would make the "wilderness...become a fruitful field" (Broadbent 1865: 204). It taught the unassuming "arts of civilization" (Mackenzie in Dachs, ed. 1975: 72), whose mundane logic worked upon the processes that most forcefully shaped the self and "natural" reality.

In fact, it was in the sphere of agricultural production that the nonconformists were to make their first tangible mark on the Tswana. Although their notion of labor had been shaped by the conditions of the urban workplace—they were themselves drawn from the ranks of artisans and the lower middle class—the iconography of the now marginalized English peasantry provided their model of preindustrial peoples elsewhere.

No sooner had they built their first station among Barolong, than the evangelists laid out fields, demonstrated the utilities of the plow, and tackled the most acute limitation of local production—uncertain rainfall. With their implements they began to dig wells, and their ability to draw water from beneath the ground made a deep impression on the Tshidi. But water, as we noted, was a symbolically charged resource in this drought-stricken land, the capacity to make rain being a crucial component of chiefly authority. Already the missionary was picking at the seams of sovereign power. Nor did his well challenge just the ruler's control over fertility; it represented a novel resource to be freely obtained through the voluntary input of labor. Such were the values held out to potential converts, whose identification with the church would be marked by the trappings of propertied individualism.

In the Methodist model of peasant production, moreover, the plow was to be the major implement, its import being as much ideological as technical. It was adopted by many southern Tswana after 1830, and this, more than any formal act of "conversion," marked their entry into a world of commodity relations. For the plow not only permitted the yield of marketable surpluses, spurred on by missionary exhortations toward self-improvement and a novel structure of wants. It also had a thoroughgoing effect on the social division of labor. Because it required animals for draught, it breached the boundary between the formerly discrete arable and pastoral sectors; and, since females were precluded from handling cattle, the prime repository of male value, men assumed direct control over plow cultivation. Women, consequently, were relegated to the devalued tasks of tending and reaping, and lost their influence over the disposal of crops. The division of labor was based increasingly on the individuated household and agriculture became subject to the same competitive inequalities that surrounded the husbandry of stock. Only some units were able to mobilize draught teams, and prior patterns of stratification became more marked. Indeed, there grew up a small category of commercial farmers whose less affluent fellows soon became vulnerable to various forms of clientage and to the impending forces of proletarianization. It was in this manner that mission cultivation anticipated the reaping of a colonial harvest.

In terms of the categories of mission culture—the nuclear family, the private estate, and marriage as a sacred contract between individuals—the natives lived in sloth and moral chaos. The point has been made repeatedly in accounts of missions in Africa. Protestant ideology presupposed the monogamous household as the elemental unit of production and consumption. Thus, at the same time as they introduced the plow, with all its social and material corollaries, the evangelists took pains to denounce such practices as polygyny and the "collective" ownership of resources. If civilization was to flourish, the "holy family" of the Christian cosmos, and its conventional, gender-based division of labor, had to triumph over "communistic" interdependence. But a more implicit pursuit of this argument was to occur in respect of the shapes and connotations of built form and organized space. For the Christians saw the concentric arcs of Tswana circular settlements—their "heaps of...huts jostled together" (Broadbent 1865: 189)—as material impediments to "healthy individualistic competition" (Mackenzie, quoted in Dachs 1972: 652).

The imposition of the square on the circle seems to have epitomized the "orientation" of cultural evangelism. Mission buildings were placed at chiefly discretion within the arc of his centralized domain, and were square, free-standing structures on securely fenced lots. The distribution and external marking of buildings dis-

JEAN & JOHN COMAROFF

tinguished the sacred from the secular, the public from the private. The spatial organization of activities among church, schoolroom, printing press, and fields was governed by European divisions of time and labor. The early evangelists, like the South African regime that followed them, were to try to "rationalize" African communities by laying upon them the geometric grid of "civilization," arguably also a form conducive to the building up of hierarchical structures. Would-be converts were encouraged to build "neat" square houses on discretely enclosed sites—models of moral and material property, cut loose from the ramifying connections of indigenous production and exchange. Of course, "civilized" homes were made of "proper" materials, "fitted up," as one contemporary observer put it, "in European style" (Holub 1881, 2: 13), and implying a new order of "needs" that hitched these communities irrevocably to the commodity market. Such standards of Christian decency also applied to dress, and converts had to ensure that their distinction from their fellows was shown in their attire.

To this end, the evangelists ensured that local communities were well served by colonial merchants. A moral discourse about bodily shame and physical modesty, rather than any material coercion (Foucault 1980), ensured a continuing demand for such "necessities" of civilization. As Etherington has noted in the Nguni context,

> The clothing which zealous missionaries thrust upon their converts for the sake of modesty...was for a time the most distinct emblem of black Christianity. Whether the convert earned his shirt by working for wages or fabricated it with European looms and needles, he was entering into new kinds of economic relationships (1978: 116).

The practical reforms initiated by the missionaries also entailed a particular conception of time (cf. Wilson 1971: 73). Thus Moffat (1842: 339) tells how, "when the place of worship was built, a wooden Dutch clock had been fixed upon the wall, for the purpose of regulating the hours of worship." The weekly schedule and annual calendar of the church ordered everyday routine in both its secular and sacred dimensions, demarcating what in the Tshidi world had been a continuous cycle of events and seasons. In the mission itself, the neophyte was set on the path to redemption when his career was objectified in time—time here being seen as a resource to be put to work in the interests of moral and material accumulation. And in its schools, as Oliver (1952: 52) has said of East Africa, "life was regulated almost as severely by the mission bell as it was in England by the factory hooter." Thomson (1967) has argued that the impersonal clock is the fundamental instrument for inculcating the organizational forms of capitalist production. It enables labor to be prized free from its embeddedness in a field of generalized social relations, rendering it measurable in terms that permit its transfer from worker to employer. This was to be the fate of the Tswana as colonial subjects, but they were first introduced to time as commodity by the evangelists, whose model of "industry" dictated that every mortal put his temporal resources to work on his own account, and whose church bells punctuated local community rhythms, announcing to one and all the worth of timeliness.

The objectification of time into a commodity, then, abstracted what had formerly been an intrinsic aspect of social practice. A parallel process occurred with the introduction of literacy, an essential component of the nonconformist mission. For Protestantism was the faith of the book, in that it required the convert to make a self-conscious commitment to "the word," that is, to a textualized truth. Chapel and school stood side by side, for learning was universally regarded by evangelists "as the door to the church" (Etherington 1978: 54); and, as has been widely acknowledged, the missionaries were perhaps the most significant agents of Western education in colonial Africa. The Methodists among the Tswana devoted considerable energy to translating, printing, and teaching the bible—by 1830, 200 pupils were being instructed on a regular basis—and gradually created an "elite" that was to step forward when the colonial government needed to staff the lower reaches of its bureaucracy. Even those not drawn by the Christian message sent their children to the mission schools (Chirenje 1976: 411).

But the effect of this literacy campaign was not merely to train personnel to minister colonial rule. The written word also has the capacity to transform the consciousness of those who come into contact with it, taking language out of its immediate context of use and reference. Like time and money, it circulates in disembodied form—in this case, as tracts available for consumption. The act of reading, of course, involves a silent, private transaction, an apparent exchange of reason between reader and message. It is an exchange which cannot but impinge on experience.

As this suggests, literacy, along with time and money, may engender a novel perception of the world and the place of the actor within it. In the case of the Methodist mission, it served to open up a discourse about the self as both subject and object, and encouraged the transcendence of a purely sensual existence. The effort to instill a sense of rational self-consciousness, so central to nonconformist evangelism, helped to create a subject divided—just as the introduction of "money" and the abstraction of "time" encouraged that divided self to seek its spiritual destiny by alienating its labor in return for wages. These processes tended to resituate the person within the material and meaningful relations of the industrial world. Not surprisingly, later generations of illiterate Tshidi were to try to regain a sense of lost mastery over their universe through the symbolic manipulation of money and the printed word. (J. Comaroff 1985: 226, 235f., 250).

Thus the seemingly disparate facets of the practical mission—agricultural reform, the reconstruction of personhood and social space, and the abstraction of time and the word—all reinforced each other, regrouping on native soil to form an analogue of their European parent culture. This unity was compelling, drawing the Tswana into its orbit however tangentially they took part in the "religious" activities of the church. Christianity first took root in the fissures of the local polity, initially attracting the marginal and the powerless; yet the mission, by its very presence, engaged all Tshidi in an inescapable dialogue on its own terms, even if they rejected its message. This dialogue had two consequences. First, it marked out a contrast between *sekgoa* (European ways) and *setswana* (Tswana ways), the latter being objectified, as never before, into a system of signs and conventions. And, second, it set in motion a confrontation between these two "systems," a confrontation that had a palpable effect on both. For Christian was received through the grid of local cultural forms and became the subject of an extended process of accommodation and struggle. In its course, Tshidi were transformed by Methodism even while they resisted or remolded its more explicit doctrines and practices. It is true that the direct appeal of the church varied within the community: as in many other African contexts, senior royals remained aloof until after

overrule; junior royals, the poor, and women of all ranks found identification more immediately congenial. But when all was said and
done, conversation with the mission engendered conversion—not
as an all-or-none commitment to Protestant ideology, but as a subtle
internalization of its categories and values. Only this can explain
why many Tswana (and others like them in South Africa; Bundy
1979) sought to participate in commodity and labor markets *before*
the formation of the colonial state, when the taxation and other
coercive measures forced them to do so.

Revelation and Resistance

We have demonstrated that the manifest "political" role of the
missionaries to the Tshidi was inherently ambiguous. Yet, we
have argued, they had a decisive impact on this chiefdom, instill-
ing in its population the signs and practices of a powerful new
order. In this respect, they played a vital part in the more general
process of colonization; for while the incorporation of a subject
people always involved some degree of material coercion, it was
the subtle inculcation of European values that was especially crucial (Schapera 1936: 225; Bohannan 1964: 22). Indeed, precisely
because this mode of penetration was ostensibly apolitical—and
rarely seen to be objectionable because it was rarely seen at all
(Bourdieu 1977: 167)—it had enormous historical force. But the
story does not end there. We also suggested, at the outset, that
it was in the relationship between the two dimensions of the historical role of the missionary that the contradictions of the
colonial process are revealed.

In patiently nurturing the Protestant subject in South Africa,
the missionary made it possible for him to become a colonial object.
Once they had been enticed, often unwittingly, into the conversation with Christianity, Tshidi were drawn into a dialogue whose
terms they could not but internalize—a dialogue that cast them as
citizens in a world of rational individualism. In this world, they were
told, they could fashion their own lives by exercising free choice;
personal achievement would be rewarded by the accumulation of
goods and moral worth. Practically speaking, this meant cultivating
for the market or selling their labor. After all, they had been taught
to put time to work, and to want what money could buy. In other

JEAN & JOHN COMAROFF

words, they were not merely prepared for wage labor and for cash cropping, the two sides of the role of peasant-proletarian that was to become the lot of most black South Africans. They were also made familiar with all the positive values said to go with the marketplace, including a series of sociocultural forms. Most notably among these was the monogamous (nuclear) family, the unit of production and consumption basic to the division of labor in industrial capitalist society. As we have noted, many Tshidi did not respond to the message exactly as the Methodists might have liked. Apart from all else, they read it through the filter of their own culture.

This, however, is where the paradox lay. The Methodist mission might have proclaimed the right of self-determination for all, and taught the Tshidi the language that colonialism compelled them to speak. But they were not in a position to deliver the liberal democracy promised by their ideology and implied by their practices. That they could not do so was due to the very indeterminacy of their role in "political" processes. Because, at the level of explicit power relations, they could be neither imperialists not liberators.

In short, the evangelists, by virtue of their politics of the spirit, introduced the Tshidi to an altogether novel world view. Yet, lacking the manifest power to consummate their project, they could not produce the world to go with it. As a result, they succeeded only in exposing native communities to more coercive forces. Thus, as the first generation of colonial subjects entered the workplace in an ostensibly Christian state, they were quickly made aware of the discrepancy between the values learned from the mission and the harsh realities of life in a racially coded society. The literate began to interrogate the biblical text, and to question how accurately it captured their own experience. It was they who were to express the first open resistance to the colonial order by pointing to its inconsistency with biblical injunction, and by freeing from the holy text itself a charter for liberation: the message of the chosen suffering in exile, whose historical destiny was to regain their promised land.

At first, this interrogation, among the Tshidi as elsewhere, occurred primarily among the small black bourgeoisie in the context of the church itself. But it did not remain long within those confines. When the South African Native National Congress (forerunner of the African National Congress) was founded in 1912, many of its leaders were alumni of the mission schools and active members of their congregations (cf. Rotberg 1965: 146-147 on Zambia). Others, however, contested the legitimacy of the orthodox denominations, and so there emerged an independent Black Christian movement (Sundkler 1961). But for adherents of this movement, no less than for their counterparts in the missions, the language of protest remained within terms that had been introduced by the evangelists (Gerhart 1978: 39ff.). Hence, the struggle was framed in the rhetoric of liberal democracy, individual equality, and the separation of church and state. In fact, the early leaders spent much time and energy claiming human rights by virtue of having proven themselves sufficiently "civilized" to act as responsible citizens. Even in its ostensible rejection, the culture of the mission, now heavily reinforced by the ideology of the South African state, had triumphed.

There was another, and eventually more widespread, statement of resistance to the hegemony of the new order. It was the response, largely if not exclusively, of the illiterate peasant-proletarian underclass and found its expression in popular cult movements such as Zionist Christianity. Here there emerged a different form of protest, one that remained largely implicit in the practices of the small churches. These churches were often more radical in their rejection of the colonial and postcolonial worlds than were other black denominations, for they set about reclaiming the everyday domains that had been transformed by the mission and the social order it heralded (Sundkler 1961; Kiernan 1976). Within such sects as the Zion Christian Church, the definition of personhood, community, work, space, and time—as well as the ostensible division of "religion" and "politics" inherent in mission culture—are all vigorously contested. But here, too, the categories of that culture provide the signs, the points of departure, for the acts of reversal and inversion that have served to mark an opposition to Protestant orthodoxy and all it represents. Indeed, this provides final evidence for the thoroughgoing efficacy of missionary colonization.

Conclusion

We began by distinguishing two forms of power, each associated with one dimension of the role of the missions among the Tswana. With respect to the first, power exercised in the domain of institutionalized politics, we showed that the historical agency of the evangelists was necessarily indeterminate. It stemmed from the fact that nonconformist Protestant ideology and the society from which it first came, were founded on a particular kind of distinction between church and state, religion and politics, spiritual and worldly authority. In the area of local politics, the enactment of this distinction unravelled the social fabric in such a way that missionaries were likely to be caught between Christian and non-Christian; they were also sometimes opposed by powerful Protestant chiefs and, ironically, were often in the end rejected by the very congregations they had spawned (cf. Rigby 1981). In the sphere of political relations among indigenous communities, the white settlers, and the imperial government, the same distinction of church and state created yet further ambivalence for the evangelists, as it rationalized a *range* of policy positions and courses of action.

But, if the balance sheet of intention and effect in this first domain is irreducibly ambiguous, the second presents a very different picture. For it is here, as we have said, that the seeds of colonial domination were most deeply planted, providing the South African state, at its birth, with a "theodicy of its own privilege" (Weber, see Bourdieu 1977: 188). This process, of course, was not a mechanical one. It was the product of an encounter between experiencing actors in which the signs and practices of Christianity became the subject of a *conversation*, refracted through the lens of native categories. Still, while the message was mediated, the signs themselves were deeply instilled—which is why the key to the historical role of the missionary lies here.

Nonetheless, this is not the end of the matter, for there was a contradiction between the two dimensions of the missionary project. This, in turn, gave rise to a discourse of resistance—or, more accurately, discourses of resistance, as there is never just one way of debating a new orthodoxy. Indeed, if there is any general inference to be drawn from this case it lies here. It is not merely that the position of the evangelist in the colonial process was always two dimensional, but that the precise relationship between the two dimensions—the manifest exercise of power and the diffuse control over everyday meaning—gave form to the missionary role in different times and places. In the South African case, the discovery by the colonized that the church had prepared them for a New Jerusalem but could only deliver them into a New Babylon (van Onselin 1982; cf. Sundkler 1980: 46-47) elicited a range of reactions and forms of protest. For a long time, those reactions made use of the terms of orthodox Protestantism, if only to invert or parody them. The ultimate power of Christianity in South Africa is enshrined in the fact that it took many decades for blacks to cast aside the language and ideology of the mission (Gerhart 1978); to move, that is, from revelation to revolution.

References

Beidelman, Thomas O.
1982. Colonial Evangelism: A Socio-historical Study of an East African Mission at the Grassroots. Bloomington: Indiana University Press.

Bohannan, Paul
1964. Africa and Africans. Garden City, NY: The Natural History Press.

Bourdieu, Pierre
1977. Outline of a Theory of Practice. Richard Nice, transl. New York: Cambridge University Press.

Broadbent, Samuel
1865. A Narrative of the First Introduction of Christianity amongst the Barolong Tribe of Bechuanas, South Africa. London: Wesleyan Mission House.

Bundy, Colin
1979. The Rise and Fall of the South African Peasantry. London: Heinemann.

Chirenje, J. Mutero
1976. Church, State, and Education in Bechuanaland in the Nineteenth Century. International Journal of African Historical Studies 9:401-418.

Comaroff, Jean
1985. Body of Power, Spirit of Resistance: The Culture and History of a South African People. Chicago: The University of Chicago Press.

Comaroff, John L.
1982. Dialectical Systems, History and Anthropology. Journal of Southern African Studies 8:143-172.

Crummey, Donald
1972. Priests and Politicians: Protestant and Catholic Missions in Orthodox Ethiopia 1830-1868. Oxford: Clarendon Press.

Dachs, Anthony J.
  1972. Missionary Imperialism: The Case of Bechuanaland. *Journal of African History* 13:647-658.
  1975. Papers of John Mackenzie. Johannesburg: Witwatersrand University Press.
Ekechi, F.K.
  1972. Missionary Enterprise and Rivalry in Igboland 1857-1914. London: Frank Cass.
Etherington, Norman
  1978. Preachers, Peasants and Politics in Southeast Africa, 1835-1880: African Christian Communities in Natal, Pondoland and Zululand. London: Royal Historical Society.
  1983. Missionaries and the Intellectual History of Africa: A Historical Survey. Itinerario 2:27-45.
Foucault, Michel
  1980. The History of Sexuality. Robert Hurley, transl. New York: Vintage Books.
Gerhart, Gail M.
  1978. Black Power in South Africa. Berkeley: University of California Press.
Heise, D.R.
  1967. Prefatory Findings in the Sociology of Missions. Journal for the Scientific Study of Religions 6:39-63.
Holub, Emil
  1881. Seven Years in South Africa. 2 volumes. Ellen E. Frewer, transl. Boston: Houghton Mifflin.
Kiernan, James P.
  1976. The Work of Zion: An Analysis of an African Zionist Ritual. Africa 46:340-355.
Linden, Ian
  1977. Church and Revolution in Rwanda. Manchester: Manchester University Press.
MacGaffey, Wyatt
  1983. Modern Kongo Prophets: Religion in a Plural Society. Bloomington: Indiana University Press.
Majeke, Nositho
  1953. The Role of Missionaries in Conquest. Johannesburg: Society of Young Africa.
Moffat, Robert
  1842. Missionary Labours and Scenes in Southern Africa. London: Snow.
Molema, Silas Modiri
  1966. Montshiwa, Barolong Chief and Patriot, 1815-96. Cape Town: Struik.
Oliver, Roland
  1952. The Missionary Factor in East Africa. London: Longmans, Green.
Ranger, Terence O.
  n.d. Religious Movements and Politics in Sub Saharan Africa. ms.
Rigby, Peter
  1981. Pastors and Pastoralists: The Differential Penetration of Christianity among East African Cattle Herders. Comparative Studies in Society and History 23:96-129.
Rotberg, Robert I.
  1965. Christian Missionaries and the Creation of Northern Rhodesia 1880-1924. Princeton: Princeton University Press.
Schapera, Issac
  1936. The Contributions of Western Civilization to Modern Kxatla Culture. Transactions of the Royal Society of South Africa 24:221-252.
  1958. Christianity and the Tswana. Journal of the Royal Anthropological Institute

88:1-9.

Shapiro, Judith
　1981.　Ideologies of Catholic Missionary Practice in a Postcolonial Era. Comparative Studies in Society and History 23:130-149.

Sillery, Anthony
　1952.　The Bechuanaland Protectorate. Cape Town: Oxford University Press.
　1971.　John Mackenzie of Bechuanaland 1835-1899: A Study in Humanitarian Imperialism. Cape Town: Balkema.

Strayer, Robert W.
　1978.　The Making of Mission Communities in East Africa. London: Heinemann.

Sundkler, Bengt
　1961.　Bantu Prophets in South Africa. London: Oxford University Press for the International African Institute.
　1980.　Bara Bukoba. London: Hurst.

Taussig, Michael
　1980.　The Devil and Commodity Fetishism in South America. Chapel Hill: University of North Carolina Press.

Temu, A.J.
　1972.　British Protestant Missions. London: Longman.

Thompson, Edward P.
　1967.　Time, Work-Discipline and Industrial Capitalism. Past and Present 38:56-97.

van Onselin, Charles
　1982.　Studies in the Social and Economic History of the Witwatersrand, 1886-1914. Vol. 1. New York: Longman.

Warner, Wellman J.
　1930.　The Wesleyan Movement in the Industrial Revolution. London: Longmans, Green.

Williams, Raymond
　1977.　Marxism and Literature. Oxford: Oxford University Press.

Wilson, Monica
　1969.　Co-operation and Conflict: The Eastern Cape Frontier. In The Oxford History of South Africa. Vol. 1. Monica Wilson and Leonard Thompson, eds. pp. 233-271. Oxford: Oxford University Press.
　1971.　The Growth of Peasant Communities. In The Oxford History of South Africa. Vol. 2. Monica Wilson and Leonard Thompson, eds. pp. 49-103. Oxford: Oxford University Press.

THE POLITICS OF TRADITION:
TOWARD A GENERIC CULTURE IN VANUATU

Jean-Marc Philibert

*T*aking a leaf out of a recent historical work on "the invention of tradition", Jean-Marc Philibert analyzes in this article the construction of traditional culture in Vanuatu, a small, newly-independent nation in the South Pacific.

In Vanuatu, as in other new states, political elites are trying to mold a culturally diverse population into a unified nation and to transform tribesmen and peasants into citizens in the modern sense of the word. This political transformation is presented, paradoxically, as a return to a traditional cultural integrity undermined by colonialism. The rhetoric is the basis of a political strategy. Inventing and popularizing a version of cultural history, the elite are able to identify themselves as those who best understand the past and are therefore best suited to lead the nation into the future.

Philibert raises two central questions. The first one deals with the link between **kastom** (invented custom) and power. Using Marx's notion of fetishization to explore the reification of the past by members of the political elite, he argues that this tactic has enabled them to disguise political discourse and thereby to foreclose political choice. It pre-empts much of the opposition and what is left is rendered virtually silent because the elite supply the vocabulary which allows people to talk about kastom and hold the seal which authenticates things as traditional. "...kastom, this son et lumière orchestration of the "past", largely conceals the differential distribution of power and its exercise."

But occasionally symbols cannot be "customized" and this leads to Philibert's second question. Why did the elite fail to enshrine **kava**, a traditional drink, within the field of kastom? His answer is to say that neo-traditional symbols cannot always be successfully imposed from above. While ni-Vanuatu may have ac-

cepted that the party in power has become the arbiter of "tradi-
tions", they have kept the right to ascribe their own meaning to
any one symbol.

> *"It may be that the profane possibilities of kava*
> *drinking were simply too numerous, too fluid one is*
> *tempted to say, for kava to become sacralized in a*
> *modern, urban context. Sacred symbols probably cannot*
> *afford to be too good, pace Levi-Strauss (1965): what is*
> *good to drink may be too good to think."*

IN AN ARTICLE WRITTEN IN the early 1960's, Geertz (1973)
describes the difficulties of new states in establishing a modern civil
polity among their citizenry, in creating a country out of an ex-
colony. The problem, as he sees it, has to do with "the great extent
to which their peoples' sense of self remains bound up in the gross
actualities of blood, race, language, locality, religion, or tradition...."
(Geertz 1973: 258). It is the dominance of primordial bonds and
sentiments over civil sentiments which makes various forms of
parochialism and tribalism so difficult to overcome in these new
states (1973: 261). Civil order, in the sense of both a new socio-cultural fabric and political peace, requires then a shift from one form
of identification to another. How to achieve this is hard to say because, although from Aristotle onward the very notion of civility
has been a concern of political scientists, we still have only a hazy
picture of how it developed in the West.

A recent book by English historians (Hobsbawm and Ranger
1983) deals with the development of civil consciousness in Europe,
particularly in the form of emerging national identity in the 19th
century.[1] One of the means employed was the invention of old,
unchanging traditions of various kinds, "ecclesiastical, educational,
military, republican, monarchical" (Ranger 1983: 211). Such invented traditions are

> a set of practices normally governed by overtly or tacitly
> accepted rules and of a ritual or symbolic nature, which
> seek to inculcate certain values and norms of behaviour
> by repetition, which automatically implies continuity with
> the past...the peculiarity of invented traditions is that the
> continuity with it [the past] is largely factitious. In short,

JEAN-MARC PHILIBERT

they are responses to novel situations which establish their own past by quasi-obligatory repetitions. (Hobsbawm 1983: 1-2)

The traditions invented in Europe since the industrial revolution seem to fall into three overlapping types:

a) those establishing or symbolizing social cohesion or the membership of groups, real or artificial communities. b) those establishing or legitimizing institutions, status or relations of authority, and) those whose main purpose was socialization, the inculcation of beliefs, value systems and conventions of behaviour. (Hobsbawm 1983: 9)

Many of these conventions pertain to a fairly recent political construct, the modern nation, to which are associated "nationalism, the nation-state, national symbols, histories and the rest. All these rest on exercises in social engineering which are often deliberate and always innovative" (Hobsbawm 1983: 13). So, far from civility being an ancient tradition in the West, it appears that civil sentiments are fairly recent here, no less so than in the new states. New forms of ruling, new "bonds of loyalty" were developed from the mid-nineteenth century onward as a result of increased bureaucratic control over the population, the development of a truly national economy, the standardization of law and administration, national political organizations, and state-controlled public primary education (Hobsbawm 1983: 264). In Hobsbawm's terse formulation this was when "state, nation and society converged" (1983: 265).[2]

Who were the inventors of neo-traditions? They were those in power, like the leaders of the Third Republic in France, whose invented traditions helped them to perpetrate a masterful act of political deception.

Yet the basic fact was that those who controlled the imagery, the symbolism, the traditions of the Republic were men of the center masquerading as men of the extreme left: the Radical Socialists, proverbially like the radish, red outside, white inside, and always on the side the bread is buttered. (Hobsbawm 1983: 270)

This raises the issue of how much political manipulation is possible by those who control public discourses. Is it, as Hobsbawm suggests, that the best examples of successful manipulation are precisely the ones which meet a "need", conscious or unconscious, among groups of citizens? In order for forms of public ritualization such as public holidays, marches, and heroes to become popular enough to carry their message, they may first have to strike a responsive chord among citizens. How much can be composed from above, and under what circumstances are, of course, empirical questions.

I wish to borrow a last item from Hobsbawm and Ranger's book, the distinction between tradition and custom.

> The object and characteristic of "traditions", including invented ones, is invariance. The past, real or invented, to which they refer imposes fixed (normally formalized) practices, such as repetition. "Custom" in traditional societies has the double function of motor and fly wheel. It does not preclude innovation and change up to a point....What it does is to give any desired change (or resistance to innovation) the sanction of precedent, social continuity and natural laws as expressed in history.... "Custom" cannot afford to be invariant because even in "traditional" societies life is not so...the strength and adaptability of genuine traditions is not to be confused with the "invention of tradition." Where the old ways are alive, traditions need to be neither revived nor invented. (Ranger 1983: 2 and 8)

Tradition, and more so the invented kind, then, is conscious custom, dead custom, empty practice.

Traditions as recent civil discourses in new states, more precisely the links between their invention and political power, are the first subject of this article. Historical revisionism cannot always be successfully imposed from above. To be adopted, neo-traditional symbols must to some extent be compatible with present-day experience. Why some symbols succeed and others fail is the second topic that will be examined. Although new states are harder to find in the 1980s, they are by no means an extinct species. The Republic of Vanuatu, known until 1980 as the Anglo-French Condominium of the New Hebrides, is such a case. Moreover, this South Pacific country is not simply an archipelago in the geological sense: it is also an archipelago of the spirit, linguistically and culturally fragmented in more ways than one would think possible in a nation of 125,000 inhabitants.[3] As such, it is an ideal place to examine the birth of civil sentiments.

1. Vanuatu Cultural Policy: the Rhetoric of Kastom

As documented in a recent issue of *Mankind*, the newly independent nations of Melanesia are developing a post-colonial identity largely by resuscitating a pre-colonial past. To create this new national identity, members of the political elite are on the one hand reaching back to a certain view of the past, while at the same time forging ahead and instituting the full apparatus of the modern nation-state. This turn toward the pre-colonial past has taken the form of reinstating "traditional"—*kastom* as it is known in Vanuatu—as a unifying political symbol. As Keesing points out, the interest of *kastom* as a political symbol derives from the fact that it is culture itself which serves as a symbol (Keesing 1982: 298).[4]

In Vanuatu, the party in power has adopted a museological view of culture, the construct it calls *kastom*. It is tradition as defined by members of an acculturated political elite living in an urban environment, many of whom were, prior to independence, Presbyterian clergymen or civil servants in the colonial administration. In other words, this *kastom* policy is endorsed by those least able to define or codify such customs. In fact, one could go further and state that it is a political symbol that could only have been devised in an urban context, away from areas where "traditional" culture has remained a lived practice because in this latter case, as Tonkinson observes, *kastom* is indeed divisive.

> In the local arena the most common uses of *kastom* as a body of lore reflect its utility in defining differences and marking boundaries among competing groups. (Tonkinson 1982: 302)

The use of *kastom* as a symbol which owes nothing to colonialism, as opposed to Christianity for example, (though the latter can be said to be, of the two, the dominating discourse, the one that has incorporated and reinterpreted the other [Philibert 1982]), started right at the beginning of the pro-independence movement. However, it received its most public airing during a National Arts Festival held in Port Vila, the capital, from December 1st to December 8th 1979. There, for the first time, ni-Vanuatu from all over the Group gathered to show their *kastom* and to watch that of others.[5] It is interesting to see the *découpage* of culture which took place by making an inventory of the activities on display and the time allocated to each one. (Most sessions were two hours long, except for traditional dances which lasted between four and six hours.) "Traditional culture" was portrayed as traditional games for 3 sessions; messages sent by slit gongs and conch shells (3 sessions); traditional dances (8 sessions); traditional ways of cooking (3 sessions); methods of food sharing (2 sessions); playing bamboo flutes (2 sessions); pottery, archery, spear throwing (1 session); traditional business, i.e. marriage and chief installing (2 sessions); fire rubbing (1 session); traditional manners and public addressing (1 session); traditional songs (1 session); display of artefacts (1 day).

To a large extent, the festival shaped a view of culture as a set of traits, "old" behaviors and beliefs, with the accent placed on culture as a spectacle such as dances and their associated paraphernalia, the performance of magical tricks, music, in short activities with a strong theatrical and ludic component. Far from being a closely integrated, functionalist view of culture, the view of *kastom* to emerge from the political circles of the capital is one of a set of survivals. This is so because those who have to decide what *kastom* was/is are precisely those who have lost theirs.

The Arts Festival accomplished two things: it showed ni-Vanuatu the diversity and thus the richness of their *kastom* and it presented this traditional knowledge in a positive light such that the *évolués*, the acculturated urbanities, felt for once their situation to be one of loss rather than advantage.[6]

Even today, the Vanuatu Cultural Center through its curator plays a pivotal role in determining what *kastom* is by mounting exhibitions, marketing artefacts, developing anthropological research policies, ensuring proper media exposure, training Vanuatu "cultural researchers" to record on cassettes and videotapes "traditional happenings" in their home communities, etc.[7]

JEAN-MARC PHILIBERT

Kastom is tradition, some invented, some not, a redefinition of a cultural past whose contour is shaped in an ongoing discourse by those in power. There are of course other views of *kastom*, for example that of the opposition party.[8] Is the process of creation of tradition by members of the Vanuatu elite captured by the following analogy with leaders of a trade union suddenly standing up for opera as an artistic genre epitomizing working class values and modes of expression? Clearly, it is not the case, yet there is a contradiction when the modernizing force committed to the making of a nation-state also controls the imagery and symbolism of the "traditional" values and virtues it now expects from compliant citizens. This intellectualization of the past is too politically self-serving not to be suspect.

Kastom amounts to a complex of symbols loosely tied together which "act as political icons of invention and convention, available for interpretation of historical contexts in this new nation, both at the national and local level" as Larcom (1982: 330) so perceptively points out. There are presumably more than one sort of social and cultural experience being articulated through *kastom*. Adolescents are shown in the national newspaper doing break dancing in the streets of the capital, Port Vila, a town with three cinemas, one of which is a drive-in, and which has now been hit by the video revolution. (There are nine video shops in this town of 12,000 inhabitants.) At the other end of the spectrum, how do ni-Vanuatu for whom *kastom* is still lived practice react to the official discourse? Are they also in the process of reifying culture into traditions, to go back to our basic distinction?

In 1979, Larcom witnessed a new local interest in *kastom* among the Mewun of Malekula, though it did not concern the *kastom* she herself had witnessed six years previously.

> *Kastom* glossed today as revealed and revitalized authentic tradition has little to do with earlier use of *kastom* in Mewun. *Kastom* as used by Mewun from their historical recollections in 1973-74 applied to knowledge and its manifestations, sold and exchanged from district to district.... The kind of *kastom* which Mewun informants described in their history had little to do with the past in the sense of traditional, continuous or authentic...*kastom* as knowledge bought and sold could be amalgamated in-

ventively as it was purchased from other districts. (Larcom 1982: 333)

The Mewun were now reading Deacon, their ethnographer, and through some sort of intellectual *glissement*, "the invention of convention now relied on the inscription of *kastom* as tradition as well as knowledge" (1982: 334). Larcom notes that

> The appeal to Deacon, to culture by the book, allows the establishment of *kastom* as a codified tradition, their culture has become ethnographic...as something like a text to be connected, integrated, taught and transmitted rather than invented. (1982: 336)

This codification, and soon perhaps ossification of culture, its transformation into a text whose merit and authenticity are defined by reference to a distant past, and the notion of the past itself as more or less an inversion of the present, an age in which precisely what is now lacking, existed in a state of plenty, none of these is entirely the result of a nationalist cultural policy. The arrival of white men, the adoption of Christianity, and the periods of indentured labour in Australia in the 19th century, were intercultural activities which had already provided Mewun with models of non-Mewun behavior (or *fasen* as it is known in *Bislama*), in other words with a vantage point from which they could see themselves. What was lacking though, was the notion of a finite text, if not a closed one; nor did there previously exist any arbiters of "true" *kastom* on the national scene with whom the Mewun had to carry a dialogue in order to produce the final text. *Kastom* is no longer lived practices for the Mewun: it is akin to the vestigial notion of culture now known in modern nations as ethnic heritage. The Mewun do not yet acknowledge that they have a culture in the anthropological sense of the word, but they now admit to having *kastom*.

In this process of indigenization of the state through the promotion of a generic culture through the Group, how much control does the political elite exercise over the symbols that are part of this civil discourse? Let us now turn our attention to kava (*Piper methysticum*), a symbol that had the potential to become a political icon, yet did not become one.

JEAN-MARC PHILIBERT

2. Kava: The Symbol That Got Away

One of the key symbols to emerge in Vanuatu after independence has been the drinking of kava. Kava appears to be the perfect neo-traditional symbol. The plant is indigenous to the country and thus fulfills the requirements of timelessness. Like wines for the French, it is something in which the country excels *naturally*. Its organic connectedness with the land is further proved by the potency of the drug, the strongest in the Pacific as ni-Vanuatu proudly state. The plant was used widely during the pre-colonial period by members of various socio-linguistic groups on many islands, though Kava drinking never developed as fully elsewhere as it did on Tanna.[9] Its use was suppressed by white men (missionaries), and can thus serve as an anti-colonial symbol and stand for the difficult and arduous anti-colonial struggle that never was. Being a root, it forms the perfect organic metaphor for soil, land, and place; it even tastes like dirt! Kava drinking was reserved to adult men, the makers and interpreters of "official culture." It was something that men did in a sort of sacrificial spirit in order to converse with their ancestors; although kava was prepared and drunk in groups of adult men, those men renounced the light of day, the familiar sounds of the village, the company of women and children and, having drunk, each other's speech. The kava ritual on Tanna which Brunton calls "the daily dissolution of society" allows adult men to reach a deeper, ontological truth. In this sense, kava was a spiritual lubricant, not a social one, connected to the sort of knowledge that matters, spiritual knowledge. In a way, it made the ancestors and spirits responsible for installing men in their dominant position. As a source of enlightenment reserved exclusively to adult men, it gave them the rod that could measure the validity of all new knowledge. Kava was the golden path to power: women and girls stayed away while young men chewed but did not drink; it testified to the irreducibility of sex and age as social categories.[10]

Finally, there was a ceremonial to kava drinking with an order of precedence among drinkers. Given all these facets of kava on Tanna, one is not surprised to hear that its use was associated with all that mattered.

> Kava carries a very heavy cultural load on Tanna...all important messages and requests should be accompanied by a piece of kava. Thus the Tannese see it as essential for actuating the roads of alliance (*suatu*), on which marriage, ceremonial exchange, dances and the division of ritual labour depend. (Brunton 1979: 97)

The potential of kava as a key symbol, as a political icon, is clear. One would thus have expected those in power to restore kava drinking to its "original" form having made the adjustments necessary to comply with a Christian view of the world. The ancestors would have had to be accommodated within a view that such spirits, whose existence is not in doubt, are pagan, *tevil,* and deadly when not handled properly.

But this is not what actually happened. What did take place encapsulates the social and cultural predicament of those neo-traditional symbols. In this case, other exigencies prevailed. Kava was promoted by the government on economic grounds to reduce the loss of foreign currency used to pay for imports of alcoholic beverages. (With a population half the size of the Solomon Is. Vanuatu imports twice as much alcoholic beverages.) It is also a crop which allows people living in rural areas to earn cash. Finally, the national distribution of the product, a most lucrative venture, is concentrated in the hands of an important member of the party in power. The ambiguous character of kava is caught in the following sentences taken from a government *précis* on how to grow the plant: "Kava represents much more than a mere species of plant. It is an integral part of the Melanesian cultural heritage....

It is a cash crop with spiritual overtones" (*Tri Independens Selebresen,* 1983: 77).

Kava is also promoted as a socially acceptable alternative to alcohol, since it induces sleep in the drinkers rather than belligerence, by a government concerned with increased alcohol-related violence against persons (wife battering, rape and assault) and against property in urban areas where the village mechanisms curtailing such violence are absent. Kava is also said by drinkers to have medicinal properties, as evidenced by the two tons of kava purchased by a German pharmaceutical firm. The national radio and press also report whenever they can on laboratory analysis being carried out in the West. It is rumored by some peri-urban villagers

JEAN-MARC PHILIBERT

to be a cure for cancer, an extraordinary claim as cancer is not yet an acknowledged disease according to local aetiology. (People have only recently started to ascribe death to heart attacks caused by over-exhaustion working for whites, but not yet to cancer.) A whole folklore is being developed around the drinking of kava, while traditionally it did not require today's justification that, like Guinness, it is good for you.

Promoted by the government as a commodity to replace alcohol, the "traditional" meaning of kava drinking is totally transformed and intoxication becomes the goal. On Tanna, kava and alcohol still belong to different social contexts, *kastom as opposed to lafet* (a modern party): drinkers of kava and alcohol exhibit different types of intoxicated behavior; different types of prestations take place in each context; the activities are even located in different parts of the village. "The two substances are contrastive symbols within a larger conceptual opposition that people make between things *kastom* and things modern" (Lindstrom 1982: 432). As this author remarks, the Tannese intellectual purism is not found in town where kava drinkers have no compunction about mixing it with alcohol. In fact it has now become the proper thing to do at wedding receptions to offer guests a choice of kava and then move on to liquor leaving no doubt as to the effects of the *mélange*.

The goal of kava drinking in town being intoxication, people endlessly debate the rules to follow to ensure that the drink is as potent as can be, such as "dry the root in the sun prior to making kava"; "never buy dry roots"; "chewed kava (à la Tannese) is stronger"; "the best kava in town comes from the Pentecost *nakamal*"; "never mix alcohol with kava, you will be sick"; "nothing works like a chaser after a bowl of kava"; "prepare the kava in the dark, it will be stronger"; "do not use electric light when drinking etc...".

How extensive is the incidence of kava drinking? In the peri-urban village of Erakor, no one drank kava in 1973. The habit had been lost following 19th century missionary proscription. By 1979, a few villagers drank it episodically; it was not generally available in town and no one grew it in the village. By 1983, every Chinese store in town sold kava as did the Erakor co-operative store. In town, there are also places selling take-away kava as well as so-called men's houses (*nakamal*) where one can drink it on the spot.

It is now even sold by the glass in the villages. Not only do a lot of people drink a lot of it, but they talk about it even more, recounting pleasant memories of being unexpectedly drugged on kava ("it was such a deceptively small root"), whether it made them throw up or not, at what point their knees buckled under them and they fell to the ground on their way home. They wear the assorted facial scratches that result as proudly as if they were battlescars.

The drinking of kava is not reserved for the less modern among villagers, quite the contrary, as it is expensive to buy. It is also among the évolués that one is likely to see women drink kava. Wealthy villagers living in concrete houses with all the modern amenities have now started to build small thatched huts in their yard where they can sit on a coral floor covered with mats, like the poor, to prepare and drink kava with friends. Such huts are miniature traditional houses. Tradition then becomes a spectacle in which one indulges to express facets of one's identity, the way preserving one's regional accent may be in many countries a statement of connectedness.

The commodization of this neo-traditional symbol in the form of a take-away product in town, its sale according to marketing devices developed in advanced capitalist economies, has transformed kava into at worst simply a locally available means of intoxication and, at best, into a sign in a discourse on culture, a form of aesthetics. There is perhaps no better expression of ambivalence of neo-traditional symbols in urban areas today than the following quote from an Erakor villager in his early 40's, an ex-policeman turned security guard, and village council member.

> It is not right for the government to push the drinking of kava as if it was only another kind of alcohol. All countries have their customs that are uniquely their own. People do not borrow the customs of the Japanese or of other people. Their custom is their way of being. Kava is important, it is central to the traditions of ni-Vanuatu and it deserves respect. And what is the government doing? It is pushing the making, the sale, and the drinking of kava so that it is now losing its importance. Today women drink it as if it was nothing. Men drink it as if it was beer or wine. They have no longer any respect for it. It is all the fault of the government. And you know what else is wrong with

this government? It won't allow pornography in the country! You cannot rent or show porno tapes on the video and you cannot buy porno magazines. If you get caught, you go to jail. Yet in Noumea, there are sex shops everywhere you go. It is all the fault of these churchmen in the government!

3. On Fetishizing One's Past

Nation-building in Melanesia has required an indigenization of the state. In Vanuatu, aloof French and British civil servants, the agents of remote colonial powers, have been replaced by a cast of Western-trained Vanuatu bureaucrats, ex-churchmen and civil servants, who have promised to build a modern country molded onto traditional ways and values. Given the cultural fragmentation of Vanuatu, clearly primordial sentiments cannot lead to the emergence of national groups of any significant size. Instead, a generic "no-name brand" culture is being codified to serve as the basis of nationalistic sentiments as well as a rallying point for a civil polity. The party in power has applied itself to inventing "traditions", *kastom*. It has also defined bad *kastom* and good *kastom*, the latter being those which challenge neither the nation-state, nor Christian dogmas. As such, the neo-traditional symbols and imagery attesting to the existence of national culture amount to a political discourse.

A reification of one's cultural past condoning the present and moulding itself to the political forms espoused by a political elite can become fetishism. The term fetish derives from the Portuguese word *feitiço* meaning charm, an object endowed with magical property and revered for this reason. Marx, in an ironic frame of mind, applied the term to the reification process found in capitalist society. Fetishism consists in attributing social efficacy to the wrong agent, such as things and money in a capitalist society, thus ignoring the social context of production and effectively placing it beyond challenge.

I now wish to borrow two ideas from Lefebvre's reading of Marx which are basic for the development of my argument. The first is that in capitalist society, commodities do not impose themselves as sets of things, but as a form in the sense of a logic, a model of society, and a mode of consciousness. Commodities are abstractions which impose their laws on men by forcing them into their logical forms, their structure, and rationality. This commodity model seeps into praxis, creating false representations, notably a sense of changelessness (Lefebvre 1968: 38-40; 83-84). Lefebvre also emphasizes the point that class relations are never direct and that it is naive at best to say that a capitalist exploits his workers; the allocation of the national income goes through the intermediary of the state and society as a whole.

> It is the bourgeoisie as a class which exploits the proletariat as a class—as well as other groups, classes and fractions of classes—by syphoning off by various means, economic, social, political, administrative, fiscal, even cultural (organization of leisure activities and of artistic production), as big a share as possible of the national income. (1968, 103: my translation).

Is there an equivalent to this process of mystification in precapitalist societies? Let us say for the sake of argument that fetishism can be found in all societies in the form of ideologies through which societies make themselves incomprehensible. Pouillon puts it somewhat more rashly when he states, "in any society, one can find fetishism, that is to say people who are alienated, and ideologues who alienate them" (1975: 115, my translation). But what form does it take, what sort of logic does it impose?

In a recent book, Taussig addresses the issue of fetishism in traditional societies in the following terms,

> ...the fetishism that is found in the economics of precapitalist societies arises from the sense of organic unity between persons and their products, and this stands in stark contrast to the fetishism of commodities in capitalist societies, which results from the split between persons and the things that they produce and exchange. (Taussig 1980: 37)

There is a magic of reciprocity exchange as well as a magic of commodity exchange. (Taussig, 1980: 124, 128). In precapitalist economies a fetishism of religion rather than one of commodity is found (1980: 121). It is a "metaphysics of persons and things" founded on the apparent inability to distinguish between people and their products. Taussig then cites Mauss of the *Essai sur le Don* and the Maori's notion of *hau*, the life-force found in the things exchanged which explains that they keep circulating.

Taussig seems to imply that people living in pre-capitalist societies entertain a natural set of relationships with the products they create, as if social experience was less culturally (arbitrarily) determined there than it is in modern societies. He fails to see that people are separated from their products and alienated from their labour in a different way. Fetishism, a form of logic which dissimulates the true nature of exploitation, is not couched in economic terms in traditional societies, though it often has an economic manifestation. The veil of illusion is not made of an economic fabric.

Fetishism consists in whatever ideology hides the creation of a surplus-value by a group which over-values its own products and under-values the products of others. Fetishism is whatever dissimulates the appropriation by a group of a greater share of the global social and cultural "income" than any other group. The mechanism of appropriation need not be relations of property. If what women and young men produce is accorded little value, they may not be separated from their product, but their labour is artificially devalued and their social worth reduced. The ideology masking this alienation becomes fetishistic when the social theory accounting for the greater worth of some and the lesser worth of others is presented as an act of nature. This political legerdemain is based on the consumption of symbolic units, symbols and classifications; it is the imposition of one group's self-serving construction of reality as the natural order of things or, to use Crick's apt formula, "the social construction of ignorance" (1982: 303). We sometimes forget the obvious, that, as Marx says, the ruling ideas are those of the ruling class, though this statement would be less of a truism if Marx had added that it is sometimes on account of its ideas that a particular class rules.

The ability to dominate derives in part from imposing one's construction of reality as the natural order of things. It is thus based on the production of exclusive knowledge by a group, on the control of the means of validation of dominant symbols, and often on the spreading of a home-spun social theory which denies the existence

of differential power and of domination. There are then as many
forms of fetishism as there are bases of symbolic domination.

Political power is thus closely linked to the acknowledgement
of one's exclusive right to produce and authenticate knowledge. The
self-proclaimed ability of a political party to retain the essence of
the past while at the same time imposing state control over the lives
of people, transforming them into citizens, is a powerful political
instrument. It pre-empts other political projects also justified by the
need to preserve local and cultural specificity, as in the case of the
Secessionists.

In Vanuatu, although one hesitates to describe the neo-traditional civil discourse know as *kastom* as hegemonic, behind the
project there nonetheless clearly lies a proto-bureaucratic class.
Members of this "class" are attempting to gain control over a symbolic code which can promote social cohesion in a wider social entity
than ever existed before and impose a form of leadership (or acquiescence, when viewed from below) modelled on that of an en-
lightened "traditional" chief who rules by virtue of his knowledge.
They are socializing ni-Vanuatu, without their knowledge, to the
values and organization of a civil polity.

Conclusion

To unravel the link between the invention of tradition and the
distribution of political power in Vanuatu was one of the objectives of this article. We saw what Collin, albeit in a very different
context, felicitously calls "la ruse de la conjugaison au passé du
projet d'avenir" (Collin 85: 33), in other words how a modern
political discourse became metaphorized as culture. When political culture becomes culture itself, that is to say when the set of
rules, values, and symbols at work in the political arena are
presented as no different from those at work in social life in
general, the by nature contentious dimension of politics is
evacuated from the field. The political discourse is no longer seen
as political which means opposition becomes difficult as there is
no terrain on which to stand. It becomes virtually impossible
when those in power also supply the vocabulary which allows
people to speak about *kastom*, that is to say when they hold the
seal that authenticates events as traditional. Moreover, when the

capillaries of power are distributed all over the social organism, *kastom*, this son et lumière orchestration of the "past", largely conceals the differential distribution of power and its exercise.

If the analysis appears to point to a conspiracy by members of a political elite to mystify the population in order to maintain their domination over them, then this is further than I wish to go. I do not believe that in Vanuatu, the invention and manipulation of neo-traditional symbols is a conscious process. The complexity of the dialectical relation between power and culture can never be accounted for by a crude conspiracy theory. Yet to endorse a consensus model and deny the existence of sectional interests on the part of the governing minority, members of the party in power and senior civil servants (the great majority of whom belong to the party), is even less acceptable. As A. Cohen (1981) shows in his study of Sierra Leone Creoles, elite groups carry on both particularistic and universalistic activities in varying proportions at different times. What I wanted to show was the irony of the situation in Vanuatu where a Westernized elite which knows least about *kastom* is busy inventing them. This is not without historical precedent in Europe as we saw earlier, yet anthropologists seem at times unaware that they are being served up with tradition rather than custom.

The second question raised was what makes forms of public ritualization popular. Is the symbolic manipulation of "old" symbols always guaranteed to meet with success? Evidently not, as we saw for kava drinking, a symbol with the potential to become the ideal political icon. Because of the government's other exigencies, the use of kava was promoted as though it was a substitute for alcohol, a drink akin to home-brewed beer, something cheaper and better for you. Before being accepted, symbols must articulate the social and cultural experience of citizens and this is not an easy task. The symbols must be equally meaningful to people living in isolated rural areas and in town, to individuals with very different recollections and practices of their "customary institutions". Ni-Vanuatu may have accepted as a matter of course that the party in power is the arbiter of "traditions", but still have kept the right to debate the validity of any symbol.

I am also unsure whether commodization has destroyed forever the symbolic potential of kava. It may yet rise some day, Phoenix-like, from the ashes of advanced capitalism to become a traditional icon!

It may be that the profane possibilities of kava drinking were simply too numerous, too fluid one is tempted to say, for kava to become sacralized in a modern, urban context. Sacred symbols probably cannot afford to be too good, *pace* Lévi-Strauss (1965): what is good to drink may be too good to think.

Acknowledgements

I *wish to thank the Social Sciences and Humanities Research Council of Canada for providing a Leave Fellowship which allowed me to spend six months in Vanuatu in 1983 researching consumption and later seven months at the Australian National University as a Visiting Fellow. Many thanks to the Australian National University for the offer of a Visiting Fellowship and to Professor Anthony Forge, Department of Prehistory and Anthropology, Faculty of Arts, at ANU for his generous hospitality. I am also indebted to Professor F. Manning and Jane Philibert for their comments and suggestions on this article.*

Notes

1.   One of the chapters is devoted to the creation of some well-known "ancient" Scottish traditions such as the kilt, the distinctive clan tartans and even the clan organization itself, all of which amount to a "bizarre travesty of Scottish history, Scottish reality" (Trevor-Roper 1983: 30). Trevor-Roper argues convincingly that the kilt or philibeg was the invention of an English Quaker industrialist from Lancashire in the 1730s. As for the identification between clans and tartans, this is how it happened. In

preparation for a royal visit to Scotland, the manufacturers of tartans for the Highland regiments prepared a "Key Pattern Book" for various clans. By the time the royal visit of 1882 was confirmed, there was no time left for the clans to choose from the samples provided.

> "The spate of orders was now such that 'every piece of tartan was sold as it came off the loom'...so Cluny Macpherson...was given a tartan from the peg. For him it was now labelled 'Macpherson', but previously, having been sold in bulk to a Mr. Kidd to clothe his West Indian slaves, it had been labelled 'Kidd', and before that it had been simply 'No. 155'." (1983: 30).

The clan organization had been dissolved by a series of acts of parliament following the unsuccessful rebellion of 1745. The clans, as part of a golden age of Highland civilization, were fraudulently revived by a pair of pedantic social climbers, the brothers Allen.

2. In France, for example, following the manifestation of radical mass politics of the Paris commune, the leaders of the Third Republic felt that "An alternative 'civic religion' had to be constructed. The need for it was the core of Durkheim's sociology..." (Hobsbawm 1983: 269).

The invention of French Republican traditions took three main forms:

> (1) "the development of a secular equivalent to the church — primary education, imbued with revolutionary and republican principles and content"; (2) "the invention of public ceremonies", such as Bastille Day whose celebration started in 1880; (3) "the mass production of public monuments" (*ibid.* 271), with the Republic represented by Marianne whose amount of clothing was proportional to the conservatism of the local citizens.

3. There is no clearer indication of the country's social and cultural diversity than its linguistic situation: there are roughly 115 languages spoken in Vanuatu, or about one per thousand inhabitants. Under the Condominium, people were further divided according to religious affiliation (Roman Catholic vs Presbyterian and Anglican), educational systems (French vs British), official languages (French vs English), and national party politics (a French-supported party for a decentralized administration and independence later vs British-supported party for a modern nation-state and independence now).

4. Many anthropologists and historians now accept that the "traditional" or "primitive" cultures described by anthropologists are partly the result of the colonial policies of the 1920s and 1930s. As Ranger points out for Africa,

> nineteenth-century Africa was *not* characterized by lack of internal social and economic competition, by the unchallenged authority of elders, by an acceptance of custom which gave every person, young and old, male and female — a place in society which was defined and protected...colonialism saw an establishment of control by elders of land location, marriage transactions and political office. Small-scale gerontocracies were a defining feature of the twentieth century rather than the nineteenth century. (Ranger 1983: 248-249)

An African historian thus writes of the invention of tribes in Tanganyika.

> Tribes were seen as cultural units "possessing a common language, a single social system, and an established common law." Their political and social system rested on kinship. Tribal membership was hereditary. Different tribes were related genealogically. (Iliffe, John as quoted in Ranger 1983: 250).

This African ideal model gained such acceptance that the best anthropologists working in Melanesia 30 years later had to justify to their colleagues not finding such groups. (Barnes 1962); the others, of course, found some.

Traditional culture was not solely the result of European codification of indigenous behaviors and the arresting of shifting social dynamics. Ranger points out that Africans also took part in the invention of their culture:

> Codified and reified custom was manipulated by such vested interests as a means of asserting and increasing control (Ranger 1983: 254).

as was the case of elders against juniors, men against women, ruling aristocracies against their subjects, and local indigenous populations against migrant populations. Clammer (1973) describes the invention of traditional culture in Fiji following the 19th century codification of "traditional" land-holding units and social groups. He writes,

> Colonialism has thus profoundly influenced the Fijians' perception of their traditional polity and its sustaining beliefs. But from the initial imposition of a system based upon, but alien to, the original traditional system, the dogma of "traditionalism" has become itself a tradition, and as such is exploited by the present political leaders of the Fijian community. (Clammer 1973: 219).

In Vanuatu, no administrative codification of customs took place, not even the codification of native laws as called for in the 1914 Protocol. The unworkable nature of the Anglo-French Condominium of the New Hebrides acted as a brake on any attempt to systematize native culture, or any other thing for that matter. So the "traditional" culture is not the result, as it is in other colonial situations of Europeans interpreting "traditions" to natives and natives in turn manipulating such models to fit (as profitably as could be managed) the colonial order. Thus if traditional customs were not sufficient to obtain the ruling expected from a colonial officer, yet older customs were unearthed during his next visit. In Vanuatu, the dialogue leading to the validation and authentification of *kastom* involves mostly (1) a Western educated elite endorsing a Third World, North-South political discourse, (2) acculturated villagers who are committed Christians, and (3) "traditionalists", those for whom "traditional culture" still amounts to a more or less systematic system of knowledge.

5.   The Prime Minister, an Anglican priest who studied in Auckland, was so taken by the Arts Festival that he had an Arts Festival organized on his own island of birth, Pentecost, according to the same format, the proceedings of which were filmed by an Australian film team. Anthropologists were later called upon to authenticate the event. I saw the film in the Department of Anthropology at the Australian National University where it was presented as an ethnographic record of traditional culture.

6.   Those coming from the islands made fun of peri-urban villagers for their lack of rituals. A villager from the peri-urban village of Erakor sent a recorded message to Radio-Vanuatu explaining that the reason they had so few traditions left was because they sacrificed them in order to bring about the new social order. Other islanders, he went on to say, now benefit from this new social order by coming in droves to Port Vila to seek employment. He then suggested to those who mocked them that, if it was really the way they felt about *kastom*, then they ought to go back home to their island to practice their beloved *kastom*.

7.   The following item was reported in *Vanuatu Weekly* of 27/4/85 under the caption, "1985 sees the promotion of Vanuatu culture". Mr. Willie Roy, in the employ of the Culture Center, explained to a reporter the purpose of the cultural activities he was organizing in the capital

> ...he said the Home Affairs Ministry, seeing the need to preserve Vanuatu's Customs, has arranged for individual islands to perform their cultural items in the Capital...The Culture activities he said, include, traditional house building, traditional medicine, traditional ways of sending messages and many other traditional items which he said, are vital for the youths of today to get to know to increase their knowledge of their individual island's colorful traditions. [sic] *Vanuatu Weekly* 27/4/85, p. 17.

JEAN-MARC PHILIBERT

In the *Bislama* section of the same newspaper, a half page is devoted to assuring the reader *kastom* is alive and well on Ambrym, an island reputed to be "traditional". On March the 5th, a *mel kon,* a sacred men's house, was erected, 40 years after the last *mel kon* had collapsed from old age. The last two paragraphs of the article state,

> All participants to the ceremony, men and women, did everything according to traditional ways (*oli makem ful kastom*). Now that the *Mel kon* is standing up again, more *kastom* will be used (*isave komaot*) in the future.

> Kirk Huffman of the of the Cultural Centre took photographs and made a video film of the proceedings which visitors to the Cultural Center can see. *Vanuatu Weekly* 4/5/85, p. 4.

8   No anthropologist has seriously studied the political discourse of those who led the secessionist attempt on Tanna and Santo. A French geographer, Bonnemaison, portrays the "rebellion" as a conflict between *kastom* and modernity, a last stand by "traditional" people against their becoming citizens of a modern state (Bonnemaison 1985b).

9.   On Tanna, kava is prepared at dusk, a period of the day that can be glossed as the time of the ancestors, on special kava-drinking grounds (Lindstrom 1982: 428). As the last mouthful is spat, the act "establishes contact with the supernatural world and precedes a prayer, request or demand, whispered to one's ancestors who are present in the surrounding dusk" (1982: 428). Having drunk kava, men eat some food and "listen" in silence to their kava.

10.   The various ways that men prepare kava, prohibitions which regulate use and non-use of the root, tease apart and order categories of people. Men divide from women, circumcised from uncircumcised males; sexually active from the inactive males; high status from ordinary men. (Lindstrom 1982: 428-429).

References

Barnes, J.
    African Models in New Guinea Highlands, *Man,* 62:5-9.

Bonnemaison, J.
    1985a. Les Fondements d'une Identité: Territoire. Histoire et Société dans l'archipel du Vanuatu. Thèse de Doctorate d'État, ORSTOM, Paris.

————
    1985b. Un certain refus de L'État, *International Political Science Review,* 6:230-247.

Brunton, R.
    1979. Kava and the Daily Dissolution on Tanna, *Mankind* 12, 93-103.

Clammer, J.
    1973. Colonialism and the Perception of Tradition in Fiji. In Talal Asad (ed.) *Anthropology and the Colonial Encounter*. Ithaca Press, London.

Cohen, A.
1981. *The Politics of Elite Culture*. University of California Press. Berkeley.

Collin, D.
Du Travail Indien au Travail Pour Les Indiens. *Culture*, 5:17-34.

Crick, M. R.
1982. Anthropology of Knowledge, *Annual Review of Anthropology*, 11:287-313.

Deacon, A. B.
Malekula, a Vanishing People in the New Hebrides. Routledge and Kegan Paul. London.

Geertz, C.
1973. The Integrative Revolution: Primordial Sentiments and Civil Politics in the New States, *The Interpretation of Cultures*. Basic Books, New York.

Hobsbawm, E.
1983. Introduction: Inventing Traditions. In E. Hobsbawm and T. Ranger (eds) *The Invention of Tradition*. Cambridge University Press, Cambridge.

————
Mass-Producing Traditions: Europe, 1870-1914. In E. Hobsbawm and T. Ranger (eds). *The Invention of Tradition*. Cambridge University Press, Cambridge.

Hobsbawm, E. and Ranger T. (eds).
The Invention of Tradition. Cambridge University Press, Cambridge.

Iliffe,
1979. *A Modern History of Tanganyika*. Cambridge University Press, Cambridge.

Keesing, R. M.
1982. Kastom in Melanesia: An Overview, Reinventing traditional culture: the Politics of Kastom in island Melanesia, R. M. Keesing and R. Tonkinson (eds.) *Mankind* 13:297-301.

Larcom, J.
1982. The Invention of Convention. *Mankind* 13:330-337.

Lefebvre, H.
1968. *Sociologie de Marx*. PUF, Paris.

Levi-Strauss, C.
1965. *Le Totémisme aujourd'hui*. PUF, Paris.

Lindstrom, M.
1982. Grog blong yumi: Alcohol and Kava on Tanna, Vanuatu. In M. Marshall (ed.) *Beer and Modernization in Papua New Guinea*. IASER, Boroka.

Philibert, J-M.
1982. Vers une Symbolique de la Modernization au Vanuatu. *Anthropologie et Sociétés* 6:69-97.

Pouillon, J.
1975. *Fétiches sans Fétichisme*. Francois Maspero, Paris.

Ranger, T.
1983. The Invention of Tradition in Colonial Africa. E. Hobsbawm and T. Ranger (eds) *The Invention of Tradition*. Cambridge University Press, Cambridge.

Taussig,
1980. *The Devil and Commodity Fetishism in South America*. The University of North Carolina Press, Chapel Hill.

Tonkinson, R.
1982. Kastom in Melanesia: Introduction. *Mankind* 13:302-305.

Trevor-Roper, H.

1983. The Invention of Tradition: The Highland Tradition of Scotland. E. Hobsbawm and T. Ranger (eds) *The Invention of Tradition*. Cambridge University Press, Cambridge.

Others:

1983. *Tri Independens Selebresen.* Port Vila, Vanuatu.

1985. *Vanuatu Weekly.*

Celebrating Cricket:
The Symbolic Construction of
Caribbean Politics

Frank E. Manning

While astute observers have long appreciated that popular sports reflect social environments, recent studies have built on this insight by exploring the character and implications of this particular type of "reflection". Conceptually, sport is neither a simple replication nor a mirror image of society. Rather, it is what Geertz terms a "text"—a product of the social imagination which gives form, feeling, and order to a people's shared traditions and experience. Like ritual, sport may function in either or both of two general ways. It may sanction the social system by consecrating its underlying beliefs and values, or it may question the social system by highlighting troubling conflicts and contradictions. Sport is also a cultural performance, a public drama that is an end in itself as well as a means for apprehending and acting upon the social world. For anthropologists, there is much to learn at the sports stadium.

In North America, sports like baseball, football, basketball, and hockey are periodic foci of mass interest. In the Caribbean, cricket enjoys a comparable status. The role of cricket in Caribbean society is complex and paradoxical. On the one hand, the sport symbolizes British colonialism and white-dominated hierarchy. On the other hand, cricket is the game at which black West Indians learned to beat their colonial masters and eventually achieve world supremacy, triumphs which made cricket a symbol of political resistance, social transformation, and cultural nationalism.

In the following piece Frank E. Manning explores the paradoxical symbolism of the cricket milieu in Bermuda. Dealing with cricket rivalries that have evolved into national celebrations, he demonstrates how the total performative environment—the game on the field, the activity of the fans, the high stakes gambling on the sidelines—represents both an exaggerated display of black cultural identity and a transparent enactment of white economic domination. This double thematic structure highlights the agonizing dilemma that Bermuda's two-party political system imposes on blacks. They must choose between committing themselves to the ideals of racial unity and solidarity by supporting the black opposition party, or gaining access to material resources and economic opportunities by developing strategic partnerships with the powerful whites who control the ruling party. Dramatizing this fundamental dilemma, cricket festivals lend performative poignancy and metaphorical meaning to the unsettling, high-risk political experience of Bermudian blacks. The culture of cricket festivals is also the culture of party politics, an ambiguous and potent significance which, on a broader level, illustrates the anthropological importance of public events and performances.

Cricket has suffered, but not only cricket. The aestheticians have scorned to take notice of popular sports and games—to their own detriment. The aridity and confusion of which they so mournfully complain will continue until they include organized games *and the people who watch them* as an integral part of their data. (C.L.R. James 1963: 191-192; emphasis in original)

THE FAILURE OF ART CRITICS to appreciate the aesthetics of popular sport has been no less myopic than the failure of anthropologists to grasp its social importance. Although folklorists and protoethnologists of the previous century showed an interest in games—much of it inspired by E. B. Tylor's evolutionary and diffusionist speculations—the anthropology of play did not advance appreciably until the late 1950s (Schwartzman 1978: 5). A great deal of the recent attention, however, has been directed at either children's play or at relatively small-scale games—a corpus pioneered by the early collaborative studies of Roberts and Sutton-Smith (1962, 1966). A significant literature on mass ludic spectacles such as popular sports events and public celebrations is only now emerging, much of it inspired by the interest of Gluckman and Turner in "secular ritual" (Moore and Myerhoff 1977) and by Geertz's (1972) paper on the Balinese cockfight.

The seminal work of these latter figures converges on a conceptual approach to the relationship between symbolic and social phenomena. For Turner (1977), "liminoid" performative genres such as festivals and carnivals are "proto-" or "metastructural", generating cultural comprehension by abstracting and recombining—often in novel, metaphorical ways—a social structure's basic principles. For Gluckman (see Gluckman and Gluckman 1977), whose views were articulated in the last article published before his death, symbolic events such as sports attractions and theatrical productions differ from traditional religious rites in being an imaginative "presentation" of society rather than a "re-presentation" or copy of it. For Geertz (1972), the cockfight is a fictive story about its social context, a "metasocial commentary" on it that is analogous to a literary text in using the devices of aesthetic license to disarrange conventional semantic contexts and rearrange them in unconventional ways. Geertz also underscores a point that is less forcefully made by Gluckman and Turner: that symbolic forms are not only a reflexive interpretation of social life, but also a means through which people discover and learn their culture. The lesson for anthropology is that symbolic inquiry, besides laying bare a social system, can also tell us a great deal about the epistemological processes whereby that system is revealed to those whose lives it shapes.

Drawing from these positions, as well as other perspectives that have thrown light on public play and mass performance, this paper examines Bermudian cricket festivals. I focus on the social history of these festivals, on the manner in which they are celebrated, and on a highly significant side activity, gambling. My contention is that the total genre dramatizes a fundamental, racially oriented conflict between cultural identity and economic interest—a conflict that is generalizable to the Caribbean (and perhaps other decolonizing areas) and that underlies the region's political situation. Consistent with Cohen's (1979: 87) observation that anthropology's chief contribution to the study of politics has been the analysis of nonpolitical symbols that have political implications and functions, I propose that celebration can provide a unique understanding of the conceptual

FRANK E. MANNING

parameters in which political awareness is developed and expressed.

Blacks in Whites

In the West Indies the game of cricket is played with elegant skill, studied with scholarly intensity, argued with passionate conviction, and revered with patriotic pride. Young boys with makeshift bats and balls play spiritedly in yards, fields, and beaches, learning the skills that in the past century have made West Indians among the world's outstanding cricketers. Organized competition begins in school and continues—often through middle age—in amateur sports clubs. Island-wide teams drawn from the clubs provide the Caribbean's premier sports attraction when they play annually in a touring series known as the Shell Shield. There is also a pan-West Indian team that represents the region in "test" (international) matches and that has been the outstanding exception to a catalog of failed attempts at West Indian unification.

One gleans the historical significance of the game in *Beyond a Boundary,* C.L.R. James's (1963) autobiography cum cricket analysis. A Trinidadian journalist, teacher, historian, political critic, and, above all, cricket devotee, James contends that in the West Indies cricket was traditionally seen as embodying the qualities of the classic British character ideal: fair play, restraint, perseverance, responsibility, and the moral inflections of Victorian Puritanism. Paradoxically, Afro-West Indians were taught to esteem those standards but were denied the means of achieving and demonstrating them. Cricket organizations—clubs, leagues, selection committees, governing bodies—conformed to the wider system of color-class stratification, and when the races occasionally played together, it was customary for whites to bat and blacks to bowl (St. Pierre 1973: 7-12).

The phrase "put on your whites" is instructive. Literally, it means to don the several items—white or cream-colored—that make up a cricket uniform: shoes, pants, shirt, sweater, protective gloves, knee pads. Figuratively, it is a metonym of the black struggle in cricket, itself a metonym as well as an instrument of the more general black struggle under British colonialism. In cricket there were a succession of black goals: to get to bat, to gain places on island-wide teams and regional tours, and, as recently as the 1960s, to be named vice-captains and captains of test teams, positions reserved for whites even after racial criteria had been virtually eliminated from selection procedures. Cricket successes brought recognition to Afro-West Indians both internationally and, more begrudgingly, in the upper strata of local society, gradually transforming the sport into a powerful symbol of black ability, achievement, and aspiration.

Bermudian cricket is a variation on these themes, but one that, like Bermuda itself, caricatures and often strikingly illuminates the Caribbean pattern. Lying a thousand miles and a climatic zone north of the West Indies, Bermuda has a five-month summer cricket season and therefore does not participate in most major West Indian tournaments, which are held during the winter. Nor do Bermudians take the game as seriously or as professionally as West Indians do. In the Caribbean, for example, festival games—occasions when a cricket match takes place in a setting of festive sociability—are relatively informal, localized, and of little general interest (James 1963: 20-21).[1] In Bermuda, however, festival games are both the highlights of the cricket season and, aside from Christmas, the calendar's most significant holidays. Bermudian festival cricket is the counterpart of Caribbean carnivals, but it enriches the spirit of celebration with the drama of a popular sporting classic.

The racial division of Bermudian cricket was shaped by an apartheidlike form of segregation, rather than by the West Indian system of color-class stratification. Introduced by British military personnel in the 19th century, the game was originally played in white sporting clubs. Blacks responded by forming neighborhood cricket clubs that have since evolved into the country's major centers of sport, entertainment, and sociability (Manning 1973). Through the clubs, blacks gained unquestioned superiority in cricket; when racial integration was nominally introduced in the 1960s, whites virtually withdrew from the game.

Two of the oldest black clubs, Somerset and St. George's, were begun primarily to promote an informal cricket contest held each August 1st in commemoration of the 1834 emancipation of slaves in British territories—an occasion marked by varied festivities throughout the Commonwealth Caribbean. Under club sponsorship the event developed into Cup Match, the oldest and most prominent cricket festival. Now held on the Thursday and Friday closest to August 1st, the game's historical identification with blacks is maintained by the white practice of observing the first day of Cup Match as Somers's Day, named after the British Admiral Sir George Somers who discovered Bermuda in 1609.

Besides Cup Match there are the Eastern, Western, and Central County Games, each involving four clubs in a series of three matches staggered between June and September. As these series progress there is a buildup of festivity and sporting interest, so that the final games—in effect, sequels to Cup Match—are like Cup Match as occasions of mass celebration. In white society the County Games are paralleled by summer yachting competitions, notably the renowned Newport-Bermuda race. Nowhere in the Caribbean is there a more striking example of the pluralistic segmentation that Smith (1965) attributed to British West Indian societies.

While Cup match commemorates emancipation from slavery, the County Games celebrate diffuse aspects of the black tradition and life-style. The Eastern and Western series, the two most popular, reflect variants in the black situation that figure in the deeper-level meaning of festival cricket. Begun in 1904, the Eastern Games involve clubs that draw from old, demographically stable neighborhoods. In each neighborhood there is a core of black extended families, typically small property owners deriving modest incomes from family stores, trades, service jobs, and, in earlier generations more than now, part-time farming and fishing. The principle of family-neighborhood integrity is the basis of Eastern County selection rules. Eligibility is based on having been born in the club's neighborhood—the usual and preferred criterion—or having been a resident of it for at least two years. Although in a number of cases current players have moved away from their ancestral neighborhoods and play for other clubs in league games, their return for the County Games makes each club roster a roll call of familiar surnames, re-creating the networks and reviving the sentiments of traditional social organization.

The Western County Games, begun in 1962, are a product of newer social influences. The Western parishes have grown appreciably since the time when the series started, as new luxury hotels have created employment and as the demand for housing among blacks short of middle age has been met by the conversion of large estates into fashionable residential subdivisions. (Newman 1972: 3). Reflecting these trends, the Western Games are touted not as neighborhood rivalries, but as slick, highly competitive all-star games. Clubs vie intensely for Bermuda's best cricketers, offering lucrative incentives that lure players from outside the Western parishes and that encourage opportunistic switching between clubs from one year to the next. The clubs have even extended recruitment into the Caribbean, scouting the region for prospects and arranging their immigration. In the mid-1970s, the final game of the Western series was extended from one day to two, a move aimed at raising the caliber of play, generating wider public interest, and boosting gate receipts. The emphasis on aggressive commercialism is also seen in other areas of club activity, notably entertainment. Two of the clubs involved in the series (as well as other clubs in the Western parishes) have built elegant lounges which remain open as late as 5 a.m., offering formidable competition to the area's hotels.

Underlying the varying inflections of the Eastern and Western County Games are changes in the terms of clientage, the basis of the black Bermudian socioeconomic condition. Traditionally, Bermuda was run by a white aristocracy whose relations to blacks were paternal in both a biological and social sense. Descendents of the original 17th-century British settlers, the aristocracy were seafarers until the 1870s, agricultural exporters from then until the 1920s, and more recently an interlocking establishment of merchants, bankers, and corporate lawyers. Functioning as a ruling class in an almost feudal sense (Lewis 1968: 323), they used the instruments of patronage—jobs, loans, credit, mortgages, charity—to maintain the allegiance and even the endearment of blacks, who make up three-fifths of the population, as well as a white underclass consisting of old "poor cousin" families, newer immigrants from Commonwealth countries, and Azorean Portuguese imported as indentured agricultural laborers. Patron-client relations were typically transacted within neighborhoods and parishes and between extended families, reinforcing residential identity and producing alliances between black and white kin groups that crosscut the system of institutionalized racial segregation. The common Caribbean metaphor of island society as a single large family (Wilson 1973: 47) was powerfully resonant in Bermuda, yielding a meaningful context in which patronage took the social form of a relationship between benevolent, although demanding, white patriarchs and filial black dependents.

Since the early 1960s, however, the power and prestige of the aristocracy have been substantially eroded. The tourist boom has made foreign-owned hotels the major employers and, along with the development of an offshore corporate business sector, brought to Bermuda a class of expatriate managers who wield an appreciable influence in local affairs. In addition, the buoyancy and expansion of the economy has allowed the aggressive rise of underclass whites, notably Bermuda-born Portuguese, and a handful of black professionals and entrepreneurs. Tellingly, many of the aristocracy's merchant houses on Front Street, the commercial frontispiece of Hamilton, are now dominated by whites whose rise to economic prominence has come about within the past two decades.

What these changes have done to the patronage system is alter its character and style while maintaining, and perhaps strengthening, its grip on the overwhelming majority of blacks. The benevolent paternalism of the aristocracy has been replaced by the bureaucratic orientation of the new elite, and largess has been escalated to include company directorships, investment opportunities, business partnerships, and well-paid managerial positions. Blacks enjoy the life-style provided by an affluent economy, but at the cost of remaining in a position of clientage and subordination.

"We black Bermudians," an old man cautioned, "can easily fool you. We're laughing on the outside, but crying on the inside." This commonplace statement derives its impact from oxymoron, the figure of speech that combines conceptual and emotional antitheses. Viewed as a collectively enacted "text", festival cricket is also built on oxymoron. Overtly and purposefully, these games articulate the meaning of freedom, family, community, club, and, above all, cricket itself—symbols that manifest to blacks their identity, their solidarity, their survival. But the games also reflect, implicitly but no less significantly, the field of socioeconomic relations in which blacks are dependent on a white power structure that has lost its traditional character but preserved its oppressive force. In this juxtaposition—this dramatic oxymoron—lies the basis of both the political system and the political imagination.

Food, Liquor, Clothing, and Money

Soliciting a description of festival cricket early in my first Bermudian fieldwork, I was told it was the time "when we eat everything in Bermuda, drink everything in Bermuda, wear everything in Bermuda, and spend everything in Bermuda." Although popular interest in the game runs unusually high, festival cricket is an occasion of participation, not spectatorship. The festival ethos is one of hedonistic indulgence, gregarious sociability, histrionic exhibitionism, lavish hospitality, conspicuous consumption—behaviors that epitomize and celebrate the black Bermudian self-image. In Singer's (1955) terms, festival cricket is a cultural performance, a dramatic spectacle in which a people proclaim and demonstrate their sense of who they are.

Like Carnival, festival cricket involves a period of preparation that is considered nearly as much fun as the event itself. For weeks before Cup Match there is intense speculation about the selection of teams. Pundits offer their personal choices in letters to the editor, and the subject is heatedly discussed in bars, in buses, and on street corners. The principal centers of activity are the black clubs, where people go, in the words of one informant, "just to hear the arguments." The arguments peak a week before the game, when the club selection committees announce their picks to the membership at a meeting in which dramatic suspense, flamboyant and often fiery oratory, and uproarious entertainment combine ritualistically to induct chosen players into the club tradition. In the final days before the game there is a general buildup of festive sociability, a flurry of shopping activity for food, liquor, and clothing, and extended expressions of team loyalty through the display of club colors on cars and items of apparel. For Country Games the scenario is similar, but on a smaller scale.

Game days begin early, as fans laden with coolers, umbrellas, collapsible chairs, and briefcase-sized portable radios arrive at the grounds several hours before the first ball is bowled at 10 a.m. Locations around the periphery of the field are carefully staked out, mostly by groups of friends who have made arrangements to contribute to a common supply of food and liquor. A more enviable location is in makeshift pavilions erected at the edge of the field or on surrounding hillsides. Wooden frames covered with canvas or thatch, the pavilions bear colorful names such as "Honey Bee Lounge" and often fly flags made of liquor banners or team insignia. Organized by club-based peer groups, the pavilions accommodate 10-20 couples who pay a set fee—as much as $100[2] for the two days of Cup Match—for food, liquor, and other amenities. Most pavilions are wired to the clubhouse, enabling the use of lights, appliances, and stereos that typically have auditorium-sized electronic speakers.

In all groups there is emphasis on extravagance, sophistication, ostentation. Bottles of brand-name liquor ranging from the 40-ounce to the 1-gallon size are set out on coolers and tables, flanked by cherries, lemons, limes, angostura bitters, and more specialized garnishes and liqueurs for concoctions that gain popularity during a particular festival season (Scotch, milk, and grenadine was the favorite one year). Food is plentiful and of two kinds: the cherished "soul" dishes built around chicken, fish, and "hoppin' john" (black-eyed peas and rice); and festive specialties, notably cassava pie and a chicken and pork filling baked pastry made from shredded cassava.) At the Eastern County Games one is also likely to see a number of festive seafood dishes, including mussel pie, conch stew, and hash shark. For those without enough food or liquor, there are at least 2 bars in the clubhouse and 2 or more bar concessions, along with 20 or more food concessions, on the grounds.

Liquor is a basis of hospitality patterns that link individuals and groups with the larger audience. People generously offer drinks to passing friends, whose visit is enlivened by joking, teasing, insult swapping, and other forms of verbal performance characteristic of Afro-Caribbean and Afro-American culture (Abrahams 1970; Kochman 1970). The visitor invariably extends an offer of reciprocal hospitality, creating an opportunity, and something of a social obligation, for the hosts to return the visit later in the day. In the pavilions persons are allowed to entertain two guests at a time, an informal rule that balances the importance of hospitality with a check against overcrowding.

The continuous traffic around the field is known as the "fashion show". Celebrants sport outfits acquired for the festival cricket season, occasionally handmade but more often purchased during the advertising campaigns that retail merchants mount in the weeks before Cup Match. Drawn from black American and West Indian trends, styles are valued for combining smartness with sexuality. A decade ago, for example, the style known in Bermuda as "black mod" was dominant. Women paraded in arousing "hot pants" outfits, suggestive two piece ensembles, bell-bottom and two-tone slacks, close-fitting pants suits, wool knit skirts and jerseys, low-slung chain belts, bubble blouses, leather collars, suede fringed handbags, large round earrings, ostentatious bracelets and necklaces, pink and yellow tinted sunglasses, and "natural" coiffures. In the same period, men wore jump suits, silk shirts slit open to expose the chest, two-tone and wide-cuffed flair pants, bolero and ruffled shirts with dog-ear collars, and suede vests over the bare skin. More recent styles have been varied, ranging from "black disco" to "unisex chic". Women have adopted pleated balloon pants, terry cloth outfits, and "cornrow" coiffures elaborated with beads and braids——a style that can cost upwards of $100 in Bermudian hairdressing salons. Men have taken to West Indian styles, notably shirt-jacs, kareba suits, and among youth, Rastafarian dreadlocks. The jewelry portfolios of both sexes center on a half-dozen necklaces of various sizes and designs. Designer jean outfits are in vogue, as are athletic shorts that are worn by women with halter tops, by men with athletic shirts, and by both sexes with inscribed T-shirts.

The popularity of T-shirts warrants special comment. The leading black dealer in the field estimates selling 1,000 to 1,500 shirts for Cup Match alone, many of them at the cricket grounds in a concession stand that he equips with his printing and dyeing machines. His most popular line is what he calls his "black" shirts— motifs about festival cricket, pan-African identity, racial solidarity, and black entertainment genres. Next in popularity, and sometimes combined with racial motifs, are sexual themes, most of them using slang double entendres for genitalia and copulation in conjunction with humorous inscriptions of invitation, challenge, and braggadocio. The manufacture of T-shirts at the game epitomizes the rapid popularization of new styles and the ready satisfaction of customer demand for them, central values in black Bermudian fashion culture.

Performative and provocative, the fashion show is closely observed by radio commentators, who mix accounts of the cricket game with animated descriptions of fashion plates. Indeed, one of the major reasons fans bring radios to the game is to hear these accounts of themselves and their fellow celebrants. Like liquor, fashion is a medium of exchange that integrates an aggregate audience into a cultural community. It is also, again like liquor, what Sapir (1934) termed a symbol of condensation: it exemplifies what it signifies, namely an ethos of affluence, hedonism, sophistication, and display. An observable result of this symbolism is that fashion evokes the black conversational mode known as "rapping", a lewd and lively exchange between men and women aimed both at enter-tainment and at the initiation or enhancement of sexual partner-ships. Like Carnival, festival cricket has a rich lore as a period of license and sexual hyperactivity.

Other modes of performance compete with fashion for public attention. Steel, brass, and rock bands play on the sidelines, stimulating impromptu dancing. Also present are Gombey Dancers, masked mummers who render a Bermudian version of the John Canoe dance to the rhythm of drums, fifes, snares, and whistles. High on surrounding hillsides are groups of Rastafarians, who smoke *ganja,* translate the festival ambience into poetry, and orate philosophically about a black millenium. A profane version of that millenium is enacted on adjacent waterways, where "boojee" (black bourgeois) yachtsmen display their boats and hold swank deck par-ties.

The cricket match concludes at 6:30 p.m., but festivities con-tinue well into the night. The clubhouse is jammed with revellers who fraternize with the cricketers, replay and comically argue every detail of the game, and get very drunk as the evening wears on. Other fans extend their merriment onto the field and may remain there all night. Several clubs run evening events ranging from dan-ces and parties to outdoor concerts featuring black American and Caribbean performers.

A final ancillary activity warrants separate discussion for both ethnographic and analytic purposes. That activity is gambling, which takes place during the cricket game on the periphery of the field in a large tent known as the "stock market". As festival cricket amplifies a mode of behavior that is manifest in less spectacular ways on a day-to-day basis, stock market gambling caricatures a general style of acquisition premised on calculated opportunism (Manning 1973: 87-114), as well as a particular fondness for gam-bling that has put soccer pool agencies and off-track betting parlors among Bermuda's lucrative businesses and has, within the club milieu, given rise to regular bingo nights, organized card games, raffles, lotteries, and so on. The significance of gambling here is twofold: first, it explicitly symbolizes a relationship between culture and money that is represented more implicitly in other phases and spheres of festival cricket; second, at a deeper level, it dramatizes the culture-money relationship in a manner that qualifies and questions the meaningful thrust of the total festival. Juxtaposed to its own content, gambling illustrates the tension that pervades black political life.

The Stock Market

Framed with wood or tubular steel and covered with canvas or sheet plastic, the stock market is a makeshift casino for a dice game known as "crown and anchor". Played on boards set atop wooden horses, the game involves betting on one or more of six choices: the four suits of cards, a red crown, or a black anchor. Three dice are rolled, their sides corresponding to the choices on the board. Winners are paid the amount of their bet times the number of dice on which it is shown, while losers have their money taken by the board. If a croupier rolls a crown and two spades, for example, he collects the money on the four losing choices, pays those who bet on the crown, and pays double those who bet on the spade.

Like cricket, crown and anchor is a game of British origin that has gained immense popularity in the Caribbean, particularly at festivals. I have personally watched it being played by Antiguans at Carnival and by Jamaican Maroons at the celebration of Captain Cudjoes's birthday in the remote mountain village of Accompong.[3] In Bermuda the game is distinguished by the amount of money that is displayed and bet. Croupiers hold thousands of dollars in their hands, and players are likely to hold several hundred. The minimum bet is one dollar, but only novices and casual players, mostly women, bet that little. Regular players tend to bet between $10 and $50 each time, although much higher bets are common. Some boards place a ceiling of $100 on bets, but the larger boards—i.e., those with bigger cash floats—generally have no ceiling. An informant lighted on the ostentatious display of cash as the chief difference between festival cricket and Christmas, the calendar's two major holidays. At Christmas, he observed, money is spent; at festival cricket, it is both spent and shown.

Crown and anchor is marked by a peculiar paradox. Although the odds marginally favor the board, regular players say that an effective strategy is to bet on choices that have not come up for two or three rolls of the dice and are therefore "due" simply by the laws of probability. A more defensive tactic, and one that is easily combined with the above, is simply to double bets on the same item until it eventually comes up and all losses, as well as the initial bet, are recouped. The only limitation is lack of ready cash, but this is minimized by the substantial sums that players carry and by the ready willingness of the boards to accept personal checks and even to loan money.

In practice, however, players tend to bet erratically and lose, often substantially. In the parlance of the stock market, they succumb to "greed" and "lose their heads" in a futile attempt to "break the board". What is potentially a game of strategy—the type associated with mastering the environment—is in effect a game of chance—the type associated with divining an uncontrollable environment (Roberts, Arth, and Bush 1959). The following example from my field notes is representative of a pattern evidenced by the stock market's "high rollers":

> Placing $10 and $20 bets unsystematically, a man lost his own money—about $60—as well as $50 that he borrowed from the board. He then borrowed another $50 and increased it to about $85 by winning a few small bets. He next bet $70 on the club, which came up on three dice to add $210 to his money. But although he owed the board $100, he kept playing rather than pay back the debt and quit with a net winning. Within half an hour he had lost all his money, as well as a third loan of $50. As he left the board he quietly told the croupier: "I owe you $150. I'll see you Monday morning."

The familiar experience of losing is offset by the claim that gambling money is expendable. As one man put it after losing $100, "If I have money to spend, I spend it. If I lose it, I don't give a fuck. I'll go back to work next week and get some more."

Although the overwhelming majority of bettors are black, the running of boards—the profitable side of the stock market—has been dominated by the Portuguese. In the 1930s, Manuel de Souza (a pseudonym), the teenage son of an Azorean-born farm laborer, watched crown and anchor being played in the segregated white section of the racetrack. Surmising the game's appeal to blacks, he started going to festival cricket matches with a dice cup, a small table, and a tarpaulin that he stretched between some trees to make a crude tent. De Souza's winnings put him on the road to acquiring a modest complex of businesses: a fleet of taxi cabs, several small farms, and a restaurant. "You can say that I owe what I have to crown and anchor," he acknowledged. "It gave me my start in life."

As de Souza's business and gambling profits grew, he began running more boards in partnership with other Portuguese. In the 1960s he was challenged by the clubs, which successfully pressed the claim that the stock market should be under their control. De Souza countered with patronage, supporting club building projects and occasionally contributing a share of his winnings. In return he was given first option on buying the entire gambling concession, an arrangement that gave the clubs a substantial cash flow to stock their bars for festivals and that made de Souza something of a "czar" or, better perhaps, "godfather", of the stock market. With his partners he ran a half-dozen tables and reports that his share of their net profits averaged $30,000 per season. He made a further profit by selling the remainder of the space in the stock market, chiefly to a growing group of Portuguese who had acquired gambling reputations in private house parties.

Although de Souza and other Portuguese board operators were generally astute enough to hire black assistants, black gamblers gradually pushed the clubs for a bigger stake in the stock market, and ultimately for control of it. Their efforts have been partially successful; for several years the concession of Cup Match and the Western County Games has been sold to a syndicate of black businessmen, while in the Eastern County series one club continues to favor de Souza and the others run the stock market themselves. The change has resulted in more blacks and fewer Portuguese, although the new concession holders sell choice space (near the outside and sheltered from the afternoon sun) to the remaining Portuguese, including de Souza, who are respected in gambling circles and known to attract heavy bettors.

FRANK E. MANNING

Yet the racial change in the stock market is less radical than it may appear. Many of the black-run boards, and a clear majority of those which have no ceiling on bets, are backed financially by whites, including Portuguese, or by racially mixed investment syndicates. The backers provide the cash float—as much as $15,000 at some boards—in return for a 40 to 60 percent share of the winnings. The parallel between the stock market and the wider economic system is frequently observed: "You know, come to think of it, I don't know a single black person in this country who has made money without having a white sponsor."

Another parallel between the stock market and the broader Bermudian situation is observed in connection with mid-1970s legislation requiring the host club to pay $500 for a one-day gambling permit and preventing the boards from taking bets later than one hour after the scheduled end of the cricket game. The cost of the permit has been passed on to the concession holders and, in turn, to individual board operators, while the time regulation has stopped boards from staying open to increase winnings, recoup earlier losses, or simply capitalize on late betting action—a restriction that has hurt mainly the smaller, black-run boards, which are on the inside and therefore wait longer for bettors. For blacks, these new statutes typify a pattern of reaction against black economic gain. As one black board operator put it, "When the stock market was run by the Portuguese, it was wide open. As soon as we boys started to get a little piece of the action, Government stepped in. That's the general trend in Bermuda."

Whatever the economic position of blacks in the stock market, their cultural presence there is highly visible and clearly dominant over whites—another correspondence, of course, to the larger society. The Portuguese play quietly and dress plainly, almost dourly. Their boards are about six feet long and staffed by two, or at most three, croupiers. They socialize with bettors or other operators, viewing the gambling relationship as an exclusively economic transaction. As de Souza explained, "People don't play at my board because they like me. They play because they want to break me." The Portuguese leave unobtrusively after the game and abstain from the evening festivities. I once went looking for de Souza after an Eastern County Game and found him working soberly in his restaurant. He said that he cleared $1,800 from his three tables—"a day's pay"—but volunteered that his lack of emotion made it impossible for most people to tell whether he had won or lost.

The image of black gamblers, by contrast, is an ideal type of the highly performative, black-oriented expressive style that Wilson (1973: 227-228) terms "reputation"—the ethos that pervades the entire festival. Croupiers dress and behave flamboyantly, standing on platforms to increase their visibility, spreading their bills like a fan, throwing their dice cups high in the air, handing out one dollar bills to passersby to engage them in the game, and barking stock invitations to bet: "Get some money for your honey.... Come in here on a bike, go home in a Rolls Royce.... Take your hands out of your pocket and put your money on the table.... Wall Street slumps, but this stock market pays double...." The black tables average eight to ten feet, with sets of betting squares on each end and often with added decorations such as the signs of the zodiac. At the larger tables there may be a staff of six, typically a "house man" who shakes the dice and holds the $50 bills, two or three assistants who collect and pay the bets, and one or two others who serve as bartenders and greeters. Both liquor and beer are freely offered to onlookers as well as bettors, and when a person's drink is half empty it will be wantonly thrown on the ground and replaced with a fresh drink.

Black gamblers extend and exploit the festival's sexual licence. At least two black operators have reportedly imported prostitutes, a commodity virtually absent from Bermuda, from the United States. The more common practice is to give gambling money to well-endowed women in return for their appearing at the board in plunging necklines, loosely crocheted blouses, diaphanous T-shirts, tight shorts, and similar fashions aimed at attracting—and distracting—male gamblers. As a sequel to this gimmick, a few black operators have begun hiring female croupiers and even forming gambling partnerships with women. Conversely, women have increasingly become regular and sometimes heavy bettors, a trend that is particularly noticeable in the western parishes where a good number of well-paid hotel positions are held by women. The effort to attract—and hold—women bettors enlivens the barking calls with colorful exchanges.

> A middle-aged woman was about to bet on heart, but withdrew the money. The operator countered: "Don't blame me if three hearts come up, lady. 'Cause you and

I—I've been looking at you for a long time—I figure our hearts could get together. We don't need no crown and anchor, honey. Our hearts could really do something."

A woman was betting, and winning, on the black choices (spades, clubs, the anchor), which are all on the bottom of the board. The operator tried to persuade her to diversify her betting: "You gotta go topside. No woman in the world is satisfied on the bottom side."

A woman in her early thirties had been breaking even on small bets and drinking heavily. Towards the end of the day she put a double entendre to the operator: "All I want is a piece of you." He took up the challenge and carried on a series of lewd but playful insults that drew raucous laughter from those at the table. But she got the last word: "Knobby, you wouldn't know what to do if you tripped and fell on top of me."

Black operators indicate that their gambling success depends on establishing their reputations within a broader context of public sociability. One prominent operator spends several hours per day outside the bar that he owns in partnership with another black and two whites, engaging passersby in brief conversation, waving at pedestrians on the other side of the street, and shouting at passing cars. This strategy, he explains, provides the exposure that is needed to attract people to his crown and anchor board (as well as to his bar and to a nightclub that he owns with his partners).

A modern Bermudian proverb is at this point appropriate: "Black is black and white is white, but money is green." Culturally different and socially divided, the races nonetheless come together for a common goal: the acquisition of money. There is no better illustration of this proverb than stock market gambling, which magnifies the unique black cultural identity that is celebrated in festival cricket at the same time that it brings the races together in a staged encounter aimed at fast and easy wealth. That scenario is a dramatic rendition of what Bermudian politics, at bottom, is all about.

Festival and Politics

Racial inversion underlies the dramatic form of festival cricket.

Blacks dress up in "whites" to play a white game that they have transformed into a celebration of black culture. Blacks take a white gambling game and make it the setting for a hyperbolic performance of their social personality. Whites enter a black milieu and badly demonstrate their superordinate position. Such inversion exemplifies the carnivalesque, a genre in which the characteristic multiplexity of symbolic expression is extended by the tendency for symbols to be used playfully and for primarily aesthetic effect. This tendency creates what Babcock (1973) calls a "surplus of signifiers," a Rabelaisian profusion of images and condensed metaphors framed in a mode of liminality.

While the range of significance is vast, fragmented, and often highly individualized, the exegete can take clues from recurrent and centrally placed symbols. A major, meaningful thrust of festival cricket, manifest in the tradition and style of celebration, is the relation of a reflexive version of black identity to hedonism, high style, and money. Turner's (1964: 29-31) contention, that dominant clusters of symbols interchange social and sensory-material themes, is appropriate. Like similar symbolic formulations in the club milieu, festival cricket contributes to the multifaceted process whereby black Bermudians are rejecting a stance of social inferiority in favor of a positive and assertive sense of self-awareness (Manning 1973: 149-183).

There is also an antithetical thrust of meaning, reminding blacks of their economic subordination and dependency on whites. The reminder is implicit in the overall emphasis on fashion and indulgence, for Bermudian blacks are acutely aware, even in festival, that consumerism keeps them in clientage. In the stock market, however, the message is explicit: big money and effective power are still in white hands. Blacks can commemorate their traditions and exhibit their ethos, but they must also deal with whites, who have the odds—mathematical and psychological—in their favor. If festival cricket is viewed as a dramatic form, the black gamblers are both heroes and clowns. In the former role they glamorize a social vision of black culture, while in the latter they enact an economic relationship in which the vision is transparently irrelevant. Like the ludic inversion of racial categories, this sense of juxtaposition and self-parody is characteristic of the carnivalesque.

As a formative feature of the black Bermudian experience, the

FRANK E. MANNING

culture-economics interplay has a variety of demonstrable references. The most clear and currently paramount, however, is the system of party politics. An arena of intense interest and extraordinarily high participation, Bermudian politics bears both a striking conceptual similarity and an uncanny ethnographic correspondence to festival cricket. Let us briefly consider this double relationship.

Party politics came to Bermuda in 1963 with the formation of the Progressive Labour Party (PLP) by black groups who had previously been active in the successful universal suffrage movement.[4] In the election of that year, the party contested 9 of 36 parliamentary seats, winning 6 of them and clearly demonstrating the practical benefits of party organization. The aristocracy responded to the challenge a year later by forming the United Bermuda Party (UBP), which was initially joined by 24 of the 30 independents in the House of Assembly, all but 1 of them white. For the remainder of the decade the UBP sought to co-opt the issues pressed by the PLP, espousing, at least nominally, constitutional reform and the bread-and-butter issues of universal free education, health and welfare benefits, and the Bermudianization of the labor force. The UBP's trump card, however, was the promise of a thoroughgoing "partnership"—the term used in campaign slogans—between blacks and whites in the running of Bermuda. The partnership was demonstrated politically by strenuous efforts to recruit black candidates in the 1968 and subsequent elections, a general tactic of putting blacks in highly visible positions in both the party organization and the Cabinet; the naming of a black premier between 1971 and 1975; the appeasement of a black-dominated parliamentary "reform" group which forced the resignation of that premier's white successor in 1977; and, from the late 1970s onward, the gradual implementation of demands put forth by an internal black caucus seeking greater leverage in both the party and the national economy.

Rhetorically, the UBP presents the partnership as a guarantee of security as well as an opportunity for gain. Only through the visible demonstration of racial integration, it is claimed, can Bermuda continue to attract tourists and international companies, the sources of prosperity. The UBP couples this appeal with an emphasis on its traditional role as manager of the economy. In the 1980 election campaign, for example, Premier David Gibbons, a white who also holds the finance portfolio and whose family controls Bermuda's largest conglomerate, told an audience:

> This election is not about personalities. It is about the conditions of people's lives. Day in and day out. People's jobs, income, housing. And, above all, the strength and stability of our economy, upon which all else depends.
>
> Look to the United Bermuda Party's management of our economy. At a time when so many nations in the West are struggling and losing ground, Bermuda maintains one of the highest rates of per capita income in the world.... Stability, security. These are facts. And they've come to pass because of experience and prudent, efficient management.

The UBP gave its economic theme a dimension of grave urgency in a full-page newspaper advertisement published on polling day:

> Today is the day when you vote...either to maintain Bermuda's economic growth and your own financial security and stability or...take a chance on the PLP. Think carefully and vote UBP.

The UBP's accommodations to black interests and its emphasis on economic security have given it an unbroken winning record at the polls, albeit by successively reduced majorities. The PLP's reaction, moderated in tone as its political position has improved, has been to emphasize its "true" blackness and therefore its legitimate and logical claim to black voter support. For the first decade of its existence, the PLP projected a posture of militant racial chauvinism, articulated through American and Caribbean "Black Power" rhetoric. In the middle 1970s, the PLP embraced the idiom of revivalist religion, a move aimed at making inroads among black church groups and, more generally, at appealing to racial consciousness implicitly rather than explicitly by stirring the powerful and pregnant association between revivalism and black culture. In the 1980 campaign, the PLP balanced the emphasis on religion with a more secular appeal to racial identity. The campaign slogan was "Xpress yourself," a black Bermudian colloquialism borrowed jointly from American soul music and Jamaican reggae lyrics and combining an allusion to the marking of a ballot paper with a slang encouragement for self-assertion. One television commercial showed a group of blacks, dancing funky style, while a singer chanted "express yourself" and an announcer extolled the merits of the PLP.

Whatever their stated differences on issues—and these have converged considerably in recent years as both parties have sought a center ground—the essential partisan distinction is racial. Recent surveys indicate that whites vote almost unanimously for the UBP, and that four-fifths of the black votes go the PLP—a division that crosscuts and overrides class, age, sex, ideological disposition, and other pertinent social factors (Manning 1978a: 199-209). The choice for blacks remains what it has always been: cultural attachment or economic security, loyalty and commitment to blacks, or strategic alignment with whites.

The distinction between the parties is manifest ethnographically in the festival setting. Hodgson (1967: 311), a black Bermudian historian and PLP polemicist, describes Cup Match as "the one and only true symbol and celebration of the black man's emancipation." Her enthusiasm, however, is offset by a scepticism that blacks will forsake such symbols in order to participate in white festivities that have now dropped the color barrier. This concern, while lacking empirical foundation, has prompted PLP politicians to present a high profile at cricket festivals, making the general environment one in which PLP supporters are familiar and welcome and UBP supporters are somewhat isolated and uncomfortable. The festival's partisan association is extended by the PLP's considerable efforts to court the club constituency (Manning 1973: 210-249), a tactic exemplified by party leader Lois Browne-Evans's speech at a club dinner in 1978.

> Your long and illustrious history...needs to be told. Essays ought to be held for your children to write what they think Daddy's club is all about....
>
> Let not economic strangulation be the cause of your enslavement. For I am convinced that you have a part to play in the Bermuda of the future, just as your forebears played a vital role in the Bermuda of the past.
>
> You must continue working until your country is free from paternalism and patronage, free from all the shackles that we know. Do not remove one form of chains for

another. You must avoid the tendency to be dependent...

The stock market, however, presents a striking contrast to the overall festival milieu. The black table operators, like their Portuguese counterparts and white backers, are primarily UBP supporters. The coterie is informally led by a black UBP member of the House of Assembly, who is also renowned, on a few occasions scandalously, for the organization of invitational crown and anchor parties in private homes. At least two prominent backers also hold UBP seats in Parliament, and it is widely known that several black board operators are being groomed as future UBP candidates. Talking to me on the street, one of the blacks who operates a table on which there is no betting limit explained his support for the UBP as follows: "There is not one black person in Bermuda with any money who is PLP. Not one..... If the [white] man looks after you, then you've got to protect him...." When a PLP member within earshot began to challenge him, the gambler yelled: "Shut the fuck up. It's niggers like you that are holding back motherfuckers like me."

PLP activists, on the other hand, tend to eschew the stock market, or at most to congregate outside or walk through without betting. Observing the action at a crown and anchor board, one PLP politician told me with a wink: "I only watch the stock market. I never invest." This avoidance is encouraged by the PLP's oft-stated position that gambling is functionally supportive of the status quo and by its general desire to adhere, publicly at least, to the strong moral condemnation of gambling made by the black churches.

Festival cricket, then, is a metapolitical commentary. It is a carnivalesque rendition of the semantic context in which Bermudian politics is conceived, institutionalized, and transacted. Through celebration, black Bermudians dramatize—and, indeed, define and discover—a fundamental aspect of their social position and its relationship, conceptual and ethnographic, to their political options. (Logically, of course, the argument is reversible; politics could be construed as a concordance for festival cricket. From a Bermudian standpoint, however, it is politics, not festival, that requires comprehension, choice, and commitment. Festival is merely for enjoyment, and perhaps profit.)

It is here that the relationship of symbolic to social phenomena, of festival to politics, is crucial, and that the convergent positions of Turner (1977), Gluckman and Gluckman (1977), and Geertz (1972), attributing creative autonomy to ludic symbolic forms, are useful. Although festival cricket evidences myriad correspondences to the political system, it is no more a mere reflection of politics than it is a functional appendage of it. The festival version of black culture is not the ideological and instrumental type of racial awareness propounded by the PLP, but a comical caricature of the black life-style and a joyous fantasy that links facial identity to the material wealth and glamor promised by a white-dominated, consumer-oriented economy. Likewise, the festival version of biracial partnership is not the liberal and pragmatic plea for partnership advanced by the UBP, but a naked dramatization of white control that lays bare both the crass acquisitiveness of blacks and their continuing subordination to whites, and that further plays on these meanings in a burlesque of the whole patronage system that transforms money from an object of need to one of show.

In Durkheimian terms—which are the ancestry of much symbolic theory—festival cricket is a "transfiguration" of Bermudian political society (cf. Nisbet 1965: 74). The semantic essence of festival cricket is that it throws the realm of politics into relief by disassembling its parts and reordering them in patterns consistent with the aesthetics of celebration, fun, and performance. Festival cricket *reveals* politics in the way that only an extended metaphor can—by creatively connecting disparate realms of experience in a manner that highlights the definitive features (in this case, the interplay of cultural identity and economic interest) on which the connection is predicated. To borrow Bateson's (1972: 177-193) classic model of cognition, festival cricket is a map for the territory of politics—not a literal, drawn-to-scale map that merely replicates its referent, but a metaphorical map, an interpretive guide, that figuratively situates its referent and conveys social knowledge about it. It is this knowledge that makes Bermudian politics a comprehensible phenomenon.

Conclusion

Like any venture into the analysis of symbolic forms as texts, the interpretation offered here rests ultimately on the anthropologist,

who "strains to read over the shoulders of those to whom they
[the texts] properly belong" (Geertz 1972: 29). In part, the
validity and value of such an interpretation depends on whether
it can be generalized, as a theoretical construct and heuristic
device, to other cultures. Limitations of space and scope make it
impractical to address that consideration here, but a few condensed examples from the West Indies may suggest the basis of
a comparative approach.

The major festival genre of the easter Caribbean is Carnival,
which evolved in Trinidad but has diffused throughout the
Windward and Leeward islands with minor changes in format.[5] Like
Bermuda's Cup Match, the historical referent of Carnival, for
blacks, is emancipation from slavery. The festival's major performative symbols—from the canboulay parade, ritualized stickfighting,
and gang warfare in earlier times, to calypso and steel bands in
recent generations—make it unequivocally black. Naipaul (1973:
364), one of the Caribbean's leading literary figures, describes Carnival as "a version of the lunacy that kept the slave alive...the
original dream of black power, style, and prettiness...a vision of the
black millenium." Calypsonians put it more simply, toasting Carnival
as the "Creole bacchanal."

But the blackness of the Carnival ethos is confronted by a strong
nonblack influence in the festival's economic organization. East Indian, Chinese, and Lebanese bandleaders predominate, as do white
and mulatto choreographers, and, of course, the government-con-
trolled Carnival Development Committee—all of these groups striving, rather successfully in recent years, to make the event an
international tourist attraction. Celebrants are exposed to the poig-
nant contrast between the revelry of "jump-up" on the streets and
the ribaldry of the calypso tent, on the one hand, and a variety of
scenarios that demonstrate the racially based socioeconomic class
system, on the other hand: the judges' stand, the paid grandstand,
the commercial nightclub scene, the maze of bureaucratic rules imposed by organizers and censors, and the presence of local elites,
and even metropolitan tourists, in the privileged sections of
masquerade bands.

Jamaica lacks a Carnival tradition but has the entertainment
idiom of reggae music, a symbol system replete with religious and
political significance (Barrett 1977; de Albuquerque 1979). One of

the best indigenous artistic commentaries on the reggae milieu is Perry Henzell's (1973) film *The Harder They Come*. Its protagonist is a country boy who comes to Kingston to learn the fast side of Jamaican life. The voyage of discovery is twofold. He becomes a reggae star and a "rudie" (rude boy), mastering expressive styles that are quintessentially black, often in a militant, even revolutionary sense. But he also learns that the music industry is controlled by Chinese, mulattoes, and other groups deemed white from the black cultural viewpoint, and that the authorities—police, government, and international economic interests—are geared to crushing the challenge that he represents. Ultimately, he is shot down by their guns.

Are such symbolic forms a metacommentary on West Indian politics? Correspondences are harder to draw than in the Bermudian case, partly because, in the Caribbean, race is a figurative more than a phenotypical category. Virtually all local political actors are generically black, and whiteness is associated less with a visible local elite than with the abstractions of foreign ownership and imperial influence. In short, a racial analysis is a more complex and problematic task in the West Indies than it is in Bermuda.

Still, it is notable that, ever since the "Black Power" wave of the early 1970s, the most dynamic and ideologically intense political conflict in most of the West Indies has come from the challenge made to established political parties by radical movements, most of them extraparliamentary. These radical movements revive indigenous linguistic terms (Morris 1973), stress cultural affinity and social solidarity with Africa, and associate themselves with Afro-Caribbean religions, notably Rastafarianism, which has spread from Jamaica throughout the Caribbean and has become a cultural rallying ground and pervasive symbol for revolutionary politics (de Albuquerque 1980). Contrastingly, established politicians are villified as "Afro-Saxon" (Lowenthal 1972: 278), imitators of white values who court foreign investment, sell out to multinational corporations, embrace the image promoted by mass tourism, and compact unholy alliances with metropolitan countries.

A litany of citations from academic, popular, and polemical literature could be introduced here, most of them familiar (and indeed, redundant), to scholars of the Caribbean. For present purposes, however, it is better to make two broad and general assertions. First, economic interest and cultural identity are often perceived in the West Indies as conflicting concerns. Second, the conflict is focused in racial symbolism, dramatized in festivity and other artistic productions, and current to political discourse. If these assertions are granted, they suggest an agenda aimed at integrating symbolic and political analyses of Caribbean societies, and perhaps of other areas that have undergone comparable historical experiences. The discussion of Bermudian cricket festivals offered here shows one direction in which such an agenda can proceed.

Acknowledgements.

I am grateful to the late Max Gluckman, cricket aficionado and analyst par excellence, whose conversations with me were an inspiration to develop this paper. Jeanne Cannizzo and Jim Freedman offered helpful comments on a draft. For fieldwork support I am grateful to the National Science Foundation (GS-2549) and to the Institute of Social and Economic Research, Memorial University of Newfoundland; grants from these bodies enabled me to witness Cup Match in 1970, 1976, and 1978, and to see 20-odd County Games since 1969. Earlier versions of this paper were presented to the Canadian Ethnology Society, in 1979, and to the Association for the Anthropological Study of Play, in 1980. Part of the present version was delivered as a guest lecture at the University of Michigan, in 1980.

FRANK E. MANNING

Notes

1. I know of no other written sources on West Indian festival cricket, but am informed by a Jamaican student that "bush cricket" in Jamaica has the same general characteristics as James's example from Trinidad.

2. The Bermuda dollar is at parity with the U.S. dollar.

3. I am told by Jeanne Cannizzo (1979: personal communication) that a version of crown and anchor is played at festivals in Sierra Leone. I have also seen it played at a number of fairs and amusement exhibitions in Canada, usually in booths where a wheel is spun, rather than dice thrown, to determine winning bets.

4. For a fuller discussion of Bermuda's recent political history, see Hodgson (1967), Manning (1973, 1978a), and Ryan (1973).

5. The most accessible general overviews of the Trinidad Carnival are those of Hill (1972) and Pearse (1956). Literature on other Caribbean Carnivals includes Abrahams (1970) on Tobago, Abrahams and Bauman (1978) on St. Vincent, Crowley (1956) on St. Lucia, and Manning (1978b) on Antigua.

References

Abrahams, Roger
1970 Patterns of Performance in the British West Indies. *In* Afro-American Anthropology: Contemporary Perspectives. Norman E. Whitten, Jr. and John Szwed, eds. pp. 163-179. New York: Free Press.

Abrahams, Roger, and Richard Bauman
1978 Ranges of Festival Behavior. *In* The Reversible World: Symbolic Inversion in Art and Society. Barbara Babcock, ed. pp. 193-208. Ithaca: Cornell University Press.

Babcock, Barbara
1973 The Carnivalization of the Novel and the High Spirituality of Dressing Up. Paper presented at Burg Wartenstein Symposium No. 59. Ritual: Reconciliation in Change. Gloggnitz, Austria.

Barrett, Leonard
1977 The Rastafarians: Sounds of Cultural Dissonance. Boston: Beacon Press.

Bateson, Gregory
1972 Steps to an Ecology of Mind. New York: Ballantine.

Cohen, Abner
1979 Political Symbolism. Annual Review of Anthropology 8:87-113.

Crowley, Daniel
1956 Festivals of the Calendar in St. Lucia. Caribbean Quarterly 4:99-121.

de Albuquerque, Klaus
1979 The Future of the Rastafarian Movement. Caribbean Review 8(4):22-25, 44-46.
1980 Rastafarianism and Cultural Identity in the Caribbean. Paper presented at the Caribbean Studies Association meeting, Willemstad, Curacao.

Geertz, Clifford
1972 Deep Play: Notes on the Balinese Cockfight. Daedalus 101(1):1-38.

Gluckman, Max, and Mary Gluckman
1977 On Drama, and Games, and Athletic Contests. In Secular Ritual. Sally F. Moore and Barbara Myerhoff, eds. pp. 227-243. Assen/Amsterdam: Van Gorcum.

Henzell, Perry
1973 The Harder They Come. Kingston, Jamaica: New World Films.

Hill, Errol
1972 The Trinidad Carnival: Mandate for a National Theatre. Austin: University of Texas Press.

Hodgson, Eva
1967 Second-Class Citizens, First-Class Men. Hamilton, Bermuda: Published by the author.

James, C. L. R.
1963 Beyond a Boundary. London: Hutchinson.

Kochman, Thomas
1970 Toward an Ethnography of Black American Speech Behavior. In Afro-American Anthropology: Contemporary Perspectives. Norman E. Whitten, Jr. and John Szwed, eds. pp. 145-162. New York: Free Press.

Lewis, Gordon
1968 The Growth of the Modern West Indies. New York: Monthly Review Press.

Lowenthal, David
1972 West Indian Societies. New York: Oxford University Press.

Manning, Frank
1973 Black Clubs in Bermuda: Ethnography of a Play World. Ithaca: Cornell University Press.
1978a Bermudian Politics in Transition: Race, Voting, and Public Opinion. Hamilton, Bermuda: Island Press.
1978b Carnival in Antigua: An Indigenous Festival in a Tourist Economy. Anthropos 73:191-204.

Moore, Sally F., and Barbara Myerhoff
1977 Secular Ritual. Assen/Amsterdam: Van Gorcum.

Morris, Desmond
1973 On Afro-West Indian Thinking. In The Aftermath of Sovereignty: West Indian Perspectives. David Lowenthal and Lambros Comitas, eds. pp. 277-282. Garden City, NY: Doubleday Anchor.

Naipaul, V.S.
1973 Power to the Caribbean People. In The Aftermath of Sovereignty: West Indian Perspectives. David Lowenthal and Lambros Comitas, eds. pp. 363-371. Garden City, NY: Doubleday Anchor.

Newman, Dorothy
1972 The Population Dynamics of Bermuda. Hamilton, Bermuda: Bermuda Government, Department of Statistics.

Nisbet, Robert
1965 Emile Durkheim. Englewood Cliffs, NJ: Prentice-Hall.

Pearse, Andrew

1956 Carnival in Nineteenth Century Trinidad. Caribbean Quarterly 4:176-193.

Roberts, John, Malcolm Arth, and Robert Bush
1959 Games in Culture. American Anthropologist 61:597-605.

Roberts, John, and Brian Sutton-Smith
1962 Child Training and Game Involvement. Ethnology 2:166-185.
1966 Cross-Cultural Correlates of Games of Chance. Behavior Science Notes 1:131-144.

Ryan, Selwyn
1973 Politics in an Artificial Society: The Case of Bermuda. *In* Ethnicity in the Americas. Frances Henry, ed. pp. 159-192. The Hague: Mouton.

St. Pierre, Maurice
1973 West Indian Cricket: A Sociohistorical Appraisal. Caribbean Quarterly 19:7-27.

Sapir, Edward
1934 Symbolism. Encyclopaedia of the Social Sciences 14:492-495.

Schwartzman, Helen
1978 Transformations: The Anthropology of Children's Play. New York: Plenum Press.

Singer, Milton
1955 The Cultural Pattern of Indian Civilization. Far Eastern Quarterly 15:23-36.

Smith, Michael G.
1965 The Plural Society in the British West Indies. Berkeley: University of California Press.

Turner, Victor
1964 Symbols in Ndembu Ritual, *In* Closed Systems and Open Minds: The Limits of Naivety in Social Anthropology. Max Gluckman, ed. pp. 20-51. Chicago: Aldine.
1977 Variations on a Theme of Liminality. *In* Secular Ritual. Sally F. Moore and Barbara Myerhoff, eds. pp. 36-52. Assen/Amsterdam: Van Gorcum.

Wilson, Peter
1973 Crab Antics: The Social Anthropology of English-Speaking Negro Societies of the Caribbean. New Haven: Yale University Press.

MICKEY MOUSE HISTORY:
PORTRAYING THE PAST AT
DISNEY WORLD

Mike Wallace

Entertainment parks highlighted by amusements, exhibits, and thematic performances have gained astounding popularity. To astute observers, these parks are not simply recreational sites; they are also complex symbolic environments that reflect and reinforce an understanding of the wider world. A few prominent parks have been interpreted as the secular equivalents of religious shrines, settings in which a society's self-understanding and sense of purpose are expressed in intense, vivid, and moving ways.

Mike Wallace develops this line of thought in an ingenious analysis of the Disney complex near Orlando, Florida. Focusing on The Magic Kingdom and the EPCOT Center, he proposes that these two sites represent alternate but ideologically consistent versions of American history. The Magic Kingdom, designed by Walt Disney himself, is an idyllic model of American society at the turn of the twentieth century, emphasizing blissful, small town values and an uncritical sense of national patriotism. EPCOT, built after Disney's death and in partnership with major business corporations, embodies a different view: the notion of an America chastened by the changes and criticisms of the past two decades and now committed to the energetic reform of its inherited values. EPCOT also looks into the future, envisioning a world in which social problems will be resolved and consumer satisfaction guaranteed through the technological leadership of the multinational corporations.

Those who have visited the Disney complex can attest to the ethnographic accuracy of Wallace's account. Indeed, he could have gone further by emphasizing the symbolic and spatial domination

*of the US pavilion within the World Showcase, an exhibition of
the social and commercial life of a dozen countries. Each country
selected is both an ally of the US and a supporter of international
capitalism. Moreover, while the items on sale as well as the
workers in each pavilion come from the countries represented, the
entire exhibition is owned, organized, controlled, and
choreographed by Disney Enterprises. The message is clear:
capitalist America runs the world. Mickey Mouse tells us why,
shows us how, and makes it seem like good clean fun.*

---

*"Industry has lost credibility with the public, the government
has lost credibility, but people still have faith in Mickey
Mouse and Donald Duck."* (Marty Sklar, vice-president,
WED Enterprises, Inc.)

WALT DISNEY NEVER GOT A PH.D., but he was, nevertheless, a
passionate historian. At Disneyland in California and Disney World
in Florida, the past is powerfully evoked for visitors—using music,
movies, robots, and the latest in special effects. It's possible that
Walt Disney has taught people more history, in a more memorable
way, than they ever learned in school. As a professional historian
interested in popular presentations of the past, I decided to review
the work of this premier interpreter of the American experience.

I soon discovered there are *two* Walt Disneys. The man we
might call "Original Walt" built the Magic Kingdom in Disneyland
in the 1950s. Later, the Magic Kingdom was cloned and transported
to Disney World in Florida. Today both kingdoms remain essentially
intact, frozen in time, their presentations of "Main Street", "Frontierland", "Adventureland", and the "Hall of Presidents" reflecting
Original Walt's 1950s-style approach to history.

Disney died in 1966—despite persistent rumors that he had himself frozen, and may yet be back. But in a way he *did* live on. As
WED (Walter Elias Disney) Enterprises, Inc., he was reincarnated
as a corporation.

In the 1970s, this "Corporate Walt", claiming it was carrying out
Original Walt's wishes, forged an alliance with other corporations
(the crème de la crème of U.S. multinationals). Together they built

EPCOT—the Experimental Prototype Community of Tomorrow—
and housed it in Disney World, next door to the Magic Kingdom.
EPCOT, too, is saturated with history, but of a remarkably different
kind from Disney's 1950s version. It is these two historical perspectives, side by side in Orlando, that I want to explore and juxtapose.
While there are intriguing continuities between them, EPCOT'S approach suggests that the sixties and seventies had an extraordinary
impact on popular historical consciousness, enough to warrant extraordinary efforts by corporate America to reconstitute a past they
could live with.

In the early 1950s Walt Disney set out to build an amusement
park that was clean, wholesome, and altogether different from the
seedy carnivals he remembered from his youth. Against great odds
(bankers frowned on the project and he had to borrow on his insurance policy to do the initial planning), he brought Disneyland
into being in 1955. At the heart of the project, right along with his
fantasy characters, Disney placed a series of history-flavored entertainments.

This was new for Walt. Aside from the spectacularly successful
Davy Crockett: King of the Wild Frontier, a few costume dramas like
Rob Roy, the Highland Rogue, and *Song of the South* (whose idyllic
depiction of master/slave relationships drew NAACP—National Association for the Advancement of Colored People, a black civil
rights lobby—fire), Walt had shied away from history. Perhaps his
turnaround was influenced by the crowds flocking to John D. Rockefeller, Jr.'s Colonial Williamsburg and Henry Ford's Greenfield
Village as 1950s Americans took to the highways in search of their
roots. Certainly his technique resembled that used at Williamsburg—he transported visitors back in time.

The minute you stroll through the turnstiles into the Magic
Kingdom you "turn back the clock," as your guidebook tells you,
"to the turn of the century." Your first steps take you to Main
Street, the heart of a small American town. It's a happy street, clean
and tidy, filled with prancing Disney characters. It has a toylike
quality, perhaps because it's built five-eighths true size ("people
like to think their world is somehow more grown up than Papa's
was"). It's like playing in a walk-in doll's house that is simultaneously
a consumer's paradise, equipped with dozens of little olde-time

MIKE WALLACE

shoppes with corporate logos tastefully affixed.

But Main Street, ostensibly, is grounded in historic reality. It was fashioned, we are told, out of Disney's recollections of his turn-of-the-century boyhood in Marceline, Missouri, a small town a hundred miles northeast of Kansas City. The intent, Walt said, was to "bring back happy memories for those who remember the carefree times it recreates." This is puzzling to those familiar with Disney's own story, which was rather grimmer.

Disney's father Elias, a hardscrabble small operator, drifted back and forth between country and city in an unsuccessful attempt to establish himself and his family. After failing at citrus growing in Florida, he moved to Chicago, where he worked as a carpenter on the Columbian Exposition of 1893, and then established a hand-to-mouth small contracting business. Walt was born in 1901, just before the business failed and the family moved again, this time to a forty-eight-acre farm near Marceline, on which Elias entered into the precarious and indebted life of the American small farmer. (Perhaps the then pervasive agrarian resentment of bankers was a source of the elder Disney's socialism—he voted consistently for Eugene Debs and subscribed to the *Appeal to Reason*). Walt was set to hard farm labor (drudgery which his two elder brothers escaped by running off) and a diet of stern patriarchal beatings. In 1910, Elias failed again. Forced to sell the farm and auction off the livestock, he moved to Kansas City, Missouri, bought a newspaper route, and set Walt and his remaining brother Roy to work as newsboys; Roy ran away the following year. After living meanly in Missouri a few more years, Elias drifted back to Chicago, where he became chief of construction and maintenance in a jelly factory, and put Walt to work washing bottles. Finally, in 1919, Walt made his own break. He spent the early 1920s in Kansas City as a commercial artist, hustling hard to stay alive and ahead of the bill collectors. In 1923 he moved to Hollywood, where his career began to click.

The confectionery quality of Magic Kingdom's Main Street thus bears little resemblance to Disney's real childhood home. And indeed a Disney official history confesses that "historically speaking, this Main Street was quite unlike the real Main Streets of yesteryear. Here, everything would always remain fresh and new. And the rows of old-time shops and the traffic vehicles and all the other elements would function together in harmony and unison unlike anything grandfather ever experienced."

Original Walt's approach to the past was thus not to reproduce it, but to *improve* it. A Disney "imagineer" (as the designers style themselves) explains how the process works: "What we create is a 'Disney Realism,' sort of Utopian in nature, where we carefully program out all the negative, unwanted elements and program in the positive elements." (This vacuum-cleaning of the past is reminiscent of Walt's film work in which he transformed Grimm's gothic horror tales into cute and cheery cartoons.) As another Disney planner puts it: "This is what the real Main Street should have been like."

The Disney people don't consider this retrospective tidying up an abuse of the past—they freely and disarmingly admit its falsification, pointing out that this is, after all, just entertainment. But they also insist they are bringing out deeper truths. John Hench, a leading member of the organization, expanded on this in an interview, explaining that Disney sought to recapture the *essence* of a period. "You take a certain style, and take out the contradictions that have crept in there through people that never understood it or by accident or by some kind of emergency that happened once and found itself being repeated—you leave those things out, purify the style, and it comes back to its old form again." Like the French architect Viollet-le-Duc, who in the 1860s and 1870s strove to restore churches to imagined Gothic purity, Original Walt aimed to strip away the accretions of time. In the case of Main Street, Hench explains, he was striving to recreate the Victorian era, "which is probably one of the great optimistic periods of the world, where we thought progress was great and we all knew where we were going. [Main Street] reflects that prosperity, that enthusiasm."

The decades before and after the turn of the century had their decidedly prosperous moments. But they also included depressions, strikes on the railroads, warfare in the minefields, squalor in the immigrant communities, lynching, imperial wars, and the emergence of mass protests by populists and socialists. *This* history has been whited out, presumably because it would have distressed and repelled visitors. As Hench noted, "Walt wanted to reassure people."

Walt's approach, though it had its roots in Hollywood, was emblematic of larger developments in 1950s America. The dominant culture, seemingly determined to come up with a happy past to

MIKE WALLACE

match its own contented present, contracted a selective amnesia. Leading academic historians downplayed past conflicts and painted optimistic, even uplifting pictures of the American past. Colonial Williamsburg's recollection of olden times conspicuously excised the presence of black slaves, 50 percent of its eighteenth-century inhabitants. Greenfield Village—another conflict-free small town— overlooked such realities of rural life as foreclosures and farmers' movements.

Walt's Main Street, therefore, can perhaps best be understood as part of a larger trend. As a stage set that cultivated nostalgia for a fabricated past, it contributed its bit toward fashioning an image— now deeply etched into popular memory—of the "gay nineties" as a world without classes, conflict, or crime, a world of continuous consumption, a supermarket of fun. Just as Colonial Williamsburg provided the model for thousands of "colonial" suburbs, Disneyland's Main Street became a model for the developing American shopping mall and the "ye olde" entertainment centers beginning to festoon the American landscape. On the face of it, Eisenhower-era citizens could assume that American's present had evolved gently, naturally, and inevitably out of its past.

There *are* places in Disneyland that recall the bumpier patches of the good old days. At Frontiertown and Adventureland, contradictions are not deleted but dwelt upon. Here we go on rides that travel to the distant and benighted places which once threatened Civilization. In the Wild West, Darkest Africa, and the Caribbean, we are in the domain of dangerous opponents—Indians, pygmy headhunters, pirates. But there is no real danger in these realms. As Hench explains: "What we do here is to throw a challenge at you—not a real menace, but a pseudo-menace, a theatricalized menace—and we allow you to win."

Scary but harmless images are a stock-in-trade of amusement parks. But it is striking that Disney's "pseudo-menaces" are all historical ones—the ghosts of once vigorous, now defeated enemies of Main Street—transformed into fun-filled characters. On the ride up the Congo River, your affable host regales you with such witticisms as "These natives have one thing in mind; they just want to get ahead." The robot pirates are agreeably wicked and the robot women seem to enjoy being ravished. In Frontierland you can hole up in an old fort and shoot Indians, with a barrage of canned gunfire as an accompaniment (this was Walt's favorite part of the park).

For all the whizzing bullets, the experience of reliving ancient passions is a soothing one. For one thing, as Hench comments shrewdly, these are "old-fashioned weapons. They're part of the safe past. Nobody worries about the past...." For another, cowboys-and-Indians is a well-established and conventional game, and historical conflict is thus shuttled into a regressive world of childhood fantasy. Frontierland and Adventureland brush up against some realities of the past, but in the end they serve as ritual reassurance of Main Street's triumph over its opponents.

The Magic Kingdom includes a direct portrayal of American history—at the Hall of Presidents. The hall has a peculiar history of its own. Designed in 1957-58, it was put on the shelf because Disney imagineers lacked the technology to produce it. Breakthroughs in "audioanimatronics" (robot building) came in the early 1960s, and at the 1964 World's Fair Disney tried out the new engineering. In collaboration with the state of Illinois, he built the "Visit with Mr. Lincoln" pavilion, starring an artificial Abe. In the 1970s, the original Hall of Presidents show was dusted off, and the Lincoln robot became its centerpiece.

The Hall of Presidents is housed at Liberty Square, in a mock-up of the eighteenth-century Philadelphia mansion. Visitors wait for the next show in the Rotunda, where paintings of the Founding Fathers establish respectful atmospherics. Then they are ushered into a theater (and told that no eating is allowed—"to maintain the dignity of the presentation"). A film begins. It shows the Founding Fathers making the Constitution. We learn that the new document was soon challenged by the Whiskey Rebels, a churlish mob, and that George Washington crushed them. Then slaveholders, an aristocratic mob, threatened it again. Andrew Jackson threatened to hang them from the nearest tree. Finally the Confederates launched the greatest challenge to date, and Lincoln took up the burden of defense. The movie implies that internal disorder remains the chief threat to America's survival.

The film ends. With great fanfare the screen goes up, revealing a stage full of robot presidents. All of them, from Washington to Reagan, are in motion, nodding or solemnly (if somewhat arthritically) gesticulating. George Washington's chair is a precise reproduction of the one in which he sat at the 1787 Constitutional Convention. Their costumes are authentic down to the last stitch. Wig-makers in Guatemala reproduced their hair strand for strand. (The attention to detail, characteristic of Hollywood costume dramas, again reminds us of Disney's cinematic roots.)

A sepulchral voice-over calls the roll of these men "who have defended the Constitution." The audience is hushed—perhaps in awe at the solemnity of the occasion, perhaps in amazement at the spectacle of thirty-odd robots twitching about on stage. When the roll call gets to FDR and the more recent presidents, there is a whisper here and there. But when it gets to Nixon, chortles and guffaws break out. The contrast between the Official History and living memories is too great—Nixon as defender of the Constitution—and the spell snaps under the strain. I asked later if this was simply a bad day for Mr. Nixon, and was told that no, the crowd always rumbles when RN takes his bow.

The Nixon disturbance is symptomatic of a larger problem with the Hall of Presidents. By the 1970s, for all its technical sophistication, its ideology was old-fashioned, less believable than it was in the heyday of McCarthyism. The Disney people deny any dissatisfaction with it, but in retrospect we can see that in the 1960s they began exploring alternatives to the nationalistic approach. The transition to the eventual solution (EPCOT) was provided by another Disney 1964 World's Fair exhibit, the Carousel of Progress, created in collaboration with General Electric.

At the Carousel of Progress, Disney takes visitors on a ride through time. After they settle down in the Carousel's small theater, the curtain rises on a robot middle-class family at home in 1900. Mom, Dad, and the kids are chatting about housework. They have the latest in labor-saving devices—gas, lights, telephones, iceboxes—and *think* that life couldn't be any easier, but *we* see that poor Mom is still subject to all kinds of drudgery. Luckily, as Dad reads in the paper, some smart fellers down at General Electric are cooking up new gadgets. At this point the theater begins to revolve around the stage (accompanied by a cheery ditty whose refrain is "Now is the best time, now is the best time, now is the best time of your life") until it reaches a new set, this one peopled with 1920s-style robots. Mom and Dad enthuse about their new machines—percolators, refrigerators, electric irons—but note that those research people at General Electric are still at it. And on we go to 1940, and finally to 1960. Things have really progressed now. Dad is cooking dinner (though somewhat clumsily) and Mom is celebrating passage of a bond issue (on which she had time to work thanks to her GE dishwasher and dryer). At ride's end a hearty voice-over concludes that we live in "the best time" ("one of the reasons is that electricity has improved our lives"), and that things will get even better ("each new year and each new day will bring a better way of life"). Finally we are shuttled toward the Kitchen of Tomorrow to see what General Electric has dreamed up for us next.

The Carousel of Progress is more than simply an extended commercial break. It is a paean to Progress—defined as the availability of emancipatory consumer goods. This was new for Disney. He had tended to political rather than commercial themes. But it was an old line of argument for industrial corporations. Even the pseudo-feminist claim that household commodities liberated women had been advanced by advertisers since the 1920s and had been a staple at the 1939 World's Fair. I would like to suggest that the Disney-GE collaboration represents an important merging of several longstanding traditions of American culture.

Consider, first, the roots of Disney's Magic Kingdom shows. They descend, in part, from the patriotic diorama, *tableaux vivants,* and waxworks of the nineteenth century. Disney upgraded the technology—viewers were hauled *into* the dioramas and robots replaced live actors or wax representations—but the red-white-and-blue spirit remained much the same.

In the 1950s, Disney married this tradition to the amusement park—a form that beer magnates, real estate developers, and transportation kings had fashioned for the urban working classes in the 1880s and 1890s, and whose culmination was Coney Island. Disney's park was a cleaned-up version, aimed at a middle-class "family" audience. He quite consciously stripped away the honky-tonk legacies of the carnival. It might be said that Disneyland represented another skirmish in a centuries-old struggle by the middle classes against popular culture's dangerous tendency to "turn the world upside down." By customary right, medieval carnivals—Twelfth Night, the Ship of Fools, Bartholomew Fair—allowed the dispossessed to ridicule the high and mighty and even (symbolically) to seize power for a day.

Disney's park erased any lingering traces of rituals of revolt and substituted highly organized, commodified fun. In this the Magic Kingdom shows were like Rockefeller Jr.'s Williamsburg and Ford's Greenfield Village, which eliminated from "history" what their sponsors found inconvenient and unwelcome. But the essence of the form, selective reconstruction of the past, goes way back: to late nineteenth-century Scandinavian open-air museums and (in spirit) to such eighteenth-century aristocratic productions as Marie Antoinette's play peasant village (complete with marble-walled dairy), French *folies* such as Parc Monceau, and the great landscape parks of the English gentry which excised all signs of daily peasant activity and eradicated any sense of time other than the artificially constructed "natural."

In the 1960s, Disney took the Magic Kingdom approach and merged it with a favorite form of the entrepreneurial bourgeoisie—the industrial exposition. These expositions, of course, go back to London's 1851 Crystal Palace (and New York City's 1853 copy). They afforded places to show off, and sell, new inventions. They were also sites of ideological production, of boasting about how technology and business would transform the future.

From the perspective of its sponsors, the exposition form had long been riven by an annoying inner tension between commercial exhortation and crowd-pleasing carnival elements. The 1893 Columbian Exposition had huge buildings devoted to transportation, manufacture, and electricity presented in historical perspective; it also had seedier entertainment pavilions, located outside the White City, including "a real Dahomey village of genuine savages."

The 1939 World's Fair overcame this dichotomy to a degree by subordinating celebration of production to fascination with consumption. Rather than the traditional presentation of awesome machinery, the Fair showcased consumer goods: companies displayed their commodities in dazzling surroundings. General Motors' Futurama shuttled visitors along in comfortable moving chairs; AT&T fostered audience interaction with a talking machine; and General Electric offered a House of Magic ("the packed audiences," it was noted, "came away thrilled, mystified, and soundly sold on the company"). Another GE show contrasted the lives of Mrs.

Drudge and Mrs. Modern, anticipating the Carousel of Progress's argument of gender emancipation through household appliances. For all this, the Fair's first year was a financial failure, partly because of the high admission price, partly because of the heaviness of the social message.

The financial and corporate sponsors presented the "World of Tomorrow" as the product of rejuvenated capitalism, a decade of depression and state intervention behind it. Entrepreneurs and technocrats would promote a rich future of mass plenty if given the opportunity, and public funds. At Futurama, as Walter Lippmann noted, General Motors "spent a small fortune to convince the American public that if it wishes to enjoy the full benefit of private enterprise in motor manufacturing, it will have to rebuild its cities and its highways by public enterprise." The agitprop turned many off, critics and visitors skirted the educational and cultural theme exhibits, and even the *New York Times* called the Fair a laboratory for "Tomorrow's propaganda." In its second year, the Fair brought back sideshows and hootchy-kootchy girls.

Twenty-five years later, the 1964 Disney-GE collaboration put sanitized entertainment at the service of business boosterism, and pointed the way to EPCOT, which would brilliantly and successfully merge *all* these techniques and traditions, retaining the advantages and shedding the liabilities of fairs, waxworks, museums, and carnivals. One of the keys to the breakthrough was the Disney ability, adroitly displayed at the Carousel, to construct highly selective versions of the past.

Walt's original vision of EPCOT had nothing to do with history. The Experimental Prototype Community of Tomorrow was to be a laboratory city in which twenty thousand people would live. Disney dreamed of "a planned, controlled community, a showcase for American industry and research," a permanent testing ground for new ideas in urban planning. Under its gigantic bubble dome, American knowhow, ingenuity, and enterprise would overcome the ills of urban life. ("In EPCOT there will be no slum areas because we won't let them develop.")

This extraordinary project might seem quite a jump from an amusement park, but the overheated reaction Disneyland evoked may have been instrumental in EPCOT's creation. Walt had been praised extravagantly as an urban planner. James Rouse, master builder of new towns and historical shopping malls modeled on Main Street (Boston's Faneuil Hall, Baltimore's Harborplace, New York's South Street Seaport), told a 1963 Harvard conference that Disneyland was the "greatest piece of urban design in the United States today." Architectural critic Peter Blake called the Anaheim park the only significant New Town built in the U.S. since World War II—"staggeringly successful"—and suggested, only half-humorously, turning Manhattan over to Disney to fix up.

All this went to Walt's head and he flowered into a utopian capitalist. This was partly a family legacy: as Michael Harrington has perceptively noted, Disney's father had been an admirer of Edward Bellamy's "warmhearted, futuristic authoritarianism." Partly, perhaps, Walt had been inspired by the 1939 World's Fair's Democracity, a scale model of a perfectly planned "World of Tomorrow"—a "vast, Utopian stage set" housed inside the great globe of the Perisphere. Whatever its roots, the hothouse atmosphere of the Kennedy-Johnson years speeded the process. Gigantic projects of social reconstruction seemed plausible in those boom years and though Walt was a Goldwater Republican (and an early financial supporter of Ronald Reagan), he too dreamed of creating a Great Society.

Disney acted boldly. By 1965 he had bought up, secretly, forty square miles (*twice* the size of Manhattan) in central Florida. The state, anticipating mammoth tourist revenues, granted him virtually feudal powers. Democracy for the residents of the Community of Tomorrow would have been a nuisance. ("There will be no land-owners and therefore no voting control.") To ensure that EPCOT ran smoothly, Walt would be King.

But, in 1966, in the midst of planning the new society, Walt died. WED Enterprises considered going ahead with his prototype city, but the company was nervous; it could see lawsuits in its future from disgruntled and disfranchised residents. So it scrapped the notion of a living city and went with a safer version. WED proposed to some of the biggest corporations in the U.S. a joint project: the construction of a permanent World's Fair. There the companies, with the help of Disney imagineers, would display evolving technologies and promote their visions of the future. EPCOT was thus transformed from utopian community to sound business proposition.

By targeting Yuppies instead of Mouseketeers, WED got itself out of an impending crisis—a looming baby bust that promised to shrivel its traditional prime market of five-to-nine-year-olds. (A similar marketing strategy recently dictated scrapping Dick Van Dyke movies for PG films like *Splash*: pre-teens no longer flocked to traditional Disney fare and the studio was forced to respond to this cultural shift. The participating companies would also profit: they could advertise new product lines and drape themselves in the mantle of Disney respectability, no small matter in the anti-corporate atmosphere of the 1970s. The corporate giants agreed. Kraft declared that sponsorship of a land pavilion was "the most effective way we can enhance our corporate identity." General Electric explained that "the Disney organization is absolutely superb in interpreting our company dramatically, memorably, and favorably to the public." Kodak observed, somewhat baldly, that "you might entrance a teenager today, but tomorrow he's going to invest his money in Kodak stock." General Motors took a broader view, noting not only that EPCOT would give them the chance "to make contact with millions of motorists," but that "it will be a good opportunity to point out how technological progress has contributed to the world and the free enterprise system."

In the end, major multinationals—notably those who had been most successful at the 1939 Fair—signed on to tell Americans what life would be like in the twenty-first century. At EPCOT, Exxon explains Energy and AT&T does Communications. Transportation is presented by General Motors, the Land by Kraft, the Home by GE, "Imagination" by Kodak. Each corporation has a high-tech pavilion, the heart of which is a ride. Seated passengers are conveyed through tunnels which open out into drive-through dioramas—stage sets crammed with robots, videos, and holograms. Supplementing each ride are exhibits, films, and hands-on demonstrations. The pavilions are grouped into an area of the park called (echoing 1939) the World of Tomorrow.

Nation-states were also invited to EPCOT. England, France, Germany, Italy, Japan, China, Mexico, Canada—usually in conjunction with national businesses (Japan Airlines, British Railways, Labatts Beer)—exhibit their wares and promote travel to their shores. Disney imagineers helped them design terrains that portray the "essence" of their culture. Presiding over this World of Nations is the host pavilion, the American Adventure (presented jointly by American Express and Coca-Cola), devoted entirely to presenting the history of the United States.

In 1982 EPCOT opened. It billed itself as "a community of ideas and nations and a testing ground where free enterprise can explore and demonstrate and showcase new ideas that relate to man's hopes and dreams." In its first year, over twenty-two million people visited. More businesses and countries signed on. By 1984, total investment had reached $1.75 billion and was still climbing.

An amazing amount of the World of Tomorrow is devoted to the world of yesterday. Virtually all the rides are time travels. Passengers settle themselves into moving vehicles which carry them from the dim past to an imagined future. Voice-over narrators, like those on TV commercials, explain the passing views and propound an interpretation of historical development.

Each multinational historian has its own style. GM's tends toward the relentlessly cheery; the past was endlessly droll, even "wacky" and "zany." AT&T's is more portentous: "Who are We? Where Are We Going?" it asks in sepulchral tones as we climb aboard our Time Machines, and informs us that the answer must be sought in the "Dawn of Recorded Time." But it is the similarities that compel attention.

There is a discernible corporate vision of history. At first blush it appears merely that of the Carousel of Progress writ large: history is a record of the invention of commodities which allow Man to master his environment. But EPCOT goes beyond this. The temporal dimensions are far grander—from the cave men to outer space. And, significantly, each corporation admits there have been Problems in the past.

Each journey begins in prehistoric times. GM's history of transportation has robot neanderthals "stumbling around" by footpower. Exxon's history of energy commences with robot dinosaurs (reminiscent of those in *Fantasia*) battling one another in a primeval swamp as fossil fuels cook beneath their feet. AT&T's history of communication starts with cave men attacking mammoths and painting on walls.

Then Man climbs out of primitive times. GM's Man does this in an unrelievedly hearty way. As we ride along (accompanied by a background ditty proclaiming that "It's fun to be free, to go anywhere, with never a care"), we watch Man slowly produce improved forms of transport—canoes, horse-drawn vehicles—until we reach that favorite corporate period, the Renaissance. Here GM's robot Leonardo turns from culture to engineering: he is shown tinkering with a flying machine while a scowling robot Mona Lisa model taps her foot. Then it's on to the Era of Inventions and a cornucopia of improvements—bicycles, horseless carriages, trains, airplanes—that bring us to the present.

AT&T's trajectory is similar. It tracks the slow progress of communications—Egyptians invent scrolls (a robot pharaoh gives dictation to a robot secretary), Greeks give birth to theater (robots declaim on stage), and monks illuminate manuscripts (one is shown cutely snoring at his desk). When AT&T hits the Renaissance, it tilts (unlike GM) toward the cultural dimension, featuring a robot Michelangelo, on its back, laboring at the Sistine ceiling. Then AT&T's Man also enters the jet stream of Progress, and inventions tumble out on what seems a self-sustaining basis.

But when the rides reach the near past, there is a sudden departure from triumphalism. Each corporation acknowledges some blemishes on the record. To be sure, many were inconsequential: one General Motors diorama jovially depicts the first traffic jam (which it blames on a horse). Other problems were serious. Kraft reminds us graphically of Dust Bowl days. Exxon reminds us that an energy crisis emerged. The past was *not* the best of all possible pasts.

The corporate histories are less than clear as to *why* problems emerged. Some seem facts of nature—dinosaur days bequeathed us limited quantities of fossil fuel. But people are responsible for others. Kraft tells us that "we" (or, occasionally, "technological man") made mistakes. "We" abused the environment. "We" polluted the air. There is a hint that "unplanned development" had something to do with it (a practice, presumably, in which multinationals do no engage).

Luckily, we are given to understand, people (or, more precisely, corporations) are working on these problems. The adjacent exhibits expand on this, and we shall return to them.

Each ride then breaks through the troubled recent past into the Future. The Future is always set in outer space. The narrative tapes

MIKE WALLACE

and ditties shut off, *Close Encounters of the Third Kind* music comes on, laser beams flash, and we are launched into awesome starry expanses in which space stations and satellites hover. In the Future, Problems have been eliminated, presumably by the corporations, whose logos are visible everywhere (as in the movie *2001*). Life in space looks remarkably like life on sitcom TV. Mom back on earth communicates (via AT&T's Network) with Sis up on the space station, and they chat about homework and boyfriends. There's a sense of serene ordinariness about the Future, which is not accidental. Hench believes "nobody worries about the future, because that's going to be up in space, in the space colonies." And Marty Sklar, WED VP, says: "We admit to being optimistic over man's future. You can call EPCOT our answer to the gloomy future predictions of the Club of Rome."

Subsidiary exhibits explain the basis for this optimism—corporate problem solvers are at work. Kraft, in full environmentalist regalia, talks about the need for "symbiosis" with the land, shows films about replanting forests and reoxygenating rivers, and explains the artificial farms of the future. AT&T approximates Bucky Fuller's environmental imagery—its geodesic dome pavilion is called Spaceship Earth—and shows how AT&T's Network will overcome communications bottlenecks on earth and in outer space. Exxon tells us it is working away at solar power (the roof of its pavilion is bejewelled with photoelectric panels). Solar, sadly, still seems far from practicable. So, Exxon explains, until the big breakthroughs come, we must rely on oil (videos sing the romance of offshore rigs and ecologically correct pipelines) and coal (films prove that strip mining can be beautiful). Exxon also wants us to keep the nuclear option open and visitors can play at running a nuclear plant. But the company is not heavy-handed about plumping for oil or atoms. All options must be kept open and in competition, including geothermal and biomass. Let the best one win.

GM, another corporate environmentalist, also believes in open options. In its "Engine of the Future" show, films project cartoon characters onto large overhead screens. Each promotes a different energy-conscious design. On the left, GM's own persona, a jolly cowboy, pitches for an improved internal combustion engine. Then alternatives are presented: an Archie Bunker sort favors coal, a Yuppie lady pushes solar, even the omnipresent Leonardo has a better idea. All these notions are shot down for one reason or another. Finally, on the extreme right, we meet a character who looks like a cross between mad scientist and Japanese dwarf, and sounds like Peter Lorre. He is working—fanatically—on a totally pollution-free and inexpensive water engine, using hydrogen. In the grand finale this crackpot blows everything up, and flames sweep across all the screens.

Then cowboy Tex gets the floor back, applauds the others, says they have a ways to go before they beat out the "good ole reliable internal combustion engine," but assures them General Motors wants them all in competition, so the consumer will benefit in the end. (Consumers are indeed never far from GM's mind; the last exhibit is a showroom of current-model GM cars. GM is the most vulgar self-promoter—a hucksterism perhaps related to declining car sales?—but even the suavest of the multinationals have their tacky moments.)

EPCOT's sensitivity to social and environmental problems is rooted in the 1970s corporate world's awareness of its image problems. Business wanted, with the aid of Disney publicists, to refurbish itself in the public mind. EPCOT designers knew Magic Kingdom boosterism wouldn't suffice. So the imagineers admitted to problems in the past but rejected corporate responsibility for them. More imaginatively still, they presented business as the cutting edge of the ecology movement. America's problems, Corporate Walt says, are technical ones; responsible corporations are the Mr. Goodwrenches who can fix them. A Kraft VP summarized the strategy: "Hopefully [visitors to our pavilion will] be aware that major organizations are working at new ways of controlling the land—without disrupting the ecology—to ensure an adequate food supply. To our benefit will be the message that here is Kraft with that kind of concern."

This is a difficult message to sell. Exxon the champion of alternative energy? General Motors the promoter of mass transit? Kraft and agribusiness the practitioners of symbiosis with the land? AT&T the savior of Spaceship Earth? As in the case of the Nixon robot, the discrepancy between claim and reality invites ridicule. Corporate Walt, a skilful communicator, tries to bridge the gap not only through bald assertion but in more indirect ways as well.

MIKE WALLACE

As in the Magic Kingdom sets, a "whiteout" approach is at work—silence blankets the sorry environmental record of the corporations. (This doesn't fool people who know better, but doesn't enlighten those—particularly children—who don't.)

Another technique is EPCOT's bravura display of technological mastery and management capacity, which seems intent on inducing awe at the capabilities of the corporations, as machines in Greek temples once impressed the populace with the power of the gods. Imagine, the place implies, what business could do if let loose on America's ills (and never mind it created many of them in the first place, or that the cost of attaining EPCOT-level efficiency—1 billion per hundred acres—seems a mite high). EPCOT thus forms a chapter in capital's longstanding attempt to control social space as it controls production space; it echoes company-town experiments from Lowell to Pullman (all of which failed—but hope springs eternal).

But the most subtle and perhaps most powerful of the methods at work is the historical analysis that permeates the entire operation. The World of Tomorrow implies that capitalist development is natural and inevitable. It does so by riding visitors, literally on rails, from a bowdlerized presentation of the past to an impoverished vision of the future. The progression goes like this: history was made by inventors and businessmen; the corporations are the legatees of such a past (their slogan might be: "From Leonardo to Exxon"); this pedigree entitles them to run Tomorrow. Citizens can sit back and consume.

Disney did not invent this approach: it had respectable academic roots in "modernization theory." This analysis, fashionable during the 1950s and 1960s, updated the Victorian belief in a march of progress from "savagery" to "civilization," substituting a trajectory from "traditional" to "modern" society, with the latterday terminus understood to be contemporary America. It is worth noting that EPCOT's popularization of modernization theory, reactionary though it is, was the product of a relatively liberal corporate culture. Had EPCOT been designed in the tooth-and-claw world of the 1980s it would probably have argued that the driving force of history was profit maximization, an approach that might make the actual version seem positively benign.

Corporate Walt's history is bad history. All historical interpretations are necessarily selective in their facts, but here the silences
are profoundly distorting. Consider, for example, that in all
EPCOT's depictions of the past as a continuous expansion of man's
possibilities through technology, there is not a word about war.
Nothing about the critical impetus it provided through the ages to
scientific development. Nor about the phenomenal destruction such
"development" wrought. And nothing about the contemporary possibilities of planetary extermination. Perhaps the imagineers stuck
their heads in the sand on this one because they wanted us to think
only the most positive thoughts. But the Magic Kingdom's justification for ostrichism ("this is only an entertainment park") doesn't
wash here—EPCOT is explicitly devoted to enhancing understanding. Perhaps, as in Fantasyland, they think the wish is parent
to the fact. Or perhaps the silences are related to the fact that many
corporations are producing armaments as well as toasters, and that
if they and Reagan have their way, the outer-space dioramas of the
Future will have to be reconstructed to include killer satellites.

Corporate Walt's history, like modernization theory, is uni-
directional. There were never any forks on the path of Progress,
never any sharp political struggles over which way to go. EPCOT
visitors would never guess that millions of Americans once objected
to motoring down the capitalist road. The implication, moreover, is
that there are no alternatives now. If there have been problems,
they have been the price of progress; the only solution is full speed
ahead on the corporate space shuttle; minor course corrections can
be left to the pilot. Corporate Walt and the multinationals have
produced a past that leads ineluctably toward *their* kind of future.

Corporate Walt's history is also a top-down version. Popular
political movements don't exist in this past. Rendering ordinary
people invisible as makers of history hardly encourages visitors to
believe they can make their own future. (And EPCOT's impact goes
far beyond visitors: its sponsors have launched a massive outreach
program to the nation's classrooms; they are mass-marketing lesson
plans and videos on land, energy, and communications.)

Corporate desire to fudge the past combined with Disney's
ability to spruce it up promotes a sense of history as a pleasantly
nostalgic memory, now so completely transcended by the modern
corporate order as to be irrelevant to contemporary life. This

MIKE WALLACE

diminishes our capacity to make sense of our world through understanding how it came to be. The Disney version of history thus creates a way of not seeing and—perhaps—a way of not acting.

Good historical analysis informs people about the matrix of constraints and possibilities they have inherited from the past and enhances their capacity for effective social action in the present. EPCOT's World of Tomorrow does the opposite: it dulls historical sensibility and invites acquiescence to what is. It should, consequently, be regarded not as a historical, but as a historicidal enterprise.

EPCOT's American Adventure—American Express and Coca Cola's direct exploration of U.S. history—is intriguingly different from the high-tech pavilions; it also marks a startling departure from Original Walt's 1950s approach to the subject.

Like the Hall of the Presidents, the American Adventure is housed in a simulated Georgian mansion, staffed by costumed hosts and hostesses. Again there is an inspirational antechamber, with quotes by authors ranging from Herman Melville to Ayn Rand. But here there are no films, no rides. The model is closer to a TV variety show, with the presentation emceed by Ben Franklin and Mark Twain robots. The American Adventure consists of a series of turns by computer-operated robot ensembles, alternately raised and lowered by a 350,000-pound apparatus below the floor boards. The technology, as usual, is stunning. The robots are the latest in lifelike humanoids. The Franklin robot actually walks up stairs. The research into details (the size of Revolutionary War cannonballs, Alexander Graham Bell's diction) is scrupulous as ever. And this dazzling technology, when set in motion, proceeds to tell, in twenty-nine minutes flat, the entire history of the United States.

At first the show seems merely a spiffed-up Hall of Presidents. It begins with an inspirational reading of the Pilgrims-to-Revolution period (robot Rebel soldiers chat at Valley Forge while a George Washington robot sits dolefully on a robot horse). But with Independence won, and westward movement underway, the show departs dramatically from the expected. Emcee Twain tells us that "a whole bunch of folks found out 'we the people' didn't yet mean *all* the people," and a Frederick Douglass robot is hoisted up on stage. As he poles (somewhat improbably) down the Mississippi, Douglass speaks of the noise of chains and the crack of the whip, and of his hope that "antislavery will unlock the slave prison." A subdued Civil War sequence follows, using Brady photographs to stress costs rather than glory.

The Civil War over, a new wave of immigrants pours in. This, Twain tells us, heralds "a new dawn to the American Adventure." But as we resign ourselves to melting-pot platitudes, a clap of thunder introduces a Chief Joseph robot. He notes that the New Dawn means a "final sunset" for his people who are being shot down like animals. He gives his famous "I will fight no more forever" speech, reminding us (as Twain says) of "our long painful journey to the frontiers of human liberty."

Then it's on to the 1876 Centennial. But before launching into a Carousel-of-Progress-type paean to inventions, a Susan B. Anthony robot surfaces. In ringing voice she says: "We ask justice, we ask equality be guaranteed to us and our daughters forever," and adds, quoting Edison (with whom she most improbably shares the stage), that "discontent is the first necessity of progress."

Edison, Carnegie, and the roll call of inventions then have their moment, but after hearing about zippers, trolley cars, vacuum cleaners, and airplanes, a robot naturalist John Muir reminds us that all this growth posed a threat to America the Beautiful, and urges robot Teddy Roosevelt to build national parks. Next comes World War I—"ready or not, we were thrust into the role of world leader"—and Lindbergh's flight. But then comes the Crash of 1929, which "tarnished the golden dreams of millions," and we are into the Depression era. Here the set is a weatherbeaten southern post office-cum-gas station. Two Black and two white robots sit on the front porch (there is a lot of implausible retrospective integration in the show). They strum "Brother, can you spare a dime," chuckle about ex-millionaires in New York, and listen to FDR on the radio talking about "fear itself." (There is also a momentary descent into tacky self-promotion: the shack is plastered with contemporary Coca-Cola and American Express ads.) Then Will Rogers plumps for military preparedness, FDR announces Pearl Harbor, and we are into World War II—which consists entirely of a stage set featuring Rosie the Riveter fixing a submarine.

The postwar material plays it safer. History becomes popular culture. A series of filmic images of personalities is projected—like *People* magazine covers—which then float up into clouds, to the

MIKE WALLACE

accompaniment of ethereal music about America spreading its golden wings and flying high. It's an eclectic and distinctly integrated assortment, including Jackie Robinson, Marilyn Monroe, Jonas Salk, Satchmo, Elvis, Einstein, Walt Disney, Norman Rockwell, John Wayne, Lucy, Billie Jean King, JFK (giving his "Ask not" speech), Martin Luther King (giving his "I have a dream" speech), Muhammad Ali, Arnold Palmer, the U.S. Olympic hockey team, and the men on the moon. We end with a blaze of traditional Disney patriotism, with Ben and Mark perched atop the Statue of Liberty foreseeing a long run for the American Adventure.

The American Adventure is thus a dramatic departure from the Hall of Presidents (and the spirit of the World of Tomorrow). American History is no longer just about great white men; indeed it seems to be largely about Blacks, women, Indians, and the ecologists. The show doesn't celebrate law and order; it recalls the words of critics. On the face of it, the American Adventure represents an extraordinary step forward.

How do we account for it? One answer is the impact, by the mid-1970s, of the Black, women's, antiwar, and environmentalist movements that had heightened popular consciousness. After a generation of protest, 1950s celebrations would no longer do for public historical presentations; even Colonial Williamsburg had to restore Blacks to its streets. As a Disney briefing pamphlet for hosts says: "we couldn't ignore certain major issues that questioned our nation's stand on human liberty and justice." Even the sponsors agreed: a Coca-Cola executive told me "the warts-and-all perspective is appreciated by most visitors because our country is not perfect and they know it." In the last analysis, I believe, shifts in popular opinion forced the Disney people to update their ideology.

The writers, though not academics, were also influenced by the new social historians who reconstructed U.S. history in the 1960s and 1970s. Dr. Alan Yarnell, a UCLA historian consulted on the project, insisted that "the Jesse Lemisch approach—history from the bottom up" replace the great-white-men verities. The corporate sponsors went along with this approach—the heavy intervention of businessmen into World of Tomorrow scripting was missing here, perhaps because it was an area of lesser political concern. Amex and Coke simply assumed from the Disney track record that nothing embarrassing would emerge from the design process.

In the end, they were right. Despite the trappings of the new social history, the American Adventure remains Disney history. The imagineers imposed a theme of "Dreamers and Doers" on the show: the past had to be portrayed in an upbeat manner. So Susan B. Anthony, Chief Joseph, and Frederick Douglass notwithstanding, American History is still a saga of progress. The dissatisfaction of Blacks, women, and ecologists are presented as having been opportunities in disguise. As Disney literature puts it: "Inevitably, Americans have overcome the tragedies of their controversies, which ultimately led to a better way of life." In the American Adventure, social contradictions are transcended as easily as are natural ones at the World of Tomorrow. The agents of change, moreover, were individual speakers and writers, not collective social movements. The spokespersons of the discontented knocked, and the door was opened.

Some "controversial" aspects of U.S. history remain completely unacknowledged—most notably, the history of labor. While the show embraces individuals associated in the public mind with the struggle for civil rights and civil liberties, i.e., the individual rights of particular groups, it finds itself unable to deal with a movement long founded on principles of collective rights and collective action—namely unions. This reluctance, perhaps, is also rooted in the ongoing challenge labor represents to the capitalist *system* as well as to the particular corporations bankrolling the exhibits.

The silences get louder the closer the show gets to the present. There are no 1960s ghetto uprisings, no campus protests, no feminist or ecology movements, no Watergate. Most notoriously, there is nothing about Vietnam. One of the designers explained that "I searched for a long time for a photograph of an antiwar demonstration that would be optimistic, but I never found one." (A picture of a helicopter was recently added—a distinctly minimalist response to complaints.)

Though willing to accept that the past was made by the discontented, the show disconnects the present from that tradition. It abandons the narrative line on reaching the postwar period—King is there, but as an icon, not as spokesman for a movement—and it implies our problems are things of the past. At show's end, Mark

MIKE WALLACE

and Ben counsel worry only about the perils of plenty, the problem of how to use leisure time, and how each individual can fulfill his or her dreams. But because the show refuses to acknowledge the social constraints on individual actors—sexism and racism, poverty and unemployment remain obstinate components of contemporary U.S. culture—it peters out into complacent boosterism. Forced to confront a changed American popular historical consciousness and to incorporate the work of radical scholars, it opts for damage control. It defuses the danger inherent in the intrusion of "real" history by redeploying it within a vision of an imperfect but still inevitable progress.

Does Corporate Walt's history have an impact? How does it affect the millions of people who visit? There is little direct evidence one way or the other. Only a few hundred have written letters, the largest single response coming from Vietnam veterans complaining about the obliteration of their experiences. But what do such cavils mean when set beside the fact that Disney World is now the biggest single tourist destination in the entire world? A tenth of the entire U.S. population travels there in a year: what accounts for this stupendous success?

Demographic statistics provide an avenue to an answer. The class spectrum of EPCOT visitors is dramatically narrow. They come from groups doing best in terms of pay and personal power on the job: the median income is $35,700, and fully three-quarters are professionals or managers. Professional and technical personnel account for 48 percent of attendees, managers and administrators for 26 percent.) This is not a working-class attraction. (Craftsmen, 4 percent; operatives, 4 percent; sales, 8 percent; service, 2 percent; laborers, 2 percent.) Nor do Blacks (3 percent) or Hispanics (2 percent) come in large numbers. (To a degree these demographics simply reflect the cost of getting there: only 22 percent of visitors come from Florida; 71 percent are from elsewhere in the U.S., chiefly the Northeast and the Midwest.)

A process of class self-affirmation seems to be at work. Certainly Disney World seems intent on providing reassurance to this class, on presenting it with its own pedigree. EPCOT's seventies style liberal corporatism seems tailor-made for professionals and technocrats. It's calibrated to their concerns—nothing on labor, heavy on ecology, clean, well-managed, emphasis on individual solutions, good restaurants—and it provides just the right kind of past for their hipper sensibilities. Perhaps, therefore, professionals and managers (many of whom, after all, function as subalterns of capital flock there because it ratifies their world. Perhaps they don't *want* to know about reality—past or present—and prefer comforting (and plausible) stereotypes.

Yet many in this class are at least potentially antagonistic to the multinationals. Their members have spearheaded the ecology movement. It was their growing sophistication that made it impossible for Disney to recycle 1950s approaches, either in films or theme parks (approaches now dismissed by a younger generation as "Mickey Mouse"). We must be suspicious of blaming messages on the receiving public, even such an affluent one as this.

Would accurate history bore or repel them? Perhaps not. Audiences often respond favorably where conventional wisdom says they won't. (A dramatic and relevant comparison might be with the spectacularly successful *Roots*—which for all its Hollywood devices and elisions was a striking departure from *Gone with the Wind*.) Do Disney's sitcoms in space work because people want reassurance, or because that's all they're being given? Are visitors getting what they want, or what corporate publicists want them to want?

There is no simple answer to these questions. Some of EPCOT's consumers may be inclined to adopt the comfortable and convenient ideologies purveyed there. Others have no vested interest in or are profoundly disserved by doing so. Regardless of predisposition, however, EPCOT's casual subordination of truth to "entertainment" impairs visitors' ability to distinguish between reality and plausible fiction. The consequences for the country are serious. George Kennan recently noted that "when an individual is unable to face his own past and feels compelled to build his view of himself on a total denial of it and on the creation of the myths to put in its place, this is normally regarded as a sign of extreme neurosis." A similar diagnosis, he argued, was warranted for a society "that is incapable of seeing itself realistically and can live only by the systematic distortion or repression of its memories about itself and its early behavior." Kennan was referring to the Soviet Union. But the United States suffers from a similar malady. If we wish to restore our social health, we had better get beyond Mickey Mouse history.

MIKE WALLACE

Postscript: Mickey Mouse Amid the Big Bad Wolves

Disney World's imagineers spin wondrous fantasies about the nature of capitalism for their twenty million visitors. But there is another Disney World story, reserved for readers of the *Wall Street Journal.* Peeking behind EPCOT's sugar plum facade reveals how the *real* capitalist world works.

In 1940, Walt found himself in a financial bind. Riding the wave of his first big success, *Snow White,* Disney had set aside his inherited distrust of bankers—his films, like Capra's, consistently portrayed them as villains—and plunged into debt to construct an expensive new studio. This and a full load of feature films ate up his capital just as war closed the crucial foreign market to him. When his debt to bankers reached $4.5 million, they shut off his credit line entirely. He was thus forced, for the first time, to make a public stock offering and dilute his control of the company. Worse yet, the stock soon started tumbling in value.

Some of the stock he had distributed to employees. Its slide worsened already bad labor relations. In 1941, a bitter strike broke out at the Disney studio, a conflict which Disney chose to regard as part of a communist plot to subvert the country. Disney stock prices fell further—from $25 to $3 a share—and only government wartime contracts for training and propaganda films kept him going. When the company slowly climbed out of the red after the war, Disney bought back outstanding stock to regain complete control.

His next encounter with finance capital came when he reluctantly sought bank backing for Disneyland. Cautious bankers turned him down: "they stepped on my neck" was the way he put it. His project was rescued by the big corporations to whom he sold concessions, and by ABC-Paramount, which bought a third of the shares of Disneyland, Inc., chartered in 1951. This time, however, Disney insisted on getting an option to repurchase the shares, and did so by 1961. He had, he thought, finally achieved financial stability and independence of the financial community.

Luckily for him, Walt died without having to witness the recent mauling and near dismemberment of his corporation by the sharks of Wall Street.

In March 1984, Saul P. Steinberg, a New York financier, began purchasing Disney stock. Rumors of a takeover bid swept Wall Street. Disney management, led by Walt's son-in-law, Ronald W. Miller, prepared for a fight. He was backed by Disney's widow, Lillian; her daughter, Sharon Disney Lund; Disney's investment banker, Morgan Stanley & Company; and a crack anti-takeover law firm. The defense team arranged to triple Disney Inc.'s $400 million line of credit with a Bank of America-led consortium.

Disney management knew it would be helpless against Steinberg in the financial jungle without a powerful outside protector. It turned out to be Bass brothers, billionaire Texas investors (and raiders in their own right). In May, Disney managers purchased a Bass real estate development firm. By paying for it with Disney stock they transferred a big share to "friendly" hands. On June 6, Disney announced plans for another acquisition—Gibson, a greeting card company—that would bring William E. Simon, the powerful former Treasury secretary (and a major Gibson stockholder) onto the defense team.

At this point Steinberg declared open war. He formally announced an attempt to buy 49 percent of Walt Disney Productions by paying stockholders between $70 and $73 a share at a time when the market value was fluctuating between $62 and $68. This would cost him about $900 million. To make the threat credible, he put together a group of raiders who lusted after parts of the Disney company. Kirk Kerkorian, the majority stockholder of MGM-United Artists, would be given Disney's rich film library to sell in the home video market. The Fisher brothers, major New York developers, would get the extensive Florida landholdings worth hundreds of millions. Steinberg also announced he would launch a proxy fight to make all stockholders who bought stock in the company after May 25 (i.e., the Bass brothers) ineligible to vote, and then unseat the Disney management.

At this point, management panicked and decided to buy Steinberg off—which may have been what he was hoping for in the first place. They agreed to pay him $70.35 a share, substantially above market value, plus $28 million for "expenses," if he would give back his block of stock and promise not to buy any more for ten years. Steinberg cleared $60 million on the deal.

Disney was not alone that year in being stung by what is called "greenmail." In the first six months of 1984, companies shelled out over $2 billion to buy off unwanted outside investors. Commenting on the incident, one institutional investor said, "I think Steinberg did exactly what you would expect someone to do, given the existing laws and free-market society we live in."

The fight to stay independent left Disney bloodied. The company's debt soared from $350 million to $850 million. Disney's stock value fell by more than 25 percent. In mid-June, with the price down to $45 a share, a new group of raiders began buying stock, this one led by Irwin L. Jacobs, a Minneapolis investor.

The Jacobs group and the Bass brothers then combined to force Disney management to renege on the agreed-upon—but as yet un-consummated—purchase of Gibson, thus freezing out William Simon, who would have shown a profit of $70 million had the deal gone through. One Paine Webber analyst, noting that management had again caved in to blackmail, suggested that "this company is going to continue to be very, very vulnerable to threats from the outside." This proved an accurate forecast: on September 7, Ronald W. Miller was forced to resign as president and chief executive.

The stage was now set for a gunfight at the Disney corral. The Bass brothers increased their share of the company to 8.6 percent, overtaking the Jacobs group's 7.7 percent. Jacobs threatened to buy enough stock to take over and break up the company. The Bass brothers countered by buying $148.2 million more stock (at $60 a share), bringing their holdings to nearly 16 percent. Jacobs, having decided there was "not a place for both of us," offered to buy out the Basses at $65 a share. They refused, and countered with an offer to buy out Jacobs at $61. He capitulated, sold at a tidy profit and left the Basses in command.

All this wheeling and dealing took its toll. For the operating quarter ending September 30, 1984, the company posted a loss of $64 million. It sought to deal with this in time-honored corporate fashion, by putting the screws to its workforce. In September, management told workers that wages had to be controlled to keep profits at an acceptable level. They announced pay cuts of 16.1 percent over the next three years and cutbacks in health benefits.

On September 25, Disneyland employees struck. Nineteen hundred picketing workers, wearing "no-Mickey" T-shirts, asked for a 2 to 5 percent increase in wages and maintenance of health benefits. The company kept the park open using clerical and managerial personnel; went to court for a restraining order against picketing; sued the unions for a quarter-million dollars; and began hiring scab replacements, who, the strikers were warned, would be taken on permanently if workers did not return. The unions responded with a boycott threat, and the Employees Association served notice it would bring class action suits against potential greenmailers or any who would dismember the organization.

Despite these militant initiatives, the workers were in a weak position, and knew it. In October, they ended their strike, accepting a two-year wage freeze and some cuts in benefits. In November Walt Disney World laid off one hundred employees.

EPCOT has no immediate plans to include a "Disney Does 'Dallas'" exhibit sponsored by the AFL-CIO.

Note

I would like to thank, for their advice, counsel, and encouragement: Jean-Christophe Agnew, Jeanie Attie, Paul Berman, Ted Burrows, Jeanne Chase, Hope Cooke, Peter Dimock, Liz Fee, Brooks MacNamara, Bob Padgug, Roy Rosenzweig, Danny Walkowitz, Jon Wiener, the summer 1984 members of the Cummington Community of the Arts, and the staff at Walt Disney World.

MIKE WALLACE

THE SYMBOLIC WEALTH OF THE WEAK: RITUALS OF RESISTANCE

GENDER AND THE STRUCTURING OF REALITY

IN TEMNE DIVINATION:

AN INTERACTIVE STUDY

Rosalind Shaw

---

*In this article on divination among the **Temne**, a Muslim people living in the Northern District of Sierra Leone in West Africa, Shaw examines ways through which social subordinates, in this case Temne Women, can restructure dominant conceptions of reality adverse to their interests. The article deals with the interrelation between conceptual structures and social strategy.*

Among the Temne, as Shaw points out, "...divination provides a vehicle for the active negotiation of meanings and categorizations which are themselves constitutive of different interests within society," in particular those of each gender. Temne males dominate their society both socially and conceptually; they think of themselves as highly civilized, though living in a world threatened by the many forms of supernatural danger inherent in women. While women do not individually think of themselves in these terms, their self-concept is not given public recognition; their world structure remains muted by comparison.

Although women cannot break their relations of dependence through divination, they can—by their choice of diviners and by maintaining the secrecy of private diagnosis—have access to more positive conceptual structures than the official ones. It would be wrong to construe such a strategy as a deliberate, conscious manipulation of symbols. The process of negotiation at work takes place at a level of "practical consciousness", of "how to behave" in everyday life; it is a level of consciousness at which actors are neither completely conscious nor entirely unconscious of the symbols they use to make sense of reality. As Shaw puts it, "Most people...are neither entirely passive victims nor entirely cynical manipulators of symbols."

Through divination, Temne women are able to objectify, if only privately, their own subjective experience and to achieve a more positive understanding of this experience. Shaw is right in pointing out that "What is at issue here is not merely the politics of definition but the politics of experienced reality."

An-Yina Musa's Diagnosis

IN JUNE 1978, FOLLOWING A SERIES OF ARGUMENTS in her marital home, a young Temne woman called Isatu travelled from her home in Makeni (a town which is the capital of Sierra Leone's Northern Province) to the village of Petbana Masimbo three miles away in order to consult a diviner about the cause. The diviner she consulted was Pa Koroma, a well-patronized Muslim diviner who was also her father's brother. Pa Koroma happened to be conducting a session of the dramatic and relatively expensive *aŋ-yina Musa* mediumship method of divination, which is commissioned by a wealthy client but which more minor clients such as Isatu can also participate in. He put a female medium, completely covered by a protective white cloth and gazing into a white bowl of water containing Islamic medicine (*mə-nɑsi*), into a trance in which she was able to communicate with *aŋ-yina Musa*, the fearful "Muslim" spirit of divination. Around Pa Koroma's central parlour, in which the divination took place, were seated members of the village, some of whom had come to ask questions, others simply to watch and, where appropriate, to interject comments on what was being said. The medium, an elderly woman called Mami Yeno, was a sister-in-law of Pa Koroma from Makaper, a village about two miles from Petbana. Each person who had come to ask about a problem addressed their question to Pa Koroma, who repeated it to Mami Yeno. Mami Yeno then silently conveyed the question to *aŋ-yina Musa* and, after a pause, returned the reply to Pa Koroma, the latter repeating and often elaborating upon her utterances to the audience.

When Isatu asked about her problems with her husband, Mami Yeno gave the following reply:

ROSALIND SHAW

If the man were present, and if he were asked, "Do you have dreams in which you have sex with a woman" he would say, "Yes." His elder brother does not like the woman, and has an *u-kərfi*(a personal spirit, which in this instance is female). During the day he pretends to be good, but at night he makes his *u-kərfi* go to bed with the husband and, in the form of a man, with the woman as well. The woman should take care that she does not have birth problems.[1] It will be hard to drive the *u-kərfi* away. In her husband's home the woman has done nothing wrong.

During overt discourse, whenever men are present, Temne almost always attribute marital problems, and usually birth problems as well, to the socially disruptive behavior of women, and it is likely that had Isatu consulted another diviner the diagnosis would have reflected this normative view. What makes the above *aŋ-yina Musa* diagnosis significant is the fact that it not only reverses this stereotyped formulation but can be seen as stemming from Isatu's relationship with this specific diviner, namely from the fact that she is Pa Koroma's brother's daughter.

The contention of this article is that this kind of selection, far from being abnormal, typifies the kinds of strategy that social subordinates in general and women in particular engage in in order to restructure disadvantageous but dominant conceptions of reality in their society. Along with other kinds of ritual and social practices, divination provides a vehicle for the active negotiation of meanings and categorizations which are themselves constitutive of different interests within society. This article, then, concerns the interrelation between conceptual structures and social strategy.

Temne Diviners and Divination: A Description

In Temne cosmology, diviners (*a-thupəs*) are a category of specialists who, together with hunters, blacksmiths, twins and secret societies officials, have "four eyes" (*aŋ ba ɛ-fər*; lit. "they have eyes"). Such people are believed to have two additional invisible eyes giving them a piercing supernatural vision of three other worlds which are normally invisible: *ro-səki*(the world of spirits), *ro-kərfi*(the world of the dead) and *ro-serəŋ*(the world of witches; see Littlejohn, 1960b, 1963. Since all witches are said to have four eyes, diviners and the other above-mentioned categories of people are regarded with ambivalence, since it is felt that they could, unbeknown to anyone else, be abusing their power by practising witchcraft.

All diviners have either a patron spirit (usually a river spirit) or, if the gift of divination has been inherited, a patron ancestor. Either of these will act as the diviner's intermediary with the inhabitants of *ro-səki* and *ro-kərfi* during divination. Individuals can become diviners through inheritance, through apprenticeship to an unrelated diviner or through a spontaneous "call," and in all three cases the crucial element in their initiation as diviners is their encounter with their patron spirit or ancestor, with whom they make a bargain to offer sacrifices periodically in return for revelations of hidden knowledge.

Both men and women can become diviners, but the great majority are men. There is greater variation in reputation and status among male diviners, since, unlike female diviners, they can carry out public as well as private divination. Only very highly regarded male diviners are hired to divine publicly, usually for a large fee ranging from twenty leones (approximately £10 in 1978) to several hundred, for problems regarded as endangering the community as a whole: theft, witchcraft, adultery and murder. These renowned diviners are called for such cases to chiefdoms outside their own, for it is said that a diviner from another chiefdom is more likely to give an impartial verdict and to be less vulnerable to attack by any medicines the guilty party may use.

Public techniques consist of various ordeals such as *ma-kobee*, in which the accused puts his or her hand first into liquid medicine, then into boiling palm oil which burns only the guilty, and what Dorjahn (1962) has called "moving vehicle" techniques, in which an object (such as a pestle, *kə-roŋp*, or a broom, *a-gbələ*) is treated with medicine and subsequently forces a bearer carrying it to beat the culprit. Added to such techniques are public witchfinding rituals and spontaneous accusations and prophecies by *ma-nɛkɛ*, the masked spirits of the men's *ra-Gbeŋle* society, which in eastern Temneland is responsible for carrying out chieftaincy rituals. All forms of public divination are described as *ka-gbay ma-thaŋ*, "to split a divination", which means the specific accusation of individuals and the public exposure of their guilt. In Temne customary law they are legally binding proofs of guilt or innocence.

Public divination is relatively rare by comparison with private divination. In nearly every village there is at least one minor diviner carrying out private divination, using either a traditional technique such as *aŋ-berɛ*, the casting and interpretation of river pebbles (see Shaw 1978), or a "Muslim" technique such as *aŋ-thasabiya*, which is based on the interpretation of numbers obtained by selecting four beads from a Muslim rosary. The initial payment or "shakehand" (*aŋ-bəra*) is very low—either forty or eighty cents—but clients who feel a diviner has helped them will give more afterwards at their own discretion. Whereas public divination is conducted in the open or on the front verandah (*aŋ-gbəŋthən*) of a house, private divination usually takes place in a small side room (*a-koŋko*), hidden from the scrutiny of others and ritually "closed" (*kaŋtha*) against witches and harmful spirits. This is said to be appropriate because private divination concerns the resolution of issues defined as being of individual rather than of community concern, although it in fact concerns the problems of those who do not have the wealth or social standing to call a public divination or a session of *aŋ-yina Musa* mediumship.

Structurally, the *aŋ-yina Musa* method falls in between public and private divination both in its location in the semi-private parlour (*aŋ-pala*), in which members of the town are gathered, and in terms of the problems brought to it, which are usually those of influential figures in the community such as household heads, sub-chiefs (*ɛ-kapər*) and occasionally paramount chiefs (*a-bay*). The fee, though not as high as that paid for public divination, is much higher than that for private divination, adding up to a total of seven or eight leones for the divination itself, plus whatever amount a grateful client may give afterwards, which can be tens or sometimes hundreds of leones.

In private divination the majority of clients are women, who typically bring such problems as their children's or their own sickness and female reproductive disorders, including barrenness, miscarriages, menstrual irregularities and any persistent pain or swelling in the abdomen. When men consult private diviners it is usually over their own sickness rather than that of their children, but they will go to a diviner if a child of theirs is seriously ill or if the mother has already taken it to several diviners and a cure has not been

GENDER AND THE STRUCTURING OF REALITY IN TEMNE DIVINATION

found. In towns, especially, other problems men bring to diviners concern unemployment, promotion and difficulties at work. Although men consult diviners about impotence, men's reproductive problems are not taken to diviners as much as those of women. Other less frequent reasons prompting the consultation of private diviners by both women and men include insanity, bad dreams, paralysis, accidents and wanting to make a journey, to get married or to win a court case.

The fact that the semi-private *aŋ-yina Musa* method is generally commissioned by male authority-holders is largely due to their greater ability to afford the higher fees involved, but is also in accordance with the Temne ideology whereby a chief embodies his community and a household head embodies his household. The problems of such figures are therefore perceived as being of wider concern and as most appropriately dealt with in the presence of other members of the town. After the main issue has been answered, these others present, both male and female, are permitted to ask about their own individual problems, as in Isatu's case above. If witchcraft or adultery is diagnosed as the cause of a client's problem in either private or *aŋ-yina Musa* divination, and if the client is a household head or chief, he is able then to call a public divination session in which specific individuals are accused and convicted. Public divinations are frequently called without any of these preliminary divinatory consultations, however, especially after a serious incident such as premature death, theft or murder, all of which are of immediate social concern.

It can be seen that the private/public and corresponding individual/social distinctions in divination are linked to that between female and male. Women comprise the majority of clients in private divinations and, although divination is generally a male preserve, some private diviners are female. In the intermediate form of *aŋ-yina Musa* divination the controlling diviner is male and the medium is usually female, while the major client is usually male and the minor clients are both male and female, in approximately equal numbers. In public divination both clients and diviners are male. This association between private/public, individual/social and female/male in divination has implications for relations between men and women and for the negotiation of definitions and identity between male and female, given the connotations of secrecy and

ROSALIND SHAW

publicity in Temne society.

The Public and the Secret in Temne Society

The distinction between public and private divination forms part of a set of contrasts between openness to and secrecy from social scrutiny whose meanings are variable and multivalent. In Temne epistemology, what is hidden from the community is highly valued, since the most powerful and effective knowledge is secret (for instance, that controlled by the secret societies, by chiefs and by ritual and occupational specialists such as diviners, blacksmiths and hunters), yet in Temne ethical belief secrecy is more often evaluated negatively as a potential danger to the community, largely because of the opportunities for witchcraft that the possession of such secret knowledge is felt to open up. Even those who have legitimized access to secret powers are suspected of using them illicitly for their own individual ends at the expense of other members of the community, secret society officials and diviners being frequently cited cases in point. The secret/open contrast thus encapsulates the tension between the conflicting claims of epistemology and ethics in Temne thought.

The hidden nature of private divination therefore renders both private diviners and their mainly female clients somewhat suspect, but public divination (and to a lesser extent, *aŋ-yina Musa* divination) is in general positively evaluated, because in it a compromise is reached between ethical and epistemological values. The secret power and knowledge of the diviner or masked spirits (and therefore their possible witchcraft) are balanced by their public exposure of the illicit secrets of witches, adulterers, thieves and murderers for the community's benefit. Both private and pubic divination is based upon the power of secret knowledge, but in public divination this power becomes socially acceptable by being publicly displayed and used ostensibly on behalf of the community. The use of private divination predominantly by women and the monopoly of public divination by men thus associates women with the pursuit of individual (and possibly nefarious) purposes and men with the upholding of community interests.

The secret/open opposition also provides structural support for the hierarchical organization of Temne society, in which men rank above women, secret society initiates rank above non-initiates, chiefs (α-bαy and ε-k$\alpha p\partial$) rank above commoners and the old rank above the young. Since in Temne belief power depends upon knowing more than others and on not being completely known oneself, relationships between superordinates and subordinates are felt to necessitate the former having greater knowledge than the latter.

At the same time, secrecy and privacy are given a definitional role in demarcating the distinction between male and female as complementary social categories. Both men and women have their own medicines and ritual activities, notably those of the male and female secret societies, which are legitimately secret from the other sex. Relations between men and women are characterized by the maintenance of areas of segregation: women and men eat separately, tend to occupy distinct spacial zones at the back and front of the house respectively, and carry out different agricultural tasks. These areas of segregation and privacy are in general willingly maintained by both sexes, women displaying as little inclination to join in men's conversations as men do to participate in women's discussions and domestic activities in the back yard, for instance. This is not to suggest by any means that Temne men and women exist in mutually isolated self-containment, but that contact between them is structured by being punctuated by crucial areas of "darkness" (α-sum), as the Temne express it, which constantly reiterate in everyday social interaction the distinction between the sexes.

As Jackson has observed for the Kuranko, this parallel maintenance of male and female secrets and areas of segregation

> generates a relationship of complementarity between the sexes which, at the level of mystical or cult activity, leads to a "horizontal" equality of male and female domains that transcends the everyday hierarchical relationship between the superordinate male and the subordinate female. (1977: 83)

Among the Temne these alternative categorizations can come into conflict, since female secrecy and the "horizontal" complementarity of the sexes which it upholds may threaten male dominance, and with it the hierarchical structure of Temne society.

ROSALIND SHAW

Male and Female World-Structures

It is clear from the above that particular conceptual categorizations and symbolic meanings may either favor or undermine the interests of different groups within society—in this instance, men and women. The interrelation between power, conceptual structures and modes of expression has been demonstrated most forcibly in Ardener's writings on male and female "world-structures" (1972, 1975), the latter being contrasting conceptual paradigms by means of which people define themselves, others and reality as a whole (see especially 1975: 22-5). Ardener characterizes the world-structures of subordinate groups as "muted" in their expression, rendered less perceptible by dominant world-structures of superordinate groups. A recurring feature of male-dominated societies, accordingly, is the prominence of the categorization of "female" with "the wild" and "the marginal", which supports a range of meanings for the role of male as symbolic of social order.

Overtly, in Temne institutions, male dominance both socially and conceptually is counterbalanced by a certain (but relatively small) measure of female influence. The keystones of Temne social organization are the paramount chiefs (*a-bay*), the sub-chiefs (*ε-kapər*) and the secret societies (see Dorjahn 1960). While among the Mende and Sherbro women can gain considerable political power as paramount chiefs (Hoffer 1972), this is not the case in Temneland, where paramount chiefs are sacred figures and must always be male, although many of the more minor sub-chiefs are female. In the village, residence and the allocation of land and labor are governed by the patrilineage (*ma-kas*). Marriage, traditionally an alliance between exogamous patrilineages, is polygynous and virilocal, involving considerable movement of women. Through payment of bridewealth a husband acquires rights over a wife's productive and reproductive capacities, thereby securing the farm labor he needs to gain personal wealth and the children necessary to ensure the continuity of his patrilineage.

Yet jural rights over women do not, of course, guarantee male control, for women are able to exert considerable control over their own economic and reproductive powers. Since men depend upon women's farm labor and reproductive capacities, the relationship between the sexes is in practice that of "horizontal" interdependence, although institutionally and jurally the "vertical", hierarchical ideology predominates. Recently some writers have stressed this ambiguity inherent in male authority:

> Even within patrilineally organized societies men ritually express anxiety about their dependence on women as regenerators of life...., and there is ample evidence that folk concepts of descent and continuity acknowledge the vital attributes of women. (MacCormack 1980a: 14)

Among the Temne, the threat to male interests represented by women's control over their reproductive potential finds expression in men's fears about several types of hidden supernatural danger inherent in women. Additionally, whereas according to Temne customary law women should not own personal property (Harrell-Bond and Rijnsdorp 1974: 37-8), they are in fact able to acquire considerable economic independence by trading and growing cash crops. This is a frequent cause of marital tension, since husbands feel that they should be given their wives' earnings, which results in women tending to keep their personal income secret from both their husbands and their co-wives.

In the Temne male world-structure, men's self-definition as supremely civilized beings contrasts with the characterization of women as representing an innocent but potentially sinister threat to order. This view is expressed in beliefs about women's weakness in the face of temptation (notably to adultery and witchcraft) and about their excessive secrecy, both of which are felt to make women potentially mystically dangerous in various ways to men, children and crops. Some of these fears are articulated in the following statement of Pa Kɑpər Bana, the sub-chief of Petbana Masimbo village:

> A man sees a woman and marries her. He does not know the behavior of the woman, whether it is good or bad. Men should have patience, because women are not people to trust... All problems in the world are caused by women. Women bear children. But there are women who go in different directions and cause problems. A woman can live with her husband and commit adultery, then she brings misfortune, and if I do farming the rice will not grow properly if she does not confess.

ROSALIND SHAW

A wife's secret adultery threatens male control, and in the male view endangers not only her husband's crops and fortune but also the welfare of her children, whether born or unborn. If she commits adultery the blessings and protection of her existing children's ancestors will be withdrawn, thereby rendering her children vulnerable to attack by witches and harmful spirits, and if she subsequently becomes pregnant she will be unable to give birth successfully until she confesses. The welfare of a woman's children is therefore, in this view, dependent upon her marital behavior (cf. Jackson 1977: 87). But, because of the connotations of secrecy in Temne society, it is only *unconfessed* adultery which is felt to be dangerous. As in all Temne relationships between subordinate and superordinate, a husband expects to know more about his wife than she knows about him. If a wife keeps secrets which her husband feels she should disclose to him, she erodes his knowledge of her, which is equivalent to his power over her, but by confessing and "calling the name" (*kə-boŋt*) of her lover, she brings what was hidden into the open and restores her husband's power. The lover is then brought to court and has to pay the fine of *way kə-bal* ("to pay for adultery") to the husband.

It is implicit, of course, that "adultery" here is that of the married woman, as in agnatic polygynous societies generally. There is no term for the adultery of a married man: *kə-bal*, "adultery", is cognate with *bala*, the verb "to marry" when referring to the marriage of a woman, rather than *nanta*, the same verb when referring to the marriage of a man. Whereas the husband of an unfaithful wife has recourse to legitimized and public retribution in the form of diviners' public ordeals, "swearing " ceremonies and the fine of *way kə-bal*, the wife of an unfaithful husband has recourse mainly to unlegitimized and secret forms of retribution. These latter are added to women's adultery as further examples of the hidden dangers to which women are believed to expose men.

A woman may, for instance, have a personal *u-kərfi*, usually a river spirit which inhabits a river pebble she keeps, to which she sacrifices in order to obtain children. Men express the fear that such a woman can "hand over" her husband to this spirit, who will then make him ill or impotent. She may also hire a private diviner to use harmful medicine against her husband. As another alternative she can use a curse such as that known as *aŋ-fisrəwəli*, "ingratitude", which she activates by urinating into a bottle while cursing the man concerned, then stopping up the bottle and throwing it away, thereby causing this man to be "stopped up" as well, to have difficulty urinating. Another perceived danger of women is witchcraft, ra-ser. The weakness and secretiveness of women in the male perception are both characteristics which are believed to make the individual more prone to witchcraft. Although the most powerful and "wonderful" witches (a-poɲinɛ and a-thekre) are said to be men, the great majority of witches are said to be women, the most common causes given for witchcraft being tensions between husband and wife and between co-wives, particularly when a wife is barren.

Women's self-categorizations are, as one might expect, rather different. The fullest expression of Temne female world-structure for which adequate documentation is available is found in the rituals of the women's aŋ-Bondo society, which, through the symbolism of domestic objects, the East and the river, reveal a conception of femaleness as associated with the social, domestic world and with birth (Lamp 1981a, b). This contrasts markedly with the male categorization of women as incipiently asocial.[2]

When asked what they think of the male view of women as excessively secretive, women often explain that their secrecy is necessary because of their relatively vulnerable position in their husband's household, especially with regard to co-wives, as two senior wives in Petvana Masimbo expressed:

> It is not all secrets that you tell your husband. If you tell all your secrets, then he might get another wife. If the three of you now live together and there is rivalry between you and your co-wife, then your husband will pay more attention to the other wife whose secrets he does not know.

> It is a good thing to keep secrets from your husband because of jealousy. If your husband has plenty of wives, you keep your own secrets, such as money. If you are earning money, you do not let your husband know, since he has other wives.

Thus while men see women's secrecy as threatening to marriage (and to the hierarchical structure of male/female relations in general), women see their secrecy as essential to their security and autonomy in marriage. According to Ya Rukoh, an elderly woman in Magburaka, the position of women in marriage rather than any "weakness" of women is the real cause of adultery:

> Some women are faithful, some are unfaithful. If your husband has more than one wife, your heart is bad and you are unfaithful.

A wife's status in her husband's household is primarily dependent upon her ability to bear children to continue his patrilineage. She is therefore dependent upon her children for her status. At the same time, the belief that the blessings of her children's paternal ancestors are conditional upon her marital behavior means that her children depend on her for their health and prosperity. This mutual interdependence of mother and child is expressed in the Temne saying "The child is the mother; the mother is the child" (ɔw-an, kɔnɛe ɔ-kara; ɔ-kara, kɔnɔe ɔw-an). Given this interdependence, it is not surprising that reproductive problems and sick children are of overwhelming concern to women and are the most common problems that women bring to diviners.

There are, of course, also problems for men, who need children to continue the patrilineage, but such problems do not threaten the identity and status of men quite as directly and profoundly as they threaten those of women, for whom "the mother is the child." The mother of a sick child may be suspected of adultery. A barren woman is unable to fulfill her expected role as provider of children in her husband's family, and is the primary suspect if her co-wives' children fall ill and die. She may then be suspected of having contributed her womb to a communal witch-feast, and to be continuing to contribute her co-wives' children as victims. When a woman with a sick child or with reproductive problems consults a diviner, therefore, she is not only seeking a cure but also seeking to avoid negative "male" interpretations of her misfortune. What is at issue here is the negotiation not only of decisions but also of world-structures and personal identity.

Divination, Interaction and the Restructuring of Reality

Divination involves the selection of particular cognitive constructions of reality and their application to everyday, practical events. It also involves the interaction of individuals who (both consciously and unconsciously) use strategies in pursuit of their interests. These interests, however, need to be viewed not simply in narrow terms of political or economic advantage but also in terms of ontology, of the definition of the self and others. Through their monopoly of public divination, for example, Temne men in positions of authority are able to projet their own interpretations of reality as if they are objective fact, while undermining their subordinates' conflicting interpretations, and thereby reassert their own social and conceptual dominance in the household, town or chiefdom. This relationship between the conceptual and the strategic in divination, as well as the interactive basis of this relationship, is evident in the extract below from a public witch-finding session (*kə-gbak*) of the male *ra-Gbeŋle* society in the town of Magburaka.

A session of *kə-gbak* is initiated by a chief or household head, who, in describing the relevant problems and their background to the *ra-Gbeŋle* head, is most likely to do so in accordance with his own perceptions and interests. During *kə-gbak* itself the masked spirits of *ra-Gbeŋle*, *ma-nɛke*, publicly interrogate the suspected witches and sing songs in eerie nasal voices extolling their own powers. They are concealed behind a mat covering the open doorway of a house and are thus audible but not visible to the audience. One by one the suspects, who are seated on the verandah, are questioned, accused and cursed. Usually, as in the following extract, they eventually confess:

> *Ma-nɛkɛ.* You are a witch, not so?
> *Accused man.* It is not true.
> *Ma-nɛkɛ.* Your foreskin.
> *Accused.* It is not true.
> *Ma-nɛkɛ.* Let those who are present listen. I want to make a bet (*kə-bəkta*) of £20 with this man that he is a witch.
> *Accused.* I have not got that £20.

ROSALIND SHAW

Ma-nɛkɛ. Do you remember making a farm with your
family at...place? Did you get rice?
Accused. I did not get rice.
Ma-nɛkɛ. What was the cause of this? Was it not you
and your witch friends who spoiled that rice?
Accused. It is true.
Ma-nɛkɛ. Well, why do you deny being a witch?

Since uncircumcized Temne men and women are classified as
children and not as full human beings, naming the accused man's
foreskin was a curse, a performative utterance (Finnegan 1969)
which categorized him as asocial. The £20 which *ma-nɛkɛ* challenged
him to put down was a deposit prior to an ordeal, which would have
consisted of the man touching the mat between him and *ma-nɛkɛ*:
guilt is proven by involuntary defecation upon doing so.

In the same session a similar process was conducted with the
man's wife. She was asked how many children she had given birth
to but were now dead, and was accused of having killed them
through witchcraft. She denied it, and was then asked if she remembered a boil on her left jaw and whether this was not a hiding place
she had used to keep human meat. When she denied this as well,
ma-nɛkɛ cursed her by saying, "Your clitoris," at which she confessed.

By such means *ma-nɛkɛ* redefined the individuals accused and
publicly restructured the accepted history of the situation. They
used a variety of techniques to effect this conceptual shift. Their
own classification as spirits meant that by definition they were
regarded as having access to hidden knowledge unavailable to
human beings. They took previously unconnected past events which
they had been told of by the household head who called them—the
accused man's crop failure and the accused woman's dead children
and boil—and reinterpreted them as evidence of witchcraft. They
used considerable drama in their eerie singing, their concealment
from the audience and their financial challenge to the accused man.
They used accusations and curses as performative utterances which
set in motion a recategorization of individuals as witches which was
eventually confirmed by the confessions of those accused. Those
who confessed, thereby renouncing their own interpretations of the
situation, were beaten and treated with anti-witchcraft medicine by

the *ra-Gbeŋle* society. Through this public reconstruction of reality, *ma-nekɛ* turned the perceptions of the household head who had called them into "objective" truths. Such "objectification" of perceptions in public divination is an important means whereby the structural hierarchy of Temne society and the corresponding conceptual dominance of male over female and senior over junior is reproduced.

Whereas in public divination there is an implicit collusion between the (usually powerful) client and the diviner(s) he hires, no such collusion can be assumed in private divination, owing to possible conflicts of interest and world-view between diviners (predominantly male) and their clients (predominantly female). Male diviners' own conceptions of the causes of misfortune generally embody the negative categorizations of women in the male world-structure. When asked about frequent causes of misfortune, and when constructing hypothetical cases in the course of teaching me *aŋ-bɛrɛ* divination, male diviners gave examples in which the hidden dangers represented by women figured prominently: children who died as a result of their mother's adultery, men made impotent by the personal spirit of a wife or girlfriend, and women who invisibly ate children by means of witchcraft but who were themselves ultimately killed by the action of a "swear" (*a-sasa* or *a-senja*), for instance. The three female diviners I was able to find offered by contrast examples in which men and independent supernatural agencies such as spirits were to blame as much as women. Ya Mari, a female diviner in Matotoka (a town south-east of Makeni and Magburaka), responded in the following way when I asked her about cases of female reproductive problems:

> Women's problems are usually not their fault. Some have spirits in a stone, a cotton tree or an anthill (i.e. personal spirits). They come to talk to them, saying, "I'm getting married. If you make me bear a child I will sacrifice a sheep to you." Then they break their promise, which makes the spirit take revenge. Often it is a man at fault. Women get diseases from them, or are beaten by them.

Because there are so few female diviners, however, the choice of female clients wishing to avoid unfavorable categorizations of themselves in diviners' diagnoses is considerably reduced. The

ROSALIND SHAW

prominence of female mediums in *aŋ-yina Musa* divination may well give female clients an advantage, but it should be remembered that such mediums are "employed" by male diviners, who would presumably cease to use a medium who consistently gave diagnoses clashing with his own perceptions. An alternative female strategy is indicated in the case of Isatu with which this article began: the consulting of a diviner with whom one has a familial relationship. Among Pa Koroma's clients a surprisingly high proportion were female relatives (approximately one in five), and in none of the cases which I observed were any of the latter given a diagnosis in which they were blamed for their problems, unlike many of Pa Koroma's unrelated clients. A diviner who is a blood relation of a female client is likely to have affective links with her and to be able to sympathize with problems she has in her husband's household and with her concern over children. He is correspondingly more likely to reach diagnoses which confirm her own perceptions than ones which express male conceptual structures by giving her a negative, asocial categorization.

Supportive diagnoses of this kind, however, are most often kept secret by women clients because of the antagonism with which their husband's families would probably react. When, for instance, I asked Pa Koroma if Isatu was going to tell her husband about the diagnosis she was given, he laughed and said, "When she goes home she should not mention this to anyone. Her father-in-law would be very angry!" A public restructuring of individuals and events is not possible because of the relatively weak position of a woman in her marital home. Further conceptual disadvantages to which female clients are subject are, firstly, the fact that the diagnosis of a diviner to whom one is related is not rated very highly precisely because it is thought likely to be partial. Secondly, the relegation of women to private divination reinforces their classification in the male view as asocial in any case.

Whereas male conceptions of reality can be publicized, objectified and legitimized, thus reproducing the dominance of both men and their world-structure, female interpretations remain private, subjective and unlegitimatized, thereby reproducing the subordinate position of women and the "muted" nature of their world-structure. Yet although women are unable to restructure unfavorable relations of dependence through divination, they can nevertheless pursue

GENDER AND THE STRUCTURING OF REALITY IN TEMNE DIVINATION

strategies in their choice of diviners and in their secrecy over diagnoses, both of which enable their own conceptual structures and their self-definition to be confirmed.

Ontology and Agency: Some Conclusions

A functionalist analysis of the above material might focus upon the role of divination in legitimizing existing power structures and realignments within them. Park, for example, argues from this position that, through the use of divination in the selection of Yoruba house sites,

> the diviner in effect provides a legitimating sanction upon a process of structural realignment which, depending as it does upon a voluntary act, would be difficult indeed to sanction in any remarkably different manner. (1963: 197)

While the manipulation of public divination by Temne household heads and chiefs is amenable to this kind of interpretation, it is extremely difficult to view Temne women's consultations of private diviners from such a perspective. Private divination is regarded with too much moral ambiguity to be an effective instrument of social legitimation, particularly where female clients are concerned. At most, where the client is male, a private diagnosis can provide the basis for the further step of commissioning a session of public divination, but this happens in only a small percentage of cases. Replacing the rather mechanical concept of legitimation with that of negotiation, however, enables us to take into account other, more internal, kinds of benefit which people can obtain from divination apart from those of social recognition and approval.

A different kind of functionalist approach is represented by Turner's analysis of Ndembu divination as part of a "ritual mechanism of redress" which helps to strengthen moral values and heal social breaches:

> He (the diviner) acts as a mechanism of redress and social adjustment in the field of local descent groups, since he locates areas and points of tension in their contemporary structures. Furthermore, he exonerates or accuses individuals in these groups in terms of a system of moral

ROSALIND SHAW

norms. Since he operates in emotionally charged situations, such norms are restated in a striking and memorable fashion. Thus he may be said to play a vital role in upholding tribal morality. (1968: 51).

Again, this view does not accord with the realities of Temne divination. Although in public divination the particular concerns of senior men are presented as the moral concerns of the community as a whole, in fact both public and private divination serve individual interests as much as social or moral ones. In some instances the statements of Temne diviners can indeed lead to a restoration of social harmony, but they can just as easily precipitate increased social conflict: the verdict Isatu received in which her brother-in-law was blamed for her marital problems is most unlikely to have improved her relations with her husband's family, which is precisely why Pa Koroma stressed to me that she should keep the diagnosis secret. By keeping her knowledge to herself, of course, Isatu would be undermining the hierarchical structure of the husband-wife relationship: her secrecy about the matter would thus be viewed as unethical according to Temne male ideology. Temne divination cannot, then, be said to play a vital moral role.

A further problem with functionalist explanations in general, including that of Turner, is that they reduce the actors to passive ciphers whose actions unconsciously contribute to the maintenance of society's equilibrium. This fails to account for the active roles played by Ndembu diviners in Turner's own description:

> diviners have learned by experience...to reduce their social system to a few basic principles and factors, and to juggle with these until they arrive at a decision that accords with the views of the majority of their clients at any given consultation. (1968: 48)

This failure adequately to confront human agency is a shortcoming which functionalist interpretations share with those of structuralist and symbolic approaches. Notwithstanding the considerable light the latter have shed upon the conceptual bases of social life, particularly ritual, their tendency to assign symbols and structure an all-powerful role in determining human behavior has engendered considerable dissent. In the words of a recent critic:

GENDER AND THE STRUCTURING OF REALITY IN TEMNE DIVINATION

> Occasionally (in such studies)...it is people who do things
> with symbols; more often it is symbols that do things to
> people. Always a person's confrontation with symbols
> seems to imply the impossibility of choosing from among
> them. (Asad 1983: 241)

In contrast, an interactive approach necessarily implies the existence of choices, and it is specifically with the possibility of exercising choices that my own study is concerned. A possible reason
for the rarity of structural/symbolic analyses of divination (in contrast to their abundance in studies of other ritual forms) may well
be that the selection and negotiation of meanings through individual
interaction are so prominent in divination, and are hardly conducive
to the deterministic orientation of such analyses.

Of interest here is a recent study of Sisala divination by Mendosa (1982), in which an emphasis on divination as legitimation is
combined with symbolic interactionist ideas concerning the creation
of meaning through interaction:

> Vuguŋ (divination) provides participants with specific cul-
> turally prescribed choices, but they do more than merely
> accept these options. They redefine them and engage in
> accommodation and compromise with each other in rela-
> tion to such principles. The outcome of any divination is
> as much a result of political struggle between involved par-
> ties as it is the result of rule enforcement. Participants take
> more than principles and rules into account when engaged
> in a divinatory confrontation with others. They also have
> personal goals, or ends that favor their particular faction
> within the group. They employ strategies to obtain these
> ends, and these particularistic interests are often cleverly
> couched in acceptable cultural terms to disguise personal
> and factional concerns. (1982: 110)

This process of the construction of the "reality of the situation"
via strategy and interaction is, I have argued, central to divination.
It should not, however, be assumed that the participants in divination who negotiate interpretations which serve their interests do not
experience these interpretations as "reality". Mendosa's language
implies that social actors deliberately utilize convenient symbols

ROSALIND SHAW

while remaining detached and unaffected by these symbols in their own experience. While conscious manipulation certainly occurs, it cannot realistically be said to characterize most instances of social interaction. Such a perspective cannot explain, moreover, what Temne women gain from a diviner's diagnosis which cannot be used to their political advantage in their marital household because it must be kept secret.

The problems outlined in these approaches derive from the assumption that people must be either largely unconscious of what they are "really" doing (as in most functionalist, structuralist and symbolic analyses) or fully conscious of what they are doing (as in symbolic interactionism). Giddens, however, has made an important distinction between "discursive consciousness", involving knowledge which can be held in consciousness and articulated at the level of discourse, and "practical consciousness", involving tacit stocks of shared knowledge of "how to act" in everyday life (1979: 5, 24-5, 57-8). This latter form of knowledge is neither unconscious nor fully conscious (i.e. discursively available), our knowledge of speech rules being a convenient example:

> There is a vital sense in which all of us *do* chronically apply phonological and grammatical laws in speech—as well as all sorts of other practical principles of conduct—even though we could not formulate those laws discursively (let alone hold them in mind throughout discourse). (Giddens 1979: 25)

It is argued here that this intermediate state of "practical consciousness" in which most social interaction takes place makes it possible for people to experience symbols as realities while at the same time being able to use these symbols and to choose between them in the pursuit of strategies in, for example, divination. Most people, then, are neither entirely passive victims nor entirely cynical manipulators of symbols.

With this perspective we can now return to our earlier question of what female clients can gain from secret diagnoses. It has been argued above that the "interests" which an individual pursues when consulting a diviner may be ontological, an interpretation pioneered by Lienhardt (1961) in his analysis of Dinka ritual. Lienhardt characterizes the Dinka diviner's task as that of bringing about a "division in experience" in which the afflicted person is enabled to separate conceptually the external agent causing his suffering from his own sense of being (1961: 151-3). More recently Parkin (1979) and Jackson (1978) have developed similar approaches to divination. Firstly, Parkin focuses upon Giriama and Swahili divinatory language, in which changes from "jumbled" to "clear" speech and from metaphors of wilderness to those of settlement dramatize a transition within the client from a state of ontological confusion to one of order and clarity. Secondly, Jackson argues that central to Kuranko divination is the process of externalization, of detachment from one's subjectivity, through the application of collective interpretive constructs to the problem and the praxis of shared social action prescribed by the diviner's diagnosis. Both the individual and the social group are thereby enabled to control their experience of the situation:

> (1) The consultor surpasses the chaotic and inchoate state in which he finds himself and, through social action, is enabled to assume responsibility for and determine his own situation;
> (2) the consultor's situation is classified according to collective dogmas of causation and, as a consequence, the group (family, subclan or village) is enabled to act decisively and systematically to determine its situation. (1978: 130-1)

Lienhardt, Parkin and Jackson, then, all focus upon an internal transition from chaos to order in the client or the afflicted person on whose behalf the diviner is consulted: a "division in experience", an inner journey from "wilderness" to "settlement", or a detachment from subjectivity. The initial ontological chaos described in these analyses is not, of course, a universal characteristic of clients at the beginning of a divination session (and none of the above writers claim it to be so), particularly in situations in which elders have a monopoly on consulting diviners. Yet even here divination has ontological consequences, since a Temne household head, for instance, whose construction of reality is "objectified" through public divination is reinforced not only politically but also, we can probably assume, in his own experience of "rightness", his sense of being.

For a female Temne client consulting a private diviner, the ontological assurance gained from a diagnosis which reaffirms her own experience of reality is likely to be of central importance. Given the threat that interpretations of misfortune deriving from the male world-structure can pose to a woman's identity and status, a female client who consults a diviner about her child's or her own sickness is considerably more likely to be in a state of internal chaos than is a household head who calls a public divination session to identify witches in his household. A sympathetic private diagnosis, while not enabling such a woman's subjective experience of reality to be publicly objectified, at least gives her some external ontological validation. Furthermore, as Jackson points out, by performing the ritual action prescribed by divination (either along or supported by members of her natal family) she is enabled to complete a transition from ontological insecurity to the control of her experience via practical action. To return to the two aspects of externalization distinguished by Jackson—the individual and the social—it can be seen that the individual transition from a chaotic to an ordered state of being is far more central to private than to public divination among the Temne. By contrast, the social transition in the divinatory process, accomplished through the collective definition of the situation and collective ritual action taken upon it, characterizes public to a greater extent than private divination. Female and junior male clients do not have access to the collective objectifying process of public divination which senior men enjoy, so for them the detachment from subjectivity through divination which Jackson describes is not as complete, yet they can find more limited but nevertheless valuable ontological validation through the selection of the "right" private diviner.

Divination, then, is not a process which affects all members of a society in the same way. Nor does it, despite the above generalizations about male and female world-structures, affect all members of the same interest group in the same way in all contexts. Women, for example, may adopt a somewhat "male" conception of the mystical dangers of female adultery when their own natal patrilineage is threatened, applauding the calling in of a private diviner to give suspected wives an ordeal, but may then adopt a very different divination strategy if they themselves are under suspicion.

GENDER AND THE STRUCTURING OF REALITY IN TEMNE DIVINATION

It is therefore important to reify neither divination nor world-structures as entities. Male and female world-structures are contrasting categorizations of reality produced by men and women as active agents who constitute different interest groups within society, and who use divination as one process whereby such categorizations can be negotiated. Yet because most people interact within "practical consciousness" rather than "discursive consciousness" most of the time, their manipulation of categorizations should not obscure for us the fact that the latter can and do have powerful effects upon them: what is at issue here is not merely the politics of definitions but the politics of experienced reality. Divination, then, is one means that allows each "reality" to be a negotiated one.

Notes

My fieldwork on Temne divination was carried out during 1977-78 (fifteen months) in the village of Petbana Masimbo (Bombali Sebora Chiefdom) and the towns of Makeni, Magburaka, Matotoka, Freetown and Koidu, Sierra Leone. Financial support was provided by a grant from the Social Science Research Council of Great Britain and additional grants from the Royal Anthropological Institute's Emslie Horniman Anthropological Research Fund and the University of London's Central Research Fund. In the preparation of this article I am indebted primarily to Keith Ray for the insights he provided during our discussions and for his criticisms of previous drafts. I am also most grateful to Professors Ivan Karp, Simon Ottenberg and David Parkin, who read previous drafts and offered invaluable criticisms and suggestions. An earlier version of the article was presented at the third Sierra Leone Studies Symposium at the University of Birmingham in 1983 and is published in its proceedings, Sierra Leone Studies at Birmingham, 1983 (Centre of West African Studies, 1984).

1.   The Temne say that sexual intercourse with a spirit (while dreaming) can cause a woman

ROSALIND SHAW

x07ml

to be barren, to miscarry or to give birth to a monstrosity.

2. In an apparent reversal, men identify themselves with the West, with the bush and with terrifying spirits in the society (see Lamp 1981c). Through this association, however, men seek to control and limit these anti-social forces.

References

Ardener, E.
1972. "Belief and the problem of women", in J. La Fontaine (ed.), *The Interpretation of Ritual*, pp. 135-58. London: Tavistock Press.
1975. "The 'problem' revisited", in S. Ardener (ed.), *Perceiving Women*, pp. 19-28. London: Dent.

Asad, T.
1983. "Anthropological conceptions of religion: reflections on Geertz", *Man* (N.S.), 18, 237-59.

Bourdieu, P.
1977. *Outline of a Theory of Practice*. Cambridge: Cambridge University Press.

Dorjahn, V.R.
1959. "The organisation and functions of the *Ragbenle* Society of the Temne", *Africa*, 29, 156-70.
1960. "The changing political system of the Temne", *Africa*, 30, 110-40.
1962. "Some aspects of Temne divination", *Sierra Leone Bulletin of Religion*, 4, 1-9.

Finnegan, R.
1969 "How to do things with words: performative utterances among the Limba of Sierra Leone", *Man* (N.S.), 4, 537-52.

Giddens, A.
1979. *Central Problems in Social Theory: action, structure and contradiction in social analysis*. London: Macmillan.

Harrell-Bond, B.E., and Rijnsdorp, U.
1974. *Family Law in Sierra Leone: a research report*. Leiden: Afrika-Studiecentrum.

Hoffer, C.P.
1972. "Mende and Sherbo women in high office", *Canadian Journal of African Studies*, 6, 151-64.
1975. "Bundu: political implications of female solidarity in a secret society", in D. Raphael (ed.), *Being Female: reproduction, power and change*. The Hague: Mouton.

Jackson, M.
1977. *The Kuranko: dimensions of social reality in a West African society*. London: Hurst.
1978. "An approach to Kuranko divination", *Human Relations*, 31, 117-38.
1982. *Allegories of the Wilderness: ethics and ambiguity in Kuranko narratives*. Bloomington: Indiana University Press.

GENDER AND THE STRUCTURING OF REALITY IN TEMNE DIVINATION

Lamp, F.
    1981a. "Cosmogramatic forms of space among the Temne", unpublished paper given at the second Sierra Leone Studies Symposium, University of Birmingham.
    1981b. "Cosmetics, cosmos and the spirit of Bondo", unpublished paper given at the African Studies Association's Annual Meeting, University of Indiana.
    1981c. "The Poro House", unpublished paper given at the African Studies Association's Annual Meeting, University of Indiana.

Lienhardt, G.
    1961. *Divinity and Experience: the religion of the Dinka.* Oxford: Clarendon Press.

Littlejohn, J.
    1960a. "The Temne ansasa", *Sierra Leone Studies* (N.S.), 14, 32-5.
    1960b "The Temne house", *Sierra Leone Studies* (N.S.), 14, 63-79.
    1963. "Temne space", *Anthropological Quarterly*, 36, 1-17.

MacCormack, C.P.
    1980a. "Nature, culture and gender: a critique", in C.P. MacCormack and M. Strathern (eds.), *Nature, Culture and Gender,* pp. 1-24. Cambridge: Cambridge University Press.
    1980b. "Proto-social to adult: a Sherbro transformation", in MacCormack and Strathern, *op cit.,* pp. 95-118.

Mendosa, E.L.
    1982. *The Politics of Divination: a processual view of reactions to illness and deviance among the Sisala of northern Ghana.* Berkeley: University of California Press.

Middleton, J.
    1960. *Lugbara Religion: ritual and authority among an East African people.* London: Oxford University Press for the International African Institute.

Park, G.K.
    1963. "Divination and its social contexts", *JRAI*, 93, 195-209.

Parkin, D.
    1979. "Straightening the paths from wilderness: the case of divinatory speech", *Journal of the Anthropological Society of Oxford,* 10, 147-60.
    1982. "Introduction" to D. Parkin (ed.), *Semantic Anthropology.* New York: Academic Press.

Rosen, D.M.
    1981. "Dangerous women: 'ideology', 'knowledge' and ritual among the Kono of eastern Sierra Leone', *Dialectical Anthropology,* 6, 151-63.

Shaw, R.
    1978. "*Aŋ-bɛrɛ*: a traditional form of Temne divination", *Africana Research Bulletin,* 9, 3-24.

Turay, A.K.
    1971. "Loan Words in Temne: a study of the sources and processes of lexical borrowing in a Sierra Leonean language", Ph.D. thesis, University of London (SOAS).

Turner, V.W.
    1968. *The Drums of Affliction.* Oxford: Clarendon Press and the International African Institute.

Skid Row Indians and the Politics of Self

E. Alan Morinis

As Abner Cohen has advised, political anthropology's most important contribution to the study of politics lies in revealing the political significance of symbolic forms and social actions that are apparently non-political. The following essay by Alan Morinis is a case in point. Most studies of Indian politics in North America have focused on the agendas of middle class Native leaders who participate formally, and often organizationally, in the institutionalized political process. Morinis proposes that a parallel type of politics is being conducted by a number of lower class Indians who inhabit the "Skid Rows" of Canadian cities. Skid Row Indians lack the resources and the bureaucratic expertise to pursue the political strategies of their middle class counterparts, but they are no less involved in preserving some of their values, attempting to symbolize control of their lives, and resisting the domination of white society.

In what is seemingly a preposterous paradox, the politics of Skid Row derives in part from a lifestyle that strikes middle class observers—Indian and whites alike—as the paragon of degradation. Morinis describes the lifestyle as follows:

> To be part of the Skid Row community is: to sleep in bug-ridden, dirty, dilapidated flop houses, eat in greasy cafes, fight in back alleys and drink in seedy bars—when there is money. And when there is not, to sink lower still, to sleep in garbage bins, eat in the "soup and salvation" mission food lines, to be beaten and rolled for the last change, to drink Lysol and Sterno or bootlegged homebrew, or to find your way to the clinic or hospital for the drugs that will stop the shakes of alcohol withdrawal. The life on Skid Row is hard; it is hardest for Skid Row Indians.

Yet Skid Row offers compensating attractions: the "bright lights" of the urban environment, which stand in contrast to the isolation and dullness of the rural reserve; a sense of solidarity with other Indians, regardless of family or social background; and an opportunity to recreate festive and ritualistic aspects of the Indian tradition. In Morinis' view, these attractions provide a cultural context in which Indians define themselves and reject control of their lives by white society, goals that compensate for the poverty, sickness, and abuse that they experience by being on Skid Row. He argues that the conventional but pejorative assessment of Skid Row Indians as being culturally deprived and undersocialized, fails to penetrate the deeper reality of their lives. The Skid Row lifestyle not only enables Indians to reject the values and goals of the wider society, but to do it in a way—unlike most of what happens on the reserves—that deeply offends the wider society and compels it to take notice. He concludes: "The Skid Row Indian...is engaged in a political action. The politics of the Skid Row Indians do not take place in the more conventional arenas of public politics, but rather through life-styling on the stage of their personal minds and bodies. Their lives are their manifestos. Their politics is the politics of self."

NATIVE INDIAN ACTIVISM IN CANADA has been increasing in recent years. Indian organizations have become stronger and more sophisticated and Indian leaders have become experienced, skillful and articulate. Representations to Royal Commissions, the Canadian Parliament, and international bodies have come to be an accepted part of contemporary Indian political affairs. Indian leaders have shown themselves to be at home lobbying the British Parliament, as they did recently over the question of patriation of the Canadian constitution.

Yet at the same time as this process of heightened political sophistication and organization has been taking place, another and apparently opposite development has been occurring. This one has received almost no publicity. We are witnessing an explosive increase in the number and prominence of Indians on the Skid Rows which are to be found in every one of Canada's major cities and in a few towns. Welfare Indians and Métis are in fact the fastest growing native grouping in the city (Dosman 1972: 68). Drunken, sick, malnourished, criminal, violent communities have long existed at

E. ALAN MORINIS

the heart of the downtown core of urban Canada. Now these are becoming heavily Indian communities. It would seem that the communities of Skid Row Indians are completely outside the sphere of attention and influence of the renascent Indian political consciousness. In this paper, I would like to explore the nature of life for Indians on Vancouver's Skid Row, and then use this ethnography to make sense of the simultaneous and apparently paradoxical increase in numbers of politically-effective Indians, and numbers of Indians on Skid Row today.

Not all, or perhaps even a majority of urban Indians spend much of their lives on Skid Row. But Indians have come to make up a sizeable proportion of the Skid Row population. The importance of studying this community lies in two factors. One is that Indians on the skids represent the current installment of Indian-White relations in this society, but it is a chapter just opened. We have reason to be concerned as an increasing number of Indians abandon the isolation and boredom of the rural reserves to seek out the exciting life of the city. Those who find a ready welcome into the established Indian community on Skid Row enter a world of poverty, sickness, abuse, racism, violence, prostitution and crime. There must be concern to find the causes of their suffering in the midst of affluence.

Secondly, it is misleading to see Indians on Skid Row as just another group of hopeless social misfits. From a dispassionate perspective, it is possible to see that the burgeoning communities of Indians at the heart of every one of Canada's cities are engaged in a struggle for the control over personal life in the face of an oppressive, immensely powerful Society that they emphatically reject but feel they lack the means to subvert. The Skid Row Indian, like the chief's delegate to Westminster, is therefore engaged in a political action. The politics of the Skid Row Indians do not take place in the more conventional arenas of public politics, but rather through life-styling on the stage of their personal minds and bodies. Their lives are their manifestos. Their politics is the *politics of self.*

This investigation has both a theoretical and an applied intent. Theoretically, I will demonstrate the limitations of accepted theories of Skid Row when applied to the unique case of Indians on the skids. Concepts such as marginality, deviance and under-socialization which are common in discussions of Skid Row communities must give way to an idea such as the *politics of self* if we are to gain real understanding of the phenomenon of Indians on Skid Row.

The applied dimension of the paper concerns Skid Row as a social and human blight. A number of schemes have been developed to improve or remove life on Skid Row. What will be the outcome if these are applied to derelict, vagrant Indians? In line with the theoretical conclusions of the paper, I suggest that a social welfare, rehabilitation approach to the Skid Row Indian perhaps may help some individuals in isolated cases, but in general will not make a major positive contribution to improving the welfare of this community because the causes underlying their situation are more socio-structural and political than such solutions acknowledge.

The Study of Skid Row

Vancouver's Skid Row is both a neighborhood and a way of life. It constitutes a community in both the physical and socio-cultural uses of the term. The clearly demarcated physical center of Skid Row is the intersection of Hastings and Main Streets. The outer boundaries of Skid Row are not clearly marked, but the community fades out as one moves away from the central focus. The few blocks around Hastings and Main are its principal territory.

To be part of the Skid Row community is: to sleep in bug-ridden, dirty, dilapidated flop houses, eat in greasy cafes, fight in back alleys and drink in seedy bars—when there is money. And when there is not, to sink lower still, to sleep in garbage bins, eat in the "soup and salvation" mission food lines, to be beaten and rolled for the last change, to drink Lysol and Sterno or bootlegged homebrew, or to find your way to the clinic or hospital for the drugs that will stop the shakes of alcohol withdrawal. The life on Skid Row is hard; it is hardest for Skid Row Indians.

The population of Skid Row is difficult to estimate. The community is fluid and transient. Census-takers primed to count people by knocking on doors at regular dwelling places are not likely to get an accurate tally of people who sleep in parks, doorways and under wrecked cars. Also, not everyone who lives at Hastings and Main is on Skid Row. There is, for example, a large Chinese population not sharing at all in the social status or life patterns of the Skid Row. Furthermore, Skid Row membership is a question of degrees, with people living on the skids to varying extents at different times.

E. ALAN MORINIS

Nevertheless, we do have a reasonably good estimate of the number of people of Indian origin living in downtown Vancouver. A recent survey of Indian people in the city (Ward 1979) estimates the innercity Indian population at between 1,940 and 3,860. A good proportion of these people would, to some degree, be living on Skid Row.

While it would only be wild guessing to try to estimate the proportion of the Skid Row population that is Indian, it is indisputable that in Vancouver the proportion is high. Indians are a regular and highly visible sub-group on Skid Row.

Before proceeding, a word about the definition of the term *Indian* as I use it is in order. On Skid Row, there is but one category of Indians, and membership is determined on the basis of subjective and social criteria. A person is Indian who looks Indian, regards him or herself as an Indian and is thought of by others as being an Indian. The legal distinction between status and non-status Indians is of no significance here.

Life on the Skids

Although the homeless, wandering vagrant has always been known to society, "Skid Row" is a uniquely North American phenomenon, the name itself having been coined in Seattle. First used to describe the road down which logs were skidded to the sawmill, it was later extended to the neighborhood of flop-houses, saloons, gambling halls and brothels that serviced the homeless workingmen of the lumber industry (Morgan 1951). Periodic economic upheavals created a group of dispossessed, rootless men, who migrated to the cities and clustered around the labor exchanges and lodging houses in the poorer districts, alternating between temporary work and idle diversion. It is estimated that in the early part of the century there were forty to sixty thousand men on Chicago's Skid Row. Estimates of the population of New York's Bowery in 1915 range from 26,000 to 75,000 (Wallace 1965: 19).

Life in Skid Row is distinctive from the rest of society in every category: economic, legal, social, cultural, nutritional, medical. I will look particularly at the patterns of social interaction within the Skid Row Indian community, and then at relations between Skid Row

Indians and the police and health care deliverers. The principles of social life depicted in these two sets of relations hold true as well for other areas not being discussed here. The police and medical workers are very distinct in outlook, purpose and practice from one another. Yet we will find that Skid Row Indians manifest basically the same attitudes and behaviors towards both. These paralleling relations are taken to imply that, from the point of view of the Skid Row Indian, the similarities between the police and medical workers outweigh the differences. Hospitals, jails, clinics and courts all represent the Society to which Skid Row Indians are hostile, and so hostility is expressed in equal measure towards a policeman making an arrest and an ambulance driver dressing a wound.

Social Life Within the Skid Row Indian Community

Vancouver's Skid Row is to a great extent an Indian community. Many of the Indians to be found there are from other provinces, but the majority are from British Columbia. They represent every band and corner of the province. This diversity could be a source of fragmentation in the community, but under the pressure of common opposition to White, middle-class, urban society, the Skid Row Indian community forges pan-Indian solidarity. One urban Indian puts it: "An Indian is an Indian no matter what kind of Indian he is."

The city is the strong attraction for the migrating Indian. *Bright lights* is how an employment counsellor described the pull, rather than employment, housing, health or the other more practical motives which can stir migration. Skid Row is a place where the Indian wins the bright lights of city living, yet he can avoid the opprobrium of alienating wage labor and the social strictures of dominant urban society. As Brody (1971: 4) puts it:

> The Skid Row community...stands between the limitations
> and constraints of a rural reserve and the rejection and
> alienation of white-dominated city life.

Three important relationships make Skid Row the natural terminus for much migration of Indians to the cities. First, Skid Row provides the contemporary Indian with an escape from the rural

E. ALAN MORINIS

backwater of the reserves while still leaving intact some important socio-cultural features of reserve life. The unemployment, welfare and drinking as well as the intense and vital interactions among people that characterize reserve society are carried over to the city.

Secondly, at the same time as the city provides the Indian with access to the urban main currents of contemporary life, Skid Row protects him from being engulfed by the forces of the dominant white, middle-class society. He does not fit into that society, and in fact is not welcome to it, his efforts at adjustment frequently being met by discrimination and rejection.

The third important relationship to influence this community is with traditional, pre-contact society. Some cultural patterns observable on Skid Row may owe something to traditional life-ways. Urban drinking patterns on the Northwest Coast have been related to traditional forms of generosity, feasting and status-building, for example (Lemert 1954). But these connections are tenuous at best. Traditional society is more a force on Skid Row by virtue of its absence. Much of the alienation and hostility towards White society manifested by Indians can be traced to evident roots in the devastation of the colonial encounter.

Skid Row is thus uniquely suited to receive Indian migrants. Because it is already home to many Indians, it is likely that the newcomer will find a friend or relation there. But Indians on Skid Row are very friendly to the newly arrived, and make him welcome anyway. Skid Row offers an "enclave of acceptance in the usually hostile milieu of the city...where they can get drunk without criticism, easily joining social groupings with little concern for outside criteria for status" (Price 1975: 20).

To a high degree, life for Indians on Skid Row revolves around alcohol, although some Indians do not drink and some are militantly anti-drinking. A poster in a downtown drop-in center reads: "Drinking is un-Indian." But drinking is a factor underlying much of the social life on Skid Row, for Indians as well as non-Indians. "Alcohol," as Blumberg *et al* (1973: 137) have put it, "is the cement of Skid Row relationships, even though it may be the solvent of other relationships in the larger community."

Much of life is spent in pursuit or consumption of alcohol. The open hours of the day are spent in the parks, drop-in centers and missions of the Skid Row area. Not an inconsiderable amount of time is spent in the *bucket* (jail) and the drunk-tank. Work tends to be seasonal and temporary; most subsist on welfare supplemented by begging, petty crime and hustling. Some cook food in their rooms, or eat in the down-at-the-heel cafes of the neighborhood. Others follow a daily trail from mission to drop-in center to hostel, getting breakfast here, coffee there, lunch and dinner elsewhere, all for the price of listening to a sermon, or perhaps not even that. Social ties in the city tend to be few, but many of the Indians retain ties with family on the reserves, whom they visit when the taste of the city sours.

But life for the Skid Row Indian focuses on alcohol. Indian and non-Indian drinking differ in several critical ways. Indian drinking tends to be more of a social event. The sullen, solitary drinker drooped over a glass is almost unknown. Indians in bars, as in fact everywhere on Skid Row, tend to be in groups, often of eight or nine, but still willing to make room for more. Drinks, loud conversation and laughter are exchanged. People move from one group to another, and the bar favored by Indians takes on the appearance of one big party. The bar-party is a context for social display, and so it is the stage for exaggerated generosity, sexual innuendo and violence. One makes, keeps and displays one's social status at the liquor feast.

The bars are also not cut off from street life—they are not forbidden places where one goes to practice vice in secret. It is a commonly reported finding that native Indians exhibit little or no guilt about drinking and drunkenness (Leland 1976). The social animation of the bar spills over into the street, and is drained off into private parties after closing time.

As has been reported of drinking on the reserves, Indian drinking on Skid Row tends towards the spree. Savings and welfare are consumed in lavish and short-lived display of conspicuous consumption lasting as long as money holds out. There are many important aspects to spree drinking, but only several concern us here. One is that the spree is an opportunity for intense social interaction, the incurring and repayment of debts and the acquisition of social status. Because alcohol is so central to Skid Row society, the spree expresses basic Skid Row values in a context which forges much social solidarity. In this way it shares many of the characteristics of a festival. But in this case, it is more an anti-festival, for the values and

E. ALAN MORINIS

displays being enacted are precisely antithetical to dominant Canadian mores: drinking, drunkenness, conspicuous displays of emotion, violence and sexuality, wanton generosity and especially the complete disregard for thrift. The spree is the sub-group's celebration of its identity as the antithesis of society.

Life within the Indian community on Vancouver's Skid Row is active and lively. Brody (1971) and Dosman (1972) found the same to be true in Saskatchewan. Even the drinking, violence and sexual informality, when divested of the stigma these activities bear in the mainstream of society, can be seen to contribute to the vitality of social interaction. Among themselves, Indians have a home on Skid Row.

But Skid Row is not the Canadian dream of home. In contrast to the middle-class suburbs, it is surely hell. For most Indians, however, that comparison is irrelevant. The only meaningful comparison is between Skid Row and the rural reserves, and in this Skid Row does not come off nearly so badly. Conditions of life may be abominable on the skids, but they are often not much worse than some people have experienced on the reserves. For some people, Skid Row is likely an improvement! And Skid Row allows for the preservation of key forms of social interaction, and especially the density of interaction, which Indians value and are accustomed to but which would be lost in the isolated alienation of suburbia and wage labor. The point I would like to emphasize is that life on Skid Row has clear positive advantages to some Indians, while the disadvantages appear more minimal to them than they would to anyone who has not experienced the reality of reserve life.

I do not want to be misinterpreted as suggesting that Indians are happy and contented on Skid Row. Most who are there frequently and easily voice their discontent. But Skid Row is the most satisfactory of all the conceivable options, some of which are worse, some unattainable. The internal satisfactions of being a member of the Skid Row Indian community are important factors. So too are the attractions of the city. The illness, crime, violence, injustice, dirt, racism and poverty are definitely regretted. Further, and less obviously, Skid Row provides an ideal stage for the forms of Indian protest that show up clearly in dealings between Indians and the police, and Indians and health care workers.

Dealings with the Police

Mean dudes is how Skid Row Indians describe the police. According to the Native Courtworkers' Association, an average of two serious complaints of police brutality against Indians in Vancouver are filed weekly. To date, not a single policeman has been suspended or reprimanded for physical abuse against Indians in custody, although one officer is said to have been transferred. It is also certain that only a very few Indians take the trouble or run the risk of reporting police wrong-doing, even if they are aware of the procedures for making such complaints. The present arrangement is that the police police the police, a situation not likely to inspire confidence of obtaining justice amongst people who have come to expect police discrimination. The well known fact that police officers resent their Internal Investigations Division and do not cooperate in its workings further exacerbates the problem.

It is also the case that neither the police nor a justice of the peace will take a report of any kind from someone who appears drunk. Since Indians on Skid Row are most likely to become the victims of crime when they are drunk, and so most vulnerable, the police are unlikely to take a complaint from them.

From the Indian point of view, the police represent oppression, discrimination and injustice. Two stories, both culled from official complaints filed with the Native Courtworkers and subject to internal police investigation, depict clearly Indian perceptions of the treatment they can expect from the police. Whether the statements are true and accurate is of much less significance than the fact that these sorts of stories are common, and reflect Skid Row Indians' attitudes towards the police.

Two young B.C. Indian men were walking on Main Street one night when a car passed by and turned in ahead of them. Realizing it was the police, the pair decided to run: "We thought we were going to get jumped" said one. They went in different directions, crossing lanes and hopping fences. One escaped, but the other became exhausted and hid behind a fence. A policeman, accompanied by a snarling, barking dog, came up and began to kick at the fence from the other side, swearing and threatening the cringing man. Eventually the fence gave way and fell, sending the Indian sprawling. The dog attacked. While the Indian pleaded for the dog to be called off, and ineffectively fended him off with his hands, the policeman stood by. His plea, he records in his statement, was, "We're not from Van and we don't have nowhere to go. We were just walking around." Eventually the dog was called to heel. A police wagon arrived with more police. The Indian was interrogated in the dark backyard by flashlight. He had sustained severe tears on his thigh, shoulder and neck. He sought hospital care the next morning, after being released from custody, a threatened armed robbery charge not having been pressed.

A forty year old Indian man entered a Skid Row bar just after midnight on a Saturday night to use the toilet, but was denied entry, on the grounds that he was wearing blue jeans. He went into another bar, ordered a drink and went to the bathroom. He was followed by three men who came into the bathroom and yelled at him, "Hey buddy, didn't you hear what I said?", and then shoved him hard against the wall. The three were not in uniform, but showed him badges as they interrogated him. They pushed and slapped him until one punched him squarely on the jaw and he fell to the floor. When he regained consciousness, he was alone again. He phoned his brother, who came and picked him up. They filed a report at the police station that night.

Indians in Vancouver complain that the police are discriminatory, abusive, violent and dishonest. If they commit a crime or are taken in as suspects, they expect to be arrested, then beaten and robbed while in custody. If a crime has been reported, Indians are frequently pulled in as suspects, regardless of the absence of evidence. Both the Indians and the police agree that Skid Row Whites also use the Indians as scapegoats, unhesitatingly pointing out Indians to the police as suspects in crimes without a shred of evidence.

Most of the police violence against Indians is said to occur in the police station. Tales of robbery abound. One old Indian sadly walking the streets in a pair of worn, glossy, black and white patent leather shoes told of having been forced to give up a new pair of boots and $180 when he was arrested. He was not given a receipt for goods or money, and never saw either again.

Indians view the police as being hostile agents. As one said: "They don't give a damn about Indians. They're just taking care of up-town folks. Six or eight years on the beat down here and they get cynical and hard. Just nothin' but another dirty, god-damned Indian." Certain named policemen are known by the community as being especially tough on Indians.

From the police point of view, Indians are a problem. More liberal policemen see the problems in socio-economic and historical context. They tend to see Indians as good, once-proud people on hard times. They acknowledge the damaging effects of the reserve system, deculturation, economic dislocation and missionizing. One said, "They have low esteem for themselves. They have low esteem for others. They've lost respect for human life and body. That's how come they can do things like put the boots to some old drunk and kick the shit out of him 'til his body is pulp." In these men one can sense a real, if stereotyping, affection for Indians. There are some "assholes, some real mean dudes", but most are "happy-go-lucky, always laughing, joking with us. They don't lose their sense of humor. Except when they've been drinking, and then they can turn mean."

But even the liberal policemen acknowledge that there are much less sympathetic members of the Department. One said, "The Indian still has pride. In a funny way, in a very preserve way, they have pride. But you can't tell that to most cops, after they've spent the evening throwing people out of bars for pissing in the corner."

The police acknowledge that physical abuse of Indians takes place. Their justification is that Skid Row is a physical place, and one has to speak that language to be understood: "You can't talk sense to a drunk." Furthermore, the police see Skid Row as an explosive place that has to be controlled or it will blow. Force is needed "to keep the lid on it. You can't give anyone the opportunity to get you. I'll give them one chance. If they fuck me, they're gone. It may not always be pretty, but down here you're the Man. You have to be the Man."

The police feel that the situation is stacked against them. They have to play rough to do their job. And just a little strong arm on an Indian and his arm or nose breaks. "It's under-nutrition," one said. "It makes them brittle and fragile. A little twist and 'snap' like a dry branch."

Many police express the same view as held by Indian social workers and leaders that 99 percent of the problems of Indians on Skid Row trace back to alcohol. Drinking exaggerates every problem area, they feel. Some policemen repeated the often heard but conclusively disproven theory that Indians are physiologically unable to hold liquor, although others stated categorically that this was a misconception.

Skid Row appears dangerous to the police, but has seldom proven so, perhaps because of the precautionary and pre-emptive measures they take. During their regular nightly bar checks, they as a rule throw into the street three categories of people: drunks, sleepers and what they call "assholes", these being anyone who makes a remark, gesture or look hinting of hostility or disrespect towards the police.

There is continual tension in these relations. One way in which this tension is diffused is through the police tolerating teasing and derogation from certain well-known characters on Skid Row. These are harmless people, for example one old Indian who is confined to a wheelchair whose joking verbal abuse of the police speaks the community's mind and is tolerated. The same words from anyone except a permitted "clown" would lead in the least to being moved along, and not uncommonly to an arrest, with perhaps a beating, a charge, a conviction and a criminal record.

The core attitude of the Skid Row Indian community is one of avoidance of contact with the police. Both sides agree that it is the police who will come out on top from any situation of conflict. Yet the police express themselves and act as if the community was poised at the brink of eruption. What they are reacting to, I think, is community-felt hostility towards what the police represent. The police are charged to enforce the law. On Skid Row this duty involves the imposition of a set of ethical and behavioral standards which the Skid Row Indian from the depth of his being rejects. He does not want to be punished for being drunk, he is on Skid Row in order to be drunk. He does not want to be jailed for robbery or breaking and entering, he sees himself as the victim of much greater social wrong-doing. The eruption that the police fear is not likely to be physically directed at them, but more likely at the moral and behavioral social principles they have the responsibility to enforce. The danger of Skid Row is the danger of all outcaste communities which live by norms and values antithetical to the codes of society and the law. Skid Row is hostile to Society, and Society responds through its police with hostility to Skid Row. This principle holds true for all people on Skid Row, but is especially true for the Indian community, which is in degrees more outcasted than its White counterpart on the skids.

Dealing with Medical Workers

When all categories of health care personnel in downtown Vancouver were asked to compare Indians and non-Indians as patients as part of our research project, 30 percent of our respondents stated that Natives were poor at keeping appointments, 23 percent found Indians non-compliant with therapy, 12.5 percent stated that Indians delayed in seeking medical care until a crisis existed, 10 percent thought Indians to be passive, 10 percent complained that Indians were poorly educated, 8 percent felt Indians were non-communicative, 8 percent considered Indians apathetic, 6 percent thought Indians were nervous as patients, 6 percent found Indians hostile and 2 percent stated that Indians were overly dependent. Twenty-one percent found no differences, 8 percent considered Indians to be better patients and 12.5 percent did not respond. In replying to another question, 23 percent of respondents indicated that communication with Indians was a problem for them.

This shows a high degree of dissatisfaction with native Indians as patients. Although the single greatest cause of this dissatisfaction is Indians' notorious irregularity in keeping appointments, in general the picture is one of poor relations between health care deliverer and recipient. Downtown Indians do not perform the patient role to the satisfaction of health professionals.

In a study of 117 tuberculosis patients at the Vancouver General Hospital, Frank (1980: 2) reveals that, slightly over half the Native patients are discharged against medical advice or for disciplinary reasons, and "of the Native people with alcohol-related problems

E. ALAN MORINIS

who are discharged in the first three months, 71 percent are against medical advice or for disciplinary reasons." Most of the Skid Row population would fall into this latter category. Compared to the 51 percent of all Indians and the 71 percent of Indians with alcohol-related problems, the over-all figure for patients discharged against medical advice or for disciplinary reasons was 34 percent. This contrast implies a large gap between the situation for Indians and the general population, but since 29 percent of all patients in the study were native Indian, the variation between Indian and non-Indian disciplinary and self-discharge problems is even greater. Further, compliance with treatment regimes after discharge from hospital "is lower for people with alcohol-related problems (30%), particularly Native people (14%)" (Frank 1980: 2). In other words, 86 percent of the population which we can reasonably expect includes Skid Row Indians is non-compliant with medical therapy for tuberculosis. It is not surprising then, that of the 94 Indians whom we interviewed on Skid Row, 16, or 17 percent, had active or past tuberculosis.

These statistics paint a picture of poor Indian health and a poor record of participation in health care relationships. In fact, the situation among Skid Row Indians is worse than these facts suggest because a sizeable proportion of this population does not bring their medical problems to the attention of health care personnel. A discussion of the interaction of downtown Indians and the health care system must include a look not only at hospitals and clinics but also at the front-line of medical care for Indians. It is the ambulance crews and the inhalator services of the Fire Department that deal with the collapses, injuries, attempted suicides, burns, accidents and acute health crises that are so typical of Skid Row Indians.

The captain of one safety and rescue team stated that the majority of their alcohol-related calls in downtown Vancouver are for native Indians. Many of the calls for stabbings and assaults also involve Indians. When asked how Indians respond to the crew's care, he said, "I find them belligerent, feeling sorry for themselves, they don't want to cooperate. So you just have to use a stronger arm on them." As a result, health care workers tend to develop a paternalistic attitude towards Skid Row Indians.

In one case, a white man had been hit by a car. The two Indian women with him sat down in the middle of the street and would not move. In the words of an attending fireman:

There was just no talking to them, they would not move. You could pick them up and they sat right down again. You had to drag them to move. That's the kind of attitude they take. On some occasions you tell them either we are going to treat you and take you to the hospital, or you are going to jail. That is the only way you can get cooperation out of them.

Other problems of treating Skid Row Indians are related to their uncommunicativeness to health care deliverers:

What makes it difficult in my opinion is the fact that when somebody is hurt and you need some information from them, they are all close-mouthed—they know nothing, they see nothing, they want to tell you nothing. When you need information because some guy is bleeding and you don't know how he was stabbed or how he was beaten, they are totally unco-operative.

Indians are reported as being non-compliant to a remarkable degree:

If you start bandaging them and you say "Leave the bandage alone", they will immediately go and knock the bandage off, as if you were doing it to aggravate them, or they are doing it to aggravate you, one of the two.

The patterns of use of health services by Skid Row Indians indicate that these services are used more as an assistance to the Skid Row way of life than to change the problem-causing features it contains. Hospitals and clinics are where you go to get patched up, or to get the pills to stop alcohol withdrawal. It is an understatement to say that there is little individual drive to health. Life on Skid Row moves in the opposite direction. Many Skid Row Indians end up receiving medical care not because of their own action but because someone else has called an emergency service. Skid Row Indians can be openly defiant against health care. When one researcher suggested to an Indian man she had interviewed that he seek medical care for his heart problem, which was flaring up, he responded: "Look, I'm a brave. I'm not afraid to die. I'm going to die soon anyway. I'll die a brave."

E. ALAN MORINIS

We can see clearly that the relationship between Skid Row Indians and medical personnel is different in degree but not in kind from relations with the police. How are we to account for this fact? Distrust of the police makes sense, given their law-enforcement duties. But why should the Skid Row Indian be non-compliant, unco-operative and even defiant to health care workers? The answer, I think, lies in the overarching relationship between this Indian community and the society which provides the police, hospitals, clinics, courts, jails, welfare offices and banks. The differences between these services are submerged in the commonality of their roots in a society that the Skid Row Indian rejects.

Discussion

In some of its most characteristic aspects, life for Indians at Vancouver's Hastings and Main is typical for all Skid Row residents. Many are homeless or transient. Alcohol abuse and drunkenness are common. Unemployment is the rule. Social ties often seem tenuous to non-existent. But these apparent consistencies do not mean that the theories that have been proposed to account for Skid Row in general automatically apply to Indian Skid Row in particular.

Both Bogue (1963) and Bahr (1973) stress the social isolation of individuals on Skid Row, thereby minimizing or ignoring the role of community. Especially in the case of Indians, there exists a distinctive sub-culture and an open, vital social solidarity which provides individuals with a satisfying sense of place and meaning within the group. Furthermore, the hostile relations between the Indian Skid Row community and the representatives of the wider Canadian society reinforce the solidarity of the group. Indians living elsewhere in the city, who may own houses or hold down steady jobs, are not infrequent visitors to the Skid Row bars, where they reconnect with community and experience the social identity lacking to them in the White-dominated world in which they survive but seldom find a comfortable place.

Indians on Skid Row are not failed, hopeless casualties of the system who have been unable to succeed despite their best attempts. Success does not seem to have been a major motivator, if by success we mean employment, financial security and social approval. One fact that is evident to all providers of services to Skid Row Indians is that members of this community have pride and dignity. Indian identity is taken seriously and appreciated. Few share the self-hate reported for Whites on the skids.

Dependency (Wallace 1965: 132), undersocialization (Pittman and Gordon 1958) and all psychoanalytical theories (*e.g.*, Myerson 1956) that have been proposed to account for Skid Row do not pertain in this cross-cultural context. The growing numbers of Indians on Skid Row represent a social fact, which cannot be explained in terms of personality defects or failures in child-rearing practices. Anyone acquainted with Skid Row Indians knows that there exists a wide range of personality types. No doubt Skid Row harbors more than its share of extreme personalities, since it offers a haven to all forms of aberration within the wider community, but the average Skid Row Indian is neither socially inadept nor psychologically dysfunctional. It has been pointed out that the social processes required to form a *bottle gang* of drinkers are not inconsiderable (Rooney 1961). Indian social life in the bars, community centers, cafes and streets is lively and vivacious. Furthermore, Skid Row is home to many Indians for only part of the year. During the summer, many return to their reserves to fish and hunt. They do not lack the practical and social skills that these activities require. An important topic for future research is the identification of the factors that lead some Indians to the alleys of Skid Row and others to the halls of parliament.

The earlier work of Blumberg and his collaborators (1966, 1973) comes closer to applicability with the idea that lack of achievement and aspiration contribute to the placing of Indians on Skid Row. He also gives credence to the community factor in Skid Row life which makes it a recognizable subculture and society. The importance given to sustenance, power and status relationships between Skid Row and wider urban society is useful and applicable to the Indian case. But his latter idea (Blumberg *et al.* 1978: xix) that Skid Row is a life-style located wherever liquor and poverty intersect generalizes the issue to the point of dilution. Liquor and poverty intersect on the rural Indian reserves, but clearly to Indians, Skid Row is a very separate socio-cultural reality from the reserves. Blumberg's theory is useful for looking at the place of alcohol in the social life of those not motivated by society's most cherished goals, but is too general to account for the specific social and cultural patterns of Indians on urban Skid Row. Nevertheless, his insistent attention to the relationship between Skid Row and wider society is well placed for our purposes as well.

Socio-economic explanations for Skid Row flounder over one unique aspect of the Indian case. The conditions of poverty and socio-economic displacement characteristic of the Skid Row Indian have not put him on Skid Row. He is likely to have been unemployed and just as poor on the rural reserve. The move to Skid Row is not so much a fall as a sideways shift for most.

A similar argument applies to alcoholism theories (*e.g.*, Jellinek 1952; Kane 1981). The Skid Row Indian tends to be a drinker, but so too does the Indian on the reserve. Both unemployment and alcohol are characteristic circumstances which the Skid Row Indian shares with other Skid Row residents, but neither can be considered a *first cause* for Skid Row membership because they tend to be general to contemporary Indian conditions, not just to Skid Row.

It is unlikely that any single factor is prior or causal of the Indian situation on Skid Row. We are dealing with a complex phenomenon. Disaffiliation, personality disorders and undersocialization are notions with at best very limited applicability to the Skid Row Indian. Alcohol, economic displacement and lack of motivation to succeed on society's terms are more useful. The terms alienated (Spradley 1970) and lumpenproletariat (Brody 1971) seem to apply, although these are very broad categories. It would probably even be possible to find individual Indians on Skid Row whose personal life histories conform to the models proposed for the general Skid Row personality. In behavior and in certain important characteristics (*e.g.*, use of alcohol, unemployment, poverty, self-neglect) Skid Row Indians are like non-Indians on the skids. These similarities are the reason why Skid Row has proven such a popular destination for so much Indian urban in-migration today. But this said, there still remain important considerations that distinguish the Indian social group from the general population on Skid Row. The behavioral similarities are not the whole picture.

One of the prime distinguishing features is the frames-of-reference for Indians and non-Indians on Skid Row. While for non-Indians Skid Row stands in contrast to the valued norms of the urban middle, or at least working class, for many Indians, especially the newly arrived transients who are swelling the Skid Row population, the main referent against which Skid Row stands is the rural reserves. The apparently deviant lifestyle and social problems of Skid Row take on a very different coloration when compared on the one hand to a middle-class suburban referent, or on the other to a rural Indian reserve.

A second consideration is the historical realities of which all Indians are conscious and which separate Indians from Whites in all contexts. When we include White society's record of treatment of Indians into our analysis, it becomes much clearer why Indians might knowingly opt for a non-participatory, non-productive lifestyle of immediate gratification coupled with active hostility and latent aggression towards the dominant White social entity. Against the background of discrimination and exploitation which Indians have been subjected to, Indians on Skid Row cannot be dismissed as psychosocial deviants whose rehabilitation requires only the application of more socio-medical services. Indians who tear off their own bandages, walk out of hospitals, are non-compliant with prescriptions, do not press criminal charges, and so on, are rejecting the extensive services already available. More services will be unlikely to have a significant impact on their life circumstances. Considering Skid Row Indians to be marginal, depressed, psychosocial deviants is not illuminating, nor has such an approach made much contribution to the health and well-being of the Indian people. Indians on Skid Row are sane and competent people. They have opted for a lifestyle of aberrant behavior. There is a very consistent message in their inverted behavior which makes sense only in the context of more pervasive Indian historical and social realities.

Conclusions: From Deviant Marginality to the Politics of Self

The life situation of the Skid Row Indian, involving poor housing, inadequate nutrition, violence, disrupted social relations, illness, injury, crime and, of course, alcohol and drugs, has made Skid Row a major preoccupation with local government and social service agencies. For the police, health workers, social service teams, churches and academics, Skid Row presents a clear-cut set of problems.

E. ALAN MORINIS

This point of view is not shared by most Skid Row Indians. While life on Skid Row is hard, it is not without its rewards, and for Indians, who are confronted with a dominant society that rejects them, a rural society that is stagnant and unsatisfying and a history that cannot be recaptured, Skid Row is not an unappealing option. It offers a vital community in the exciting city, plus the bonus that one can survive there without having to join the wage-labor world. True, Skid Row comes with illness, crime, dirt, violence, racism and poverty, but those conditions are common on the rural reserves as well. The benefits of the city redeem the difficulties.

I suggest that the problems of Indian people on Skid Row are less the unfortunate symptoms of a depressed people than they are acts of defiance, rejection and opposition to society. No matter how loud the protests from the rural reserves, they will not catch the ear of modern Canada.

In general, Indian-White relations can be characterized as an opposition. While some Indians have chosen to grapple with this opposition by meeting the White world on its own ground, and have become experienced and skillful lawyers, politicians, lobbyists and media propagandists, a much larger number have chosen another route to protest. These latter reject even the fundamental premises of contemporary, bureaucratic, middle-class culture which the Indian lawyer must master and use in his political dealings with the dominant society. The Skid Row Indians' protest is more profound. Their defiant statement of opposition denies them even the possibility of participating in the values, norms or behaviors of the Society they reject. To be drunk in a Vancouver alley, to neglect your TB follow-up, to court arrest, to act out all of the other dis-valued behaviors so common on Skid Row is to grapple with political realities of a much deeper sort than the Constitution. The consistency and determination with which Skid Row Indians adhere to their lifestyle, and the extent to which membership in the community depends on performance according with the values and norms of Skid Row, which invert dominant mores and principles, indicate clearly the force of social protest movement underway on Skid Row. The Skid Row Indian lives out his statement which may doom him, but perhaps in a very real sense within the flow of history, any other form of action offers only a more painful form of death.

The Skid Row Indian provides an example of behavior which I
would call the *politics of self*. In this politics, political processes are
enacted on the stage of individual minds and bodies. There are no
rallies or organizations or parties. There are rather groups of people
agreeing on certain principles of action as strategies for contending
with widespread and powerful social and political realities. Skid Row
Indians face a culture and society which oppress them, which they
reject but which they lack the power to subvert. The individual life
is then transformed into the locus of rejection, opposition and
defiance more familiarly known to be staged in less personal, more
public, arenas.

The politics of the Skid Row Indian are not reasoned and intellectual. They are lifestyle politics emerging naturally from personal history and the imprint of social forces. There is no stated
immediate aim for these politics. Rather, they are the politics of
protest. These may be unfamiliar politics, but I venture that labelling
the consistent demonstrative behavior of Skid Row Indians to be
political rather than problematical permits us to see more clearly
why every form of service provided to that community has not succeeded in eradicating its problems. Be they medical, legal, emergency, social, economic or other forms of service, they share the idea
that Skid Row is a social problem. The thrust of their programs has
been to cure the individual Skid Row resident. The Indians have
not cooperated. To give up their problems is to give up their protest.
To surrender to rehabilitation is to yield the political field. Skid
Row Indians want a better life, with health, peace and prosperity,
but not at all costs. The root causes of their protest must be addressed if they are to gain a better life, as is their due, and these
causes are political.

Society is at present very far from addressing this reality. More
typical are the comments of Dr. Edward L. Margetts in the introduction to a symposium on Canada's Native Peoples published in
the *Canadian Psychiatric Association Journal* (1974: 33):

> The Indian has high rates of alcoholism and drug addic-
> tion....Migration to towns may lead to problems of pros-
> titution and criminality. Explanations of these phenomena
> have been mostly sociological, but that is only part of the
> story—there may also be biological susceptibilities, and
> these have been minimized in research so far.

E. ALAN MORINIS

He later criticizes psychiatrists for having recourse to sociological explanations for Indian deviancy and illness:

> The answers to illness syndromes lie in individual psychodynamics, psychopathology and pathology and not in social stresses, most of which can be taken by people in their stride if they are individually healthy in their total makeup of genetic and constitutional endowments, with normal growth and development in mental and physical facets.

The implication about the faulty genetic and constitutional makeup of Indian people is clear.

As a direct result of this sort of perception, all of the resources directed towards Skid Row people go either to protecting society from the blight of Skid Row, or towards rehabilitating the individual. There has long been a call to organize the vagrant transients into labor armies. In Vancouver, Reverend Andrew Roddan, the Superintendent of the First United Church, which is located right in Skid Row, proposes in a book entitled *Canada's Untouchables* (1932: 13) that rather than police action against transients and vagrants, as had been ordered by Prime Minister R.B. Bennett, "The men ought to be organized into a working army and put to work for reasonable wages under proper conditions."

In the 1960s the thrust of approaches to the Skid Row problem shifted to *urban renewal,* that is, tear it down. The justification for such drastic measures is the protection of society (Bogue 1963).

Few studies have acknowledged the social or sub-cultural reality of Skid Row. The community is seen as a collection of deformed individuals, and the route to transforming Skid Row is through the servicing of individuals (B.C. Department of Social Welfare, 1960). This dominant view of Skid Row as a place of problems at the individual level has given rise to solutions which consist of the provision of services to lead the individual from being a useless, deviant parasite to being an upstanding, responsible working citizen (Vancouver City Council, 1966).

These approaches to the Skid Row problem differ from one to the next, but they share the strong implicit notion that Skid Row is a wound in need of cleaning up. The remedies address superficial symptoms only. They ignore the political dimension of the Skid Row

Indian's lifestyle, and their "adequate socio-medical services" are tantamount to the stifling of that protest, which is raised through the inverted, perverse and defiant behavior of those at Hastings and Main. In this light, no amount of services provided by society will have any impact on the situations they are intended to change until the basic relationship between Indians and Canadian society is resolved. Until such time, we can expect that Indians will continue to practice the politics of self, that Skid Row will thrive, and that a portion of Canadian society will suffer a high incidence of illness, incarceration, inhumanity, violence and degradation.

On a theoretical note, the politics of self is not a phenomenon exclusive to Skid Row Indians. The concept sheds light as well on other contemporary social movements, *e.g.*, punk rockers and Buddhist meditators. Wherever members of social groups jointly enact behaviors which have as their essence a statement about wider social patterns, but do so outside the realm of conventional political action and instead through their personal dress, eating habits, health behavior, language, etc., then they are practising the politics of self.

References

Bahr, H.M.
1973 *Skid Row: an Introduction to Disaffiliation.* New York: Oxford University Press.

Blumberg, L., T.E. Shipley, Jr., I.W. Shandler and H. Niebuhr, Jr.
1966 The Development, Major Goals and Strategies of a Skid Row Program, *Quarterly Journal of Studies on Alcohol,* 27:242-258.

Blumberg, L., T.E. Shipley, Jr., and I.W. Shandler
1973 *Skid Row and Its Alternatives.* Philadelphia: Temple University Press.

Blumberg, L., T.E. Shipley, Jr., and S.F. Barsky
1978 *Liquor and Poverty: Skid Row as a Human Condition.* New Brunswick, NJ: Rutgers Center for Alcohol Studies.

Bogue, D.
1963 *Skid Row in American Cities,* Community and Family Study Center, Chicago: University of Chicago.

E. ALAN MORINIS

British Columbia Department of Social Welfare
1960 *Report on Homeless Transients in the Province of British Columbia.*

Brody, H.
1971 *Indians on Skid Row.* Northern Science Research Group, Ottawa: Department of Indian Affairs and Northern Development.

Caplow, T., H.M. Bahr and D. Sternberg
1968 Homelessness. In David Sills (ed.), *International Encyclopedia of the Social Sciences* 6:494-499. New York: Macmillan.

Dosman, E.J.
1972 *Indians: The Urban Dilemma.* Toronto: McClelland and Stewart.

Frank, R.
1980 *Proposal for a Comprehensive Management Program for Tuberculosis Patients: Hospital, Halfway House and Follow-up Components.* Vancouver: Vancouver General Hospital.

Jellinek, E.M.
1952 Phases of Alcohol Addiction, *Quarterly Journal of Studies on Alcohol* 13:673-684.

Kane, G.P.
1981 *Inner City Alcoholism.* New York: Human Sciences Press.

Leland, J.
1976 *Firewater Myths: North American Indian Drinking and Alcohol Addiction.* New Brunswick, NJ: Rutgers Center of Alcohol Studies.

Lemert, E.M.
1954 Alcohol and the Northwest Coast Indians, in *Culture and Society.* Berkeley: University of California Press.

Marriage, A.
1957 *The Police Court Drunkenness Offender.* Vancouver: The Alcoholism Foundation of British Columbia.

McClelland, D.C., J.W. Atkinson, R.A. Clark and E.L. Howell
1953 *The Achievement Motive.* New York: Appletone-Century-Crofts.

McSheehy, W.
1979 *Skid Row.* Boston: Hall.

Mears, B., K. Pals, K. Kuczerpa, M. Tallio and E.A. Morinis
1981 *Illness and Treatment Strategies of Native Indians in Downtown Vancouver: A Study of the Skid Row Population.* Vancouver: Health and Welfare Canada.

Morgan, M.
1951 *Skid Road: An Informal Portrait of Seattle.* New York: Viking Press.

Myerson, D.J.
The "Skid Row" Problem, *New England Journal of Medicine* 254 (25):1168-1173.

Pittman, D.J. and C.W. Gordon
1958 *Revolving Door: A Study of the Chronic Police Case Inebriate.* New Haven: Yale Center of Alcohol Studies.

Price, J.A.
1975 An Applied Analysis of North American Indian Drinking Patterns, *Human Organization* 34 (1):17-26.

Roddan, A. (Rev.)
1932 *Canada's Untouchables.* Vancouver: First United Church.

Rooney, J.F.
1961 Group Processes Among Skid Row Winos; Re-evaluation of the Under-

socialization Hypothesis, *Quarterly Journal of Studies on Alcohol* 22:444-460.

Rosenman, S.
1955 The Skid Row Alcoholic and the Negative Ego Image, *Quarterly Journal of Studies on Alcohol* 16 (3):447-473.

Spradley, J.
1970 *You Owe Yourself a Drunk*. Boston: Little Brown.

Vancouver City Council
1966 *Skid Road: The Chronic Drunkenness Offender.*

Walker, R.D.
1981 Treatment Strategies in an Urban Indian Alcoholism Program, *Journal of Studies on Alcohol, Suppl.* 9:171-184.

Wallace, S.E.
1965 *Skid Row as a Way of Life.* Totowa, NJ: The Bedminster Press.

Ward, B.
1979 *A Study of the Native Indian Population of Vancouver, B.C. In Relation to the Vancouver Indian Centre*, Vancouver: Department of Secretary of State/Pacific Region.

THE ANTISTRUCTURE OF RESISTANCE:
CULTURE AND POLITICS IN A
TORONTO HIGH SCHOOL

Peter McLaren

Si recte calculum ponas, ubique naufragium est.

Petronius Arbiter

The politics of self that underlies the resistance of Skid Row Indians is echoed in the resistance strategies of students in a Toronto inner city Catholic school. Drawing on Victor Turner's classic distinction between structure and anti-structure, Peter McLaren demonstrates here how junior high school students evoke the symbols and behavioral styles of their own anti-structural "streetcorner state" to withstand and subvert the structural "student state" that is imposed on them by the institutionalized practice of education. The cultural conflict that ensues is a pervasive and politically charged aspect of the school setting:

> *...Teachers were faced each day with a spectrum of resistances and reprisals to their instruction—a series of ineluctable acts of ritualized disjunction and reritualization...designed to rupture and erode the authority of the teacher. In fact, student resistance in inner city schools has been one of the largest sustained guerrilla warfare campaigns since the advent of mass literacy.*

Rooted in the complex relationship between ritual and politics, McLaren's analysis exemplifies the Manchester tradition of anthropology; it also parallels developments in Gramscian theory and contemporary cultural studies. The school, viewed as a cultural system, is an instrument of hegemony. Its purpose is to make "good Catholics" and "good workers" out of the students, who are the children of Portuguese and Italian immigrants. Hence the school reproduces Canada's famed "vertical mosaic" in which non-Anglo ethnics are seen as naturally fitting on the lower rungs of the class hierarchy. At the same time, the school is a contested terrain. Counterhegemonic cultural and political forces pose a constant challenge to the designs of the institution. Like impoverished peasants, Skid Row Indians, and many others who hold subordinate and relatively powerless positions in society, students from apparently "underprivileged" circumstances exemplify the symbolic wealth of the weak and the extraordinary capacity of that wealth to generate political resistance.

MONDAY, 23 MARCH

A SMALL NUMBER OF STUDENTS AND TEACHERS joined hundreds of protesters from all walks of life in order to converge en masse on the Litton factory in Rexdale, an industrial complex that was— and still it—making parts for the US nuclear missile euphemistically know as the "cruise". The march outside the plant, which was organized by a variety of anti-nuke groups across Canada, constituted a rite of revitalization by reinforcing the growing Catholic position (as exemplified in many recent statements made by the Catholic bishops) against nuclear weaponry. During the march, the students walked in a circle outside the plant, armed with a huge banner of the Virgin Mary. Also on the banner were pictures of miniature cruise missiles with Xs crossing them out. The words HAIL MARY were written in block letters on one side of the banner.

There was a tremendous surge of spontaneous communitas throughout this powerful symbolic protest. An unmistakable feeling of solidarity among the protesters made them seem invulnerable. Freed temporarily from structural constraints and legislated encumbrances of role, class, reputation, sex and status, the students shed the institutional armour of the student state and talked openly and animatedly with other groups who had gathered to protest. Some students even defied the police—who were present in a startling display of force. I watched as several students, arms akimbo, stood before the police and insisted on knowing why they supported nuclear armament. Walking arm in arm to display their solidarity

PETER MCLAREN

for a common cause, teachers and students chanted anti-nuclear slogans, their voices rising in confidence as the march progressed.

The march on the Litton factory was equally a rite of intensification since the direct confrontation with the police served to stimulate and motivate the students as much as the anti-nuclear sentiments that they were espousing.

Student: I really got nervous when we shouted at the cops. My heart started to pound. It was fun. I wish more St. Ryan students showed up.

After several hours the students took a bus back to the school. During the ride home, I overheard teachers from Brother Regis discuss animatedly how they planned to follow up on the protest march in their forthcoming lessons.

The ideological hegemony of school life was not monolithically impregnable—an iron-clad system which held captive students' subjectivities and agency. There were considerable resistances on the part of students to engagement in the macro and micro rites. The very existence of school rules and shared symbols intimated their profanation or violation. The classroom, with all its hydra-like symbolic dimensions, became a highly contested territory—a Homeric battlefield where struggles were continuously waged over existing power relations and symbolic meanings. The seeming harmony that pervaded life in the classroom existed at the imaginary level only; when one began to scratch the surface of this apparent solitude one quickly realized that ritual meaning often lurks in subtle negation, opposition and resistance as well as affirmation of the status quo: it is conflictual as it is consensualist.

Despite the fact that, on the whole, students were compliant and acquiesced to teacher-sponsored rules which were presented as salient, real and natural, teachers were faced each day with a spectrum of resistances and reprisals to their instruction—a series of ineluctable acts of ritualized disjunction and reritualization (Erikson's term) designed to rupture and erode the authority of the teacher. In fact, student resistance in inner city schools has been one of the largest sustained guerrilla warfare campaigns since the advent of mass literacy.

By the term "resistance" I refer to oppositional student behavior that has both symbolic, historical and "lived" meaning and which

THE ANTISTRUCTURE OF RESISTANCE

contests the legitimacy, power and significance of school culture in general and instruction in particular (e.g. the overt and hidden curriculum).

Organized resistance to school policy in the form of student unions or grievance committees is largely the preserve of the children of the ruling class, not the children of the dispossessed. Resistance among working-class students rarely occurs through legitimate channels of checks and balances that exist in educational organizations. Rather, resistances among the disaffected and disenfranchised are often tacit, informal, unwitting and unconscious. This is because they are resisting more than just a formal corpus of rules and injunctions: they are resisting the distinction between the "lived" informal culture of the streets and the formal, dominant culture of the classroom.

Resistances were, in Turner's idiom, "liminal" experiences; they occurred among students who had begun to traffic in illegitimate symbols and who attempted to deride authority by flexing, as it were, their countercultural muscles. The provenance of resistances was located in the antistructure where contradiction and conflict competed with the continuity of ritual symbols and ritual metaphors— and where students attempted to disrupt, obstruct and circumvent the incumbent moral demands of the instructional rites. The terrain of resistance was the world of Burroughs and Genet. It was a world devoid of approved symbolic arrangements—a world filleted of traditional meanings and associations. Here students would scoff at and deride the accepted syntax of communication. The antistructure of resistance was a dialectical theater in which meanings were both affirmed and denied simultaneously. Whatever sense of identity was stripped from the student during class time was returned through the torn seams, fissures and eruptions of the resistant and liminal self. In both subtle and overt ways, recusant students exhibited actions which undermined the consensually validated norms and authorized codes of the school—norms and codes which made up the bric-à-brac of institutional life. The performances of resistance in the suite consisted of ritualized acts of *sparagmos* or dismemberment which comprised a spectrum of modes: from the stirring frenzy of a class "going wild"; the carefree abandonment of students at play (which generally moved through prescribed limits); the lugubrious whining of students who felt "cheated" or "hard done by"; to the orderly resistance of collective struggle. Added to these resistances were various other ritualized modes of conflict, dramatic confrontative performances, and the release of anarchic behavior— all assaults on the established order. During times of acute distress, teachers would occasionally suspend the rules (e.g. the class would be given a period of "goof off", to engage in a game or read a book). This type of teacher ploy served as a steam valve effect which diffused growing frustrations in the class.

It was not difficult to understand why students resisted schooling in the student state through rites of transgression since the student state was the path to apathy, passionlessness and emotional and spiritual emptiness. It was, furthermore, a denigration of their identity as a social class. The norms of how one related to life in the student state were drawn from the requirements of the culture to maintain the status quo—a situation found by the students to be overwhelmingly oppressive. Breaching the rules was a logical response to the oppressive conditions of the student state and occurred most often when the naked authoritarianism of the teacher became too much to bear.

But resistance went beyond reactions to bureaucrats high on the aphrodisiac of power: it was a reaction to the separation between the lived cultural meaning of the streetcorner state and the thing-oriented, digital approach to learning of the student state—an approach in which thinking skills were stressed over political and moral values and individual feelings.

It is important to understand school resistance as a form of what Turner calls "social drama". The four cultural markers of the social drama are: breach, crisis, redress, and either reintegration or recognition of schism. Rituals traditionally associated with breach are those dealing with life crises, marriage and death. Redressive rituals include divination, curative rituals and initiatory rites.

The breach in the classroom social drama became manifested through subtle and not-so-subtle acts of subversion undertaken by a group of students known as the "cool guys" and "class clowns"— acts which I refer to as "working the system".

Student: The cool guys wear the leather jackets and act tough. They like to talk back to the teacher. The guys who like to work are the browners. Lots of them are wrist guys.

THE ANTISTRUCTURE OF RESISTANCE

Peter: What are "wrist guys"?

Student: You know—the fairies, fags.

Student breaches were typical reactions to the anti-incarnational characteristics of school instruction. Consisting of a variety of behaviors which were marshalled in opposition to the *pro forma* curricular declarations of the suite, resistances often took the form of buffoonery, ribaldry, raillery, hoopla, open disputation, the occasional affray, a plethora of anti-teacher verbiage (usually muttered in muted or whispered tones), the thwarting of a lesson through brusque remarks, constant carping at the classroom rules, non-negotiable demands, sabotaging lessons by taunting teachers, incessant jabber, insouciant slapstick, engaging in conversations with peers unbeknownst to the teachers, marvellously inventive obscenities and general intransigence—"streetcorner" characteristics which threatened to make hay of established codes of classroom propriety.

TUESDAY, 20 JANUARY

I was tired at the end of the day. As I approached the subway entrance, yawning, I noticed Rocko standing near the door with a group of kids. He noticed me and came up to me, his tongue flicking like an Iguana.

"Hey sir, wanna see some of these?" He flashed a set of cards in his hand.

"What have you got there, Rocko?"

"Nice, eh?" He started peeling the deck, card by card. There were various shots of nude women smiling and pinning their labia against their legs.

"Donchya wanna see some more?" Rocko asked gleefully.

"Sorry Rocko," I said.

Rocko shrugged. "See you at mass on Friday, sir."

PETER MCLAREN

To breach classroom instruction was to thwart an obligation or unwritten contract with Christ and constituted a fundamental immoral act. More passive resistances occurred obliquely and figuratively through streetcorner argot (e.g. whatever slang was *de rigueur* in order to be a "cool guy"). Gestures of resistance included clenched fists, pursed lips, and arms folded defiantly across the chest. These gestures did not symbolize student "interiority" (as if thoughts somehow precede gesture). Gestures are not (following Merleau-Ponty) weak translations of thoughts. Gestures of resistance *are* student anger, fear and refusal expressed in an incarnate or corporeal mode. *The aim of the breach was to fight to establish the streetcorner state inside the suite* (whose precinct is the student state). The most common instances of resistance were: leaning back on chairs so that students nearly fell over (and often did); knocking each other on the backs of the knees and other forms of "masculine" jostling; leaning over the desk and talking to other students; lollingly sitting at your desk and looking around the room with a bored expression; insurrectionary posing such as thrusting out the chin and scowling at the teacher; being in a restricted space without permission (such as a hallway or washroom) during a classroom lesson or activity; obeying a teacher's command but performing the required task in slow motion (symbolic stalling); "horsing around" or fighting in class; and wearing "intimidating" clothing. Occasionally students would wear stained sweatshirts with sleeves ripped off over the shoulders as forms of stigmata or symbols of self-exile. They would affect the bravado and histrionic self-consciousness of the aggressive and "macho" male.

Teacher: There is really nothing wrong with sitting and doing nothing, the question is sitting there and doing nothing for how long. And at what point does it become inappropriate behavior? It's the same thing as going to the washroom. How long before one should ask? How long can a person sit without doing anything?

Peter: Can you think of any others [acts of resistance]?

Teacher: They constantly change. What you have with one group and what one group figures they can get away with is different from another group. For example, this year there is

THE ANTISTRUCTURE OF RESISTANCE

a lot of kicking each other in the back of the legs. That never happened before and it is something I have difficulty dealing with here because it is not something we are used to. Everyone is doing that and because it is so prevalent it's hard to stop it. It's just fooling around but it does get serious sometimes. Where does it become inappropriate? There is a great big area, to be perfectly honest. I felt that I managed to deal with it. I said to one of the boys: "Franko, I want you to keep your hands to yourself for the rest of the day or you're going to get a detention!" That worked for the rest of the day.

Peter: Can you see different forms of resistance?

Teacher: OK, putting one's hands up. In some groups there is a lot of shouting out. Other groups are hesitant. That could, in some cases, be a form of resistance. To refuse to put your hands up shows resistance. Or leaning back in chairs and shouting out answers. Again, it's sometimes hard to condemn them when they are showing enthusiasm. Other things, leaning back in chairs, chewing gum, are all forms of resistance...

There are limits to the resistance that they [should be] allowed to show. My discomfort in sitting in this chair causes me to lean back and sit properly again—totally acceptable. I'm not going to make any comments about it. The person who leans back in their chair and stays that way—well, I'm going to point it out to them.

Seldom would physical violence erupt during the frequent and overt displays of odiousness and scurrilousness among the students, although tempers would routinely and uncomfortably flare. Natural bodily functions—such as farting ("honking") or belching—became a popular method of extending the streetcorner state into the oppressive confines of the student state.

Other instances of breach reported to me by students included: stealing the supply room keys when the teacher was absent; plugging the toilet with paper towels or stolen clothes; and vandalizing the washroom walls and ceiling. A favorite trick involved putting a full garbage can on the lever that releases the water into the sink. While the water was running, students plugged the sink with toilet paper and fled the washroom. Fifteen minutes later there is a flood.

Student: Sir, did you hear what happened in the washroom? Some-
one broke the tank. There's about an inch of water. The teachers think some guy in my class did it.

Peter: I never heard about it. What other things do people do?

Student: Where we wash our hands, people put a garbage can there and it fills up with water.

Peter: How does that happen?

Student: They take paper and plug the drain holes.

A mini-crisis occurred when I intervened in a fight after school in which a gang of "cool guys" were pummelling a student about the head and kidneys for telling the administration the name of the washroom vandal. I was surrounded by a group of very big "cool guys" who asked me how well I could defend myself. When I told them I had studied martial arts and offered them the name of a well-known martial arts club, their provocation ceased as suddenly as it had begun, and I left the scene unchallenged.

TUESDAY, 22 DECEMBER

A festive and communicative event, the mass is the heart of the Church's life, the fulcrum of the Church's ministries and apostolates. Containing a power and a significance born of centuries of hallowed worship—like the Passover meal—the celebration of the Eucharist is both sacrifice and sacred meal. It functions to shrink the range of one's world in order to keep one's mind focused on particular sacred or transcendental symbols. In the way that it selects or "brackets" a particular segment of the symbolic universe, the mass somewhat resembles Husserl's "drive" towards consistency.

The schoolwide Christmas mass certainly did not appear to capture the attention—let alone the commitment—of a large number of students. In fact, this mass was one of the shallowest I have ever experienced; it utterly failed to engender feelings much different than the most perfunctory instructional rite.

Student: What a bore, man. We might just as well have been doing math.

A sombre, highly structured occasion, with teachers "scanning" the aisles and watching for students who were moving or talking, the mass became a forum of student resistance. Students laughed, joked, discussed the latest drug deals and bumped into each other. During the sign of peace, hands were squeezed hard; some students even tried to pull each other over the pews—all this despite the strict controlling forces of the teachers. Resistances were "variations" within the liturgy—indexical indicators of the present commitment of the students to this particular orchestration of religious meaning.

Carol singing was led by a sister who told the students when to lower their pitch and when to raise it. Verses to the carols were projected on to a screen from an overhead projector. During the sermon, the priest spoke condescendingly to the students using a vituperative rhetoric. He upbraided them for not attending mass with greater regularity. He spoke to the students as if they were toddlers; the message of the sermon was presented as a pathetic analogy about travelling on the road to salvation and driving to Lisbon in a car; if you stop the car and leave it unattended while you stroll on foot somewhere to enjoy the scenery, thieves will undoubtedly notice your absence and steal the tires of your car. The message was: do not get out of the car; you must stay on the road and avoid distractions at all costs, so that you can get to heaven. The sermon constantly went over the same points again and again until the priest's voice became, in T.S. Eliot's words, like the "rattling of dry bones". It is no wonder the students avoided attending Sunday mass. Some students felt, however, that mass was even more important than school: "It's where we can talk to God quietly—not like at school." However, many of the students saw the mass as "just another boring lesson".

It appeared that, for many students, there was little response to what was usually an evocative display of language, gesture, and symbolism. There was almost no engagement of the students at a level of felt and intuitive meaning—despite the presence of the Portuguese priest who presided. On this occasion, the dominant symbol was not the sacrifice of Christ on the cross but the lectern from which the priest "lectured" to the students about their inadequacies. (It is rather ironic that there were four school lecterns in the church on the day of the schoolwide confession.) Responses from the students appeared to confirm Scheff's notion of ritual overdistancing.

Student: I believe in Jesus and all that but in Church I just can't concentrate. Like it gets too distracting all the time.

The students could hardly be faulted for their apathy. Indeed, the majority of the students had yet to undergo Confirmation. In addition, the overall performance of the mass was made oppressive by the structure of unconscious coercion manifest in the control functions of both priests and teachers. One of the most telling moments for me was when a teacher, standing with his legs apart and his hands on his hips, "guarded" the entrance to the aisle where the pupils genuflected towards the altar as they filed into the pew. In effect, the students were literally kneeling submissively at the feet of the teacher, who wore a look of unmistakable self-satisfaction. Whom were the students really prostrating themselves before at that very moment? To which God(s) were they paying greatest homage? Was it the bureaucracy of the Separate School Board, or Christ—or both? Instead of becoming a celebration in the temple of God, mass became just another "subject" in the pedagogical repertoire of the schooling process (process in the sense of being "processed"?) Teacher patrols flanking the pews invoked a feeling of restrictedness and confinement; it was like being in a prison instead of the house of God. To construct such an ambience constituted a type of "forced feeding" of sacred symbols.

However, teachers felt that it would be more beneficial for the students to attend mass rather than not attend at all.

Teacher: It's important for students to attend mass. They learn the proper responses and also learn how to act appropriately. But they also need to communicate with the eternal. They need the forgiveness that the mass provides.

It was as if the mass were supposed to spiritually soak up sins on contact—and with an absorption capacity of a transcendental sponge.

The usual sense of union, intimacy and affirmation of faith were absent from this particular celebration of the mass. In fact, the entire performance was immersed in a sense of bathos. The richness, depth and mystery of a potentially magnificent event—perhaps one of the most hallowed events known to man—was reduced to no more than a shallow lecture. At its height, the mass resembled a dithrambic eulogy more than an inspirational event. What was potentially a privileged moment became an abortive one.

Classroom rituals possessed a collective function other than simply fostering a sense of organic solidarity. As both organized and spontaneous opposition to instruction, rituals of resistance served both to flush out dead symbols from the clotted cultural conduits of the ritual system—those which had grown ossified and retarded and which no longer provided channels for addressing the needs of students—and replace them with more meaningful symbols, those that lay a "fiduciary hold" (Turner's words) on the student. For instance, symbols of prime ministers, saints and historical figures were ignored in the streetcorner state in favor of the motorcycle rider, the hockey hero, "Mr. T.", the cool guy and the "break dancer."

THURSDAY, 19 FEBRUARY

Today was the first dance of the year. It was a spontaneous, festive and carnivalesque event— a wildly beautiful display of the streetcorner state freighted with symbolic overload and a surfeit of signifiers. As opposed to the sporadic episodes of institutionalized communitas occasionally experienced during a rare engaging lesson, this was a paradigmatic instance of spontaneous communitas. The paradox of freedom co-existing within the structure became temporarily resolved for a number of students:

Student: School's not so bad when they let you have fun. Hard work makes more sense when you get some time to laugh and have fun. That's what working is all about, I guess.

PETER MCLAREN

While the dance was structured through the orchestration and sequencing of songs by a West Indian disc-jockey, it was more novel than formulaic; both students and teachers unashamedly tapped the vitality of the streetcorner state. The dance allowed for emotional contagion and status inversion; it was one of the few occasions during which students could display their superiority: through movement. While bodies were on sexual display during the fast dances, there remained a sense of sanctified prurience. Some teachers admitted feeling threatened by the fluidity, pleasing eurhythmics and unrestrained indulgences of student performances. Laughter was explosive and feet tapped the ground in a delicate frenzy. Several students started to emit wild groans and before long the whole gym was an orgy of pre-verbal utterances. Students formed small circles and danced around the gym. Some bodies joined together in contagious hysteria: writhing, twisting and sliding across the floor in a human snake. Boys slow danced tenderly with girls although girls usually danced with other girls. One teacher admitted being "shocked" and "horrified" at witnessing some boys dancing with other boys.

Several other teachers were affronted by the screaming, the sweat, the shrieks and the guttural groans emanating from the dance floor. One athletic-looking male teacher danced with an attractive female student during a slow dance—much to the delight of the students who whistled and cheered them on. Time collapsed into the strains of the music: "When you get into the music you forget you're in school or what time it is." A student exclaimed: "The dance made me feel a part of everything." It was good "to not think all the time in your head". Another student remarked: "I wouldn't mind learning so much if we could just feel good about living. You gotta have some fun." Students lamented the fact that there were so few dances. And so the dance ended with teachers clutching each other minuet style, their arms moving mincingly while their students swirled around them with unfettered gusto.

The dance echoed Worgul's assertion that a social structure high in communitas will survive whereas social structures with diminished communitas will be vulnerable to challenge and to dissolution (1980: 216). It would appear that events such as the school dance are more important for sustaining the school system than one would otherwise think without an adequate theory of ritual to inform him.

THE ANTISTRUCTURE OF RESISTANCE

The Untamed Eye

Student: I like to pretend that I'm workin'. Like move my pencil
and that kind of thing. But I'm really outside [of the class]
in my head...you know...I'm makin' my moves but I'm not
movin' but my body can still feel the muscles workin'... The
teacher sometimes catches you because she sees you starin'
at the wall. Then she screams at you: "Eyes on your work!"

Refusing to do work was one of the formidable methods of resistance: it was a scandal of absence, a silent insurrection, a withdrawal
into the dark interiority and ludic caverns of imagination. Sitting
motionless and pretending to be thinking about an assignment was
more than just a policy of clandestine provocation, it was fundamentally an ontological rebellion, a breaking free from a constrictive
and crippling moral perfectionism divested of the liminal attributes
of the streetcorner state. To be "on task", as the teachers call it,
was to be preoccupied with the known, the tangible, the safe.

The silence and stillness that was part of the refusal to work
was a feedback-seeking pause which acted as a form of "zero sign"
that signified by the absence of movement (cf. Poyatos 1981: 153).
To refuse to work was to exist beyond the frontiers of subordination
by locating human agency and individual volition in the vesperal
and chthonic antistructure of the mind where the rational gives way
to the surreal, the indicative to the subjective, the metonymical to
the metaphorical. Staring straight ahead into blank space was not
vegetative. Rather it became a mental mutiny, an inert agitation, a
silent upsurge against the extermination of the corporeal being; it
was to shriek soundlessly against the betrayal of the mind and flesh.

The eye, as a mirror of the mind, was the most phenomenologically subversive organ of student resistance. To be faced with an
"untamed eye" was, in mythological terms, to confront the Medusa-
like horror of raw being.

The wandering eye meant a mind disembodied from the rational
discourse of assignments: a mind detached, and critical, and therefore threatening. The wandering eye promoted the incantation of
the eternal teacher retort: "Keep your eyes on your work!"

Refusing to work was subversive in that it altered the rhythm

PETER MCLAREN

of the instructional rite, effectively bringing it to a halt. It was the inchoateness, the formlessness, the not-yetness surrounding the refusal to do work that competed with the redundancy and certainty of the instructional rite.

It was a rather grim paradox that when students were not working, they became active participants in resistance, and when they were at the mercy of the bleak self-effacement of instruction, they remained, for the most part, passionless observers and passive recipients of over-packaged (and over-cooked) information.

The Class Clown: Arbiter of Passive Resistance, Inversion and Meta-Discourse.

Situated in the context of more passive ritual resistance to the normative order of the school was the class clown.

Peter: We've talked about the different types of students. Barbie was talking about the "clown". How would you describe the clown, Brock? Is there a type?

Brock: The class clown would be someone who is a verbal clown who is fairly witty and can see certain things that you might be saying or doing and see the humor in it or the different side of it and can make a fool out of you on occasion and on the other hand can really add something to the lesson. It depends on the situation and your attitude towards it but I don't think we have too many of those kinds of kids; we don't have many kids who have a quick wit. What we have are more acting-type clowns who act out that side of themselves and maybe Vinnie might be an example of that, but I don't think he is a witty clown. It is interesting that I was talking on the weekend, actually on Thursday, to a last year teacher who told me what a nice kid he is which is interesting in that he apparently got in trouble constantly last year. And yet the teacher's impression of him was really nice and yet he was constantly getting detentions so there seemed to be a frustration on the part of the teacher last year with him because I guess Vinnie disrupted the class, disrupted the instruction, but at the same time, after it is all over, the teacher's impression is: "He's a nice kid."

Throughout the course of my fieldwork, I identified several class clowns (one of whom I shall call Vinnie, a student in Brock's class). Vinnie was capricious, vacillating and frequently obstreperous. His behavior could be described in terms of the way it changed the context of the classroom setting which was shaped by the instructional rituals. Without the benefit of pratfalls, custard pies or *commedia dell'arte* masks, class clowns arrogated to themselves—often unconsciously—the function of deconstructing the familiar. They achieved this through sarcastic comments, a Trickster-like prankishness, buffooning the teachers, parody and burlesque.

Punning, facetious and irreverent, Vinnie would shift vagariously from farce to satire, and even to mawkishness. Like a character in one of Genet's plays, he was the epitome of pure, stylized action—a performer of wordless skills in the tradition of the *mimus*.

Watching Vinnie act in non-accordance with the school norms made me aware of just how boring school really was. He also revealed the tenuousness and arbitrariness of the codes that prevented possible chaos from breaking out in the suite. Thus, Vinnie's task was not solely buffoonery, but teaching.

Vinnie nearly always smiled, despite the various degrees of seriousness of the occasion, and despite continued admonishments from the teacher. Although Vinnie was often ignored by his classmates, a large number of students either wilfully followed his antics or else they were engagingly distracted by him.

Vinnie would do zany things when the teacher's attention was somewhere else: he would roll his eyeballs sarcastically, throw a pen in the air or joke with his friends. He would frequently make bizarre faces—always incorporating some type of twisted smile. On numerous occasions I watched him gingerly roll a baseball across the floor, between the desks, while others were hard at work or at prayer.

Vinnie's performance as the class clown appeared to be consistent with Bouissac's (1982) observations that the actions of the clown constitute an "acted meta-discourse" on the tacit rules of the social order. In other words, they mirrored or expressed "the basic but unwritten rules" on which our construction of a culturally bound meaningful universe depends. Along these lines, it could be said

PETER MCLAREN

that the classroom clown trivialized instructional transactions and demonstrated the arbitrariness of the "sacred" cultural axioms and enshrined protocols that held together the symbolic universe of the suite. This profanation of the sacred rules by the clown was more than just the breaking of classroom decorum; it was the blatant exposure before all of the classroom's cultural code—the Rosetta Stone which revealed the hallowed and revered rules—the "tacit axioms or silent dogmas" from which all the other rules were derived. The sacred binding axiom of the suite could be stated thus: "Whatever your individual inner beliefs and/or quality of faith may be, never betray any disrespect for what your teachers regard as useful or sacred." It was not the breaking of the code itself which was important (everybody at least intuitively knew what the sacred rules were), but the knowledge that the clown knew and could communicate through satire and humor what the rules were—and that he understood the secret of their arbitrariness and the fact that they were not handed down from the heavens.

Like the dadaists and surrealists, his counterparts in the world of art, the clown changed the meaning of conventional axioms by dramatically shifting the context. The antics of the clown became a Damoclean sword continually poised above the teacher's head; it threatened at any moment to swoop down and cut through the teacher's "bullshit", forcing the teacher to keep "honest".

One of Vinnie's methods of abrogating convention was to silently mock the prayers. With Thespian expertise he would at first appear splendidly indifferent, then suddenly crack a smile and cross himself perfunctorily. Sometimes he would prefer to play with a pen or inspect his lapel while the rest of the class stood with bowed heads. He would, on occasion, clasp his hands in front of his face as if in prayer, and then vigorously explore his nostrils with his index finger while licking his lips. This was a signal to the other students that he could slip out of the sacred shackles of the "sanctity state" whenever he felt like it; for Vinnie, his performance was invariably a "high"—a demiapotheosis. Another one of Vinnie's tricks was to knock over all the chairs that had been placed on top of the desks at the end of the day. Once, during mass, I observed several class clowns (including Vinnie) pull each other over the pews during the sign of peace.

As he mocks, scoffs, lampoons and parodies the foibles of both teachers and fellow students, the class clown may be said to "play" with the internal inconsistency and ambiguity of the ritual symbols and metaphors. He amusingly bridges the gap between the world of classroom life and the inversion of that order. Possessing a disproportionate zeal for "being an ass", the class clown symbolically undoes or refracts what the instructional rituals work so hard to build up—the student state and its concomitant reification of the cultural order; indeed, he tacitly de-reifies the cultural order. The clown serves to attenuate the rootedness of classroom reality; he diminishes the authoritative hold which the master symbols have on the students. Unable to maintain equanimity in the culture of the student state, the clown inverts the classroom *Lebensraum*. What distinguishes the class clown's actions from more typical forms of resistance are his amusing methods of rule profanation, his ingenuous personality, and his often outrageous flouting of the ordinary canons of moral conduct. The clown is a rupture in the classroom social system, Derrida's *aporia* somaticized metaphorically. He is a minus sign placed before expected classroom protocol.

While the clown manipulates the context of classroom life, he never becomes fully reified above context to the extent that he becomes, in Frathoff's (1970) terms, a "symbolic type". Although he resists transmogrification into a symbolic type, Vinnie's antics would seem to support the notion set forth by Handleman and Kapferer (1980) that ritual clowns are liminal figures and thus can be transformative and retransformative of context.

Students did not have to be informed of the unstated, sanctified rules of the suite beforehand in order to know what they were. For instance, no student ever hung a crucifix upside down in Black Mass fashion or painted a moustache on the picture of the pope. Students did not wear the sacrilegious fashions of the public school punk rockers (who occasionally sported priests' collars worn with swastikas or inverted crucifixes). They did not repair to the washrooms to smoke dope and abjure the Trinity. Desecrating holy images was too blatant an act of profanation. Respect for the sacred was too strong among students (including the clowns)—to test it outright. And thus the power of the sacred embodied in prayers, in religious symbols and in the religious studies curriculum continued to force consistency upon the context of classroom events. The most that the clowns achieved was to reduce this consistency and further

PETER MCLAREN

endow these sacred symbols and themes with ambiguity. In short: they symbolically "lightened" the dead weight and oppressive themes of the dominant ritual relations. They softened the "certainty" of the moral order and opened the suite to oppositional meanings. Most of the clowns' profanations were so understated and so subtle that the teacher could shrug them off more often than take action against them.

In terms of the instructional activity in the suite, the clown offered more than just comic relief. He was threatening in the way that he symbolically stripped the teachers naked and demythologized the classroom power structure. Every morning the classroom clown symbolically sat in the boardroom of the Ministry of Education and wagged his tongue (at a risk, perhaps, of being streamed into a basic level program). Because he was often amusing, the clown was not perceived as a direct threat, yet his antics could not go totally unpunished. He was sometimes described by teachers as "a bit of a nut"—a label which conveniently permitted teachers to place him outside the context of the "normal student", so that the punishment meted out to him need not appear as severe as that which was inflicted upon the rank-and-file deviant. The clown demanded that the teacher laugh at himself or herself and all that the teacher represented. To a certain extent teachers met this demand (by often engaging in some self-effacing humor) for fear of incurring extended antics from the clown or reprisals from other, more dangerous students. The only way a clown could be severely punished was if the teacher believed with his indomitable soul that the clown was actually dangerous, that he was working to effectively contravene the ordinances of the school; then the teacher would be forced to take whatever measure was necessary to curtail the clown's antics.

The Laughter of Resistance

The laughter of resistance is unlike any other. It occurs when the entire class—or a significant number of students within the class—spontaneously turn against the teacher. Usually the students wait patiently for an opening—a "slip-up" on the teacher's part (however slight)—and, when the time is right, they begin to howl with laughter. Yet the laughter that is directed against the teacher is qualitatively different from other forms of laughter. For instance, it is different from the laughter that follows the antics of the clown: a communal laughter that signals approval; a sign of social solidarity which states that the class is "with" the clown. And unlike the laughter of merriment, which brings the body into a state of unalloyed euphoria, or the laughter of the saint, which fills the universe as it celebrates a sense of certainty hiding behind the randomness and tenuousness of worldly events, the laughter of resistance serves to mock and denounce. It is a hostile act, an insurgent symbol, one which inscribes the *via rupta*. There is a vicious harmlessness about it. It starts high in the chest, shudders forth from the throat like sparks from an engine, and curls around its victim like wafts of thick smoke. It envelops the power of the teacher and neutralizes it. It forces the teacher to question—and abrogate—his self-typification as leader. Nothing can erode self-confidence more profoundly than the banshee-like laughter of resistance that chillingly penetrates the teacher's sense of sacral self.

The laughter of resistance reflects Mish'alani's remark that "the demonstrative material of laughter, the open mouth, the exposed teeth, the spasmodic contractions, the roar or chuckle, always reproduces an aspect or phase of predation, conquest, and even ingestion..." (1984: 151). It further echoes Mish'alani's description of the sneer and jeer as "contemptuous because it renounces the possibility of actual harm to its victim by way of commenting on his insufficiency to merit the expenditure of force, as if the text of its self-referential comment were: 'The strength brandished herewith is not being hereby deployed because you are too insignificant to merit its use'" (*idem*: 152). For the teacher who is at the mercy of the laughter of resistance, "the mocking jeer, the cackle of ridicule, does not lose force by distance, but persists in the imagination of its victim, pursuing him wherever he flees, haunting him, insinuating itself into him, undermining his self-complacence" (*idem*: 153).

Yet it is important to understand the laughter of resistance as more than wanton cruelty on the part of the students. It is not some form of jocular blood lust. It is, in its essence, a form of redefining the power structure of the class. It is a way for the students to reclaim their sense of collective identity. The laughter of resistance takes on the force of a group exhortation. It is an "argument" that cuts across class and gender boundaries yet remains culturally tied to whatever group employs it. Victims of the laughter of resistance are placed in a no-win situation. If a teacher reacts against it, or tries to deny it, then the students can prolong its effect. If the teacher acknowledges it, then he or she only confirms or reinforces the collective power behind it.

The laughter of resistance can flail and bludgeon the spirit and can only be deflected when the teacher "goes" with it. Brock was able to survive the laughter of resistance by laughing at himself or even responding with a one-liner that the class found amusing. Penelope, however, found it difficult to protect herself from the laughter of resistance and would only prolong her agony through her attempts to force the class into silence.

Tua, Vita Mea

From the perspective of the teachers, many of whom were convinced of the intellectual obliquity of the Azorean student, instructional ceremonies attempted to elevate the Portuguese student from the status of illiterate, belligerent immigrants to well-mannered, literate, middle-class Canadians. The untransformed and unelevated residues of the streetcorner knowledge of the uninstructed were to be replaced by academic knowledge. Minds tenacious of age-old superstition and ignorance were to be opened. Attitudes towards learning which were supposedly built on archaic presuppositions were to be radically reshaped. Instruction became the secular correlative to Kenneth Burke's theological formula of victimage and redemption: the unfortunate Portuguese are degraded (failed and/or punished) as part of their transformation into docile, well-mannered citizens.

Teacher: We try to get them through. Even if only a few of them become doctors and lawyers—it's at least a start.

Through the coldly efficient and hyper-rational rites of instruction, teachers attempted to transform the behavior of their students from what they perceived as stubbornness, impudence and resistance into docile, pliable, volitionless, obedient and beneficent behavior which enabled students to be easily conditioned to the mind-deadening and spirit-breaking norms of the factory or machine shop. Students were made, like Christ, into criminals, underlings; they were mocked and abused. And then, once vilified, these "primordial victims" were to be raised out of their material and cultural poverty and redeemed into the sanctified world of the educated. The persistent failure of many woebegone Azorean students served as a sacrifice that purged the school community of its academic ills and helped to ensure that students from non-working-class/cultural strata would avoid contagion. To fail the student is a ritual vaccination against a potentially larger outbreak of social malaise. The sacrificial aspect of the rites of instruction can be lucidly summed up in a teacher's remark:

Teacher: It would be ridiculous to imagine every student here making it as far as a corporate executive. How many teachers make principals or VP? Somebody's got to do the dirty work.

It appeared to one teacher only "natural" that the Azorean students should be sacrificed for at least another generation.

Teacher: It will probably take a few generations before we see a greater influx of Azorean lawyers and doctors and what have you....It's the same situation with any immigrant group. You can't expect them to step right in and take over.

Not only were Azorean students victimized, but they were blamed for their own victimization—a key scenario in the apologetics of capitalism (cf. Ryan: 1976). The pervading assumption that working-class students were only intermittently creatures of reason became transmuted into educational ideology through the setting up of basic level programs to accommodate such underlings. By blaming the academic failure of the Azorean student on his individual deficiencies, the teachers further turned the tables on those who were suffering because of their class and ethnic location in the larger society by implying that they were the cause of their own misfortune. The ideology of blaming the victim views student insolence and provocation as solely gratuitous—not as actions which are mediated by wider relations of class, authority and power. This is a continuation of the Renaissance tradition of individual achievement which fails to see the larger sociocultural context which the individual inhabits.

Observations that the Azorean students were sacrificed to the system strangely mimic Girard's argument that all institutions (including modern ones) grow out of the body of the victim and that the surrogate victim is "the ideal educator of humanity..." (1977: 306).

The sacrificial dimension of schooling functions as a type of purity rite: a social mechanism which protects the educational system by projecting its excrement on to its enemy or those who in some way are perceived to be threatening or jeopardizing the system. Sacrifice permits aggression to be deflected from more dominant social groups while allowing them to retain their privileged sphere of domination. The academic failure of the Portuguese student becomes a form of expiation for the "good of the system" (whatever benefits the white, Anglo-Saxon population). But why is this so? Why should the victims pay for this injustice?

I believe that the answers lie in the deep-seated conviction on the part of many members of the dominant class that the social system would somehow malfunction if everyone had the same chance for academic success. Not only would the powerful lose their power to dominate the poor, but society would somehow grind to a halt. The standards and quality of our schools (and, by implication, our society) would decline appreciably—some would argue drastically—in an attempt to accommodate "inferior" races. The failure of the disempowered thus becomes, for the ruling class, a crucial factor in the maintenance and evolution of the social order. This perspective provides the ideological base that allows the inferiority of the Azorean immigrant to become part of the social heredity of the dominant culture.

Purgation through victimage is part of the ritual of school instruction and in a multicultural society there exists an abundance of victims to help cleanse the system of its foreign impurities. Not surprisingly, these victims are often the children of the poor, and usually from minority backgrounds. Put less functionally, sacrifice is part of the social logic of schooling that is inscribed not only in the residues of social Darwinism but also, more alarmingly, in the current resurgence of neo-Conservative discourse. The social logic of sacrifice works through educational rituals as it seeks to manifest

THE ANTISTRUCTURE OF RESISTANCE

itself materially in the failure of minority students. As long as educators refuse to interrogate this logic and the ways that it contributes to the failure of minority groups, the general populace can rest comfortably in assuming that the system must continue to exclude the indigent and disaffected if our educational standards and way of life are to persist and evolve productively.

The ritual frame that is constructed around the sacrifice of the working-class immigrant student is one that can be described as follows: "Knowledge acquired through the instructional rituals (the cultural 'sacra') amounts to power—the key to becoming the successful working Catholic. We, the teachers, are the dispensers of that knowledge. Just as 'many are called but few are chosen', not everyone is worthy of receiving the sacred wisdom imparted by the teacher. If we watered down the curriculum so every group could succeed, schooling would lose its present status and power."

Given the somewhat cynical attitude of the teachers in the suite towards the capabilities of the Portuguese student, and given the rather dull, busy work the teachers often administered to the students, it could be argued that the teachers were simply reinforcing the academic competencies which the students already possessed and which the teachers felt would be adequate for the type of job the students would most likely seek. This would account for the pronounced isomorphism between the suite and the factory.

Teaching to the lowest common denominator of the academic program further reinforced student apathy, since the students could not help but wonder why they were not moving "upstream" as opposed to floundering in the stream in which they were placed by the teachers at the beginning of the year—one that meanders through the basic level groups and basic level courses and ends up eventually in the reservoir of despair known as the factory floor.

Regrettably, most parents accepted the fate of their children whom they fully entrusted to the teachers.

Parent: Look, the teachers know the best thing for the students. The students got to work in Canadian society so they must do as the Canadian teachers say. But the teachers aren't as strict as they were back home and that's the problem here.

Parents were generally conformist-minded, urging a "no-frills" core curriculum which stressed maths and reading. They wanted their children to achieve high standards but this desire was clouded in a value system which stressed strong teacher control.

Parent: Portuguese students are used to being pushed. If teachers don't push them, then they turn out to be lazy. They hang out at the plaza with those big radios and don't think about their responsibilities...[to]...their families.

The reaction of most parents to the prospect of economic advancement was one of a passive acceptance of their lot in life.

Parent: Not too many Portuguese can become rich here in Canada until they've been here three or four generations. It takes that long before you're accepted by the Canadians.

Several months after completing my observations at St. Ryan, a number of grass roots Portuguese groups began to mount a public protest against the fact that their children were outranked in the competition for academic rewards. For these fledgling critics of the system, school was hypostasized as an antagonist to the future success of their children in the labor market.

Parent: Our kids don't get the same breaks as Canadian kids. They stream our kids into low-level programs that don't lead to university. They look at us as less intelligent just because we don't come from an industrialized country. So our kids pay for it here.

References

Bouissac, P.
   1982 "The profanation of the sacred in circus clown performance", Paper presented at Symposium on Theatre and Ritual, Wenner-Gren Foundation for Anthropological Research.

Girard, R.
   1977   *Violence and the Sacred.* Baltimore: Johns Hopkins University Press.

Grathoff, R.
   1970   *The Structure of Social Inconsistencies.* The Hague: Martinus Nijhoff.

Mish'alani, J.K.
   1984   "Threats, laughter and society", *Man and World* 17:146-56.

Poyatos, F.
   1981   "Towards a typology of semantic signs", *Semiotic Inquiry* 1 (2):136-56.

Ryan, W.
   1976   *Blaming the Victim.* NY: Vintage Books.

Worgul, G.
   From Magic to Metaphor: A Validation of the Christian Sacraments. NY: Paulist Press.

PETER MCLAREN

EVERYDAY FORMS OF PEASANT RESISTANCE

James C. Scott

James C. Scott, a political scientist with long-term research interests in Asian peasants, is now pursing his work with the help
of anthropological tools. Ethnography reveals the importance of
everyday life, an anthropological commonplace insufficiently appreciated in other social sciences. As a result of his anthropological
fieldwork in Malaysia, Scott is now dissatisfied with recent work—
including his own—on peasant rebellion and revolution. Large
peasant rebellions against those who extract deference, rents, taxes,
labor, food, and conscripts from them are few and far between, no
doubt because such uprisings are usually so savagely repressed.
According to him, the arena of class conflict and peasant resistance is not to be found in acts of collective defiance, but rather
in the use of the weapons of the weak: "footdragging, dissimulation, false-compliance, pilfering, feigned ignorance, slander, arson,
sabotage, and so forth."

While such Brechtian, everyday forms of resistance may be
insufficient in themselves to transform the unequal power relations
between peasant and their extracting masters, they are by no means
trivial. Scott examines two examples of a silent and anonymous
form of economic and political struggle in a Malaysian rice-farming village. In the first case, poor village women try to stop the
growing mechanisation of rice harvesting by threatening to boycott
landowners who use combine-harvesters. The second case concerns the increasing theft of threshed paddy left overnight in the
fields during harvest. In both cases, no collective action was attempted, nor was there an open challenge to the system of property
and domination, in either political or symbolic terms.

Scott argues in favor of a definition of peasant resistance that
recognizes such anonymous and seemingly petty acts of defiance
as constituting a form of class-based collective action. To do other-

> *wise and to insist that the only acceptable evidence of class resis-*
> *tance should be formally organized activities is to blind ourselves*
> *to daily acts of self-defence. Because organized economic and*
> *political action is unlikely to be found among members of a social*
> *class as politically uncoordinated as the peasantry, the alternative*
> *to Scott's position is to continue to perceive peasants as an*
> *apathetic mass and to understand their political action through*
> *the familiar image of the abused dog which, in sheer rage and*
> *desperation, every so often flings himself at his master's throat.*

I. The Unwritten History of Resistance

THE ARGUMENT WHICH FOLLOWS originated in a growing dissatisfaction with much of the recent work—my own as well as that of
others—on the subject of peasant rebellion and revolution. It is only
too apparent that the inordinate attention to large-scale peasant
insurrection was, in North America at least, stimulated by the Vietnam war and something of a left-wing academic romance with wars
of national liberation. In this case interest and source material were
mutually reinforcing. For the historical and archival records were
richest at precisely those moments when the peasantry came to pose
a threat to the state and to the existing international order.[1] At
other times, which is to say most of the time, the peasantry appeared
in the historical record not so much as historical actors but as more
or less anonymous contributors to statistics on conscription, taxes,
labor migration, land holdings, and crops production.

The fact is that, for all their importance when they do occur,
peasant rebellions, let alone peasant "revolutions", are few and far
between. Not only are the circumstances which favor large-scale
peasant uprising comparatively rare, but when they do appear, the
revolts which develop are nearly always crushed unceremoniously.
To be sure, even a failed revolt may achieve something: a few concessions from the state or landlords, a brief respite from new and
painful relations of production[2] and, not least, a memory of resistance and courage that may lie in wait for the future. Such gains,
however, are uncertain, while the carnage, the repression, and the
demoralization of defeat are all too certain and real.

JAMES C. SCOTT

In a larger sense one might say that the historiography of class struggle has been systematically distorted in a state-centric direction. The events that claim attention are the events to which the state and ruling classes accord most attention in their archives. Thus, for example, a small and futile rebellion claims an attention all out of proportion to its impact on class relations while unheralded acts of flight, sabotage, theft which may have far greater impact are rarely noticed. The small rebellion may have a symbolic importance for its violence and for its revolutionary aims but for most subordinate classes historically such rare episodes were of less moment than the quiet, unremitting guerrilla warfare that took place day-in and day-out. It is perhaps only in the study of slavery that such forms of resistance are given due attention, and that is clearly because there have been relatively few slave rebellions (in the antebellum South at any rate) to whet the historian's appetite. It is also worth recalling as well that even at those extraordinary historical moments when a peasant-backed revolution actually succeeds in taking power, the results are, at the very best, a mixed blessing for the peasantry. Whatever else the revolution may achieve, it almost always creates a more coercive and hegemonic state apparatus—one that is often able to batten itself in the ironic position of having helped to power a ruling group whose plans for industrialization, taxation, and collectivisation are very much at odds with the goals for which peasants had imagined they were fighting.[3]

A history of the peasantry which only focused on uprisings would be much like a history of factory workers devoted entirely to major strikes and riots. Important and diagnostic though these exceptional events may be, they tell us little about the most durable arena of class conflict and resistance: the vital, day-to-day struggle on the factory floor over the pace of work, over leisure, wages, autonomy, privileges, and respect. For workers operating, by definition, at a structural disadvantage and subject to repression, such forms of quotidian struggle may be the only option available. Resistance of this kind does not throw up the manifestos, demonstrations, and pitched battles that normally compel attention, but vital territory is being won and lost here too. For the peasantry, scattered across the countryside and facing even more imposing obstacles to organised, collective action, everyday forms of resistance would seem particularly important.

EVERYDAY FORMS OF PEASANT RESISTANCE

For all these reasons it occurred to me that the emphasis on peasant rebellion was misplaced. Instead, it seemed far more germane to understand what we might call *everyday* forms of peasant resistance—the prosaic but constant struggle between the peasantry and those who seek to extract labor, food, taxes, rents, and interest from them. Most of the forms this struggle takes stop well short of collective outright defiance. Here I have in mind the *ordinary* weapons of relatively powerless groups: footdragging, dissimulation, false-compliance, pilfering, feigned ignorance, slander, arson, sabotage, and so forth. These Brechtian forms of class struggle have certain features in common. They require little or no co-ordination or planning; they often represent a form of individual self-help; and they typically avoid any direct symbolic confrontation with authority or with elite norms. To understand these commonplace forms of resistance is to understand what much of the peasantry does "between revolts" to defend its interests as best it can.

It would be a grave mistake, as it is with peasant rebellions, overly to romanticise these "weapons of the weak". They are unlikely to do more than marginally affect the various forms of exploitation which peasants confront. Furthermore, the peasantry has no monopoly on these weapons, as anyone who has observed officials and landlords resisting and disrupting state policies which are to their disadvantage can easily attest.

On the other hand, such Brechtian (or Schweikian) modes of resistance are not trivial. Desertion and evasion of conscription and of corvée labor have undoubtedly limited the imperial aspirations of many a monarch in South-east Asia[4] or, for that matter, in Europe.

In a similar fashion, flight and evasion of taxes have classically curbed the ambition and reach of Third World states—whether precolonial, colonial, or independent. Small wonder that such a large share of the tax receipts of Third World states is collected in the form of levies on imports and exports; the pattern is, in no small measure, a tribute to the tax resistance capacities of their subjects. Even a casual reading of the literature on rural "development" yields a rich harvest of unpopular government schemes and programs which have been nibbled to extinction by the passive resistance of the peasantry. On some occasions this resistance has become active, even violent. More often, however, it takes the form

JAMES C. SCOTT

of passive non-compliance, subtle sabotage, evasion and deception. The efforts of peasants in self-styled socialist states to prevent and then to mitigate, or even undo, unpopular forms of collective agriculture represent a striking example of the defensive techniques available to a beleaguered peasantry. Again the struggle is marked less by massive and defiant confrontations than by a quiet evasion that is equally massive and often far more effective.

The style of resistance in question is perhaps best described by contrasting paired forms of resistance, each aimed at much the same goal, the first of which is "everyday" resistance in our meaning and the second the more open, direct confrontations that typically dominate the study of resistance. In one sphere lies the quiet, piecemeal process by which peasant "squatters" have often encroached on plantation and state forest lands; in the other a public invasion of property that openly challenges property relations. In one sphere lies a process of gradual military desertion; in the other an open mutiny aiming at eliminating or replacing officers. In one sphere lies the pilfering of public or private grain stores; in the other an open attack on markets or granaries aiming at the redistribution of the food supply.

Such techniques of resistance are well adapted to the particular characteristics of the peasantry. Being a diverse class of "low classness", geographically distributed, often lacking the discipline and leadership that would encourage opposition of a more organised sort, the peasantry is best suited to extended guerrilla-style campaigns of attrition which require little or no co-ordination. Their individual acts of footdragging and evasion, reinforced often by a venerable popular culture of resistance, and multiplied many-thousand fold may, in the end, make an utter shambles of the policies dreamed up by their would-be superiors in the capital. The state may respond in a variety of ways. Policies may be recast in line with more realistic expectations. They may be retained but reinforced with positive incentives aimed at encouraging voluntary compliance. And, of course, the state may simply choose to employ more coercion. Whatever the response, we must not miss the fact that the action of the peasantry has thus changed or narrowed the policy options available. It is in this fashion, and not through revolts, let alone legal political pressure, that the peasantry has classically made its political presence felt. Thus any history or theory of peasant

EVERYDAY FORMS OF PEASANT RESISTANCE

politics which attempts to do justice to the peasantry as an historical
actor must necessarily come to grips with what I have chosen to call
"everyday forms of resistance". For this reason alone it is important
both to document and to bring some conceptual order to this seeming welter of human activity.

Everyday forms of resistance make no headlines. Just as millions
of anthozoan polyps create, willy-nilly, a coral reef, so do thousands
upon thousands of individual acts of insubordination and evasion
create a political or economic barrier reef of their own. There is
rarely any dramatic confrontation, any moment that is particularly
newsworthy. And whenever, to pursue the simile, the ship of state
runs aground on such a reef, attention is typically directed to the
shipwreck itself and not to the vast aggregation of petty acts which
made it possible. It is very rare that the perpetrators of these petty
acts seek to call attention to themselves. Their safety lies in their
anonymity. It is *also* extremely rare that officials of the state wish
to publicize the insubordination. To do so would be to admit that
their policy is unpopular and, above all, to expose the tenuousness
of their authority in the countryside—neither of which the sovereign
state finds in its interest. The nature of the acts themselves and the
self-interested muteness of the antagonists thus conspire to create
a kind of complicitous silence which all but expunges everyday forms
of resistance from the historical record.

History and social science, written by an intelligentsia using written records which are also created largely by literate officials, is
simply not well equipped to uncover the silent and anonymous
forms of class struggle which typify the peasantry.[5] In this case, its
practitioners implicitly join the conspiracy of the participants who
are themselves, as it were, sworn to secrecy. Collectively, this unlikely cabal contributes to a stereotype of the peasantry, enshrined
in both literature and in history, as a class which alternates between
long periods of abject passivity and brief, violent, and futile explosions of rage.

> He had centuries of fear and submission behind him, his
> shoulders had become hardened to blows, his soul so
> crushed that he did not recognise his own degradation.
> You could beat him and starve him and rob him of every-
> thing, year in, year out, before he would abandon his cau-
> tion and stupidity, his mind filled with all sorts of muddled

JAMES C. SCOTT

ideas which he could not properly understand; and this went on until a culmination of injustice and suffering flung him at his master's throat like some infuriated domestic animal who had been subjected to too many thrashings (Zola, 1980: 91).

There is a grain of truth in Zola's view, but only a grain. It is true that the "onstage" behavior of peasants during times of quiescence yields a picture of submission, fear, and caution. By contrast, peasant insurrections seem like visceral reactions of blind fury. What is missing from the account of "normal" passivity is the slow, grinding, quiet struggle over rents, crops, labor, and taxes in which submission and stupidity is often no more than a pose—a necessary tactic. What is missing from the picture of the periodic "explosions" is the underlying vision of justice which informs them and their specific goals and targets which are often quite rational indeed. The "explosions" themselves are frequently a sign that the "normal" and largely covert forms of class struggle are failing or have reached a crisis point. Such declarations of open war, with their mortal risks, normally come only after a protracted struggle on different terrain.

II. Two Diagnostic Examples

In the interest of pursuing the analytical issues raised by everyday forms of resistance, I offer a brief description of two examples, among many encountered in the course of field research in a Malaysian rice-farming village from 1978 to 1980. One involved an attempt by women transplanting groups to boycott landowners who had first hired combine-harvesters to replace hand labor. The second was a pattern of anonymous thefts of harvested paddy which appeared to be increasing in frequency. Each of these two activities had the characteristic features of everyday resistance. Neither the boycott, as we shall see, nor the thefts presented any *public* or symbolic challenge to the legitimacy of the production and property arrangements being resisted. Neither required any formal organisation and, in the case of the thefts of paddy, most of the activity was carried on individually at night. Perhaps the most important characteristic of these and many other such activities in the village is that, strictly speaking, they had no authors who would publicly take responsibility for them.

BACKGROUND

Before examining the two proposed examples of resistance more closely, a brief sketch of the village in question and its recent economic history should help to situate this account. The village, which we shall call Sedaka, is a community of some 74 households (352 people) located on the Muda Plain in the state of Kedah, Malaysia. The Muda region has been, since the fourteenth century, the main rice-producing area on the peninsula and rice production is by far the dominant economic activity. Village stratification in Sedaka can be read, for all practical purposes, directly from the data on paddy-land ownership and farm size. The land-poor half of the village in 1979 owned only three percent of the paddy-land farmed by villagers and farmed (including land rented in) 18 percent of the cultivated acreage. Average farm size for this poorest half of the village was barely over one acre, less than half the paddy-land judged necessary to provide a minimum standard of living to a family of four. Ten families are entirely without land and just over half Sedaka's households have incomes below the government-established poverty line. At the other end of the stratification the ten best-off households own over half the paddy-land held by villagers and cultivate, on average, over eight acres. These households constitute the economic elite of the village. Those among them (seven) who belong to the dominant Malay party (UMNO) dominate the quietly contentious political life of the village.

For our purposes, the major change in the economic and social life of Sedaka during the past decade was the beginning of double-cropping in 1971 and the mechanisation of the paddy harvest which came in its wake. Double-cropping, by itself, was something of a boon to virtually all strata of the village; landlords got double rents, owner-operators and tenants increased their annual profits, and even the roughly 28 families who depended on field labor for a substantial share of their income prospered as never before, transplanting and harvesting two crops. In a brief period of euphoria, homes were repaired and rebuilt, heads of households who had left earlier to find work elsewhere in the off-season found they could remain at home, and everyone had enough rice to feed their family the year round. Other consequences of double-cropping were, however, working to undermine the gains made by poorer villagers and they were decisively compounded by the introduction of combine-harvesters.

In 1975, virtually all the paddy in Muda was cut and threshed by hand. By 1980, huge western-style combines costing nearly M$200,000 and owned by syndicates of businessmen, were harvesting roughly 80 percent of the rice crop. If it is hard to imagine the visual impact on the peasantry of this mind-boggling technological leap from sickles and threshing tubs to clanking behemoths with 32-foot cutting bars, it is not so hard to calculate their impact on the distribution of rural income. Paddy wage-labor receipts have been reduced by nearly half and transplanting remains the only major operation which still requires manual labor. The losses in income have, of course, been greatest among those most in need: smallholders, marginal tenants, and above all landless wage laborers. If the impact of mechanisation is added to the effects of stagnant paddy price for producers, rising input costs and rising consumer prices, the poorest half of Sedaka's households has lost nearly all of their original gains from double-cropping. Income distribution, meanwhile, has worsened appreciably as the gains of double-cropping have gone largely to the big farmers who own most of the land and local capital.

As with many technological changes, the secondary effects of combine-harvesting have been at least as important as its primary effects. To reduce what is a very complex story to its barest essentials, the following major consequences of combine-harvesting may be noted.[6]

(1) It virtually eliminated gleaning by grinding up the stalks which were previously left beside the threshing tubs. Gleaning had been a subsidiary food for many poor village families.

(2) It favored the substitution of broadcast sowing for hand transplanting since the machine could more easily harvest paddy sown broadcast and of uneven height and maturity. By 1980 nearly half the paddy acreage was sown in this fashion thus eliminating

that much employment for hand transplanting.

(3) It greatly reduced the demand for harvest labor thereby allowing a reduction in the effective wage-rate for the employment still available.

(4) It made it easier for larger landowners inside and outside the village to dismiss the tenants they had previously rented to and resume cultivation themselves by hiring machine services.

(5) It created a new class of wealthy, entrepreneurial leasehold tenants willing and able to rent in large tracts for many seasons at a time, paying the advance rent in a lump sum.

The transformations in paddy-growing since 1971 have not only resulted in the relative impoverishment of poorer villagers but also in their *marginalization* so far as production relations are concerned. Until even 1975 rich landlords and farmers had more paddy-land than they could cultivate alone; they needed tenants, ploughing services, transplanters, reapers, and threshers. To ensure a reliable supply of labor it was common for better-off villagers to "cultivate" the goodwill of their labor force as well as their land. They did this by giving occasional feasts, by extending *zakat* (the Islamic tithe) bonuses to harvest laborers, by small loans or gifts, and by socially tactful behavior. Now, the well-to-do have little need to take on the poor as tenants or laborers. Correspondingly, they have little incentive to continue to cultivate their goodwill and the marginalization of the poor is reflected in a much remarked decline in feast giving, in *zakat* and charity, and in overt respect flowing from the rich to the poor.

OBSTACLES TO OPEN, COLLECTIVE RESISTANCE

Despite the economic reverses experienced by Sedaka's poor, despite the deteriorating quality of class relations evident behind the scene, there have been no striking instances of overt class conflict. The reasons why this public silence should prevail are worth mentioning briefly precisely because they are, I believe, common to so many contexts of agrarian class relations as to suggest that the resistance we shall find here is the rule and not the exception. The situation the poor confront in Sedaka and on the Muda Plain is, after all, part of the ubiquitous and undramatic struggle against the effects of capitalist development in the countryside; the loss of access to the means of production (proletarianisation), the loss of work (marginalization) and income, and the loss of what little respect and recognised social claims that went with their previous status. Most readings of the history of capitalist development, or simply a glance at the odds in this context, would indicate that this struggle is a lost cause. It may well be just that. If so, the poor peasantry of Sedaka finds itself in numerous and distinguished historical company. The *quiet* resistance of the victims in this case may be traced to two sets of reasons: one concerns the nature of the changes confronted by the poor as well as the nature of their community while another concerns the effects of repression.

Forms of resistance in Sedaka reflect the conditions and constraints under which they are generated. If they are open, they are rarely collective, and, if they are collective, they are rarely open. Here the analogy with small-scale, defensive, guerrilla skirmishes is once again appropriate. The encounters seldom amount to more than "incidents". The results are usually inconclusive, and the perpetrators move under cover of darkness or anonymity, melting back into the "civilian" population for protective cover.

Perhaps the most important "given" that structures the options open to Sedaka's poor is simply the nature of the changes which they have experienced. Some varieties of change, other things being equal, are more explosive than others—more likely to provoke open, collective defiance. In this category we might place those massive and sudden changes which decisively destroy nearly all the routines of daily life and, at the same time, threaten the livelihood of much of the population. Here in Sedaka, however, most of the changes that constitute the green revolution have been experienced as a series of *piecemeal* shifts in tenure and technique. Painful as the changes were, they tended to come gradually and to affect only a small minority of villagers at any one time. When landlords decided to resume cultivation themselves or to lease (*pajak*) their land to wealthy commercial operators, only a few tenants were threatened at a time and their difficulties at first seemed an individual misfortune rather than a general trend. Much the same can be said for the raising of rents and for the substitution of broad-casting for transplanting. The screws were turned piecemeal and at varying speeds so that the victims were never more than a handful at a time. In this case as in others, each landlord or farmer insisting on the change represented a *particular* situation confronting one or, at most, a few individuals.

The only exception to this pattern was the introduction of combine-harvesting and, as we shall see, it provoked the nearest thing to open, collective defiance. Even in this case, however, the impact was not instantaneous, nor was it without a certain ambiguity for many in the village. For the first two seasons the economic impact on the poor was noticeable but not devastating. Middle peasants were genuinely torn between the advantage of getting their crop in quickly and the loss of wage earning for themselves or their children. At no single moment did combine-harvesting represent a collective threat to the livelihood of a solid majority of villagers.

Another striking characteristic of the agricultural transformation in Kedah—one that serves very powerfully to defuse class-conflict is the fact that it simply removes the poor from the productive process rather than directly exploiting them. One after another, the large farmers and landlords in the Muda Scheme have *eliminated* terrains of potential struggle over the distribution of the harvest and profits from paddy-growing. In place of the struggle over piece-rates for cutting and threshing, there is now only a single payment to the machine-broker. In place of negotiations over transplanting costs, there is the option of broadcasting the seed and avoiding the conflict altogether. In place of tense and contentious disputes over the timing and level of rents there is increasingly the alternative of hiring the machines and farming oneself or of leasing to an outsider for a lump sum. The changes themselves, of course—dismissing a tenant, switching to the machines—are not so simple to put across. But once they have been put across, the ex-tenant or ex-wage laborer simply ceases to be relevant; there is no further season-by-season struggle because the poor have become redundant. Once the connection and the struggle in the realm of production has been severed it is a simple matter also to sever the connection—and the struggle—in the realm of ritual, charity, and even sociability. This central aspect of the green revolution, by itself, goes a long way toward accounting for the relative absence, here and elsewhere, of

JAMES C. SCOTT

mass violence. If the profits of the green revolution had depended on squeezing more from the tenants, rather than dismissing them, or extracting more work for less pay from laborers, the consequences for class conflict would surely have been far more dramatic. As it is, the profits from double-cropping depend far less on exploiting the poor than on ignoring and replacing them. Class conflict, like any conflict, is played out on a site—the threshing floor, the assembly line, the place where piece-rates or rents are settled—where vital interests are at stake. What double-cropping in Muda has achieved is a rather massive bulldozing of the sites where class conflict has historically occurred.

A related obstacle to open protest is already implicit in the piecemeal impact of double-cropping. The impact of each of the changes we have discussed is mediated by the very complex and overlapping class structure of Sedaka. There are well-off tenants and very poor tenants; there are landlords who are (or whose children are) also tenants and laborers; there are smallholders who need wage-work to survive but also hire the combines. Thus each of the important shifts in tenure and production creates not only victims and beneficiaries but also a substantial strata whose interests are not so easily discerned. Sedaka is not Morelos where a poor and largely undifferentiated peasantry confronted a common enemy in the sugar plantation. It is in fact only in comparatively rare circumstances where the class structure of the countryside was such as to produce either a decisive single cleavage or a nearly uniform response to external pressure. The situation in Sedaka is, I believe, the more common one. The very complexity of the local class structure militates against collective opinion and, hence, collective action on most issues.

The obstacles to collective action presented by the local class structure are compounded by other cleavages and alliances which cut across class. These are the familiar links of kinship, faction, patronage, and ritual ties that muddy the class waters in virtually *any* small community. Nearly without exception, they operate to the advantage of the richer farmers by creating a relationship of dependence that restrains the prudent poor man or woman from acting in class terms.

Lest one gain the impression from the foregoing that the obstacles to class conflict in Sedaka are entirely a matter of the complex local stratification and the piecemeal character of changes in production relations, I hasten to add that repression and the fear of repression are very much involved as well. Here it is sufficient simply to note that popular efforts to halt or impede the growth of combine-harvesting occurred in a climate of fear generated by local elites, by the police, by the "Special Branch" internal security forces, by a pattern of political arrests and intimidation. Open political activity was both rare and firmly repressed. A popular demonstration in Alor Star, the state capital, in early 1980, demanding an increase in the farm-gate paddy price was greeted with arrests of many opposition figures, threats of detention, and promises of even more draconian action if the protests continued. The fear of reprisal or arrest was mentioned explicitly by many as a reason for maintaining a low profile.

A final obstacle to open defiance might be called "the duress of the quotidian." The perspective I have in mind is best expressed in the words of Hassan, a poor man who was given less than the expected wage for filling paddy sacks. Asked why he said nothing to his wealthy employer, he replied, "Poor people can't complain; when I'm sick or need work, I may have to ask him again. I am angry in my heart." What is operating here is something which Marx appropriately termed "the dull compulsion of economic relations"— a compulsion which can occur only against a background of expected repression (Marx, 1970: 737). Lacking any realistic possibility, for the time being, of directly and collectively redressing their situation, the village poor have little choice but to adjust, as best they can, to the circumstances they confront daily. Tenants may bitterly resent the rent they must pay for their small plot, but they must pay it or lose the land; the near-landless may deplore the loss of wage-work, but they must scramble for the few opportunities available; they may harbor deep animosities toward the clique which dominates village politics, but they must act with circumspection if they wish to benefit from any of the small advantages which that clique can confer.

At least two aspects of this grudging, pragmatic adaptation to the realities merit emphasis. The first is that it does not rule out *certain* forms of resistance, although it surely sets limits that only the foolhardy would transgress. The second is that it is, above all, pragmatic; it does not at all imply normative consent to those

JAMES C. SCOTT

realities. To understand this is simply to grasp what is, in all likelihood, the situation for most subordinate classes historically. They struggle under conditions which are largely not of their own making and their pressing material needs necessitate something of a daily accommodation to those conditions. If much of the "conforming" day-to-day public behavior of the poor in Sedaka reflects the realities of immediate power relations, there is surely no need to assume that it drives from some symbolic hegemony, let alone, consensus. The duress of the quotidian is quite sufficient.

THE EFFORT TO STOP THE COMBINE

The introduction of combine-harvesting, the most sudden and devastating of the changes associated with double-cropping, also stirred the most active resistance. This resistance went well beyond arguments about its efficiency, the complaints over lost wages, and the slander directed against those who hired the combine. Throughout the rice bowl of Kedah there were efforts physically to obstruct its entry into the field, incidents of arson and sabotage, and widespread attempts to organise "strikes" of transplanters against those who first hired the machine. All of these actions ultimately failed to prevent the mechanisation of the paddy harvest, although they undoubtedly limited and delayed it somewhat.

Sabotage and obstruction of the combines began as early as 1970 when a few small experimental machines were used in field trials. It was only in 1976, however, that large-scale commercial machine harvesting—and therefore widespread acts of vengeance—began. Officials of the Muda Agricultural Development Authority chose to speak simply of "vandalism". Batteries were removed from the machines and thrown into irrigation ditches, carburettors and other vital parts such as distributors and air filters were smashed; sand and mud were put into the gas tank, and various objects (stones, wire, nails) were thrown into the augers. At least one combine was burned. A small group of men awoke the night watchman sleeping in the cab, ordered him down, and, using the kerosene they had brought along, set the machine on fire. In a good many villages, veiled rumors of possible violence persuaded many large farmers to hesitate before hiring a combine. Such tactics in one village actually prevented any machine harvesting for three full seasons. Two aspects of this sabotage and associated threats deserve particular emphasis. First, it was clear that the goal of the saboteurs was not simple theft, for nothing was actually stolen. Second, *all* of the sabotage was carried out at night by individuals or small groups acting anonymously. They were, furthermore, shielded by their fellow villagers who, if they knew who was involved, claimed total ignorance when the police came to investigate. As a result, no prosecutions were ever made. The practice of posting a night watchman to guard the combine dates from these early trials.

At about the same time there were the beginnings of a quiet but more collective effort by women to bring pressure to bear on the farmers who hired the machines. Men and women—often from the same family—had, of course, each lost work to the combine, but it was only the women who still had any real bargaining power. They were, for the time being, still in control of transplanting. The group of women (*kumpulan share*) who reaped a farmer's land was typically the same group that had earlier transplanted the same field. They were losing roughly half their seasonal earnings and they understandably resented transplanting a crop for a farmer who would use the combine at harvest time. Thus, in Sedaka and, it appears, throughout much of the Muda region, such women resolved to organise a boycott (*boikot*) that would deny transplanting services to their employers who hired the combine.

Three of the five "share groups" in Sedaka made some attempts to enforce such a boycott. Each group was composed of anywhere from six to nine village women. The remaining two groups did not participate but they refused to help break the boycott by planting for any farmer who was being "boycotted" by one of the other three gangs. Why the groups of Rosni, Kokiah, and Mariam took the initiative is not entirely clear. They are composed of women from families which are, on average, slightly poorer than those in the remaining two groups, but only slightly. If we rely on local explanations for the pattern of resistance, the consensus is that Rosni and Kokiah depend heavily on wage labor to support their families and are, at the same time, "courageous" (*berani*).

The boycott actually represented a very cautious form of resistance. At *no* time was there ever an open confrontation between a farmer who used the combine and his transplanters. Instead, the anonymous and indirect approach of rumors and hints (*cara sembunyi tau*) with which we are familiar was employed. The women *let it be known* through intermediaries that the group was not pleased (*tak puas hati*) with the loss of harvest work and would be reluctant (*segan*) to transplant the fields of those who had hired the combine the previous season. They also "let it be known" that when and if a combine broke down in the course of the harvest, a farmer who then wanted to get his crop in by hand could not count on his old workers to bail him out.

When it came time, at the beginning of the irrigated season of 1977, to make good this threat, circumspection again prevailed. None of the three groups refused outright to transplant paddy for those who had harvested with the combine in the previous season. Rather, they delayed; the head of the share group would tell the offending farmer that they were busy and could not get to his land just yet. Only a dozen or so farmers had used the combine the previous season, so the share groups had a good deal of work to occupy them just transplanting the crops of those who had not mechanised. The transplanters thus kept their options open; they avoided a direct refusal to transplant which would have provoked an open break. Fully abreast of the rumors of a boycott, the farmers who had been put off became increasingly anxious as their nursery paddy (*semai*) was passing its prime and as they feared their crop might not be fully mature before the scheduled date for shutting off the supply of water. Their state of mind was not improved by the sight of their neighbor's newly transplanted fields next to their own vacant plots.

After more than two weeks of this war of nerves—this seeming boycott that never fully announced itself—six farmers "let it be known" indirectly that they were arranging for outside laborers to come and transplant their crops. The six were large farmers by village standards, cultivating a total of nearly 70 acres. They claimed in their defence, that they had pressed for a firm commitment for a transplanting date from their local share group and, only after being put off again, had they moved. At this point, the boycott collapsed. Each of the three share groups was faced with defections as women feared that this transplanting work would be permanently lost to outsiders. They hastily sent word that they would begin transplanting the land in question within the next few days. Three of the six farmers cancelled their arrangements with the outside gangs while the other three went ahead either because they felt it was too late to cancel or because they wished to teach the women a lesson. Transplanters came from the town of Yan (just outside the irrigation scheme) and from Singkir and Merbuk, further away. One farmer, Haji Salim, using his considerable political influence, arranged with local authorities to bring in a gang of Thai transplanters—a practice he has continued and for which he is bitterly resented.

The brief and abortive attempt to stop the combine by collective action was the subject of demoralised or self-satisfied post-mortems, depending on which side of the fence one happened to be. Aside from the pleasure or disappointment expressed, the post-mortems converged on the inevitability of the outcome. Even those with most to lose from mechanisation had realised that if their bluff were called, it would be nearly impossible to move beyond talk and vague threats. They agreed sadly that "it was just talk and we planted anyway. What could we do?" To have continued to refuse to transplant once outside laborers had been brought in would have meant further jeopardising an already precarious livelihood. The futility of such a refusal was more than once characterised by the use of a Malay saying closely approximating the English "cutting off your nose to spite your face". Or as the villager who became the local machine-broker put it: "The poor have to work anyway; they can't hold out." A healthy interest in survival required them to swallow their pride and return to work. In fact, the possibility of this outcome was implicit in the indirectness with which the boycott was conducted; an open confrontation and boycott would have meant burning bridges behind them. Instead they left open an avenue of retreat. In terms of public discourse the boycott was a non-event; it was never openly declared; it was thus never *openly* defeated; the use of delays and barely plausible excuses meant that the intention to boycott itself could be disavowed.

The goals of the attempted "strike" in Sedaka and innumerable other villages on the Kedah Plain were ambitious. The women aimed at nothing less than blocking a momentous change in production relations. Their means, as we have seen, however, were modest and disguised. And while they certainly failed to stop the mechanisation of the harvest, their attempt has not been completely futile.

JAMES C. SCOTT

There is little doubt that combine-harvesting would have been adopted more rapidly had it not been for the resistance. For poor villagers living at the margin the time gained has proved vital. Five years after the introduction of combines there are still five or six farmers who hire hand labor for some or all of their paddy harvest because, they say, their neighbors need the work. There is little doubt that they have been influenced by the underground campaign of slander and defamation waged against those who invariably hire the machines.

THE THEFT OF PADDY: ROUTINE RESISTANCE

The attempt to halt combine-harvesting, while hardly the stuff of high drama, was surely out of the ordinary. It took place against a rarely noticed background of routine resistance over wages, tenancy, rents, and the distribution of paddy that is a permanent feature of life in Sedaka and in any stratified agrarian setting. A close examination of this realm of struggle exposes an implicit form of local trade unionism which is reinforced both by mutuality among the poor and by a considerable amount of theft and violence against property. None of this activity poses a fundamental threat to the basic structure of agrarian inequalities, either materially or symbolically. What it does represent, however, is a constant process of testing and renegotiation of production relations between classes. On both sides—landlord-tenant, farmer-wage-laborer—there is a never-ending attempt to seize each small advantage and press it home, to probe the limits of the existing relationships, to see precisely what can be got away with at the margin, and to include this margin as a part of an accepted, or at least tolerated, territorial claim. Over the past decade the flow of this frontier battle has, or course, rather consistently favored the fortunes of the large farmers and landlords. They have not only swallowed large pieces of the territory defended by wage-workers and tenants but, in doing so, they have thereby reduced (through marginalization) the perimeter along which the struggle continues. Even along this reduced perimeter, however, there is constant pressure exerted by those who hope to regain at least a small patch of what they have grudgingly lost. The resisters require little explicit co-ordination to conduct this struggle, for the simple imperative of making a tolerable living is enough to make them dig in their heels.

The dimensions and conduct of this more "routine" resistance could fill volumes. For our purposes here, however, most of the basic issues raised by resistance of this kind can be seen in a particularly "popular" form it takes: the theft of the paddy. Rural theft by itself is unremarkable, it is nearly a permanent feature of stratified agrarian life whenever and wherever the state and its agents are insufficient to control it. When such theft takes on the dimensions of a struggle in which property rights are being contested, however, it may become an essential element of any careful analysis of class relations.

The amount of paddy stolen over a single season, while not large as a proportion of the total harvest, is alarming to the large farmers and, what is more, they believe that it is growing. No firm statistics are available, of course, but I made an effort to record all the losses of paddy reported to me during the 1979-80 main season. By far the largest category of thefts was the whole gunny sacks of threshed paddy left in the fields overnight during the harvest. These are listed below:

REPORTED THEFTS OF THRESHED PADDY BY THE SACK IN MAIN SEASON 1979-80	
Farmer	Reported Loss Gunny Sack(s)
Shahnon	1
Haji Kadir	1
Samat	1
Abu Hassan	2
Ghani Lebai Mat	1
Amin	2
Tok Long	2
Idris	1
Lebai Pendek	2
Fadzil	1
total	14

(Approximate cash value = M$532)

JAMES C. SCOTT

To this total one must add paddy that was spirited away in other ways. At least four gunny sacks of paddy drying in the sun on mats disappeared. Two very well-off farmers each lost a gunny sack which was stored beneath their respective houses. Something like the same quantity of paddy was reported stolen from rice barns (*jelapang*) in the course of the season. A small amount of paddy was reported taken on the stalk from the fields. How much is difficult to say, but the quantity is not substantial; villagers point out that the sound of threshing and the disposal of the straw would present a problem for the thief, while the rich claim that thieves are too lazy actually to put themselves to the trouble of threshing. Finally, a thorough accounting of paddy thefts would have to include some estimate of the grain which threshers are said to stuff into their pockets and inside their shirts at the end of the day's work. Such pilfering is "winked at" by most farmers and I have made no attempt to calculate how much paddy is appropriated in this way during the harvest.

Certain facts about the pattern of theft are worth noting. The first is that, with the exception of two farmers who are only modestly well-off, all of the victims are among the wealthiest third of Sedaka's households. This may indicate nothing more than the obvious fact that such households are likely to have more paddy lying in the field at harvest time and that smallholders, who can ill afford the loss, take pains to get the threshed paddy to their house quickly. It is certainly true that large farmers with plots far from their houses that cannot be threshed (and hence stored) in a single day are the most prone to such losses. But here it is significant to realise that the pattern of theft is an artifact of the pattern of property relations prevailing in Sedaka. The rich, by and large, possess what is worth taking while the poor have the greatest incentive to take it. No one doubts either that poor men, *local* poor men at that, are responsible for the vast majority of the paddy thefts.

The total amount of paddy stolen, perhaps 20 to 25 gunny sacks, is less than one-hundredth of the paddy harvested in a season by all village farmers. By this measure, the losses are fairly trivial and are borne largely by those who produce a substantial surplus. If, however, we measure its significance by what it may add to the food supply of a few of the poorest families in the village, then it may be quite significant. If is of some interest that these 20 to 25 gunny sacks of paddy are more than half the quantity of grain given *volun-*

tarily by farmers as an Islamic tithe (*zakat peribadi*) after the harvest. The comparison is apt precisely because I twice heard poor men refer smilingly to paddy thefts (*curian padi*) as "*zakat peribadi* that one takes on his own" (*zakat peribadi, angkat sindiri*). This evidence is certainly not conclusive—but it is entirely possible that some of the poor, at any rate, consider such acts not so much as theft but as the appropriation of what they feel entitled to by earlier custom—a kind of forcible poor tax to replace the gifts and wages they no longer receive. In this connection, two other items of circumstantial evidence are relevant. Only one of the farmers who lost paddy (Samat) was among those ever praised by the poor for their reluctance to hire the combine, while all the others have used the machine whenever possible. There is also some indication that paddy thefts may be used as a sanction by disgruntled laborers. Thus Sukur once told me that farmers were careful to hire the threshers they had customarily invited since anyone who was omitted might, in his anger, steal paddy from the fields. If, indeed, the theft of paddy has a certain element of popular justice to it, the scope for such resistance has been considerably narrowed by the use of combines which make it possible to gather and store (or sell) a farmer's entire crop in a single day. Combines thus not only eliminate hand reaping, hand threshing, in-field transport, and gleaning; they also tend to eliminate theft.

The attitude of wealthy farmers toward such thefts is a combination of anger, as one might expect, and also *fear*. Haji Kadir, for example, was furious enough over his loss to consider spending the following night in the fields guarding his paddy with his shotgun. He did not follow through because he reasoned that the mere rumor that he might lie in wait would be sufficient to deter any thief. The element of fear can be gauged, in part, by the fact that no police report of a paddy theft has ever been made in Sedaka. Wealthy farmers explained to me that if they made such a report and named a suspect, word would get around quickly and they feared that they would then become a target for more thefts. Haji Kadir, the wealthiest farmer in the village, once spied someone stealing a gunny sack at night from a neighbor's field. Not only did he fail to intervene to stop the theft, but he would not even inform his neighbor, even though he was certain about the identity of the thief. When I asked him why, he replied that the thief had seen him too, would know he was the informer, and would steal his paddy next. In an earlier season, Mat Sarif lost two gunny sacks but told me that he did not *want* to know who did it. Old and quite frail, he added simply, "I'm afraid of being killed (*takut mampus*)." For a handful of the more daring village poor, it would appear that something of a small balance of terror has been struck that permits such limited pilfering to continue.

Other forms of resistance by the poor of Sedaka vary in particulars but not in general contour. One distinguishing mark of virtually all resistance in Sedaka is the relative absence of any open confrontation between classes. Where resistance is collective, it is carefully circumspect; where it is an individual or small group attack on property, it is anonymous and usually nocturnal. By its calculated prudence and secrecy it preserves, for the most part, the on-stage theatre of power which dominates public life in Sedaka. Any intention to storm the stage can be disavowed and options are consciously kept open. Deference and conformity, though rarely cringing, continue to be the public posture of the poor. For all that, however, backstage one can clearly make out a continuous testing of limits.

Resistance in Sedaka has virtually nothing that one expects to find in the typical history of rural conflict. There are no riots, no demonstrations, no arson, no organised social banditry, no open violence. The resistance we have discovered is not linked to any larger outside political movements, ideologies, or revolutionary cadres—although it is clear that similar struggles have been occurring in virtually any village in the region. The sorts of activities found here *require* little co-ordination, let along political organisation, though they might benefit from it. They are, in short, forms of struggle that are almost entirely indigenous to the village sphere. Providing that we are careful about the use of the term, these activities might appropriately be called *primitive* resistance. The use of "primitive" does not imply, as Hobsbawm does, that they are somehow backward and destined to give way to more sophisticated ideologies and tactics.[7] It implies only that such forms of resistance are the nearly permanent, continuous, daily strategies of subordinate rural classes under difficult conditions. At times of crisis or momentous political change they may be complemented by other forms of struggle which are more opportune. They are unlikely, however, to disappear altogether so long as the rural social structure remains

EVERYDAY FORMS OF PEASANT RESISTANCE

exploitative and inequitable. They are the stubborn bedrock upon which other forms of resistance may grow and they are likely to persist *after* such other forms of resistance have failed or produced, in turn, a new pattern of inequity.

II. What counts as Resistance

But can the activities we have described and others like them be seen as resistance? Can we call a boycott that was never even announced, class resistance? Why should we consider the theft of a few gunny sacks of paddy as a form of class resistance; there was no collective action nor was there any open challenge to the system of property and domination. Many of the same questions could be raised about gossip and character assassination which is one of the principle means by which the poor of Sedaka consistently try to influence the behavior of the well-to-do.

As a first approximation, I propose the following definition for peasant class resistance—one that would include many of the activities we have discussed. The purpose behind this definition is not to settle these important issues by fiat, but rather to highlight the conceptual problems we face in understanding resistance and to make what I believe to be a plausible case in a rather wide understanding of the term.

> Lower class resistance among peasants is any act(s) by member(s) of the class that is (are) intended either to mitigate or to deny claims (e.g. rents, taxes, deference) made on that class by superordinate classes (e.g. landlord, the state, owners of machinery, moneylenders) or to advance its own claims (e.g. work, land, charity, respect) vis-à-vis these superordinate classes.

Three aspects of the definition merit brief comment. First, there is no requirement that resistance take the form of collective action. Second—and it is a very nettlesome issue—intentions are built into the definition. We return to this problem again but, for the moment, the formulation allows the fact that many intended acts of resistance may backfire and produce consequences that were entirely unanticipated. Finally, the definition recognizes what we might call sym-

JAMES C. SCOTT

bolic or ideological resistance (for example, gossip, slander, rejecting imposed categories, the withdrawal of deference) as an integral part of class-based resistance.

The problem of intentions is enormously complex and not simply because the as-yet-unapprehended paddy thieves of our earlier example are unwilling to be identified, let alone to discuss their intentions once they have been located. The larger issue has to do with our tendency to think of resistance as actions that involve at least some short-run individual or collective sacrifice in order to bring about a longer-range collective gain. The immediate losses of a strike, a boycott, or even the refusal to compete with other members of one's class for land or work are obvious cases in point. When it comes to acts like theft, however, we encounter a combination of immediate individual gain and what *may* be resistance. How are we to judge which of the two purposes is uppermost or decisive? What is at stake here is not a petty definitional matter but rather the interpretation of a whole range of actions which seem to me to lie historically at the core of everyday class relations. The English poacher in the eighteenth century *may* have been resisting gentry's claim to property in wild game, but he was just as surely interested in rabbit stew. The South-east Asian peasant who hid his rice and possessions from the tax collector may have been protesting high taxes, but he was just as surely seeing to it that his family would have enough rice until the next harvest. The peasant conscript who deserted the army may have been a war resister, but he was just as surely saving his own skin by fleeing the front. Which of these inextricably fused motives are we to take as paramount? Even if we were *able* to ask the actors in question and even if they could reply candidly, it is not at all clear that they would be able to make a clear determination.

Students of slavery, who have looked into this matter most closely, if only because such forms of self-help were frequently the only option open, have tended to discount such actions as "real" resistance. "Real" resistance, it is argued, is (a) organised, systematic, and co-operative, (b) principled or selfless, (c) has revolutionary consequences, and/or (d) embodies ideas or intentions that negate the basis of domination itself. "Token", incidental, or epiphenomenal "activities" by contrast are (a) unorganised, unsystematic and individual, (b) opportunistic and "self-indulgent", (c)

have no revolutionary consequences, and/or (d) imply, in their intention or logic, an accommodation with the system of domination.
Now these distinctions are important for any analysis which has as
its objective the attempt to delineate the various forms of resistance
and to show how they are related to one another and to the form
of domination in which they occur. My quarrel is rather with the
contention that the latter forms are, ultimately, trivial or inconsequential, while only the former can be said to constitute real resistance. This position, in my view, fundamentally misconstrues the
very basis of the economic and political struggle conducted daily by
subordinate classes—not only slaves, but peasants and workers as
well—in repressive settings.

Let us begin with the question of actions which are "self-indulgent", individual, and unorganised, because such acts intrinsically
lack revolutionary *consequences*. This *may* often be the case, but it
is also the case that there is hardly a modern revolution that can
be successfully explained without reference to precisely such acts
when they take place on a massive scale. The Russian Revolution
is a striking case in point. Growing desertions from the largely
peasant rank-and-file of the Tsarist army in the summer of 1917
were a major and indispensable part of the revolutionary process
in at least two respects. First, they were responsible for the collapse
of the main institution of repression of the Tsarist state—an institution which had earlier, in 1905, put down another revolutionary
upheaval. Second, the deserters contributed directly to the revolutionary process in the countryside by participating in the seizures
of land throughout the core provinces of European Russia. And it
is abundantly clear that the haemorrhage in the Tsarist forces was
largely "self-indulgent", "unorganised", and "individual"—although
thousands and thousands of individuals threw down their arms and
headed home. The attack into Austria had been crushed with huge
losses of troops and officers; the ration of bread had been reduced
and "fast-days" inaugurated at the front; the soldiers knew,
moreover, that if they stayed at the front they might miss the chance
to gain from the land seizures breaking out in the countryside.
Desertion offered the peasant conscripts the chance of saving their
skins and of returning home where bread and, now land, were available. The risks were minimal since discipline in the army had dissolved. One can hardly imagine a set of more "self-indulgent" goals.

JAMES C. SCOTT

But it was just such self-indulgent ends, acted on by unorganised masses of "self-demobilized" peasant soldiers which made the Revolution possible (Carr, 1966: 103).

The disintegration of the Tsarist army is but one of many instances where the aggregation of a host of petty, self-interested acts of insubordination or desertion, with no revolutionary intent, have created a revolutionary situation. The dissolution of the Nationalist armies of Chiang Kai-shek in 1948 or of Saigon's army in 1975 could no doubt be analysed among similar lines. And long before the final debacle, acts of insubordination and non-compliance in each army— as well as in the US Army serving in Vietnam, it should be added— had set sharp limits on what the counter-revolutionary forces could expect and require of their own rank-and-file. Resistance of this kind is, of course, not a monopoly of the counter-revolution as George Washington and Emiliano Zapata, among others, discovered. We can imagine that the eminently personal logic of Pedro Martinez, a some-time soldier with the Zapatista forces, was not markedly different from that of the Tsarist soldiers leaving the front.

> That's where [battle of Tizapán] I finally had it. The battle was something awful! The shooting was tremendous! It was a completely bloody battle, three days and three nights. But I took it for one day and then I left. I quit the army...I said to myself, "It's time now I got back to my wife, to my little children. I'm getting out...." I said to myself, "No, my family comes first and they are starving. Now I'm leaving." (Lewis, 1964: 102).

The refreshing candor of Pedro Martinez serves to remind us that there is no necessary relationship between the banality of the act of self-preservation and family obligations on the one hand and the banality of the consequences of such acts. Multiplied many times, acts that could in no way be considered "political" may have the most massive consequences for states as well as armies.

The issue here is by no means confined to desertion from armies which has been chosen only as a diagnostic illustration. It applies with nearly equal force to the tradition of peasant flight, to theft, to the shirking of corvée labor; the consequences of such acts of self-help may be all out of proportion to the trifling intentions of the actors themselves.

To ignore the self-interested element in peasant resistance is to ignore the determinate context, not only of peasant politics, but of most lower class politics. It is precisely the fusion of self-interest and resistance that is the vital force animating the resistance of peasants and proletarians. When a peasant hides part of his crop to avoid paying taxes, he is both filling his stomach and depriving the state of grain. When a peasant soldier deserts the army because the food is bad and his crops at home are ripe, he is both looking after himself and denying the state cannon fodder. When such acts are rare and isolated, they are of little interest; but when they become a consistent pattern (even though uncoordinated, let alone organised) we are dealing with resistance. The intrinsic nature and, in one sense, the "beauty" of much peasant resistance is that it often confers immediate and concrete advantages while at the same time denying resources to the appropriating classes *and* that it requires little or no manifest organisation. The stubbornness and force of such resistance flows directly from the fact that it is so firmly rooted in the shared material struggle experienced by a class.

To require of lower class resistance that it somehow be "principled" or "selfless" is not only a slander on the moral status of fundamental human needs. It is, more fundamentally, a misconstruction of the basis of class struggle which is, first and foremost, a struggle over the appropriation of work, production, property, and taxes. "Bread-and-butter" issues are the essence of lower class politics and resistance. Consumption, from this perspective, is both the goal and the result of resistance and counter-resistance. This is then the self-interested core of routine class struggle: the often defensive effort to mitigate or defeat appropriation. Petty thefts of grain or pilfering on the threshing floor may seem like trivial "coping" mechanisms from one vantage point; but from a broader view of class relations, how the harvest is actually divided belongs at the center.

A further advantage of a concept of resistance which begins with self-interested material needs is that it is far more in keeping with how "class" is first experienced by the historical actors themselves. Here, I subscribe wholeheartedly to the judgement reached by E.P. Thompson on the basis of his own compelling analysis of working class history.

In my view, far too much theoretical attention (much of

JAMES C. SCOTT

it plainly a-historical) has been paid to "class" and far too little to "class-struggle". Indeed, class struggle is the prior, as well as the more universal, concept. To put it bluntly, classes do not exist as separate entities, look around, find an enemy class, and then start to struggle. On the contrary, people find themselves in a society structured in determined ways (crucially, but not exclusively, in productive relations), they experience exploitation (or the need to maintain power over those whom they exploit), they identify points of antagonistic interest, they commence to struggle around these issues and in the process of struggling they discover themselves as classes, they come to know this discovery as class-consciousness. Class and class consciousness are always the *last*, not the first, stage in the real historical process. (1978: 149).

The inclination to dismiss "individual" acts of resistance as insignificant and to reserve the term of "resistance" for collective or organised action is as misguided as the emphasis on "principled" action. The privileged status accorded organised movements, I suspect, flows from either of two political orientations: the one, essentially Leninist, which regards the only viable class action as that which is led by a vanguard party serving as a "general-staff", the other more straightforwardly derived from a familiarity and preference for open, institutionalised politics as conducted in capitalist democracies. In either case, however, there is a misapprehension of the social and political circumstances within which peasant resistance is typically carried out.

The individual and often anonymous quality of much peasant resistance is, of course, eminently suited to the sociology of the class from which it arises. Being scattered in small communities and generally lacking the institutional means to act collectively, it is likely to employ those means of resistance which are local and require little co-ordination. Under special historical circumstances of overwhelming material deprivation, a break-down in the institutions of repression, or the protection of political liberty (more rarely, all three) the peasantry can and has become an organised, political, mass movement. Such circumstances are, however, extremely rare and usually short-lived. In most places at most times these political options have simply been precluded. The penchant for forms of resistance that are individual and unobtrusive are not only what a Marxist might expect from petty commodity producers and rural laborers, but they also have certain advantages. Unlike hierarchical formal organisations, there is no center, no leadership, no identifiable structure that can be co-opted or neutralized. What is lacking in terms of central co-ordination may be compensated for by flexibility and persistence. These forms of resistance will win no set-piece battles but they are admirably adopted to long-run campaigns of attrition.

If we are to confine our search for peasant resistance to formally organised activity we would search largely in vain, for in Malaysia as in many other Third World countries, such organisations are either absent or are the creations of officials and rural elites. We would simply miss much of what is happening. Formal political activity may be the norm for the elites, the intelligentsia, and the middle classes in the Third World as well as in the West, who have a near-monopoly of institutional skills and access, but it would be naive to expect that peasant resistance can or will normally take the same form.

Nor should we forget that the forms of peasant resistance are not just a product of the social ecology of the peasantry. The parameters of resistance are also set, in part, by the institutions of repression. To the extent that such institutions do their "work" effectively, they may all but preclude any forms of resistance other than the individual, the informal, and the clandestine. Thus, it is perfectly legitimate—even important—to distinguish between various levels and forms of resistance: formal-informal, individual-collective, public-anonymous, those which challenge the system of domination—those which aim at marginal gains. But it should, at the same time, be made crystal clear that what we may actually be measuring in this enterprise is the level of repression which structures the options which are available. Depending on the circumstances they confront, peasants may oscillate from organised electoral activity to violent confrontations, to silent and anonymous acts of footdragging and theft. This oscillation may, in some cases, be due to changes in the social organisation of the peasantry, but it is as, if not more, likely to be due to changes in the level of repression. More than one peasantry has been brutally reduced from open, radical political activity at one moment to stubborn and sporadic acts

JAMES C. SCOTT

of petty resistance at the next. If we allow ourselves to call only the former "resistance", we simply allow the structure of domination to define for us what is resistance and what is not resistance.

Many of the forms of resistance we have been examining may be "individual" actions, but this is not to say that they are uncoordinated. Here again, a concept of co-ordination derived from formal and bureaucratic settings is of little assistance in understanding actions in small communities with dense informal networks and rich, and historically deep, sub-cultures of resistance to outside claims. It is, for example, no exaggeration to say that much of the folk-culture of the peasant "little tradition" amounts to a legitimation, or even a *celebration,* of precisely the kinds of evasive and cunning forms of resistance we have examined. In this and in other ways (for example, tales of bandits, peasant heroes, religious myths) the peasant sub-culture helps to underwrite dissimulation, poaching, theft, tax evasion, avoidance of conscription and so on. While folk-culture is not co-ordination in the formal sense, it often achieves a "climate of opinion" which, in other more institutionalised societies, would require a public relations campaign. The striking thing about peasant society is the extent to which a whole range of complex activities from labor-exchange to house moving to wedding preparations, to feasts are co-ordinated by networks of understanding and practice. It is the same with boycotts, wage "negotiations", the refusal of tenants to compete with one another, or the conspiracy of silence surrounding thefts. No formal organisations are created because none are required; and yet a form of co-ordination is achieved which alerts us that what is happening is not just individual action.

In light of these considerations, then, let us return briefly to the question of intention. For many forms of peasant resistance, we have every reason to expect that the actors will remain *mute* about their intentions. Their safety may depend on silence and anonymity; the kind of resistance itself may depend for its effectiveness on the *appearance* of conformity; their intentions may be so embedded in the peasant subculture *and* in the routine, taken-for-granted struggle to provide for the subsistence and survival of the household so as to remain inarticulate. The fish do not talk about the water.

In one sense, of course, their intentions are inscribed in the acts themselves. A peasant soldier who, like others, deserts the army is, in effect, saying by his act that the purposes of this institution and the risks and hardships it entails will not prevail over his family or personal needs. To put it another way, the state and its army has failed sufficiently to commit this particular subject to its enterprise so as to retain his compliance. A harvest laborer who steals paddy from his employer is "saying" that his need for rice takes precedence over the formal property rights of his boss.

When it comes to those social settings where the *material interests* of appropriating classes are directly in conflict with the peasantry (rents, wages, employment, taxes, conscription, the division of the harvest) we can, I think, infer something of intentions from the nature of the actions themselves. This is especially the case when there is a systematic pattern of actions which mitigate or deny a claim on their surplus. Evidence about intentions is, of course, always welcome but we should not expect too much. For this reason, the definition of resistance given earlier places particular emphasis on the effort to thwart material and symbolic claims from dominant classes. The goal, after all, of the great bulk of peasant resistance is not directly to overthrow or transform a system of domination but rather to survive—today, this week, this season— within it. The usual goal of peasants, as Hobsbawm has so aptly put it, is *"working the system to their minimum disadvantage"* (1973: 12). Their persistent attempts to "nibble away" may backfire, they may marginally alleviate exploitation, they may amount to a renegotiation of the limits of appropriation, they may change the course of subsequent development, and they may more rarely help bring the system down. These, however, are possible consequences. Their intention, by contrast, is nearly always survival and persistence. The pursuit of that end may require, depending on circumstances, either the petty resistance we have seen or more dramatic actions of self-defense. In any event, most of their efforts will be seen by appropriating classes as truculence, deceit, shirking, pilfering, arrogance—in short, all the labels devised to denigrate the many faces of resistance. The definition of appropriating classes may, at other times, transform what amounts to nothing more than the unreflective struggle for subsistence into an act of defiance.

It should be apparent that resistance is not simply whatever peasants do to maintain themselves and their households. Much of what they do is to be understood as compliance, however grudging.

JAMES C. SCOTT

Survival as petty commodity producers or laborers may impel some to save themselves at the expense of their fellows. The poor landless laborer who steals paddy from another poor man or who outbids him for a tenancy is surviving but he is surely not resisting in the sense defined here. One of the key questions that must be asked about any system of domination is the extent to which it succeeds in reducing subordinate classes to purely "beggar thy neighbor" strategies for survival. Certain combinations of atomisation, terror, repression, and pressing material needs can indeed achieve the ultimate dream of domination: to have the dominated exploit each other.

Allowing that only those survival strategies which deny or mitigate claims from appropriating classes can be called resistance, we are nevertheless left with a vast range of actions to consider. Their variety conceals a basic continuity. That continuity lies in the history of the persistent efforts of relatively autonomous petty commodity producers to defend their fundamental material and physical interests and to reproduce themselves. At different times and places they have defended themselves against the corvée, taxes, and conscription of the traditional agrarian state, against the colonial state, against the inroads of capitalism (for example, rents, interest, proletarianisation, mechanisation), against the modern capitalist state and, it should be added, against many purportedly socialist states as well. The revolution, when and if it does come, may eliminate many of the worst evils of the ancien régime, but it is rarely if ever the end of peasant resistance. For the radical elites who capture the state are likely to have different goals in mind than their erstwhile peasant supporters. They may envisage a collectivised agriculture while the peasantry clings to its smallholdings; they may want a centralised political structure while the peasantry is wedded to local autonomy; they may want to tax the countryside in order to industrialise; and they will almost certainly wish to strengthen the state *vis-à-vis* civil society. It therefore becomes possible for an astute observer like Goran Hyden to find remarkable parallels between the earlier resistance of the Tanzanian peasantry to colonialism and capitalism and its *current* resistance to the institutions and policies of the *socialist* state of Tanzania today (Hyden, 1980: *passim*). He provides a gripping account of how the "peasant mode of production"—by footdragging, by privatising work and land that have been appropriated by the state, by evasion, by flight, and by "raiding" government programs for its own purposes—has thwarted the plans of the state. In Vietnam, also, after the revolution was consummated in the south as well as in the north, everyday forms of peasant resistance have continued. The surreptitious expansion of private plots, the withdrawal of labor from state enterprises for household production, the failure to deliver grain and livestock to the state, the "appropriation" of state credits and resources by households and work teams, and the steady growth of the black market, attest to the tenacity of petty commodity production under socialist state forms. The stubborn, persistent, and irreducible forms of resistance we have been examining may thus represent the truly durable weapons of the weak both before and *after* the revolution.

Notes

1. See, for example, Barrington Moore, Jr., *The Social Basis of Dictatorship and Democracy* (Boston: Boston Press, 1966); Jeffrey M. Paige, *Agrarian Revolution: Social Movements and Export Agriculture in the Underdeveloped World* (New York: Free Press, 1975); Eric R. Wolf, *Peasant Wars of the Twentieth Century* (New Haven: Yale University Press, 1976); Samuel L. Popkin, *The Rational Peasant* (Berkeley: University of California Press, 1969).

2. For an example of such temporary gains, see the fine study by E.J. Hobsbawm and George Rudé, *Captain Swing* (New York: Pantheon Books, 1968), pp.281-99.

3. Some of these issues are examined in Scott, "Revolution in the Revolution: Peasants and Commisars", *Theory and Society*, Vol. 7. Nos. 1, 2 (1979). pp.97-134.

4. See the amount and analysis by Michael Adas, "From Avoidance to Confrontation: Peasant Protests in Precolonial and Colonial Southeast Asia", *Comparative Studies in Society and History*, Vol. 23, No. 2 (April 1981), pp.217-47.

5. R.C. Cobb, *The Police and The People: French Popular Protest, 1789-1820* (Oxford: Clarendon Press, 1970), pp.96-97. For a gripping account of self-mutilation to avoid conscription, see Emile Zola, *La Terre*, translated by Parmée. (Harmondsworth: Penguin, 1980).

6. For a fascinating account of such resistance in Tanzania, see Goran Hyden, *Beyond Ujamaa In Tanzania* (London: Heinemann, 1980). For the consequences of short-sighted agrarian policy imposed from above see Robert Bates, *Markets and States in*

Tropical Africa: The Political Basis of Agricultural Policies (Berkeley: University of California Press, 1981).

References

Adas, Michael
1981 "From Avoidance to Confrontation: Peasant Protest in Precolonial and Colonial Southeast Asia", Comparative Studies in Society and History, Vol. 23, No. 2, April, pp.217-47.

Bates, Robert
1981 Markets and States in Tropical Africa: The Political Basis of Agricultural Policies, Berkeley: University of California Press.

Carr, E.H.
1966 The Bolshevik Revolution: 1917-1923, Vol. 1, Harmondsworth: Penguin.

Cobb, R.C.
1970 The Police and the People: French Popular Protest, 1789-1820 Oxford: Clarendon Press.

Davies, R.W.
1980 The Socialist Offensive: The Collectivisation of Soviet Agriculture, 1928-1930, London: Macmillan.

Ferro, Marc
1971 "The Russian Soldier in 1917: Undisciplined, Patriotic, and Revolutionary", Slavic Review, Vol. 30, No. 3, Sept.

Genovese, Eugene
1974 Roll, Jordan Roll, New York: Pantheon Books.

Ghee, Lim Tech
1977 Peasants and their Agricultural Economy in Colonial Malaya, 1874-1941, Kuala Lumpur: Oxford University Press.

Hobsbawm, Eric J. and George Rudé
1968 Captain Swine, New York: Pantheon Books.

Hobsbawm, Eric J.
1965 Primitive Rebels: Studies in Archaic Forms of Social Movement in the 19th and 20th Centuries, New York: Norton.
1973 "Peasants and Politics", Journal of Peasant Studies, Vol. 1, No. 1.

Hyden, Goran
1980 Beyond Ujamaa in Tanzania, London: Heinemann.

Lewis, Oscar
1964 Pedro Martinez: A Mexican Peasant and his Family, New York: Vintage Books.

Marx, Karl
1970 Capital, Vol. 1. London.

EVERYDAY FORMS OF PEASANT RESISTANCE

Moore, Barrington, Jr.
   1966   *The Social Basis of Dictatorship and Democracy*, Boston: Beacon Press.
   1978   *Injustice*, White Plains, New York: M.E. Sharpe.

Mullin, Gerald
   1972   *Flight and Rebellion*, New York: Oxford University Press.

Nonini, Donald M., Paul Diener and Eugene E. Robkin
   1979   "Ecology and Evolution: Population, Primitive Accumulation, and the Malay Peasantry", unpublished ms.

Paige, Jeffrey M.
   1975   *Agrarian Revolution: Social Movements and Export Agriculture in the Under-developed World*, New York: Free Press.

Patnaik, Utsa
   1979   "Neo-populism and Marxism: The Chayanovian View of the Agrarian Question and its Fundamental Fallacy," *Journal of Peasant Studies*, Vol. 6, No. 4, July.

Popkin, Samuel L.
   1969   *The Rational Peasant*, Berkeley: University of California Press.

Rudé, George
   1964   *The Crowd in History, 1730-1848*, New York: Wiley and Sons.

Scott, James C.
   1976   *The Moral Economy of the Peasant*, New Haven: Yale University Press.
   1979   "Revolution in the Revolution: Peasants and Commisars". *Theory and Society*, Vol. 7, No. 1.
   1984   *Everyday Forms of Peasant Resistance*, New Haven: Yale University Press.

Skocpol, Theda
   1979   *States and Social Revolutions*, Cambridge: Cambridge University Press.

Thompson, E.P.
   "The Crime of Anonymity" in Douglas Hay *et al.*, *Albion's Fatal Tree*.

Thompson, E.P.
   "Eighteenth-Century English Society: Class Struggle Without Class?", *Social History*, Vol. 398-399.

Wildman, Allan
   1970   "The February Revolution in the Russian Army", *Soviet Studies*, Vol. 22, No. 1, July.

Wolf, Eric R.
   1969   *Peasant Wars of the Twentieth Century*, New York: Harper and Row.

Zola, Emile
   1980   *La Terre*, translated by Douglas Parmée, Harmondsworth: Penguin.

Consuming Culture:
A Study of Simple
Commodity Consumption

Jean-Marc Philibert

Anthropologists have from the start been interested in non-Western economic systems as the work of Malinowski (1922), Mauss (1923), and Firth (1936) shows. However, they focused their research almost exclusively on traditional forms of exchange and reciprocity, therefore neglecting production and consumption, the other two components of economic systems. Moreover, the theoretical debate which raged on for almost 40 years in the field of Economic Anthropology over the usefulness of concepts derived from formal Economics to understand non-market forms of exchange was particularly sterile and, when seen from the perspectives of the 1980s, a little silly.

The 1960s brought a welcome respite from this debate in the form of French neo-Marxism which, by shifting the focus to pre-capitalist modes of production, produced an analytic breakthrough. It is in part to this influence that we owe the present-day concern with social contexts of appropriation, power and domination in pre-capitalist societies. More recently, as a result of anthropologists growing increasingly dissatisfied with a mode of production approach that reifies the economic domain to the neglect of other dimensions of culture, some have turned to the study of consumption. For this to happen, consumption had to cease to be seen as the largely unproblematical provisioning of natural and social "needs". In other words, a way had to be found to move away from a theory of needs, without a doubt the least theoretically promising way to look at this rich social phenomenon.

Jean-Marc Philibert tries in this article to put forward a programmatic statement of areas we should investigate. He

*proposes to look at consumption as an ideological act, rather than
a material one, through which people construct messages about
themselves, thus approaching it from the perspective of Symbolic
Anthropology; he is at the same time concerned with consumption
at the interface of Western and Third World societies, so bringing
it within the sphere of political economy. When members of Third
World societies consume Western goods, they borrow at the same
time ideas and perceptions responsible for the existence of these
goods in the first place: the consumption of Western goods is also
the consumption of signs and ideas associated with international
capitalism. This raises the issue of whether or not the people
studied by Anthropology can resist this sort of ideological penetration; do they have the cultural means to refuse or oppose foreign
systems of ideas, from clothes and transportation to medical and
educational systems; finally, must the end product necessarily be
a sort of cultural subjugation.*

*This article is made up of three parts: the first is a brief review
of existing models of consumption in pre-capitalist and capitalist
societies; the second examines the tie between consumption and
power in the shape of hegemony; the third looks at consumption
as at a form of "silent production". Throughout this article,
Philibert relies on ethnographic data from Vanuatu to illustrate
the process of cultural categorization at work in patterns of consumption.*

*Neo-Marxist theory has forced us to confront the culture of
capitalism which underpins our social theories and significantly
limits our sociological imagination. Philibert suggests that the
study of consumption in societies located at the periphery of the
First Third World is particularly important in this respect as it is
there that the capitalist structure of comprehension underpinning
our social theories is more easily apprehended.*

Introduction

THE TERM SIMPLE COMMODITY CONSUMPTION will no doubt
amuse or annoy, depending on how punctilious one is towards Marxist terminology. This pseudo-Marxist concept is used first to suggest
that insights into consumption can profitably result from a neo-Marxist approach and, second, to ask whether or not there is in the
field of consumption an analog to simple commodity production.

It may not seem obvious at first that an approach considering

JEAN-MARC PHILIBERT

production as the diagnostic dimension of economic systems has a great deal to contribute to an understanding of consumption. But it has, if one is willing to set aside for a moment the dimension of utility, the materialistic aspect of consumption as it were, and to examine it as a cultural act. One of the advantages of a neo-Marxist framework is that it highlights power relations in societies that anthropology has been content for too long to portray as integrated cultures. Anthropologists have been lax in pointing out, on the one hand, that the "official culture" they described in any given society was not necessarily everyone's culture and, on the other, that knowledge is an important political resource. Crick (1982: 303) makes the latter point simply but effectively when he writes, "One of the important aspects of everyday knowledge is that it keeps certain people in power and certain others in the dark".

Marxism has always had a critical attitude to knowledge, although, as we shall see, the role of ideology and culture was perhaps not fully appreciated before Gramsci. Though all Marxists (and some non-Marxists as well) believe that in the "last instance" economic factors are determinant, it is obvious that some writers reach this stage of final analysis sooner than others and are quicker to bring the economic base into play. Anthropologists like myself who sit uncomfortably between the two stools of cultural anthropology and neo-Marxism put up with the tension inherent in the refusal to commit themselves exclusively to either paradigm because each tradition complements the other in important ways: Marxism offers a welcome corrective to the politically aseptic view of culture found in cultural anthropology; anthropology points to the 19th century materialism of Marxism and its subsequent failure to appreciate the role of culture. One way of applying the insights found in each tradition is to focus on the cultural content of intergroup relations. In this perspective, one believes there is more to class relations than mere relations of production. As Worsley (1981: 234) remarks,

> ...Groups and categories of people are allocated to roles
> and sectors not just in the economic order but in a total
> societal and cultural division of rights and duties, division
> of labor, and differential access to valued goods, including
> power and immaterial goods.

This brings us to a second reason for coining the term simple

commodity consumption. The study of peasant societies shows that
the capitalist penetration of pre-capitalist economies has not
resulted in the predicted disappearance of non-capitalist modes of
production; it has led instead to the emergence of complex social
formations in which dominant (capitalist) and subordinate
(precapitalist) modes of production coexist. The social groups
studied by anthropologists often have social systems in which
economic relations are commodified, except for labor power, and
yet these groups have managed to retain a use-value perspective.
The analytical focus of neo-Marxist anthropologists concerned with
the study of interclass relations of production is of course the maintenance of such non-capitalist labor systems.

Let us assume for the sake of argument that there are patterns
of consumption occupying an intermediate position between pre-
capitalist and capitalist forms of consumption in a manner analogous
to the position held by simple commodity production halfway between pre-capitalist and capitalist modes of production. Such an
assumption would naturally direct our attention to the ways in which
the partial commoditization of social life in peasant societies affects
the role played by consumption in the social and cultural ordering
of social groups. At the risk of unduly testing the reader's patience,
let us indulge for the moment in a tripartite model of consumption:
pre-capitalist consumption; petty or simple commodity consumption; and commodity consumption.

How does someone interested in simple commodity consumption study interclass relations of consumption? First by acknow-
ledging that capitalist penetration and domination are not simply of
a material nature. To quote Worsley (1981: 245) again,

> Among the Third World mass, cultural nationalism, and
> even political ideology, has long been displaced by con-
> sumerist values.... Workers are now psychically incor-
> porated, not via a Protestant work ethic so much as via
> their transmutation into consumers.... The atomization of
> society produced by consumerism is now countervailed by
> new forms of mass identity and solidarity (e.g., World Cup
> soccer, Disneyland).

This capitalist penetration also takes the form of penetration of
industrially produced goods. The borrowing of such goods (food,

clothing, means of communication or transportation) is not entirely explained by their greater convenience or utility value. Underpinning such goods are classificatory schemes, sets of ideas and perceptions, which gave rise to these items being produced in the first place.

A symbolic, but all too real, capitalist penetration takes two forms: (1) that of status-giving goods and activities borrowed from a prestigious Western world in order to share in this highly valued state of modernity; (2) the largely unforeseen insertion of Western classificatory schemes in local symbolic systems when such goods and activities become accepted. These cognitive structures assert themselves through the process of utilization. I am describing here a process that may appear to some as singularly anthropomorphic, something almost in the nature of a conspiracy theory, but no more so than the operation of any formal organizational context such as an educational system for example. A structure of recognition underpins the use of these goods and activities; once this structure is in place, it then frames and limits other alternatives. Perceiving such structures is of course more difficult than understanding the use of goods as status symbols, a well-known process.

Can peasants resist ideological penetration? Do they have the means to refuse, incorporate, or subvert foreign classificatory schemes? Is the end product necessarily cultural subjugation? These are the questions raised here according to a model of society in which social groups, classes and fragments of classes, not the individuals/households/firms of liberal economics, are the main protagonists and in which culture is the terrain on which group struggle takes place. The article is divided into three parts: in the first part, some models of consumption in pre-capitalist and capitalist societies are reviewed; in the second, the link between consumption and power is analyzed; and in the last, the idea of consumption as "silent production" and a form of hidden resistance is examined.

Models of Consumption

A good starting point is the valuable model of consumption developed by Douglas and Isherwood in their anthropology of consumption. According to these authors, objects create meanings. They are needed to make the categories of culture visible (Douglas and Isherwood 1979: 74). Consumers choose goods as part of a process of "cognitive construction", as part of a "classifying project". Goods are markers, counters in a competition in which advantage accrues to those who are well-placed in the system. Knowledge is power, an anthropological commonplace if there ever was one. Going beyond the obvious level of utility, consumption for Douglas and Isherwood amounts to a ritual activity that has to do with social inclusion and exclusion. In this activity, one is called upon to give as well as to receive marking services. The consumer, "instead of being regarded as the owner of certain goods, should be seen as operating a pattern of perodicities in consumption behavior" (1979: 123). Throughout, the motivation of the consumer is to obtain as well as to control information about the "changing cultural scene" (1979: 95). There is finally a feedback from consumption to employment as those who belong to the top consumption class obtain a higher rate of earnings than others (1979: 181).

Douglas and Isherwood advocate the use of an information model to understand the rituals of consumption. In this way they attempt to go beyond a purely utilitarian approach to consumption. The fact that people eat for sustenance hardly explains how many meals a day they consume, the people they eat with, or the classification of appropriate food for different occasions. It is with food as it is with sex: the satisfaction of a biological need is encoded in a set of cultural prescriptions and possibilities.

Douglas and Isherwood contrast the meaning encoded in sets of objects in complex industrial societies (and in different consumption classes within those societies) with consumption in small-scale, simpler societies. This has been cited as both one of the book's strengths at the level of an illuminating analogy, and one of its greatest weaknesses (Rosman 1982: 212). The root of the problem is that the authors have constructed no theoretical foundation for assuming that consumption is conceptually the same in industrial societies and in the Third World. This is crucial to their view that consumption is a system of meanings. Their conclusions are consequently equivocal—"Where the argument leads is hard to see"— and evasive—"Anthropology is not the discipline for finding solutions to problems"(1979: 202). "The next steps which should

JEAN-MARC PHILIBERT

follow from this argument are in philosophy, in econometrics, and in sociology" (1979: 204).

While Douglas and Isherwood concerned themselves with commodity consumption, some French sociologists have attempted to develop models of consumption in the Third World corresponding to our categories of pre-capitalist consumption and simple commodity consumption. (See *L'Homme et la Société*, No. 55-58, 1980). These authors propose to look at the agents of consumption, be they individuals, social classes or states, and at the categories of consumed objects, the factors stimulating various forms of consumption including conspicuous consumption, and the means of diffusion of new patterns of consumption (Lombard 1980: 143).

In traditional societies, goods are often signs of an ascribed social identity expressed in, as well as delineated by, rights of resistance and ownership, position in a kinship system, participation in networks of exchange, and custody of parts of a shared symbolic universe. As D'Haene observes, "The object has no [semiotic] value except as a sign of the relationship it memorizes" (1980: 183, my translation). The semiological value of an object, then, is as a sign of an underlying social identity; it is the signifier of social reality. To ensure correspondence between signifiers of social status, conspicuous consumption is often regulated: the right to wear certain clothes, to display certain ornaments, to live in particular places may be reserved for given categories of individuals. However, with the advent of capitalism and the commoditization of social life, social statuses are no longer fixed by custom but are acquired temporarily through convention. The symbols of such social statuses themselves become commodities that are now accessible to all through the medium of money. As Adam (1980: 155) points out, this causes a true semiological displacement: the use of money that makes it possible to acquire the signs of a given function or status creates at the same time the illusion that the full function or status itself is acquired by extension. The object now comes ahead of what is signified: no longer a sign, it becomes an image or a dream.

As one moves from the logic of consumption found in traditional societies to the logic of consumption in Westernized societies, new images displace traditional symbolism. Following the privatization of social life, individuals and groups find themselves isolated and in competition with one another by means of object-signs. Acculturated individuals purchase objects in order to attain what their image suggests, but there is never enough behind the image. Their desire is forever renewed but never satisfied. Their quest for social identity requires that they spend more and more, yet the logic of consumption itself cancels the sign-effect of their acquisitions (D'Haene 1980: 183). This is so because of the double function of consumption, that of social integration as well as segregation. People express or mark their status by manipulating objects to form a discourse, manipulating signs to signal membership in a reference group. Goods and wants thus filter down from a model group to those deemed socially inferior. Yet these desires and the means to satisfy them also maintain distance and exclude. As Baudrillard (1970) argues, objects that are commercialized and serialized derive their semantic value from a prototype that is the sign of high social status. However, when the objects become readily available, the impact of their ownership is diminished. This has happened in the West to reduce the *cachet* of television sets, video recording units, hi fi sets, calculators, digital watches, and even personal computers. In efforts to counteract this tendency, people pay thousands of dollars for a Swiss watch, now transformed into a jewellery item, that is no more accurate than an inexpensive Japanese quartz watch. Everyone but the very rich is always one step behind. Indeed, "the social paradigm is also the paradigm of consumption which first presupposes wealth" (Adam 1980: 153, my translation).

In the Third World, the bureaucratic neo-bourgeoisie acts as a relay for the diffusion of the Western way of life. The ruling class often adopts a modernist stance, but members of this class do not simply mimic Western archetypes; the nationalist consciousness developed at the time of independence from former colonial masters leads to syncretism in this matter. One finds designer sunglasses but also traditional dress. A few years in Vanuatu[1], a rebel leader who advocated a return to traditional ways was sighted in a government building with his assistants. The leader wore khaki trousers with matching safari shirt and a French beret. His men were naked except for customary loincloths that proclaimed the traditional legitimacy of the movement, yet they also carried attache cases to show they were nonetheless sophisticated and not to be taken for local yokels. In effect, they were claiming equal competence in two cultural worlds through their consumption of clothes

JEAN-MARC PHILIBERT

and accessories. This juxtaposition of symbols derived from the powerful West with those found in the weak, local culture; in other words, the simultaneous pariahization and brahmanization of a political movement represents a potent manipulation of cultural codes.

The desire for Western goods, not only consumer goods, but also productive goods from mining equipment to oil rigs to medical and educational systems, is most clearly expressed by those in power. This elite has its own practice of objects based on Western models of consumption. Although the ruling elite does not share the position of the Western bourgeoisie, it may nonetheless have equivalent aspirations.[2] In fact, members of this group must state their legitimacy by using the required object-signs. Such an elite has often assimilated the values and way of life of Western society (D'Haene 1980: 185).

Anthropologists will no doubt feel uncomfortable with a sociological model contrasting consumption in traditional and modern societies along the only too predictable lines of ascription versus achievement. While the general validity of this distinction is not disputed, it does not facilitate the task of anthropologists who must differentiate between "traditional" societies. Moreover, what does one find among those who are not members of a ruling elite or in those parts of the Third World where capitulation to capitalism does not seem either natural or inevitable? Consumption is fundamental to understanding those cultures in the Third World where petty commodity production for the capitalist market is well-established while at the same time the capitalist mode of production is kept at a distance.

If we start from the premises that, among other considerations, (1) consumption amounts to an appropriation of meanings symbolized in the use of particular objects; (2) people consume according to a code of recognition, a semiotic chain invested in a (bound) series of objects; and (3) people speak about themselves in their consumption choices, then we can begin to deconstruct the "texts" that consumers create. In other words, we can proceed beyond the utility value of objects to the messages inscribed with and within them in the Third World. As Hall and Jefferson (1976: 55) put it,

> Objects and commodities do not mean any one thing, they "mean" only because they have been arranged, according

to social use, into cultural codes of meaning.

Tweed jackets, corduroy trousers and Clark Wallabies do not naturally go together though they have now become as indispensable to the male professorial role as developing, early in one's career, a pronounced academic stoop. Compare the following "patterns of significance" from Vanuatu, one found in a "traditional" setting, the other in an urban context.

You can't trust people with trousers!

Some important social and cultural contrasts were drawn when, during the 1983 Vanuatu electoral campaign, a member of Parliament addressed his rural constituents on the radio in the following terms:

> If you vote for me, I know that I can look after your needs. I am a member of Na-Griamel party and I know your traditional culture well. I am a member of Parliament, but I am really on the side of traditions. During the electoral campaign, there will be much talk, many lies and a lot of different political signs. If you see someone who goes naked, this man is one of yours, naked people of Santo. Someone who goes naked you can vote for. Such a man will defend you, look after your needs, protect your land. You shall hold on to these for the rest of your life.

While the first reaction to this statement may be to ponder the disquieting implication that all politicians really sound alike in all societies, let us consider the sets of contrasts used to "speak" to rural constituents: on the one hand, a traditional notion of political legitimacy is expressed through the set of nakedness, truth, traditional knowledge, and land; on the other, people who wear trousers, lies, modernity (parliamentary nation-state), and land spoliators are grouped together. To belong means to possess natural rights to land by virtue of membership in a discrete group which has a culture of its own and is associated with tutelary spirits found in the local landscape. The term sometimes applied in this insular world to those without traditional land rights is drift wood, something that has lost its roots and is washed ashore on foreign land. This strong, dichotomous view of tradition and modernity informing rural politi-

JEAN-MARC PHILIBERT

cal legitimacy contrasts with the code found in a peri-urban village.

On "good houses"

I have for many years been interested in the conspicuous consumption of Erakor villagers (Philibert 1981, 1984, 1986). There was only one concrete house in 1973 in this peri-urban village which then numbered some 800 inhabitants. The number grew to 20 in 1979 and 31 in 1983. The villagers' understanding of what constitutes a modern house is surprisingly thorough. *Haos i kamplit*, a fully furnished house, means having all the specialized furniture/implements found in rooms with specialized functions (living rooms, dining rooms...) such as buffets, bookshelves, curtains in windows, tiles on the floor, plastic tulips in plastic crystal-like vases, and pseudo-traditional artifacts, of the sort bought by tourists, on the walls. This form of housing is very much at odds with the "traditional" design of a one-room hut made up of split palm trees with a thatched or corrugated iron roof (to catch rain water).

As Baudrillard (1970) points out, objects organize themselves into panoplies, into collections. An object is not simply purchased for its utility value, but for its position in a series of objects with a signification of its own. Brand names play in our society an important part in imposing a coherent vision of the whole seen as made up of indissociable parts. It is a chain not simply linking single objects but signifiers as well. Together, they amount to a super-object yet more complex. Consider the matching green or almond appliances in our kitchens (refrigerator, stove, dishwasher, kettle, toaster, mixer...) which carry a more coherent message than the same implements in mixed colors or simply white, because the relation between each appliance and the user is now mediated through the whole. The merchandise becomes culturalized, its utility value becomes sublimated into "ambiance", a sort of neo-culture. We are familiar with this phenomenon in our society with objects of consumption reproducing our cultural frames, our map of understandings. Our own culture specifies various constitutions of social identity (sex, age, class), which are expressed in and through the social uses of commodities.

Wealthier villagers in Erakor living in concrete houses with all the modern amenities have recently started to build small thatched huts in their yard where they can sit on coral floors covered with mats, like the poor, to prepare and drink kava (*Piper methysticum*) with friends. The line between tradition and modernity is drawn differently in this example, emphasizing the open-ended way in which signifiers fit together in a commodity-based society. As Sahlins puts it, the code works as an open set. (1976: 185).

Moving from objects to their underlying reality as signs, we are confronted by different classificatory schemes which are at the very heart of the cultural representations of social groups. Acculturation is in a sense the borrowing or the imposition of someone else's symbolic order. This brings us to relations existing between cognitive structures. Gramsci's notion of hegemony is useful to explore the cultural dimension of interclass relations and the role played by ideological domination.

On Ideology

Gramsci's thought, as jotted down in the form of notes in his *Prison Notebooks* written during his incarceration from 1926 to 1937, must be pieced together: Gramsci died before he could accomplish this task himself. Moreover, to add to the difficulty, what he wrote was censored and many ideas could not be expressed plainly. His thought has been submitted to a great deal of exegesis and, as expected, there exists more than one interpretation of his ideas. I am basing this brief presentation of Gramsci's ideas on Simon (1982) and Mouffe (1979).

Gramsci uses the term hegemony in a special sense and the following is the simplest exposition of it that I have come across:

> The starting point for Gramsci's concept of hegemony is that a class and its representatives exercise power over subordinate classes by means of a combination of coercion and persuasion.... Hegemony is a relation, not of domination by means of force, but of consent by means of political and ideological leadership. It is the organization of consent (Simon 1982: 21).

For some Marxists, ideology is closely associated with the interests of a particular social class and is dealt with as false consciousness, the result of mystification, when an already established class manages to impose its perspective and world view on other social classes which then accept them as their own. Gramsci believes that a class, in order to rule, must go beyond its narrow class interests to take into account the interests of other classes or fractions of classes in order to develop broad-based alliances. It must develop a role of national leadership by articulating popular aspirations so that its class' interests and world view appear to represent general interests and the general will. It is ideology which gives such varied social groups and forces their unity. For him,

> Ideologies are not individual fancies, rather they are embodied in communal modes of living and acting...they are the uncritical and largely unconscious way in which a person perceives the world...and are compounded of folklore, myth and popular experience (Simon 1982: 25).

In other words, ideology has to do with the way individuals and groups phenomenologically construct and understand their reality, what has here been called classificatory schemes. For Gramsci, all men have a "spontaneous philosophy" made up of language, "common sense", "good sense", popular religion and "the entire system of beliefs, superstitions, opinions, ways of seeing things and acting... collectively bundled together under the name of folklore" (SPN: 323). (See *The Study of Philosophy* and also *Critical Notes on An Attempt at Popular Sociology*.)

According to Gramsci, class relationships are located in the sphere of economic production (economic coercion) and in state control (political coercion), but also in what he terms "civil society", institutions such as churches, political parties, trade unions, mass media, educational systems, cultural organizations... His contribution as a Marxist thinker is to show clearly that civil society is one of the terrains of class struggle and that it is there that hegemony develops and is exercised.

Anthropologists will have no difficulty accepting the idea that "subjects are not originally given but are always produced by ideology through a socially determined ideological field, so that subjectivity is always the product of social practice" (Mouffe, 1979: 186). It also implies, when consciousness is derived from ideologies and when such ideologies are the world view of "social blocks" (class alliances), that all forms of consciousness are in effect political. This means that the project of anthropology, like that of other social sciences, is by nature political: there is no neutral, ideologically-free terrain on which to stand, nor has there ever been any. This led Gramsci to consider seriously the role of the intellectual: the symbolic ordering of social life and the social ordering of symbols and ideas are part of the same process, albeit a very complex one which cannot be apprehended by such simple notions as projection from one level of reality to another. We must allow for a large amount of indeterminacy and contradiction here.

Bourdieu's (1977: 83) notion of *habitus* helps us to understand the social determination of consciousness. *Habitus* is

> a system of lasting, transposable dispositions, which integrating past experiences, functions at every moment as a *matrix of perceptions, appreciations, and actions* and makes possible the achievement of infinitely diversified tasks, thanks to analogical transfers of schemes permitting the solution of similarly shaped problems...

Let us examine a practice of objects to try to see what the relationship between objects represents and how the objects are transformed, contrasted and consumed. The following example from Vanuatu illustrates the embedded quality of the metaphors with which people transform an anomalous object into something both new and familiar. At the end of World War II, a Small Nambas tribesman on Malekula Island received, as a parting gift from an American serviceman, a lipstick in a gold colored metal case inscribed with the word "Hollywood". Its new owner covered the case with spider webs, made the required incantations to give it magical power, and transformed the lipstick into a traditional means to transport himself instantaneously from island to island.

The mental reconstruction of the lipstick as a means of transportation occurs through a practice of *bricolage*. The statements constructed with the lipstick concern metaphors of value, efficacy and agency, at the very least. They assert that a lipstick is an object of value to be traditionally protected and concealed in spider webs; that a lipstick can be a magical vehicle; that the power to effect this transformation rests with the owner, the recipient of a gift. Clearly, this construction employs an established vocabulary and syntax: only the object itself and the event of categorizing it are new. The act

JEAN-MARC PHILIBERT

of using the lipstick in a way its manufacturers never envisioned establishes a here and now that is fertile ground for analysis. This created present is highlighted for us by distance in time and space between the serviceman and the tribesman, between World War II with its aircraft as agents of global violence and magical flight in a tiny, insular world, between the meanings we associate with lipstick and Hollywood magic on the one hand and traditional magical objects that create magical movement on the other. We would not presume that the Vanuatu tribesman experienced the same contrasts or that he structures his practice of objects according to our rules. But we would assume that categorizing this alien lipstick is a process that creates contrasts and requires a structuring that occurs in its use.

A second example of consumption practices from Vanuatu will illustrate some of the dialectical relations between hegemonic structures and allow us to reflect on the ways social consciousness is objectified in cultural action. Jolly (1982) has recently examined the relation between cultural traditions (*kastom*)[3] and modernity among members of a traditional society, the Sa speakers of South Pentecost. She describes the recent penetration of the cash economy and wonders what the commoditization of food practices will do to the Sa culture in which food production and consumption are constitutive of gender identity through a division of labor, food taboos, and mythical associations.

Jolly also believes that another threat to the Sa speakers' symbolic integrity lies in the performance for tourists of an important ritual, the *Gol* or Pentecost land dive.[4] The staging of this spectacular ritual for tourists is particularly tempting for the Sa speakers as they can earn hard-to-get money by doing what they do best, that is to say by being themselves. The question is, are they remaining themselves? Jolly expresses concern that "the selling of traditional life-styles converts lived practices into folkloric spectacles" (Jolly 1982: 352).

We confront here the Sa speakers in their role of producer and consumer of a cultural web. We find a dissociation in their practice as they now produce two rituals: one for themselves which is deemed efficacious, and one for tourists which is a staged or empty ritual. A cultural phase displacement must occur: people do not theatricalize their lives for others without taking, for at least the length of the representation, an altered view of themselves. If there is, as is often the case, contempt toward a public which does not know enough to be able to distinguish between the real performance and its simulacrum, some of this scorn is also heaped on the actors themselves for having to play to such a poor public. The ritual statements made in the staged *Gol* are grammatical, they follow the sytactic rules, yet the ritual *parle pour ne rien dire:* it is an empty discourse.

At issue here is not the fetishization of a culture as against symbolic integrity: traditional societies are no more, and no less, natural than modern societies in this respect, as both state various constitutions of identity, place, gender, local politics, etc. What takes place is a code switch. Commoditization converts the land dive into a sign with a different meaning, and power attaches itself differently to commodities than to other sorts of signs. In commodity-based societies, one finds control of the code while constant supervision of signs is abandoned. Clothing provides an illustration of this. In our society, social actors (designers and consumers) are given a large amount of freedom "to make fashion statements", as the advertisers call it, using what appear to be endless permutations of fabric, color, cut and accessories to signify, for example, the respective qualities of masculinity and femininity. Some social groups may even challenge the cultural code by manipulating the signs, as in the unisex style. In pre-capitalist societies, both signs and codes are controlled. Hence, in staging a ritual, it is not only the valence of the signs that is changed; a switch is also being made to a new, more open system, a sort of symbolic free trade system. As the principles encoding signifiers change, so does the signified.

The Sa speakers are also consumers of this ritual, and the act of consumption establishes a present relative to time and space. The presence of spectators, and European spectators at that, vastly increases the spatio-temporal referent, although it is hard to say how much actors and spectators take in of the "other". The symbolic interchange takes place between actors who do not know their public and spectators who do not speak the actors' language. A comedy of errors, Jolly would say. Yet we must be careful not to over-emphasize the cultural impact of the West on "simpler" societies. The lack of communication mentioned above, the intellectual equivalent of ships passing in the night, can be an asset as

JEAN-MARC PHILIBERT

well as a liability. How is staging rituals for tourists different from manufacturing artifacts for sale in the capital, something most anthropologists would probably encourage because it maintains traditional craft production? In both cases, the makers, ignorant of the uses to which the product is put, are equally alienated from their product.

Meaning and Power

Commodities are cultural signs that reproduce the cultural frames, the sets of understandings, which gave rise to their being produced in the first place. What is the relationship between dominant and subordinate systems of classification? Let us turn briefly to the link between meaning and power. The work of members of the Centre for Contemporary Cultural Studies at the University of Birmingham (Hall & Jefferson 1982) is particularly useful in this respect.

According to them,

> ...just as different groups and classes are unequally ranked in relation to one another, in terms of their productive relations, wealth and power, so *cultures* are differently ranked, and stand in opposition to one another in relations of domination and subordination, along the scale of "cultural power". The definitions of the world, the "maps of meaning" which express the life situations of those groups which hold the monopoly of power in society, command the greatest weight and influence, secrete the greatest legitimacy. (Clark, Hall, *et al*, 1976: 11)

How classes gain a monopoly of social authority for their own definition of reality and how they are able to reproduce it is what Gramsci was on to.

> A hegemonic cultural order tries to *frame* all competing definitions of the world within *its* range. It provides the horizon of thought and action within which conflicts are thought through, appropriated...obscured...or contained. A hegemonic order prescribes, not the specific content of ideas, but the *limits* within which ideas and conflicts move

and are resolved. (Clark, Hall *et al* 1976: 39)

The underlying classificatory schemes are of course unconscious. As Bourdieu observes (1979: 559), they are objectified only when they have ceased to work in a tacit, practical manner, when the guardians of the established order, rather in the way grammarians attempt to guide and order "proper" speech, believe such principles must be codified and explained. It then becomes the official system whose principles are clearly expressed in the hegemonic apparatuses of school, church, law and other social and cultural agencies. Durkheim's sociology was part of such an objectifying effort (Hobsbawm 1985: 269).

I have documented in a recent article (Philibert 1986) the development of hegemonic discourse in Vanuatu. Members of the Vanuatu political elite are now socializing their fellow countrymen, without their knowledge, to a new political culture, that of the nation-state. They are attempting to develop a national identity by putting forward a generic, "no-name brand" of culture based on the invention of neo-traditions (see Hobsbawm and Ranger 1983). A bureaucratic neo-bourgeoisie is in the process of establishing its intellectual, moral and political role of leadership. In its hands, modern political culture has not only become metaphorised as culture itself, which has the effect of denying the existence of sectional interests, but what is more, it is presented as a collage of the best of what traditional culture has to offer. What is constitutive of Vanuatu social identity, the image of the past as well as that of the future, is now controlled, as never before, by one group of *ni-Vanuatu* (people of Vanuatu). Through various cultural policies, members of this incipient social class have become the arbiters of what tradition is; they now hold the seal that authenticates practices as traditional.

Cultural hegemony is not simply restricted to one's own society. Are the peasants importing Western goods not also importing cultural signifiers, and if so, does this necessarily lead to a self-inflicted cultural subjugation? The expected consequences of imported goods need not always be some form of consumerism. The tendency may be diverted by rejecting or altering the objects or by using them with respect to goals and contexts alien to the imposed system. Peasants may respond to encroaching capitalism by transcending or outwitting the dominant social order without necessarily leaving it.

After all, this is what happened in the field of production. De Certeau (1984) considers consumption to be a kind of production, a "secondary, silent" production hidden in the process of utilization. De Certeau's objective is to evaluate the production of images and representations against the secondary production that occurs in their consumptions. To expanding, more invasive systems of production "corresponds *another* production, called 'consumption'. The latter is devious; it is dispersed, but it insinuates itself everywhere, silently and almost invisibly, because it does not manifest itself through its own products, but rather through its *ways of using* the products imposed by a dominant economic order" (de Certeau 1984: xiii).

Reading offers a prototype for rethinking other kinds of consumption in which the user has often been seen as passive but is in fact creative, appropriating the written text and "inventing" memories: "a different world (the reader's) slips into the author's place" and makes itself at home, transforming the borrowed space of the text like a tenant furnishing an apartment with acts and memories (de Certeau 1984: xxi). Readers wander through an imposed system helping themselves: "Readers are travellers: they move across lands belonging to someone else, like nomads poaching their way across fields they did not write despoiling the wealth of Egypt to enjoy it themselves." (de Certeau 1984: 174).

This process of "poaching" can be subversive in reference to the ways products imposed by a dominant economic order are used. This is especially evident today in those parts of the Third World where an obvious contrast exists between a persistent traditional way of life and the capitalist mode. There, the concealed subversion that occurs through consumption can encourage the independence of the very people that capitalist production would co-opt.

De Certeau (1984: xiii) refers to South American reaction to the Spanish conquest in the following terms:

> Submissive, and even consenting to their subjection, the Indians nevertheless often made of the rituals, representations, and laws imposed on them something quite different from what their conquerors had in mind; they subverted them not by rejecting or altering them, but by using them with respect to ends and references foreign to the system they had no choice but to accept. They were

other within the very colonization that outwardly assimilated them; their use of the dominant social order
deflected its power, which they lacked the means to challenge; they escaped it without leaving it. The strength of
their difference lay in procedures of "consumption".

Not only in South America, but also in Oceania, the per-
meability of systems of ideas to foreign constructs in economic,
political, and religious spheres may paradoxically also be a source
of strength.

There are not, to my knowledge, a large number of studies of
the semiotics of consumption in the Third World. In a recent one,
Adam (1984) recants somewhat his earlier view of consumption as
the direct *assujettissement consommatoire* (subjection through consumption) of the Third World, a self-imposed form of cultural
alienation. Though commodity consumption still amounts for him
to an enormous social theater with individuals putting on, as if they
were on stage, the very social statuses they lack in real life, he now
feels one must not overestimate the impact of borrowed Western
signifiers. Many semantic displacements occur when Western signs
are borrowed to fit a symbolic grid foreign to their production. In
order to express their upward social mobility, African consumers
will imitate one of the prestigious local models (well-known
musicians, wealthy merchants or upper cadres in the civil service),
rather than the archetype derived from the European ruling class.
According to Adam, sociocultural signs are never arbitrary in the
manner of linguistic signs: they describe and stipulate the attributes
of prestige-carrying tasks and functions in the social hierarchy (1984:
7).

A successful example of the way a local culture is able to appropriate imported elements is found in Janglish or Japanese
English. In a tongue in cheek article, the journalist R. Whymant
reports cases of borrowed English such as "creap" for coffee
creamers, a wedding hall calling itself "a green and human plaza",
a beverage named "pokhari sweat", etc. Janglish is "cheap chic",
meaningless English used for adding local color to commercial
goods. According to Whymant, "Janglish makes the pushers of
Franglais seem like small time crooks. The French have the decency
to leave the pirated words more or less intact. Not so the
Japanese..." (Manchester Guardian Weekly, March 30, 1986: 9). Ex-

amples of language misappropriation are "tatchi gaymu" (petting games), "imejji-uppu" (to improve one's image) and "no pan kissa" (coffee shop with panty-less waitresses). Not satisfied with such mutilations, the Japanese further claim borrowed English words as their own: "sebiro" is Japanese for a suit, a term originally derived from the Japanese pronunciation of "Savile Row".

One feels duty bound to point out that there exist other cases of linguistic borrowing in which local cultures have contained with less success the penetration of their vehicular language, such as *Franglais* or various sorts of pidgin English. Moreover, the empirical evidence available to me of the ability of local groups to outwit the dominant cultural order is far from reassuring. I have for some years now studied an undeservedly neglected sociological type in Melanesia, the peri-urban village, because it represents a natural laboratory in which to monitor the ever-shifting boundaries of rural and urban life. Peri-urbanities are neither peasants, nor proletarians: they occupy a social world which inwardly remains a village, while outwardly it has taken on the appearance of a town neighborhood. Established on their own land, peri-urbanities are wage earners who have retained corporate solidarities in that some food, labor, forms of mutual help, and land circulate among villagers in an uncommoditized fashion; they have also preserved the sort of discourses consonant with this form of ownership of means of production. Moreover, the village studied is endowed with considerable natural resources so that villagers cannot truthfully be said to be driven to paid employment by the specter of poverty and famine.[5]

Up to the mid-1960s, Erakor had essentially a rural economy with its inhabitants relying on subsistence gardening and fishing for most of their food, while using copra making, the marketing of produce in town, and occasional wage earning to raise the little money needed for church, school fees, clothes, imported food items, tobacco and alcohol. A drastic fall in the price of copra allied to unprecedented economic development in the capital following the establishment of a tourist industry and greater spending by the two colonial powers led the villagers to abandon petty commodity production for paid employment over a period of little more than five years. By 1972, wage labor outside the village was accounting for about 90% of the cash inflow in the village. The increased dis-

CONSUMING CULTURE

posable incomes were quickly invested in new houses, modern furnishings, means of transportation, small businesses, and increased leisure activities (dancing and drinking in town). However, this economic boom was short-lived and was soon followed by economic recessions: a first one brought on by the 1973 world oil crisis, and a subsequent one by political troubles surrounding the country's accession to independence in 1980. One would have expected Erakor villagers to react to a contradiction in the labor market by reducing their consumption of store-bought goods and by relying to a greater extent on subsistence activities to achieve some measure of self-sufficiency.

But that is not what happened. The villagers' "consumerist" urge did not ease off between 1972 and 1983, as can be seen from the tables below, and this, despite the fact that acquiring such consumer items had become harder (Philibert 1984b).

Women fared better than men on the labor market during the period of recession: the percentage of women among wage earners increased from 37% in 1972 to 45% in 1983. However, these aggregate figures only tell part of the story, as not all women were equally affected. The proportion of wage earners among able-bodied women of the 25-34 age group jumped from 23% (1972) to 51% (1983); during the same period, the proportion of salaried workers among the 35-44 year old women fit to work also increased appreciably from 18% to 27%. These women are precisely those who belonged to the 15-24 age group studied in 1972 and who, having moved to better paying semi-qualified and qualified work in the interval, remained employed after their marriage. For the first time in village history, a category of Erakor women, much like Western women, work outside their home and raise a family at the

VILLAGE POPULATION			
	1972	1979	1983
Number of Residents	628	836	1006
Number of Households	92	123	154

same time.

Such changes in the occupational structure, made in order to preserve the earning power of households, have had an impact on family organization. It has already had distressing consequences for child-rearing practices: a 1982 national public health study has found evidence of malnutrition among children in Erakor, ironically one of the wealthiest villages in Vanuatu. It was found among the bottle-fed children whose absent working mothers could no longer nurse. Whoever was left at home to mind the children either did not know how to prepare the milk formula or the formula was replaced by condensed milk to reduce expenses.

Some social costs have been incurred as well, although these will not be felt for a while. Women may play a pivotal role in loosening, if not severing altogether, the tie between some villagers and their land, in other words in transforming part of the next generation of villagers into proletarians. (See Philibert 1988 for an extended development of this argument.) Let us consider the likely outcome of these occupational changes for women's production

COMMODITY CONSUMPTION IN ERAKOR

Consumer Items	Number of Households		
	1972	1979	1983
Refrigerators	2	24[*]	40
VCR and TV	N/A	N/A	5
Cars/Light Trucks	14	48[1]	44[2]
Concrete House	1	20	31
Boys[**]	0	7	11

1   19 late models
2   20 late models

*   Electricity and running water were installed in Erakor in 1979. Electric refrigerators then replaced costlier kerosene-run refrigerators.

**   Boys is the pidgin term applied to agricultural workers hired by wage-earning villagers to work the fields for them. As labor is uncommoditized among villagers, these agricultural workers come from other islands. The employer-employee relationship is a highly paternalistic one.

function before examining the effect on their reproductive role. Land owners in Erakor must exercise their rights to parcels of land if they wish to resist the yearly encroachment of neighbors on their garden land. Women normally carry out many of the gardening activities which become severely curtailed by wage labor outside the village. Wage earners are thus at a disadvantage in the long term as their rights to a valuable uncommoditized resource are left more or less unprotected. The solution is of course to use *boys,* but not every household can afford them. There are today households in Erakor which do not garden at all.

Work in town is indirectly related by villagers to a drastic change in family organization, a four-fold increase of consensual unions in the village between 1972 and 1983. There were, in 1972, 7 couples living out of wedlock in Erakor, a behavior much frowned upon by village authorities in this Presbyterian Christian village. Their number grew to 31 by 1979 and it remained at this level in 1983. In the majority of cases, one of the partners is not from the village. During the 11 year period studied, the failure rate of such consensual unions, in the sense that the unions did not result in an eventual church marriage, was 30 to 40%. Unless paternity is acknowledged by an Erakor father, the children born of these unions are unlikely to obtain rights to garden land in the village or, at the very least, their rights will be less extensive than those of children born in wedlock. Land is transmitted patrilineally in Erakor with sons obtaining the lion's share. Consensual unions literally bear the seeds of a class of landless villagers.

The increased participation of young women in the labor force is responsible for their going to town not only to work but also to live. Although Erakor is only 10 km from the capital, some young women cohabit in town with non-villagers. They seem to prefer other islanders to Erakor men: in 1983, of the 26 Erakor women living with men in town, married or unmarried, only 2 had an Erakor partner. Erakor women, who have the reputation of being urban sophisticates, are attracted to men with well-paid jobs: almost half of them hold white collar jobs. These young women, breaking away from the expectation of marrying in the village, soon enter the social networks of their partners and are drawn further away from Erakor social life. The children of these women will have no access to land in the village. The Erakor women living in town will produce the first generation of *de facto* proletarians in Vanuatu, the first truly urban ni-Vanuatu.

Villagers' response to the recession has been to maintain their living standards at their current level by making greater use of women on the labor market. Villagers then acquiesced to changes in subsistence activities and in the division of roles within the family, and to a new form of family organization in order to reach their objective. Women have now become the unconscious vector of change-for-the-worse in the village economy; they are the agency through which important social relationships will no longer be reproduced as they stood in the past. This will lead to the abandonment of a tried and proven Melanesian adaptation to the modern world, the refusal to commit oneself entirely to the market economy (Brookfield 1973). An atrophied subsistence sector will leave villagers with only one economic leg to stand on, thus destroying the very condition which allows them to participate in the market economy under largely favorable terms. What is more, land being absolutely central to the Melanesian notion of identity, the greater impoverishment will first and foremost be a cultural one.

An order (levels, patterns, norms, modes) of consumption is linked to a given order of production, though it would be naive indeed to reduce consumption in a mechanistic way to the functional requirements of a system of production. It would be clearly wrong to conceptualize the relation between the two as that of a plug and a wall socket. The two systems are mediated by the domain of culture, a semi-autonomous dimension between on the one hand the consciousness, and thus motivation, of social agents and the structural requirements of a society on the other. To make things yet more complex, there are also "deep disjunctions and desperate tensions within social and cultural reproduction", as Willis (1980: 175) remarks.

The Erakor material does not call into question de Certeau's view of the power of the powerless to deflect a dominant social order: Melanesians also engaged in passive, and at times not so passive, resistance during the colonial period. It does however remind us that ideology cuts both ways, that it leads to acceptance as well as resistance. What permitted South American Indians to resist the Spanish cultural order while outwardly accepting it is also what is leading some Erakor villagers to embrace a capitalist political economy now that they have tied their modern-day self-image to the ownership of industrial goods (Philibert 1982, 1984a).

Conclusion

Whether or not there is such a thing as Simple Commodity Consumption, our assuming that there is has enabled us to focus on the process of cultural categorization revealed in patterns of consumption. It is perhaps not so surprising that consumption obeys a different logic or follows a different sort of social calculus in societies that are not yet fully incorporated into a capitalist political economy. After all, unlike ourselves, people living in peasant societies do not necessarily see themselves as equals facing a world of goods obeying its own impersonal laws, and their social experience, in this sense, is not always expressed the way our own is, through a reification of the economic domain.

The following points have been briefly, too briefly, touched upon here: the social role of consumption in pre-capitalist and capitalist economies; the link between consumption, as a type of social notation shaping consciousness, and Gramsci's notion of hegemony; the relation between meaning, in the form of social classification, and power; the notion of consumption as silent production and hidden resistance. In a rather discursive fashion, it has been an attempt to examine the consumption of goods as the consumption of signs that are the social product as well as the agent of capitalist penetration of Third World countries. I hope to have convinced others that each of the above-mentioned themes deserves fuller treatment in its own right and that to approach consumption purely in terms of utility, marginal or otherwise, leaves out some of its most significant dimensions.

A comparative framework appears essential here, not simply to help us understand the diversity of modes of consumption, but more importantly to remind us that consumption is no less culturally determined in our own society. Anthropologists should not let economists get away with a naturalised, unproblematical model of consumption deemed universally applicable. It is in societies located at the periphery of the capitalist system that this can be achieved, because it is there that the capitalist structure of comprehension underpinning our social theories is more easily apprehended, the way poor novels rather than good ones serve as unwitting pastiches of an era, encapsulating faithfully the ideas and values of their time.

Notes

I wish to thank the Social Sciences and Humanities Research Council of Canada for providing a leave fellowship which allowed me to spend six months in Vanuatu in 1983 researching consumption and later seven months at the Australian National University as a Visiting Fellow. Many thanks to the Australian National University for the offer of a Visiting Fellowship and to Professor Anthony Forge, Department of Prehistory and Anthropology, Faculty of Arts, at ANU for his generous hospitality. I am also indebted to Professors F. Manning, C. Creider, J. Cannizzo, M. Spence and M.E. Smith, and to Jane Philibert for their comments and suggestions. I am grateful to Erakor villagers for their benevolent tolerance of my never-ending curiosity about their life, the way one puts up with flaws of character in one's friends. Much credit for the ideas expressed here goes to Dr. Margaret Rodman, a fellow Vanuatu anthropologist, who, at one time, was a co-worker in this research on consumption in Vanuatu. She co-authored a first draft of this article and I gratefully acknowledge her contribution here.

1. The Republic of Vanuatu is a South Pacific archipelago with a population of some 130,000 inhabitants situated between the Solomon Islands and New Caledonia. Prior to gaining independence in 1980, the group was known as the Condominium of the New Hebrides, a territory jointly administered by France and Great Britain. I carried out fieldwork in Vanuatu in the peri-urban village of Erakor from 1972 to 1973, and again in 1979 and 1983 for a duration of 24 months.

2. Consumption is significant with respect to class analysis. The economics of less developed countries (LDCs) far from match those of nineteenth century Western countries. As Rivière (1975) remarks, modernization in LDCs is to a large extent planned and controlled by those holding political power. In such an instance, the ownership of the means of production matters less than the effective control of those

means. If there is a bourgeoisie at all, it is a politico-bureaucratic bourgeoisie and it is their control of the means of production allied to their control of the legal and political structures of the state that allows them to claim a larger share of the social income. Such a Third World bourgeoisie is well known for its propensity for spending, unlike the saving and investing bourgeoisie of nineteenth century Europe. With a generally limited agricultural and industrial production, the differential amount of privileges in such countries is expressed in consumption. Social differentiation is thus better expressed by the appropriation of consumer goods than by ownership of the means of production. Rivière feels that the Marxist problematic must be corrected in Africa where the ownership of the means of production does not necessarily overlap with the ownership of the means of coercion, where economic power may rest less with production than consumption, and where access to wealth is regulated primarily by politics. Another factor that makes consumption crucial for the understanding of social classes is the enlargement of the tertiary sector following independence with the establishment of a national administration and a universal educational system. This leads to the emergence of a large number of public employees, those most concerned in LDCs with living standards and social position. Finally, as opposed to nineteenth century Europe, workers in LDCs are not to be considered a social class in the process of becoming impoverished, an emerging proletariat. Quite the contrary in fact, since wage labor raises the social status of an individual rather than lowering it.

3. Traditional culture, called *kastom* in Pidgin throughout Melanesia, has seen a great deal of political service in such newly independent countries as Vanuatu and the Solomon Islands. See Keesing and Tonkinson (1982), Philibert (1986).

4. "The land dive is part of an ensemble of rituals performed in association with the yam harvest. There is an intimate relationship between the harvest of yams and the dive. The quality of the crop determines the safety and efficacy of the *gol*, and the performance of the *gol* simultaneously ensures the worth of the harvest in the next year. This identity is based on the metaphysical identity of men and yams...the ritual is seen as a powerful statement of the strength and sanctity of men...The rite celebrates a "hot" dimension of masculinity...It is a statement both of men's potency and of resistance to European domination." (Jolly, 82: 352-353)

5. Erakor, the second largest village community in Vanuatu, is a modern, prosperous village located on the island of Efate, some 10 km from Port Vila, the administrative and commercial capital. The village land, which covers an area of 1,409 ha, is bordered on the northern and western sides by a lagoon where villagers find fish and shellfish. Village households are involved to varying degrees in subsistence gardening (slash-and-burn cultivation of root crops mostly), with a majority of them self-sufficient with regard to native produce. In 1983, 248 villagers were also employed in town or in the two international-class hotels located across the Erakor lagoon. Villagers showed themselves to be particularly entrepreneurial during the colonial period, often taking the initiative in establishing links with European newcomers. They were the first on their island to welcome Christian teachers in 1845. A Canadian Presbyterian missionary who resided in Erakor from 1872 to 1902 exerted a strong influence on the villagers. They renounced the use of magical stones, intertribal warfare, dancing, men's houses, polygyny, and the drinking of kava (*Piper methysticum*). In return, the villagers found in the Presbyterian mission a powerful ally willing to protect native rights in the frontier situation prevailing during the early phase of colonial history. The mission also provided a social and intellectual framework within which villagers could react effectively to the colonial situation (see Philibert 1982). In 1884, Erakor villagers ceded the village land to the Presbyterian mission in order to prevent further land alienation. Encouraged by the mission, they started as early as 1910 to develop their own coconut groves as an alternative to wage labor on

JEAN-MARC PHILIBERT

European plantations. In the mid-1960s, the villagers were the first Melanesians to become involved in the nascent tourist industry in the country. Twenty years later, they were the first ni-Vanuatu to be part-owners of a small hotel and restaurant sited on village land. Erakor villagers like to think of themselves, at their best, as culture brokers for their whole island. This is how an informant put it: "When a large wave comes from far away on the sea, it must first break on Erakor reef. It has always been so."

References

Adam, M.
1980 La contre-culture coca-cola. Le mirage des objets et la dépendence du consommateur dans le Tiers-Monde. *L'Homme et la Société*, 56-58:149-160.
n.d. Le développement comme Signe. To appear in *Tiers-Monde*.

Baudrillard, J.
1970 *La Société de Consommation*. Paris: Gallimard.

Bourdieu, P.
1977 *Outline of a Theory of Practice*. Cambridge: Cambridge University Press.
1979 *La Distinction. Critique sociale de jugement*. Paris: Les Editions de Minuit.

Clarke, J., S. Hall, T. Jefferson and B. Roberts
1976 Subcultures, cultures and class. In Hall, S. & T. Jefferson (eds.) *Resistance through Rituals*. London: Hutchinson.

Crick, M.R.
1982 Anthropology of knowledge. *Annual Review of Anthropology* 11:287-313.

de Certeau, M.
1984 *The Practice of Everyday Life*. Berkeley: University of California Press.

d'Haene, S.
1980 Essai d'analyse du fonctionnement des modèles de consommation dans les pays sous-developpés. *L'Homme et la Société*, 56-58:179-187.

Douglas, M. & Baron Isherwood
1979 *The World of Goods*. Harmondsworth: Penguin.

Gramsci, A.
1971 *Selections from the Prison Notebooks*. New York: International Publishers.

Hall, S. & T. Jefferson (eds.)
1976 *Resistance through Rituals*. London: Hutchinson.

Hobsbawm, E.
1985 Mass-producing traditions: Europe, 1870-1914. In Hobsbawm, E. & T. Ranger (eds.) *The Invention of Tradition*. Cambridge: Cambridge University Press.

Jolly, M.
1982 Birds and banyans of South Pentecost: *Kastom* in anti-Colonial struggle. In

Keesing, R.M. & R. Tonkinson (eds.) *Rethinking Traditional Culture: The Politics of Kastom in Island Melanesia.* Special Issue of *Mankind* 13(4):338-356.
n.d.   From corporeality to commodity: food and gender in South Pentecost, Vanuatu.

Keesing, R.M. and R. Tonkinson (eds.)
1982   *Reinvesting Traditional Culture: The Politics of Kastom in Island Melanesia.* Special Issue of *Mankind* 13(4).

Lombard, J.
1980   Modèles sociaux et comportements de consommation. *L'Homme et la Société* 56-58:141-148.

Mouffe, C. (ed.)
1979   *Gramsci and Marxist Theory.* London: Routledge & Kegan Paul.

Philibert, J-M.
1981   Living under two flags: selective modernization in Erakor Village, Efate. In Allen, M. (ed.) *Vanuatu. Politics, Economics and Ritual in island Melanesia.* Sydney: Academic Press.
1982   Vers une symbolique de la modernisation au Vanuatu. *Anthropologie et Sociétés* 6(1):69-98.
1984a   "Affluence, Commodity Consumption and Self-Image in Vanuatu." In Salisbury, R.F. and E. Tooker (eds.) *Affluence and Cultural Survival.* The American Ethnological Society.
1984b   Adaptation à la récession économique dans un village péri-urbain du Vanuatu. *Journal de la Société des Océanistes,* Tome XL, No. 79:139-150.
1986   The politics of tradition: toward a generic culture in Vanuatu. *Mankind* 16(1):1-12.
1988   Women's Work: A Case Study of Proletarianization of Peri-Urban Villagers in Vanuatu. *Oceania,* 58:161-175.

Riviere, C.
1975   Classes et Stratifications Sociales en Afrique noire, *Cahiers Internationaux de Sociologie,* Vol. LIX:285-314.

Rosman, A.
1982   Review of Douglas and Isherwood's *The World of Goods. American Anthropologist* 84(1):211-212.

Sahlins, M.
1976   *Culture and Practical Reason.* Chicago: The University of Chicago Press.

Simon, R.
1982   *Gramsci's Political Thought.* London: Lawrence & Wishart.

Willis, P.E.
1980   *Learning to Labour.* Westwead: Gower.

Worsley, P.
1981   Social class and development. In Berreman, G.D. (ed.) *Social Inequality.* New York: Academic Press.

CONCLUSION

AN ITINERARY REQUIRES BOTH a point of departure and a point of arrival. In the realm of ideas, the latter is much more difficult to identify than the former. Yet the reader who has come this far is surely entitled to know where we go from here.

To some extent, each of the chosen articles speaks for itself as it demarcates areas of research worth pursuing. It is probably clear by now that our anthropological approach owes much to non-anthropologists, to cultural Marxists such as Raymond Williams and to British sociologists like Paul Willis and Stuart Hall. If like them we focus on ideology, it is because ideology is the old concept of culture grasped in a political (mine)field. The advantage of treating parts of culture as ideology is that it emphasises the situated nature—in time, space, social positions—of the ideas put forward by members of social groups, as well as the link between such ideas and power. It also implies an active view of culture, as it is caught, if the image is not too risqué, in the act of reproduction. Culture, for us, is always at the stage of project; it is a never completed task. This view stresses actors' roles as they question, challenge, refuse or bow to accepted meanings, or, alternatively, invent new ones as they reproduce social and cultural forms. Because such cultural forms are close to the way subjects experience their life, they are normally contested. The process, which may seem placid when expressed in terms of structural determinants, is in fact fraught with the stress and tensions found in the movement of tectonic plates.

One of the theoretical problems facing social scientists in the 1990s has already been outlined by the cultural Marxists: one cannot derive cultural forms from structural (economic, social or political) constraints. Willis puts it very simply,

> Just because there are what we call structural or economic
> constraints it does not mean that people will unproblemati-

> cally obey them. In some societies people are forced at the
> end of a machine gun to behave in a certain way. In our
> own this is achieved through apparent freedoms. In order
> to have a satisfying explanation we need to see what the
> *symbolic* power of structural determination is within the
> mediating realm of the human and cultural. It is from the
> resources at this level that decisions are made which lead
> to the uncoerced outcomes which have the function of
> maintaining the structure of society and the status
> quo....macro determinants need to pass through the cul-
> tural milieu to reproduce themselves at all. (1977: 171)

Anthropologists will find in authors such as Willis the analytical
tools associated with Marxist class analysis combined this time with
an appreciation of cultural forms or factors as the mediating realm
between people's subjectivity and structural factors. The result is
that the objectionable air of conspiracy theory often found in Marxist analyses has evaporated. Gone as well is the Marxist view that
cultural production is less real than material production, that culture
is but epiphenomenal.

At a more general level, this type of study, which we suggest
anthropologists can profitably borrow from, attempts to find solutions to more general problems that social theorists like Giddens
have outlined for us: how to overcome the old conceptual oppositions inherited from the nineteenth century between synchrony and
diachrony, emic and etic descriptions, the local reality and a world
system, the individual and structural levels. In a nutshell, how to
move away from teleological explanations of social systems and
come to understand the reproduction of social institutions in a way
that acknowledges the considerable amount of freedom of action
of social actors who understand far more about the reproduction
of social groups than social scientists imagine. This makes the relation between power and agency an essential focus of analysis and
this is where Marxism can be useful.

It also points to the role of ideologies in deflecting actors' understanding or discursive penetration, as Giddens calls it, of social
systems, thus limiting their ability to change it. This is where Symbolic Anthropology can be most helpful. We believe that the tension
existing between cultural Marxism and Symbolic Anthropology will
be fruitful ground for the development of the discipline in the 1990s.

References

Willis, P.E.
    1977   *Learning to Labour*. NY: Columbia University Press.

CONTRIBUTORS

Turner, V. 1920-1983

Cohen, A. Department of Anthropology, University of London, England

Manning, F.E. Department of Anthropology, University of Western Ontario, London, Ontario, Canada

Myerhoff, B. 1936-1985

DaMatta, R. Department of Anthropology, University of Notre Dame, Notre Dame, Indiana, USA

Coggeshall, J. Department of Sociology, Clemson University, Clemson, South Carolina, USA

Finn, G. Cultural Studies Program, Carleton University, Ottawa, Ontario, Canada

Shamgar-Handelman, L. Department of Sociology, School of Education, Hebrew University of Jerusalem, Jerusalem, Israel

Handelman, D. Department of Sociology & Anthropology, Hebrew University of Jerusalem, Jerusalem, Israel

Comaroff, Jean Department of Anthropology, University of Chicago, Chicago, Illinois, USA

Comaroff, John Department of Anthropology, University of Chicago, Chicago, Illinois, USA

Philibert, J-M. Department of Anthropology, University of Western Ontario, London, Ontario, Canada

Shaw, R. Department of Sociology and Anthropology, University of Edinburgh, Edinburgh, Scotland

Morinis, A. Anthropologist and Film maker, Vancouver, British Columbia, Canada

McLaren, P. Center for Education & Cultural Studies, Miami University, Oxford, Ohio

Scott, J.C. Department of Political Science, Yale University, New Haven, Connecticut

SOURCES

Victor Turner (1965), "Ritual Symbolism, Morality, and Social Structure Among the Ndembu." In M. Fortes and G. Dieterlen (eds.), *African Systems of Thought*. London: Oxford University Press, for the International African Institute. Reprinted with permission.

Abner Cohen (1979), "Political Symbolism." Adapted, with permission, from *Annual Review of Anthropology*, volume 8. © 1979 by Annual Reviews Inc.

Frank E. Manning (1977), "The Salvation of a Drunk." In *The American Ethnologist*, vol. 4, no. 3, August 1977. Reproduced by permission of the American Anthropological Association. Not for further reproduction.

Barbara Myerhoff (1984), "A Death in Due Time: Construction of Self and Culture in Ritual Drama." In J. ManAloon (ed.), *Rite, Drama, Festival, Spectacle*. Philadelphia: Institute for the Study of Human Issues, pp. 149-178. Reprinted with permission.

Roberto DaMatta (1984), "Carneval In Multiple Planes." In J. Mac-Aloon (ed.), *Rite, Drama, Festival, Spectacle*. Philadelphia: Institute for the Study of Human Issues, pp. 208-240.

John Coggeshall (1990), "Those Who Surrender Are Female: Prison Gender Identities as Cultural Mirror." Also in K. Nyberg (ed.), *Transcending Boundaries*. Amherst, Mass.: Bergin & Garvey Publishers.

Geraldine Finn (1988), "Women, Fantasy and Popular Culture: The Wonderful World of Harlequin Romance." In R.B. Gruneau (ed.), *Popular Cultures and Political Practices*. Toronto: Garamond Press, pp. 51-67. Reprinted with permission of Garamond Press.

Lea Shamgar-Handelman and Don Handelman (1986), "Holiday Celebrations in Israeli Kindergartens: Relationships Between Representations of Collectivity and Family in the Nation State." Published by permission of Transaction Publishers, from *The Frailty of Authority*, by Myron Aronoff (ed.). Copyright © 1986 by Transaction Publishers.

Jean Comaroff and John Comaroff (1986), "Christianity and Colonialism in South Africa." *The American Ethnologist*, 13:1, pp. 1-22. Reproduced by permission of the American Anthropological Association. Not for further reproduction.

Jean-Marc Philibert (1986), "The Politics of Tradition: Toward a Generic Culture in Vanuatu." *Mankind*, vol. 16, no. 1, pp. 1-12. Reprinted by permission of the author.

Frank E. Manning (1981), "Celebrating Cricket: The Symbolic Construction of Caribbean Politics." In *The American Ethnologist*. Reproduced by permission of the American Anthropological Association. Not for further reproduction.

Mike Wallace (1985), "Mickey Mouse History: Portraying the Past at Disney World." *Radical History Review*, no. 32, Spring 1985, pp. 33-57. Reprinted by permission.

Rosalind Shaw (1985), "Gender and the Structuring of Reality in Temne Divination: An Interactive Study." *Africa*, 55 (3). London: International African Institute, pp. 286-303. Reprinted with permission.

Alan Morinis (1986), "Skid Row Indians and the Politics of Self." *Culture*, vol. 2, no. 3, pp. 93-105. Reprinted by permission.

Peter McLaren (1986), "The Antistructure of Resistance: Culture and Politics in a Toronto High School." In P. McLaren, *Schooling as a Ritual Performance*, chapter 4. London: Routledge and Kegan Paul, pp. 141-147, 151-162, 171-174.

James C. Scott (1986), "Everyday Forms of Peasant Resistance." In J.C. Scott and B.J. Tria Kerkvliet (eds.), *Everyday Forms of Peasant Resistance in South-East Asia*. London: Frank Cass., pp. 5-35. Reprinted by permission.

Jean-Marc Philibert (1989), "Consuming Culture: A Study of Simple Commodity Consumption." In H.J. Rutz and B.S. Orlove (eds.), *The Social Economy of Consumption*. New York: University Press of America. Reprinted by permission of the author.

Nota Bene: The Editors of this book and the Publisher have made every attempt to locate the authors of the copyrighted material or their heirs or assigns, and would be grateful for information that would allow them to correct any errors or omissions in a subsequent edition of the work.